Guerrilla Warfare
in the Irish War of
Independence, 1919–1921

ALSO BY JOSEPH MCKENNA
British Ships in the Confederate Navy (McFarland, 2010)

Guerrilla Warfare in the Irish War of Independence, 1919–1921

Joseph McKenna

McFarland & Company, Inc., Publishers
Jefferson, North Carolina, and London

LIBRARY OF CONGRESS CATALOGUING-IN-PUBLICATION DATA

McKenna, Joseph.
Guerrilla warfare in the Irish War of
Independence, 1919–1921 / Joseph McKenna.
p.   cm.
Includes bibliographical references and index.

ISBN 978-0-7864-5947-6

1. Ireland — History — War of Independence, 1919–1921.
2. Political violence — Ireland — History — 20th century.
3. Guerrilla warfare — Ireland — History — 20th century.   I. Title.
DA962.M48   2011   941.5082'1— dc22   2010047839

British Library cataloguing data are available

© 2011 Joseph McKenna. All rights reserved

*No part of this book may be reproduced or transmitted in any form
or by any means, electronic or mechanical, including photocopying
or recording, or by any information storage and retrieval system,
without permission in writing from the publisher.*

Front cover: Sean Keating (1889–1977). *Men of the South*,
1921, oil on canvas, 127 × 203.4 cm, Crawford Art Gallery, Cork

Manufactured in the United States of America

*McFarland & Company, Inc., Publishers
Box 611, Jefferson, North Carolina 28640
www.mcfarlandpub.com*

To my mother,
Mary McKenna née Cunningham,
who drove the last Black and Tan
from Republican territory with her house broom.

Acknowledgments

My thanks to former colleagues in the Social Sciences and Local Studies and History departments of the Central Library, Birmingham, England. Thanks also to the staff of the Imperial War Museum, London, and the National Library, Dublin.

Contents

Acknowledgments vi
List of Acronyms ix
Preface 1
Introduction 3

1. The Easter Rising, 1916   11
2. Political Reorganization   31
3. Military Reorganization   38
4. Passive Resistance   66
5. The Intelligence War   73
6. Urban Warfare   97
7. The Splendid Women   109
8. Guerrilla Warfare   116
9. 1919: The War Begins   125
10. 1920: The Second Year of the War   132
11. 1921: The Last Year of the War   184
12. Between Truce and Treaty   250
13. Conclusion: Prelude to Civil War   265

Appendix I: "Patrolling in the City" (from Record of Rebellion in Ireland 1920–1921*)* 273
Appendix II: Tom Kelleher's Account of Crossbarry 275
Appendix III: Analysis of Crossbarry by Tom Barry 278
Chapter Notes 279
Bibliography 283
Index 285

List of Acronyms

AC: Armored Car
AIR: Army of the Irish Republic
ASU: Active Service Unit
BCS: British Cooperative Society
CSB: Crimes Special Branch
DMP: Dublin Metropolitan Police
DORA: Defence of the Realm Act
FDE: Federation of Dublin Employees
GAA: Gaelic Athletic Association
GHQ: General Headquarters
GL: Gaelic League
GOC: General Officer Commanding
GPO: General Post Office
ICA: Irish Citizen Army
IO: Intelligence Officer
IRA: Irish Republican Army
IRB: Irish Republican Brotherhood
ISD: Irish Self-Determination League
ITGWU: Irish Transport and General Workers' Union
IV: Irish Volunteers
KOSB: King's Own Scottish Borderers
MC: Military Cross (Officers)
MM: Military Medal (Other ranks)
MP: Member of Parliament
NCO: Noncommissioned Officer
NUR: National Union of Railwaymen
OC: Officer Commanding
RAF: Royal Air Force
RDS: Royal Dublin Show
RIC: Royal Irish Constabulary
ROI: Restoration of Order in Ireland
RUC: Royal Ulster Constabulary
S/Ldr: Squadron Leader
SIS: Secret Intelligence Service
TUC: Trades Union Conference
USC: Ulster Special Constabulary
UVF: Ulster Volunteer Force
VC: Victoria Cross
WWU: Women Workers' Union

We are not establishing or attempting to establish a regular force on the lines of the standing armies of even small independent countries of Europe. If we undertake any such thing we shall fail. Our object is to bring into existence, train and equip as riflemen scouts a body of men, and to secure that these are capable of acting as a self-contained unit. — Michael Collins, *An t Oglach,* 1920.

Preface

The Irish War for Independence was an unnecessary and often brutal little war. It was unnecessary in that the democratic wishes of the Irish people should have been adhered to, especially by a country that holds democracy so dear. The original aims of both the Irish National Party and Sinn Fein was for a modest form of self-determination known as Home Rule. Both parties, and indeed all the people of Ireland, were not seeking complete separation from Britain, just the right to run their own affairs while remaining part of the British Empire. When Home Rule, passed into law by the British Parliament, was deferred for the duration of World War I, discontent in Ireland led to anger and anger led to the Dublin Rising of 1916. The British military's response in executing the Irish leaders of the Rising hardened attitudes in Ireland. In the general election of December 1918 some 72 percent of the population of Ireland voted for independence—but democracy was again denied. The British politicians, including men like David Lloyd George and Winston Churchill, rightly saw that to give independence to Ireland would see the breakup of the British Empire, which of course happened within fifty years. When democracy fails, as it did, not once but twice, all that remains is to take up arms.

This present work looks at the recruiting, training and arming of a people's army that took on the might of the British Empire and forced it to a stalemate. It is a story of ordinary young men, of their triumphs and tribulations. I have used a number of sources, in particular the works of Tom Barry, Ernie O'Malley, Sean Moylan and Dan Breen, and the personal witness statements of ordinary Irish soldiers collected in the 1940s and 1950s, when passions were spent. Where possible I have sought to balance their versions by using British sources now housed in the Public Record Office in Kew, and the Imperial War Museum in London. In book form I have used William Sheehan's recently published accounts, *British Voices* and *Fighting for Dublin*. I have also used contemporary London newspaper accounts, balancing viewpoints expressed by the right-wing *Times,* the more liberal *Observer* and *Manchester Guardian,* and the socialist *Daily Herald.* In my research I have come across the works of a number of pro–British revisionist historians who, regrettably, in their bid to give an alternative history of these times have, though not in every case, distorted accounts to fit their own hypotheses. Where they have made honest and valid statements contrary to accepted belief, I have included them for balance. This then is my account of the raising of a guerrilla army and of the war that army fought, an action dignified with the name of the Irish War for Independence.

Introduction

In the second decade of the 20th century the hopes and aspirations of the Irish people were about to be realized. The Home Rule Bill of 1912 had been passed by the House of Commons, the lower house of the British Parliament, and had been sent to the upper house, the House of Lords, for approval. By the Parliament Act of 1911, the upper house could not delay the bill from becoming law beyond 1914. After 114 years of direct British rule, brought about by a forced Act of Union in 1800, Ireland would have her own parliament restored. She would be given greater autonomy as a nation, but remain within the British Empire. The act had been brought about not by violence and disorder, but by the massive commitment of the Irish people to the democratic process, pursued by the Irish National Party in Parliament. Erskine Childers, perhaps best known as the author of the 1903 novel *Riddle of the Sands*, developed, through his Irish relatives, an interest in Irish Home Rule. Comparing the policies of the Parliamentary party with those of the lesser known, more radical party Sinn Fein, he reflected the opinion of most Irish people of the day, when he wrote, "If the Sinn Fein alternative meant anything at all, it meant complete separation, which Ireland does not want, and a final abandonment of constitutional methods."[1] What the parliamentarians were seeking was a degree of autonomy within the British Empire as a free state, based on the South African model, not an Irish Republic.

The majority of Protestants in the north of Ireland were bitterly opposed even to this modest form of Home Rule, which still would have kept Ireland within the Empire. Back in 1886 and later in 1893, Home Rule bills had produced anti–Catholic riots in Belfast. Bigots and morally bankrupt opportunistic Conservative politicians like Lord Randolph Churchill had preached that "Home Rule is Rome Rule," playing on Protestant fears that under a Dublin parliament their religion and very way of life would be threatened. It was a far cry from the time of the Protestant-led rebellion of 1798, when the United Irishmen, inspired by the American War of Independence, sought Ireland's freedom as a republic. Protestant leader Theobald Wolfe Tone summed up a greater vision of what they sought to achieve:

"To unite Protestant, Catholic and Dissenter under the common name of Irishmen in order to break the connection with England."

Such idealism was now forgotten. In 1912 a new Protestant leader arose, Sir Edward Carson, a successful Dublin lawyer. He organized resistance to Home Rule, with the backing of the British Conservative Party. On 28 September 1912, religious services were held throughout Protestant Ulster, and a Solemn League and Covenant was signed by over 218,000 men, some using their own blood. They pledged themselves to use "all means which may be found necessary to defeat the present conspiracy to set up a home-rule parliament in Ireland." The Ulster Volunteers were established as the physical means of resistance and were armed with guns from Germany: 35,000 Mausers and 2,500,000 rounds of ammunition. In September 1913 a "Provisional Government" was set up in Ulster to come into being on the day that Home Rule passed into law. Their actions were treasonable, but Carson declared, "I am told it will be illegal. Of course it will. Drilling is illegal ... the Volunteers are illegal and the government know they are illegal, and the government dare not interfere with them.... Don't be afraid of illegalities."[2]

Carson was assured that no action would be taken, because he had the backing of the Conservative Party and of its leader, Bonar Law, who vied with the extremist Ulster Unionists in his violent rhetoric. Carson also had the support of the British Army in Ireland. General Sir Hubert Gough, commanding the 3rd Cavalry Brigade at the Curragh Camp, refused to move against the Ulster Unionists. Other officers followed suit, preferring to resign their commissions than to fight the Ulstermen. The officers were summoned to London, where after forceful objections were raised by them the secretary of state for war, Colonel Seely, gave a written assurance to Gough that the Forces of the Crown would not be used against the provisional Ulster government or the Ulster Volunteers.

John Redmond, Irish Parliamentary Party leader.

In the face of a military mutiny, the Liberal government under Prime Minister Herbert Asquith sought a compromise. John Redmond, leader of the Irish National Party at Westminster, was persuaded to accept Home Rule by stages as the price for peace. Asquith convinced him that the Unionists would bring about their own downfall by their actions, and Home Rule for all of Ireland would eventually be achieved by a parliamentary majority.

In response to the formation of the Ulster Volunteer Force, and the British Army's unwillingness to move against them, the Irish Nationalists formed their own volunteer army to force through Home Rule. It was pointed out that since the British government had not interfered with Carson it could hardly prohibit Nationalist Ireland from doing the same. The initiative came from the Irish Republican Brotherhood, a secret society founded in 1858 by James Stephens. The IRB had considerable influence in Nationalist affairs, with fingers in all aspects of Irish social and cultural life. At an inaugural meeting held in Dublin, on 25 November 1913, a total of 4,000 men enrolled in the Volunteers. In Ireland's provincial towns and cities, other companies of Volunteers were also raised. In County Kildare the Volunteers mustered for the first time at Gibbet Rath on 7 June 1914. Up to

1,000 Volunteers attended, with companies from Athy, Newbridge and Kildare. This muster attracted fresh recruits, and a second muster was held on the 11th of the same month at the County Agricultural Society grounds. The Athy Battalion itself had grown to four full companies, numbering 1,000 men and including a mounted troop. By the end of the year, the Volunteer strength had grown to 10,000 men.

In English cities with Irish Roman Catholic populations, the Volunteer movement rose out of such organizations as the Gaelic League and the Gaelic Athletic Association. The young Michael Collins, from County Cork, then working in London, attended the inaugural meeting of the Volunteers, held in the German gymnasium near King's Cross Station. He was enrolled on 25 April 1914. A large number of young Irishmen in London joined the Irish Volunteers, about 2,000 in all. Following a split in the Volunteer ranks at the outbreak of World War I, one hundred of these London-based Volunteers remained true to the original ideal. Ironically the majority of these one hundred young men were English-born, and they formed part of the garrison that held the GPO during the Easter Rising.

Sir Edward Carson addressing an anti–Home Rule meeting in 1913.

On 4 December, nine days after the inauguration of the Volunteers, the British government prohibited the importation of military arms and ammunition. This outraged the Nationalists, not only because of its seeming bias, but also because the Liberal Party government maintained power only because it had the support of the Irish Party at Westminster, meaning that Redmond and his fellow MPs had agreed to the ban. At home many Redmondite supporters transferred their allegiance to Sinn Fein at the seeming betrayal of the national interest.

The Volunteers grew in numbers as a consequence. Unlike the UVF with its class-bound structure, being officered by retired British army personnel, the Nationalist army was a very democratic organization. Men were grouped according to locality, irrespective of class or creed. Any competent Volunteer might be elected as an officer, though in practice many turned out to be IRB men. Squads of men were grouped into sections, and sections into companies of 100 men, each under a captain. Later companies were organized into battalions and battalions into brigades. Colonel Maurice Moore of the Connaught Rangers became inspector general of the Volunteers. Bulmer Hobson was appointed secretary to the Volunteers and the humanitarian but flawed Sir Roger Casement, who had exposed Belgian atrocities in the Congo, became its treasurer. Arms were secured from wherever possible, but many Volunteers began their military careers armed only with wooden guns or hurley sticks. The UVF had shown the way in their disregard of the ban with their illegal importation of guns; now the Irish Volunteers did the same. They obtained 1,500 Mausers and 49,000 rounds of ammunition from Hamburg, Germany, in the early summer of 1914. Erskine Childer's yacht, *Asgard,* Conor O'Brien's *Kelpie* and Sir Thomas Myles' *Chotah* were used to bring the guns into the country. The guns aboard the *Asgard* were landed at Howth on Sunday, 26 July at 12:45 P.M. Within twenty minutes the cargo was unloaded and cars and trucks were used to whisk away arms to prearranged caches. Some 1,000 Volunteers, with guns on their shoulders but devoid of ammunition, marched south to Dublin. At Clontarf, the Volunteers found themselves confronted by a mixed force of armed Dublin Metropolitan Police and soldiers of the King's Own Scottish Borderers. Without ammunition the Volunteers could not defend themselves. Their officers went forward to negotiate. Though ordered by their superiors to seize the arms, many of the constables with Volunteer sympathies refused to do so. In the seeming chaos, the Borderers acting as observers only, the Volunteers melted away in all directions. Only 19 guns were seized, and these were later recovered by Colonel Moore. A week after the landing at Howth, 600 additional rifles were landed at Kilcoole in County Wicklow.³

A third army came into being in 1913, and with it a socialist dimension arose for any future Irish Republic. In August there were a series of strikes in Dublin over the failure by employers to recognize the Irish Transport and General Workers' Union, founded by James Larkin. Industrialist William Martin Murphy locked out some trade unionists on 19 August 1913. In response Larkin called for an all out strike on Murphy's Dublin United Tramway Company. At an open air meeting in O'Connell Street, addressed by Larkin on 31 August, baton-wielding members of the Dublin Metropolitan Police charged into the crowd to break it up, killing two men and wounding scores of others in the process. Larkin, not enjoying the same immunity as Carson, was arrested for "using seditious language." The Federation of Dublin Employers, representing 400 companies in the city and led by Murphy, pledged themselves to break the union by refusing to recognize it or its members. A lockout followed. There were sympathetic strikes by other workers across Dublin, violent clashes between workers and the police ensued, and there were evictions of strikers for nonpayment of rent. By 27 September there were estimated to be 24,000 people out of work. Estimates of their dependants could probably be magnified by a factor of five. The British Cooperative Society sent food and clothing to the starving, and the emergent British Labor Party gave the strikers its support.

The young Michael Collins joined the Volunteers in London, where he was working at the time.

Mrs. Erskine Childers and Mary Spring-Rice aboard the Asgard, *1914.*

As a result of public clamor, Larkin was released from prison after a few weeks. At a public meeting in October, encouraged by a Protestant Ulsterman, Captain Jack R. White,[4] a man with socialist leanings, Larkin called upon the workers to form a Citizen Army to protect themselves against police assault. Armed only at first with hurling sticks, Captain White, a former British Army officer, agreed to train them. Guns and rifles were smuggled in later for their use from Glasgow, Liverpool, Holyhead and London by sailors and stewards aboard the ferries that crossed the Irish Sea. In January 1914, after six months, the strike was broken, and hungry defeated workers were forced back to work, many on lower wages.

Ireland had always fascinated the socialists of mainland Europe. Marx, Engels, and now Lenin watched to see what would happen next. The Irish Transport and General Workers' Union had organized the people in an anticapitalist movement. They now had a military wing in the Citizen Army. If any country was ripe for overthrowing the existing social order it was Ireland; and if Ireland did so, Great Britain would surely follow. How soon before Russia followed them?

A raffle ticket issued by the Volunteer movement. First prize was a rifle. From such beginnings the Irish Republican Army grew.

The Communists watched and waited. Like Lenin, union organizer James Connolly hoped that should war come the socialists in Germany, France and England would refuse to fight. But when war was declared they all fell in like sheep and went out to fight against the workers of other countries, much to Connolly's disgust.

In mid–1914, Jack White resigned as ICA Commander, to join the Redmondite National Volunteers. James Larkin left Ireland for America to form a trade union there, and in his absence he was replaced by James Connolly, ITGWU's representative in Belfast and a committed Marxist. Connolly also became commander of the Citizen Army. He changed the army from a workers' self defense militia into a 220-member strong revolutionary army, dedicated to the establishment of an Irish socialist republic through physical force. In July 1914 the ICA obtained German Mausers, having assisted the Volunteers at the landings at Howth. The ICA, unlike the other two "illegal" armies in Ireland, introduced a policy of equality between men and women. Both sexes were trained in the use of arms. Countess Markievicz (Constance Gore-Booth), daughter of an Irish aristocratic family, became treasurer and an officer within the ICA. She wore a uniform and carried a sidearm. Army headquarters was established at the ITGWU building, Liberty Hall. In October 1915 armed units of the ICA gave protection to striking dockers in the Port of Dublin, preventing the police from breaking up the picket lines or interfering with open air meetings.

It was now the second year of the war. Right from the outbreak of World War I, Connolly had railed against it as an imperialist/capitalist war. In 1915 he began to call for insurrection in his newspaper, the *Irish Worker*. When this was banned for sedition he founded another, the *Workers' Republic,* and continued in the same vein. His call for insurrection was closely watched by the IRB, which had similar plans.

The Irish Citizen Army grew from a defense force into a Marxist army dedicated to the overthrow of British rule in Ireland and the establishment of an "Irish Socialist Republic."

Throughout Ireland there were garrisons of British troops, even in wartime. The Dublin Garrison itself numbered nearly 2,500. In addition there was the Royal Irish Constabulary, an armed paramilitary force 10,000 strong and operating out of barracks all over Ireland, except in Dublin. These were independent of the local authorities and answered directly to Dublin Castle. The RIC was composed of Irishmen, transferred away from their native counties to avoid any clashes of local loyalty. They were conscientious and intelligent in the discharge of their duties and developed a thorough understanding of the ways of the people they policed. They were faithful to the British government, efficient and eager. In an unarmed country it was easy for them to dominate the populace. Within the RIC was the Crimes Special Branch, which concerned itself with political work. It gauged the strength of political organizations opposed to British rule, recorded seditious speeches, and followed suspects. The Dublin Metropolitan Police Force, which policed the capital, was very similar to the British police forces in England, Scotland and Wales. They were unarmed, but had access to arms should they be required. The DMP had a plainclothes detective force, including G Division, its political branch. This branch consisted of about a dozen men, a number that increased to twenty by 1920. The division kept records of dissidents, shadowed suspects, watched meetings, and checked on the arrivals and departures of suspects at railway stations and ports. By 1916 Ireland was an armed camp, with five armies, legal and illegal. It was a powder keg just waiting to explode. But when it did, it was totally unexpected.

1

The Easter Rising, 1916

Upon the outbreak of war with Germany, John Redmond, leader of the Irish Nationalists in the British Parliament, promised the government the support of his party and of his country. His rash announcement split the Nationalists in two. Arthur Griffith, writing in the newspaper *Sinn Fein* five days later, protested at Redmond's failure to consult the people of Ireland in his decision: "Ireland is not at war with Germany. She is not at war with any continental Power. England is at war with Germany.... [W]e are Irish Nationalists and the only duty we can have is to stand for Ireland's interests, irrespective of the interests of England or Germany or any other foreign country.... If Irishmen are to defend Ireland they must defend it for Ireland, under Ireland's flag, and under Irish officers. Otherwise they will only help to perpetuate the enslavement of their country."[1]

Griffith's attitude was shaped by Britain's prevarication over Irish Home Rule. Two years earlier, the latest Home Rule bill had been introduced in Parliament but had been held up in the House of Lords. The Parliament Act was later passed to curtail the power of the lords in their attempts to thwart democracy, and the bill finally became law on 18 September 1914 — but with a curtailment. A Suspensory Act was inserted whereby the original act would not become law until the end of the war with Germany. While Redmond and his supporters represented the passing of the act as a triumph, more skeptical Nationalists, including some in his own party, did not. On 20 September, while speaking at Woodenbridge in County Wicklow with the passing of the Home Rule Act very much in mind, Redmond caused a split in the ranks of the Volunteers by asking them to join with Britain in its war against Germany, in the defense of "small nations." He declared that it would be to Ireland's eternal shame if her young men did not go and fight. A convention was called by those Volunteers opposed to Redmond's recruitment drive. In a vote, the majority of the Volunteers, now some 180,000 strong, gave their support to Redmond and became known as the National Volunteers. Some 12,000, most of them the original founding members, reaffirmed their allegiance to Ireland and Ireland alone. They became known as the Irish Volunteers. James Connolly's newspaper, the *Workers' Republic*, was scathing of Redmond's splitting the Nationalist movement, and in one jingle prophetically outlined the outcome:

> Full steam ahead John Redmond said
> that everything was well chum;
> Home rule will come when we are dead
> and buried out in Belgium.[2]

At a meeting of the Supreme Council of the IRB in August 1914, it was decided that there must be an insurrection in Ireland before the end of Britain's war with Germany. There is an old saying that "England's difficulty is Ireland's opportunity." This was very much in the minds of the Council of the Irish Volunteers when they met. They were all IRB men:

Chief of Staff
Eoin MacNeill

Director of Organization	**Director of Military Operations**	**Director of Training**
Patrick Pearse	Joseph Plunkett	Thomas McDonough*
Quartermaster General	**Director of Communications**	
Bulmer Hobson	Eamonn Ceant	

*Also commandant of the Dublin Brigade.

After the split, the policy of the Irish Volunteers remained as it had always been from its inception: to resist if attacked by British forces, otherwise to remain as the guardians of Irish national rights. This meant resisting the partition of Ulster and resisting the conscription of Irish men into the British armed forces. By 1916 the membership of the Irish Volunteers had grown to 15,000, with functioning brigade and battalion staffs in Dublin, Cork and Limerick. Two garrisons were established in Dublin: in the north at the Keating Rooms in North Frederick Street near Parnell Square and in the south at Larkfield, Kimmage, at a disused stone mill built on 8 acres of land on the river Poddle, the property of Joseph Plunkett's family. The garrison here was mainly made up of Liverpool and London-Irish Volunteers. It was at the Kimmage garrison that munitions were prepared. As London-born Volunteer Joe Good relates, "The mill was an excellent training place for men likely to go into battle. The food was simple, wholesome and plentiful.... George [Plunkett] kept us busy, taking us nightly on route marches.... Some of us were busiest for most of the time making crude hand-grenades out of 2" × 4" cast-iron down-pipe, with a flange-end through which a long bolt passed. A small hole penetrated one of the flanges, through which a fuse was inserted. The fuse was of sulphur or match type.... [I]t was estimated to be a three-second bomb.... There were only two crude brass moulds for the shot-gun pellets, which turned out ten lead pellets. One man held the pellet mould, and another poured the liquid lead.... [T]he output of hand-grenades, when we had enough material, would be twenty an hour."[3]

Discovering that James Connolly's Citizen Army, some 220 strong, was also intending a rising, the IRB informed Connolly of their own plans, and an agreement was reached. Though smaller than the Irish Volunteers, the Citizen Army was better disciplined and better trained. It was ideologically committed to an independent Irish Socialist Republic. The guiding principle of the ICA was that "the ownership of Ireland, moral and material, is vested by right in the people of Ireland." Connolly was a Marxist, and this worried the right-wing Roman Catholic element within not only the Volunteers but also the IRB. Connolly very skillfully assured the leaders of these two organizations that these ideological differences could be overcome, and both armies were forged into one.

Connolly, a former soldier in the British army, carefully studied popular uprisings from the past with a view to adapting their successes and failures in a war against Britain to bring about Irish independence. This interest gave rise to a series of articles on revolutionary warfare that appeared in the *Workers' Republic* (29 May–24 July 1915). These articles took the form of a narrative, followed by an assessment of why revolutions succeeded or failed. The examples chosen included the Moscow Insurrection in 1905, Tyrol in 1809, Brussels in 1830, the Alamo in 1836, Paris in 1830, Lexington in 1775 and Paris in 1848. It is clear from his writings that the Rising of Easter 1916, was not, as far as he was concerned, intended as some "blood sacrifice" but was to have been the start of a nation-wide revolutionary war. A detailed plan was drawn up by Connolly and the Volunteer leaders, using the lessons of history. Dublin was to be seized by an initial force of 3,000, while in the provinces a force of 13,000 were tasked with preventing British reinforcements from marching on the capital. The Rising, intended to begin on Easter Sunday, hinged on the arrival of German arms, to be landed at Tralee Bay. With their German rifles the Volunteers in the provinces were to keep British troops and the armed Royal Irish Constabulary occupied. The British garrison in Enniskillen was to be surrounded by Volunteers from Belfast. Other Volunteers were to engage the British Army at the Curragh and in Athlone. Any Volunteers that could be spared were to be drafted to reinforce the Dublin Brigade. Key points within the city were to be seized, and approach roads blockaded. These comprised:

Eoin MacNeill, president of the Irish Volunteers.

(1) The IRB Military Council was to seize and occupy the General Post Office in Sackville Street (now O'Connell Street) and there establish the Headquarters of the Provisional Government. This task was entrusted to a combined force of Volunteers and Citizen Army under the command of James Connolly.
(2) The First Battalion under Edward Daly was to occupy the Four Courts.
(3) The Second Battalion under Thomas MacDonagh was to seize the strategically important Jacob's Biscuit Factory.
(4) The Third Battalion under Eamon de Valera was charged with occupying Boland's Bakery, which commanded the main road leading from Kingstown Harbor (Dun Laoghaire) to Dublin, the route which British troops landing from England/Wales would approach. They were also to cover the railway line from Lansdowne Road to Westland Row.
(5) The Fourth Battalion under Eamonn Kent, with Cathal Brugha as second in command, were charged with securing Kingsbridge Station, the terminus of the railways from the south, with Con Colbert of that brigade detailed to seize Rowe's Distillery. Further sections of the brigade were ordered to occupy the South Dublin Union, a collection of poor houses and administrative buildings, with other Volunteers taking up encircling sniper positions.
(6) The Citizen Army was to occupy and establish entrenchments in St. Stephen's Green. Chief of staff Michael Mallin was to command, with Constance Markievicz as second in command. Units of Cumann na mBan, the women's

movement attached to each battalion, were to act as couriers and first-aiders and provide meals.

The German trawler *Aud* sailed from Luebeck, with a crew of 21 officers and men, commanded by Captain Carl Spindler, on the afternoon of Sunday 9 April 1916. She had a cargo of 20,000 captured Russian rifles, 10 machine guns, a million rounds of ammunition and explosives destined for the west coast of Ireland. Sir Roger Casement, who had been liaising with the German government, now discovered that no German officers, on whom the Volunteers were counting, would be sent. He also became concerned that the *Aud* would not succeed in running the British blockade. So concerned was he in fact that he persuaded the German government to supply him with a submarine. He led them to believe that it was vital that he return to Ireland in order to take part in the Rising and that his presence was essential there. In reality it was his intention to persuade the IRB to call off the Rising. The submarine left Kiel on 12 April. Its commander's orders were to rendezvous with the *Aud* in Tralee Bay on Good Friday, two days before the Rising. Aboard the *Aud*, Spindler's orders were to arrive off Inishtooskert Island between Thursday, 20 April and Easter Saturday. The *Aud* sailed under the Norwegian flag, ostensibly with a cargo of timber. The one vital piece of equipment she lacked was a radio. Despite gales off the north of Scotland, and the Royal Navy blockade, the *Aud* reached her destination at 4:00 P.M., on Holy Thursday.

Everything had gone to plan, but now the Supreme Council of the IRB changed that plan. As Dorothy Macardle disingenuously remarks in her book, "The Irish leaders had made a slight — very slight — alteration in their plan."[4] What they did was to doom the Rising to failure, and full blame must rest with them. Mobilization and exercises of the Irish Volunteers were planned for Easter Sunday, 23 April. These exercises were an accepted norm, and the British authorities would not have been unduly alarmed at the presence of the Volunteers on the streets of Dublin and elsewhere. These maneuvers were designed as a cover for the launching of the Rising. Orders had gone out for Volunteers to assemble at 6:30 P.M. on Easter Sunday. These orders were now rescinded and mobilization was postponed by one day. The Military Council of the IRB reasoned that on Easter Monday most of the officers of the Dublin Garrison would be out of town at the Fairyhouse Races, thus giving the enterprise greater chance of succeeding. A telegraph was sent to Berlin that the arms should not be landed before the night of Easter Sunday. Unfortunately the message could not be sent to the *Aud*, which lacked a radio. Unaware of this, orders were sent by Volunteer GHQ to the commandant in Limerick warning him to expect the German arms on Sunday night. Austin Stack, commandant of the Kerry Brigade and responsible for the landing and distributing of the arms to the Volunteers in Cork, Tipperary, Limerick and the West of Ireland, was likewise notified of the change and withdrew his spotters.

Unbeknownst to the Volunteers, British Naval Intelligence had broken the German naval code back in February, and all messages transmitted between Ireland, Germany and the United States were intercepted and decoded. Now aware of the presence of the *Aud*, 29 Royal Navy ships began to look for her. On Good Friday she was boarded by sailors from a patrol boat, but her captain was able to convince them that he was a neutral. However, later in the day another patrol boat, the *Bluebell*, approached. She put a shot across the *Aud*'s bow and ordered her to lay in a course for Queenstown (Cobh). In Queenstown harbor, Captain Spindler blew up his ship, with the loss of 20,000 stand of arms. On the previous evening, Casement, Robert Monteith, his ADC, and a Volunteer named Daniel Bailey, alias Beverley (who later turned king's evidence against Casement) had been landed from the German submarine U-19, commanded by Kapitanleutnant Raimund Weissbach,[5] at Banna Strand. Exhausted in coming ashore, Casement was left to rest in a nearby field, while the other two traveled to Tralee to meet Austin Stack. Casement was found and arrested. Word arrived in Dublin of what had happened, and MacNeill cancelled all previous orders. Bulmer Hobson, Irish Volunteer quartermaster, was given authority over all the Volunteers in the city, and Commandant O'Connel was given authority to supersede all authority in the rest of the country, in the process canceling all previous orders.

Still unaware that the *Aud* had been captured, Pearse, MacDonagh, and Sean MacDermott of the

> **POBLACHT NA H EIREANN.**
> **THE PROVISIONAL GOVERNMENT**
> OF THE
> **IRISH REPUBLIC**
> **TO THE PEOPLE OF IRELAND.**
>
> IRISHMEN AND IRISHWOMEN: In the name of God and of the dead generations from which she receives her old tradition of nationhood, Ireland, through us, summons her children to her flag and strikes for her freedom.
>
> Having organised and trained her manhood through her secret revolutionary organisation, the Irish Republican Brotherhood, and through her open military organisations, the Irish Volunteers and the Irish Citizen Army, having patiently perfected her discipline, having resolutely waited for the right moment to reveal itself, she now seizes that moment, and, supported by her exiled children in America and by gallant allies in Europe, but relying in the first on her own strength, she strikes in full confidence of victory.
>
> We declare the right of the people of Ireland to the ownership of Ireland, and to the unfettered control of Irish destinies, to be sovereign and indefeasible. The long usurpation of that right by a foreign people and government has not extinguished the right, nor can it ever be extinguished except by the destruction of the Irish people. In every generation the Irish people have asserted their right to national freedom and sovereignty; six times during the past three hundred years they have asserted it in arms. Standing on that fundamental right and again asserting it in arms in the face of the world, we hereby proclaim the Irish Republic as a Sovereign Independent State, and we pledge our lives and the lives of our comrades-in-arms to the cause of its freedom, of its welfare, and of its exaltation among the nations.
>
> The Irish Republic is entitled to, and hereby claims, the allegiance of every Irishman and Irishwoman. The Republic guarantees religious and civil liberty, equal rights and equal opportunities to all its citizens, and declares its resolve to pursue the happiness and prosperity of the whole nation and of all its parts, cherishing all the children of the nation equally, and oblivious of the differences carefully fostered by an alien government, which have divided a minority from the majority in the past.
>
> Until our arms have brought the opportune moment for the establishment of a permanent National Government, representative of the whole people of Ireland and elected by the suffrages of all her men and women, the Provisional Government, hereby constituted, will administer the civil and military affairs of the Republic in trust for the people.
>
> We place the cause of the Irish Republic under the protection of the Most High God, Whose blessing we invoke upon our arms, and we pray that no one who serves that cause will dishonour it by cowardice, inhumanity, or rapine. In this supreme hour the Irish nation must, by its valour and discipline and by the readiness of its children to sacrifice themselves for the common good, prove itself worthy of the august destiny to which it is called.
>
> Signed on Behalf of the Provisional Government.
> THOMAS J. CLARKE.
> SEAN Mac DIARMADA.   THOMAS MacDONAGH.
> P. H. PEARSE.   EAMONN CEANNT.
> JAMES CONNOLLY.   JOSEPH PLUNKETT.

The Declaration of Irish Independence.

IRB went to see MacNeill and persuaded him that everything was still alright. MacNeill agreed to revoke his countermand. As Bulmer Hobson was made of sterner stuff, he was arrested by the triumvirate. On Saturday morning, the news of the landing of three men from a boat in Kerry, the arrest of one of them, the arrest of Austin Stack, and the destruction of the *Aud* at Queenstown reached Republican headquarters. Word was also received that the British authorities intended to undertake the widespread arrest of Volunteers. MacNeill called a meeting of his senior staff and told them that he had decided once again to call off the mobilization. MacDonagh, who was present, reported back to the Military Council of MacNeill's change of mind. In his absence, MacNeill sent messengers around the country to inform the Volunteers that all movements were cancelled. Notices to this effect were given to the press.

The expectation was that the British authorities in Ireland would now act — but they

The signatories of the proclamation: (a) Thomas James Clarke, (b) Patrick Henry Pearse, (c) James Connolly, (d) Thomas Mac-Donagh, (e) Sean MacDiarmada, (f) Joseph Mary Plunket, (g) Eamonn Ceant.

did not. British Intelligence had infiltrated the various Irish resistance movements, including the Volunteers. They were aware that a rising was planned to take place soon after the landing of Casement and the German arms. But Casement had been arrested, and the arms had sunk with the *Aud*. Lord Wimborne, the lord lieutenant of Ireland and the king's representative, was informed of this. He proposed the arrest of between 60 and 100 of the Irish leaders. Had this been done successfully, it seems highly unlikely that the Rising would have taken place. Sir Matthew Nathan, the principal assistant secretary and a civil servant with considerable colonial administrative experience, persuaded Wimborne that there was no need for action, given MacNeill's cancellation of all movements. What Nathan was unaware of was the split within the higher ranks of the Volunteers and the IRB's support of Patrick Pearse, who was prepared to go ahead with the Rising.

Nationally there was complete chaos within the Volunteer movement over orders and counterorders. MacNeill's last minute cancellation of the Rising was transmitted by messengers and reported in the newspapers. Early on the morning of Easter Sunday, the Military Council met in Liberty Hall, the headquarters of the Citizen Army. The old Fenian Thomas Clarke presided. He announced that he was in favor of the Rising going ahead. Pearse, MacDermott and Connolly agreed with him. Their opinion prevailed, and the council decided that it would go ahead, despite the fact that they would be seriously short of arms and that the initial Rising would be confined to Dublin. What might perhaps have succeeded with German arms and a national rising was now turned into a gesture — a blood sacrifice. Even Connolly recognized this. Asked what the chances of success were, he is said to have replied, "The chances against us are a thousand to one." On the day of the Rising one of his men asked if there was any hope of winning. He replied, "None whatever." Seldom in history have men and women been so willing, some might say eager, to throw away their lives for an ideal.

Monday

Easter Monday, 24 April, was a sunny bank holiday. The streets of Dublin were crowded with people out enjoying themselves. At 12:00 noon, small bodies of Volunteers, units of the Citizen Army and members of the Hibernian Rifles marched through the city to seize their various strongpoints. Their hope was that one of three things might occur: the country would rise in response, the British might recognize that they could not control the country and they would not take any action, or the Germans might somehow come to their assistance. Five important buildings, or groups of buildings, were seized north of the river Liffey and nine south of it, as outlined in the original plan. All were occupied and defenses were prepared. Windows were knocked out, to be replaced by mail bags, books and anything that could be used as a barricade. As yet there was no response by the British authorities in Dublin, who had been taken completely by surprise. The Volunteers' headquarters was established in the General Post Office in Sackville Street. Snipers were placed in all corner houses commanding the approaches. Kelly's ammunition shop at the corner of Bachelor's Walk and Hopkins' jewelry shop at the corner of Eden Quay were likewise garrisoned. Connecting walls between these two buildings were knocked down as far back as Abbey Street, some one hundred yards away, to enable reinforcements and arms to be moved in safety. An unarmed British soldier, investigating what was going on, was shot and wounded. A little later four British Army Lancers came trotting down Sackville Street, completely oblivious to the danger. Volunteers snipers opened up, and within seconds the four troopers and three of their horses were dead. As the fourth horse just stood there, it too was shot and killed. This tragic little group remained there until the end of the battle.

Meanwhile, about ten minutes past twelve noon, a column of men, with two young women in the rear, barely 20 in number, were sent to picket Dublin Castle to prevent

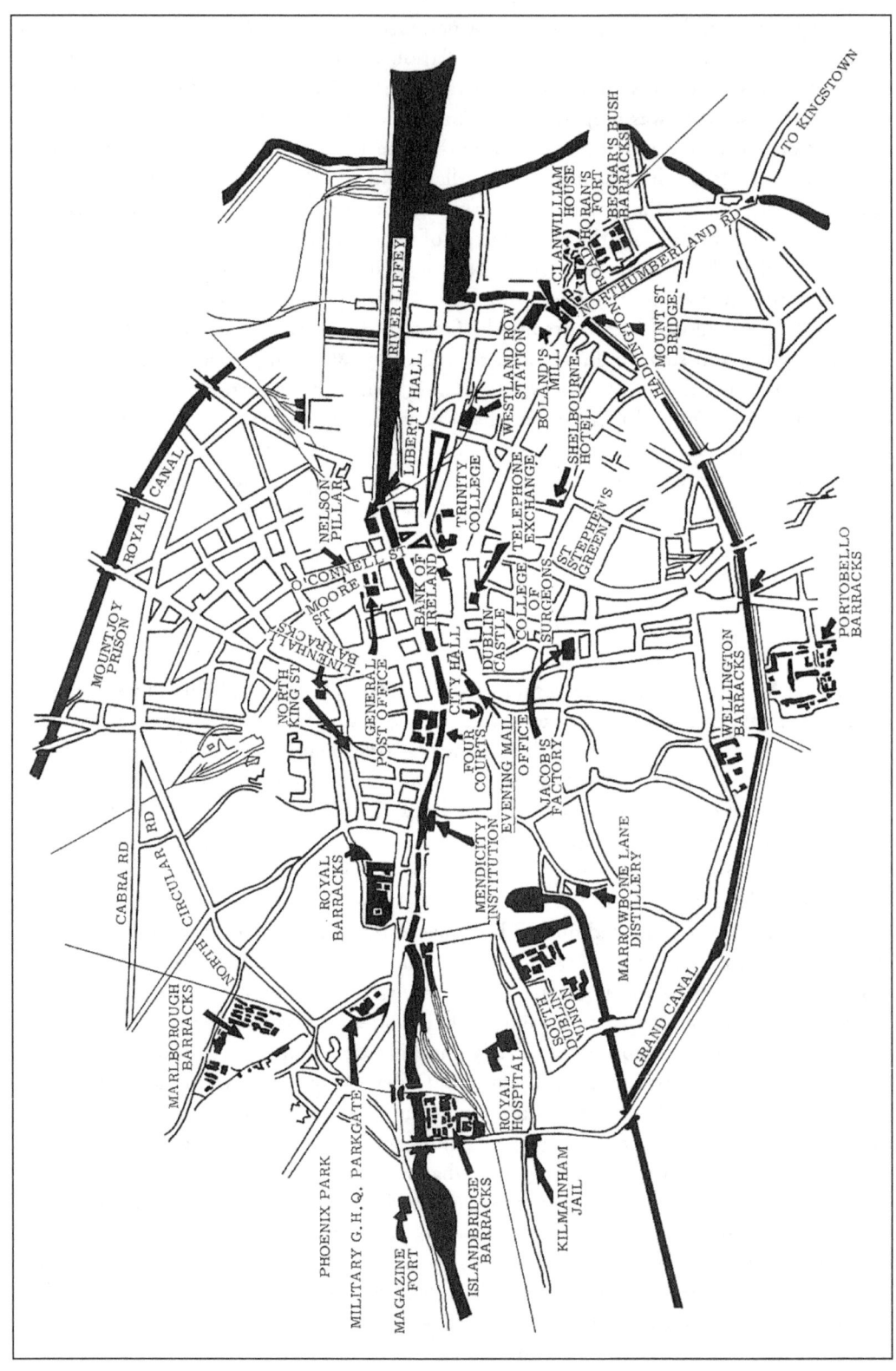

British troops from leaving. Seeing that it was so poorly guarded, they decided to try to capture it. A policeman on duty at the entrance was shot, and the Volunteers entered the yard. Hearing the shot, the few soldiers on duty ran out to the yard and drove off the Irishmen, who withdrew to city hall and the joint newspaper office of the *Daily Express* and *Evening Mail* overlooking the castle, in accordance with their original orders.

The main railway terminuses in the city were seized. Westland Row Station and Harcourt Street Station were taken over. At Lansdowne Road on the Kingstown line, the rails were torn up. Harcourt Station, it was found, could not be adequately garrisoned and was abandoned later that afternoon. At the Amiens Street, Kingsbridge and Broadstone terminuses, railway bridges and lines were blown up. The Great Northern Railway line was cut at Fairview. All train communications with the city were cut for a week. An attempt by the boys of Fianna Eireann to capture a large quantity of arms and ammunition from the Magazine Fort, an arsenal in Phoenix Park, was only partially successful before they were driven off. At other places telephone and telegraph wires were cut, briefly isolating Dublin Castle in the process.

At twelve o'clock, a combined force of Citizen Army and Volunteers took possession of St. Stephen's Green. All civilians were cleared from the park, and the gates were locked. Trenches within the park were dug, and barriers were thrown up. A number of houses overlooking the green were commandeered, including the Royal College of Surgeons at the corner of York Street and Little's public house at the corner of Cuffe Street. Snipers were placed in these and other buildings nearby. The Four Courts, home of the Irish judiciary, was occupied without any resistance. The adjoining Four Courts Hotel was also seized. On the bridges over the railway on the North Circular and Cabra roads, strong barricades were erected. Portobello Bridge, which commanded the approach to the city from the military barracks, was the site of one of the first skirmishes, shortly after midday. An outpost of the Four Courts was established at Davy's public house close to the bridge and facing the barracks. Seeing what was happening, a British officer raised the alarm. An initial attempt to dislodge the Volunteers was repulsed, but strong reinforcements succeeded in driving off the Volunteers.

The South Dublin Union in James' Street and the nearby Rowe's Distillery in Marrowbone Lane were occupied by units of the 4th Battalion under Eamonn Kent. Later in the day they came under attack, and after stiff fighting, during which both sides suffered casualties, they were driven from part of the building complex. Reinforcing the remaining buildings, they held out until the struggle ended on Sunday.

At 12:15 the Castle ordered troops up from the city barracks at Portobello, Kingsbridge, Richmond. The strength of these troops is given as follows: 3rd Royal Irish Regiment—18 officers, 385 other ranks; 10th Royal Dublin Fusiliers—37 officers, 430 other ranks; 3rd Royal Irish Rifles—21 officers, 650 other ranks.

At 12:30 telephone messages were sent to the Curragh and other barracks outside of Dublin, including Templemore and Athlone. London was notified, and reinforcements were requested. Lord French, the British Army commander-in-chief and himself an Irishman but a committed Unionist, ordered four divisions to be prepared for embarkation to Ireland. The first objectives of the British troops were (1) to take possession of the Magazine Fort

Opposite: *Dublin 1916, showing the Volunteer positions.*

in Phoenix Park, (2) to strengthen the guards at the Viceregal Lodge, and (3) to relieve Dublin Castle.

At 4:45 P.M. the first train of British reinforcements from the Curragh arrived at Kingsbridge and by 5:30 the whole cavalry column, numbering 1,600, was in the city. In addition a battery of four 18-pounders was ordered from Athlone. The 4th Dublin Fusiliers from Templemore, a composite battalion from Belfast, and an additional 1,000 more from the Curragh also arrived. By Thursday there were almost 20,000 British troops in Dublin, with machine guns and artillery. Earlier, at about 4:00 P.M., the Dublin Home Defense Force or the Georgius Rex, so called because of their cap badges but more derisively known by the people of Dublin as the "Gorgeous Wrecks"), returning to their Beggars Bush barracks, came under attack. Approaching down Northumberland Road in two columns they came under heavy fire from outposts of de Valera's 3rd Battalion. Unarmed as they were, many of the force were killed.

Exploratory probes by British troops were initiated on Monday afternoon, producing skirmishes at St. Stephen's Green, the North Wall and the Castle. Meanwhile Volunteer commandant Daly of the First Battalion, based at the Four Courts, captured the Linen Hall Barracks. Following the news that several of his men had been shot by the Volunteers, the chief commissioner of the Dublin Metropolitan Police ordered the withdrawal from the streets of his entire uniformed force. In their absence, looting began in the city. Shop windows in Lower Sackville Street were smashed and crowds of looters stole clothes and other goods. Sweet shops — Noblett's at the corner of Earl Street and Lemon's in Lower Sackville Street — were ransacked by children. Into Earl Street and on to Henry Street the looters moved unhampered by the police.

Shortly after 5:00 P.M. troops from Dublin Castle launched an assault on the ICA garrison of twenty-two Volunteers in city hall. By the use of machine guns they were able to pin the Citizen Army soldiers down as they rushed into the building, which was in total darkness. On the ground floor they took the surrender of a small group of wounded men and Citizen Army women from the hands of Dr. Kathleen Lynn, the senior ranking officer. They proceeded up through the building with caution, clearing each floor in turn, so that it was early Tuesday morning before the building was totally secured.

Tuesday

By Tuesday, some 5,000 British troops had arrived in Dublin. In almost every instance the soldiers could be conveyed only to within five or six miles of the city, owing to the disruption caused by damaged rails. There was comparative calm at first as the British military analyzed the situation. By the evening the British had thrown a cordon around Dublin and cut the city in two along the river Liffey, controlling the quays and all bridges and making it impossible to get from the north side to the south side of the city without challenge. British troops and artillery were moved into Trinity College, and it became British Military Headquarters. It was a natural fortress that the Volunteers had intended to seize, but lacked the numbers to do so. Fired from here, artillery was used to knock out some of the minor Republican outposts, drawing the cordon tighter. When St. Stephen's Green came under sniper fire from the surrounding houses, the Republicans, approximately 130 men and women, withdrew to the College of Surgeons. The British surrounded a Republican outpost at nearby Cork Hill, and at the *Daily Express* building artillery was brought to bear, prior to a successful assault by a detachment of the 5th Royal Dublin Fusiliers under the command of Second Lieutenant F. O'Neil.

A little four-page newspaper, *Irish War News,* appeared on the streets of Dublin. In it Pearse appealed to the citizens of Dublin to come to their aid. The people were too busy looting, though. Martial law was proclaimed by the British.

By late afternoon further British reinforcements arrived at Kingstown (now Dun Laoghaire) from mainland Britain. A little later Volunteer outposts near Phibsborough in north Dublin were attacked. The barricades at the railway bridges on the North Circular and Cabra roads were destroyed by shell fire. Volunteer casualties were reported as 40 killed or wounded, with 100 prisoners captured. By the end of the day the British had control of the North Circular Road and were pushing south towards the city center, hindered only by sniper fire.

Wednesday

Fresh reinforcements had now brought the British army strength up to a point where they outnumbered the Republicans by twenty to one. The battle now began in earnest. A machine gun placed high on the tower of the Fire Brigade Station opened up on Liberty Hall. Shell fire from the gunboat *Helga* was brought to bear, and Liberty Hall burst into

Liberty Hall headquarters of the Irish Citizen Army, was shelled by the gunboat Helga.

flames. It had been evacuated a little earlier, and there were no casualties among the Citizen Army. The British gunners on the Liffey and elsewhere opened up with a reckless abandonment at several commercial buildings. The gunfire was inaccurate, and many unintended buildings were hit and civilians killed. At one point a 9-pounder gun was fired against a single sniper. As British troops moved south towards the river, they came under sniper fire from Kelly's shop, at the corner of Bachelor's Walk. An 18-pounder was brought into Brunswick Street (today's Pearse Street) and anchored to the pavement by lifting some of the sets. Trained on the shop, the gun sent eleven shells the length of D'Olier Street that penetrated the brick walls of the premises, forcing the Volunteers, under Peader Bracken, to evacuate the position. Fires broke out in the city. Isolated as Dublin now was by a cordon, food could not get in and people began to go hungry. At St. Stephen's Green, the Citizen Army, having lost seven of its soldiers to sniper fire, evacuated its outposts around the park and sought protection in the surrounding buildings. Leading an assault on an enemy outpost near the Russell Hotel, Citizen Army officer Margaret Skinnider was badly wounded in her back and shoulder.

That evening battalions of the Sherwood Foresters arrived at Kingstown. One column entered by the Stillorgan road and reached the Royal Hospital in Dublin without any opposition. The other attempted to reach Dublin by the Ballsbridge road and came under heavy fire from de Valera's Third Battalion of Volunteers in Boland's Bakery and a number of other nearby houses. General Sir John Maxwell, the newly appointed commander-in-chief and a relative of the Countess Markievicz, who was fighting with the Citizen Army at St.

The burned-out shell of the General Post Office.

Stephen's Green, reported that his men had met with "great opposition."[6] The fighting lasted for about five hours. An Irish Republican tricolor had been hoisted on a distillery that de Valera hadn't enough men to occupy, and this was bombarded by shell fire from the gunship *Helga* on the Liffey. De Valera had barely 130 men, but by carefully dispersing them, he was able to hold a considerable area against a force of vastly superior numbers. About 20 men held the bakery, while others in two or three man units occupied houses along Haddington and Northumberland roads. A seven man unit held Clanwilliam House, commanding Lower Mount Street Bridge, over which the British troops had to cross. Eventually, by a concerted attack, the Sherwood Foresters were able to drive the Volunteers back. Clanwilliam House was set on fire and its defenders evacuated the building, losing three of their men in the fire. The British troops were able to cross the bridge and continue on to Dublin. They lost 4 officers killed and 14 wounded; other ranks had 216 killed and wounded. The Republicans lost 6 men. In Dublin that night, the atrocities began. The Foresters began shooting male citizens on sight in revenge at their losses.

Thursday

As day dawned the British made a successful assault on Boland's Mill. At the South Dublin Union the Volunteers were forced to evacuate against overwhelming odds. The cordon was drawing even tighter. Artillery was brought into play at every point. All day long the bombardment continued. The General Post Office was shelled and began to burn from the top down. Connolly, while out reconnoitering in the streets around the post office, was wounded twice by bullets. His foot was shattered. Dosed with morphine to deaden the pain, he continued to direct the battle from a stretcher. Whole streets were now ablaze in the capital. Throughout the day the battle continued, the post office continually under shell fire. Outside, the whole of Sackville Street from Nelson's Pillar to O'Connell Bridge was thickly strewn with debris. In the GPO Michael Rahilly ("The Rahilly," as he was known) sang patriotic songs to encourage the defenders. As yet, no Republican stronghold had surrendered, but the leaders of the Rising were becoming aware that without outside support they could not win.

Friday

Realizing that defeat was inevitable, Pearse issued the following statement to what was now the Irish Republican Army: "If we accomplish no more than we have accomplished, I am satisfied. I am satisfied that we have saved Ireland's honor...." He now ordered the withdrawal of the women and girls before the post office was completely encircled. Shaking hands with each one he thanked them for all they had done, telling them that they deserved a foremost place in the nation's history. Later that day, with the greater part of the building ablaze, Pearse ordered its evacuation. The plan was to escape out of a side door, cross Henry Street into the lane beyond, and into Moore Street and up it to Parnell Street, where the plan was to occupy Williams & Woods Jam Factory. From there the plan was to open communications with the Four Courts and then act in unison. The dash was not without incident. Henry Street was being raked by small-arms fire, and a British artillery post in Parnell Street commanded the lane into which they proposed to run. At dusk they hauled a horse van across Henry Street to give them some protection, and the evacuation got under way. Unknown to them, the Four Courts was completely cut off. There were seventeen casualties in the evacuation, killed or wounded. A house at the corner of Moore Street was entered, and the wounded were cared for. Meanwhile a group of Volunteers began burrowing through the partition walls in a bid to dig their way through to Parnell Street. At No. 16, Moore Street, they were halted by debris, and could not continue. A new headquarters was established here.

Saturday

British bombardment of the city continued. The post office was completely gutted when the roof fell in. Civilians running from burning buildings nearby were shot dead in the street, even though some carried white flags. Fighting intensified around the Four Courts, with a last battle fought for King's Street. Some 5,000 British soldiers, accompanied by armored cars and artillery, took 28 hours to advance about 150 yards against some 200 Republican fighters. In revenge for their heavy losses, troops of the South Staffordshire Regiment bayoneted and shot civilians hiding in cellars.

About midday the leaders of the Rising made the decision to surrender unconditionally to avoid any further loss of life. At half past three Pearse surrendered his sword to Brigadier General Lowe. A message was sent to the Republican commandants: "In order to prevent further slaughter of Dublin citizens, and in the hope of saving the lives of our fol-

The surrender document signed by Pearse and countersigned by Connolly.

lowers now surrounded and hopelessly outnumbered, the members of the Provisional Government present at Headquarters have agreed to an unconditional surrender, and the Commandants of the various districts in the City and Country will order their commands to lay down arms."

James Connolly countersigned the order on behalf of the Citizen Army. There was a reluctance on the part of some commandants to surrender, particularly where their defenses had not been penetrated and indeed they had extended their positions. It was Sunday before the last of the commandants, Thomas MacDonagh, surrendered. The insurrection was over.

The Provinces

At ten o'clock on Easter Monday, Thomas Ashe, commandant under James Connolly, mobilized the 5th Battalion at Knocksedan, in the north of County Dublin. By evening there were between 60 and 70 men assembled under Ashe's command. Their arms were an odd assortment: fifteen modern service rifles, twelve Martini single-shot rifles, some Mausers and twenty or thirty shotguns and revolvers. Ashe's orders were to disrupt and destroy enemy communications in north County Dublin. At Rogerstown Bridge he blew up the Great Northern Railway line, destroying communications between Belfast and Dublin. At Howth Junction, with its connections with Belfast and Britain, the telegraph lines were cut. On Tuesday morning, following a request from Connolly, Ashe sent 20 men under the command of Captain Richard Coleman to reinforce the garrisons at the GPO. The remainder, some 45 men, began a series of raids on RIC barracks. The town of Swords was captured and its arsenal distributed among the volunteers. Donabate Barracks added to their supply of modern arms. Garristown Barracks was also captured.

By Friday most of the north of the county was in Republican hands. Ashe's plan was to capture Asbourne barracks, then cut the Midland Great Western Railway line at Batterstown in order to hold up British reinforcements expected from Athlone. The barracks was a large two storey building fronting onto the main road. Ashe divided his forces into two sections. One section moved unobserved to the rear of the barracks. Ashe with the remainder of his men, using whatever cover they could find, advanced upon the front of the building. Moving forward they surprised a sergeant and two constables. One of the constables took to his heels and escaped. The sergeant was persuaded, under a white flag of truce, to approach the barracks and call upon the men inside to surrender. As he approached , he too took to

Eamon de Valera (right) under arrest following the failure of the 1916 Rising.

his heels and escaped. By now the men within the fortified barracks were aware of the situation. Ashe's call to surrender was met by a fusillade of rifle fire. The Volunteers opened up in response. Two homemade hand grenades were thrown at the building, but to little effect. The garrison had been reinforced, its windows protected with steel shutters, with loopholes for defensive firing. Barriers had been erected in front of the building. Nevertheless after half an hour's assault, the garrison decided to surrender. A rifle with a white flag attached was pushed through an upper window. Ashe ordered his men to cease fire. Cautiously a number of Volunteers approached the building. Then, a short distance away to the northwest, the Volunteers heard the hooting of car horns and saw a convoy of some twenty motor vehicles approaching. They were full of RIC reinforcements, estimated at 80 in number.

Ashe reacted quickly to the new danger. He sent a man to the Volunteers at the rear of the building, to get them to attack the approaching RIC on their left, while he and the men at the front dashed down to the crossroads to hold them, to prevent the police from disembarking and spreading out. The Volunteers got into position first, using ditches and the higher bank on the opposite side. The police convoy was halted along the road and pinned in by the smaller force. The police disembarked from their vehicles and dived into the ditches on either side of the road, returning fire. Firing had continued for about half an hour when the Volunteers who had been attacking the barracks from the rear came up on the police left flank and opened fire. Ashe then sent a runner for reinforcements. Their orders were to divide their forces, one group to attack the right flank and the others to the rear and thus surround the police. With the reinforcements in position the Volunteers tightened their grip. By rapid, systematic fire and good use of the terrain, the Volunteers were able to disguise their inferior numbers. For five hours the battle continued. The Volunteers were fearful that more British reinforcements would appear — but they did not come. At about 4:00 P.M., during a lull in the firing, a shout went up — "Charge!" — and Lieutenant Richard Mulcahy of the Irish Volunteers and about seven of his men, with fixed bayonets, charged at the police. The police panicked and broke ranks. They fled from the road towards a farm

Thomas Ashe (center) under arrest in Kilmainham Prison, 1916.

laborer's cottage, continually under fire. After ten minutes the police agreed to surrender, on the understanding that they would not be killed, and Ashe ordered a ceasefire. Soon after, the barracks' garrison, some twenty in number, likewise surrendered.

Ashe felt a keen sense of admiration for the foe when, asking the barracks' commanding officer why he had not opened fire during the battle, the commander replied that he had already surrendered and would not break his word. The police lost eleven men killed, and almost twenty wounded. Two Volunteers were killed and five wounded. Over 90 rifles and a large supply of ammunition was captured. Ashe treated his prisoners honorably. The wounded were taken to the hospital. The others were lined up and told that they might return to their homes but should not ever again be found in arms against the Irish Republic. Ashe moved his men off in good order, and they found quarters that night at Borranstown. The next day, continually on the move, they quartered for the night at Newbarn. The following morning, Sunday, some of the outer pickets intercepted a police officer carrying a white flag. He carried with him a handwritten note, bearing Pearse's signature, with an order for them to lay down their arms.

Elsewhere in the provinces, hope had turned to despair, as orders for the Rising were countermanded by MacNeill. Then came news that in Dublin fighting had broken out. The commandants in the provinces were faced with the dilemma of whether they could, or should, lead their men, inadequately armed, against an enemy who was now forewarned. Some individual companies from the southwest, two hundred to three hundred in number all told, made their way to Dublin. In Cork, plans had been made for the Volunteers to link up with those of Kerry and receive the German arms. On Good Friday, with the capture of the *Aud* and MacNeill's cancellation of maneuvers, it appeared that the Rising had been postponed. The Volunteers were stood down. Then came the countermand from MacNeill that the Rising would take place.

Thomas MacCurtain and his deputy, Terence MacSwinney, anguished over what to do, given that the British forces, both military and police, were now fully prepared to counter any rising in the southwest. The RIC had instigated arrests of known Volunteers. To order men out would have been suicidal. Added to this a bitter civil war might have developed. Redmond had instructed his National Volunteers to support the British military, and they were out on the streets in support. Neither Cork nor Kerry took part in the Rising.

In Meath and Louth there were skirmishes between Volunteers and the police. In Wexford some 600 Volunteers under the command of Robert Brennan seized control of the town of Enniscorthy. Detachments of Volunteers under Commandant Paul Galligan took up positions in the countryside of North Wexford. Wexford was held until Pearse's surrender, and even then the Volunteers refused to surrender until emissaries escorted to Dublin were personally ordered to surrender by Pearse.

It was Easter Tuesday when the Rising in Galway began. To a prepared plan Commandant Liam Mellows ordered the assault on police barracks throughout the county, the erection of barricades, destruction of bridges, and the cutting of telegraph wires. The town of Athenry was seized by some 1,000 volunteers. Throughout the county there was loss of life on both sides in the skirmishes that took place. Once organized, the British counterattacked with ruthless efficiency. At Moyvore, the Volunteers were trapped in an encirclement by soldiers and police. The local parish priest, under a white flag, was persuaded to speak to them, asking them to lay down their arms. While some managed to break out of the encirclement hundreds of them were captured following their surrender and deported as prisoners to England.

Exact numbers of casualties in the Easter Rising are unknown. British casualties are estimated at 500, with almost twice that number, including civilians, on the Irish side. Included in the British casualties were six of Redmond's National Volunteers, who had fought for the British, and three members of the Dublin Metropolitan Police Force, who though unarmed, had been shot by the Volunteers. Fifteen civilians were shot or bayoneted to death in cellars in North King Street by soldiers of the 26th South Staffordshire Regiment (Territorials). General Maxwell, in a statement in the *Daily Mail*, admitted that brutalities had been committed: "Possibly some unfortunate incidents, which we should regret now, may have occurred.... [I]t is even possible that under the horrors of this attack some of them 'saw red'; that is the inevitable consequence of a rebellion of this kind." Three noted Dublin citizens, Francis Sheehy Skeffington, Thomas Dickson and Patrick McIntyre, were arrested, taken to Portobello Barracks and there shot by order of Captain Bowen-Colthurst. On their journey to the barracks the three prisoners witnessed Bowen-Colthurst personally shoot a boy called Coade, at Rathmines. At the instigation of a senior British officer, Sir Francis Vane, Bowen-Colthurst was eventually court-martialled, but was found to be of unsound mind at the time. He was committed to Broadmoor Criminal Asylum. Damage to buildings was estimated at about £2½ million. Large parts of Dublin lay in ruins. As the arrested rebels were marched across the city they were met by the jeers and boos of the crowds, particularly in the slum areas. The mass of public opinion was against them. But then the reprisals began.

The United States government expressed "their hope that Great Britain would exercise clemency in the treatment of Irish political prisoners generally." John Redmond, and Sir Edward Carson, that arch–Unionist, appealed for clemency in the House of Commons. "No true Irishman calls for vengeance," Carson said. "It will be a matter requiring the greatest wisdom and the greatest calmness in dealing with these men. Whatever is done, let it be done not in a moment of temporary excitement but in a moment of deliberation."[7] Prime Minister Herbert Asquith and his cabinet were deaf to their entreaties. The leaders of the Rising were tried by court-martial and shot in secret. Pearse, MacDonagh and Clarke were shot at dawn on the morning of 3 May 1916 in the yard of Kilmainham Prison. On the 4th, just prior to his execution, Joseph Plunkett was permitted to marry his fiancé, Grace Gifford. With him on that day were executed Edward Daly, Michael O'Hanrahan, and Willie Pearse. On the 5th, Major John MacBride was shot. On the following Monday, 8 May, Eamonn Kent, Michael Mallin, J.J. Heuston and Cornelius Colbert died. Finally, on Friday, 12 May, Sean MacDermott and James Connolly were executed. Willie Pearse was not one of the leaders, and it is generally believed that he was shot simply because he was the brother of Patrick Pearse. Most disgusting of all, perhaps, to the Irish of all persuasions, was the execution of James Connolly, who was dying. He was shot in a chair, since he could not stand. The death sentences on Countess Markievicz, Thomas Ashe and Eamon de Valera were commuted to life imprisonment. After a highly dubious trial in which he was found guilty of treason committed outside of England, Sir Roger Casement was hanged at Pentonville Prison, London, on 3 August 1916. The rank and file of the Irish Volunteers proceeded through a series of prisons before being interned at Frongoch in Wales.

The Rising was a failure. Connolly, in his series of articles on insurrectionary warfare, had carefully analyzed why and how previous risings had failed. The Republicans' best hope was to emulate the Moscow insurrection of 1905, having learnt from its mistakes. Instead, their plans in shambles because of MacNeill's countermand, they opted for a blood sacrifice which, following their executions, united the people behind the Republican cause. The failure of the south and west to rise in support of Dublin meant that there remained the potential of an Irish Republican army in the field. A later Royal Commission investigating the Rising expressed the concern that the presence of such an army would have been formidable. Once committed to a Rising in Dublin, Connolly certainly did not believe that the British would use artillery. Some have claimed that it was his opinion that a capitalist nation would not wantonly destroy commercial buildings. Connolly's belief in the nonuse of artillery was a military judgment, in that it went against all the teachings of military science. Bringing artillery into the close quarters of street fighting could well have resulted in the seizure of the guns. A general bombardment of the city from a distance, thus not risking seizure of the guns, would have been possible only if the entire nonbelligerent population could be removed. Doing this would have delayed final victory and given the Volunteers in the provinces time to capture strategic points in their own areas before marching to the aid of their comrades in the capital.

In Dublin, just as in Moscow, government troops made slow progress at first. In Moscow this was because of the multitude of barricades that had been erected over a period of time, sometimes several in the same street. They were erected everywhere. This had the double purpose of preventing cavalry charges and making it impossible for the advancing troops to tell which were defended and which were mock barricades. This greatly hindered the government troops, who had to treat every barricade with caution before they dared to pass it. At the approaches to the center of the city, there were more substantial barricades constructed of telegraph poles, the iron supports to the overhead wires of electric trams, doors, railings, even tramcars to give the barricades solidity. The whole lot was lashed together with wire, making them difficult to tear down. In Dublin this was not done to the same extent, no doubt because of the time constraint. In Dublin, as in Moscow, the barricades themselves were not defended. Instead, as the troops approached the barricades they found themselves coming under sniper fire from both sides of the street. All they could do was to retire and call up the artillery pieces which would then bombard the house and barricade, by which time the insurrectionists had withdrawn to another ambush site. The troops would then advance once more to the next barricade and so on. All fighting on the part of the defenders was done at close quarters rather than at long range, where the superior weapons of the

Michael Malin, commander of the St. Stephen's Green garrison, was executed for his part in the Rising.

government forces would tell. While the Russian government forces proceeded with caution and eventually succeeded in crushing the rebels, the British acted more ruthlessly and to an organized plan, dividing up the city into sections and using artillery to a greater extent before mopping up with ground troops.

Connolly based his account of the Moscow insurrection on the work of the journalist H.W. Nevinson, from his book, *The Dawn of Russia*. A far more useful account, if Connolly had only known about it, was Lenin's analysis, *The Lessons of the Moscow Uprising*.[8] As Lenin saw it, the rising in Moscow provided lessons in new tactics and organization. Military tactics had changed since the 19th century, and those planning insurrection had to take this into account. Rebels could not defend barricades or buildings with revolvers and rifles against enemy artillery. It required a new strategy—guerrilla warfare, using small mobile units, which Lenin suggested might consist of ten-, three- or even two-man detachments. These would use hit and run tactics. One could not ignore, Lenin wrote, "the new question of tactics and organization called forth by street fighting under the conditions imposed by modern military technique."

The Dublin Volunteers did exactly what Lenin had advised against. They garrisoned buildings—they became static. This led to enemy artillery being used against them with the inevitable consequences. The implications of their activities, or lack of them, have perhaps not been fully considered. For example, though they cut telegraph and telephone wires isolating Dublin from the rest of the country, telephones and telegraph services within the city remained unhindered. The Telephone Exchange in Crown Alley was neither seized nor destroyed, though it was in the original plan to blow it up.[9] Failure to do so resulted in the British forces being able to use the system to draw down artillery fire on specific buildings. If any building had to be used as a static headquarters, then Trinity College would have been a better choice. It was a building intended to be occupied, but lack of Volunteers prevented this. The building and its ample grounds was the most central and commanding position within the city. It was built like a fortress, but more important it contained the arsenal of the Officer Training Corps and housed some one hundred service rifles and many thousands of rounds of ammunition. Perhaps the greatest example of the Republicans' military naivety was the placing of troops in the park at St. Stephen's Green. It was an open enclosure surrounded by tall buildings on every side, and from which almost every corner of the park could be fired upon by snipers.

The British were more efficient than their Russian counterparts. Initially they concentrated on containment until their forces could be built up. They greatly outnumbered the Republicans, and with a modern rail network could quickly call on more reinforcements from other parts of Great Britain if necessary. They also had superior, up-to-date weapons, and they were better trained. The Easter Rising was an exercise, and a lesson, in what not to do when taking on the might of the British Empire. Comfort could be drawn by the Republicans from the exploits of Thomas Ashe at Ashbourne. He had shown how a war of independence could be won: not cooped up in confined city streets, in buildings that could be destroyed by shell fire, but out in the countryside, in battles of their choosing, gaining ground, but never statically occupying it.

2

Political Reorganization

Under a new prime minister, David Lloyd George, the British government reviewed its policy on Ireland. In a spirit of appeasement it released many of the three thousand men and women arrested after the Rising. The new prime minister called an Irish Convention to solve, as he described it, "the Irish Problem." Since Sinn Fein, the now dominant Irish Republican party boycotted it, the convention was a complete failure. The House of Commons then proposed enforcing conscription on Ireland. The Irish Nationalists in the Commons voted against the bill. Nevertheless it was passed into law on 16 April, by 301 votes to 103. In protest the Nationalists left the Commons and returned to Ireland to organize resistance there. During 1917 Sinn Fein won a series of by-elections, including East Clare (Eamon de Valera) and Kilkenny City (William Cosgrave). British policy reverted to its former position, and during July and August 1917 spokesmen of the Republican movement were arrested for sedition in the form of speeches. Caught up in these arrests was Thomas Ashe, the hero of the skirmish at Ashbourne. He was found guilty of sedition, and sentenced to one year's hard labor. In Mountjoy Prison he and the other Sinn Feiners campaigned to be treated as political, rather than common, criminals. Refusal of such status led to a hunger strike on the part of the prisoners. The prison authorities responded by force-feeding, which tragically led to the death of Ashe. His funeral on 30 September 1917 was attended by tens of thousands of mourners. Twelve Volunteers fired three volleys over his grave in salute, and Michael Collins stepped forward to deliver the oration. It was brief: "Nothing additional remains to be said. That volley which we have just heard is the only speech which it is proper to make above the grave of a dead Fenian."[1]

In the spring of 1918 further arrests were made in the so-called German Plot. Evading capture, Michael Collins, a junior officer in the GPO during the Rising, began to establish his position within both the Volunteers and Sinn Fein, the political party. With the Republican movement apparently leaderless, the British authorities set about breaking the will of those remaining. Drilling by Volunteers was prohibited, as was the wearing of unauthorized military uniforms. On 21 June a by-election was held in East Cavan in Ulster that was seen as a litmus paper of the state of the country. The British authorities expected it to be won by the Parliamentary Nationalists rather than the Unionists, but to their consternation it was won by Arthur Griffiths, the imprisoned Sinn Fein leader, with a majority of 1,200 votes.

To prevent Nationalist outpourings, certain districts in Ireland with strong republican tendencies were proclaimed as Special Military Areas, and all public meetings, including fairs, were prohibited. On 4 July, Sinn Fein, the Volunteers, Cumann na mBan (the women's movement), and the Gaelic League were all proclaimed as dangerous associations, and meetings of these organizations were banned. In the following months the police broke up meetings, sporting events and concerts, using baton and bayonet charges in some cases. During September 1918 ninety-six members of Sinn Fein were imprisoned by civil and military court-martial on political offenses.

At the general election of 14 December 1918, Sinn Fein triumphed at the polls: Sinn Fein 67, Irish Nationalist 6, Unionist 26. The people of Ireland as a whole had voted for a Republic by a majority of 73 percent. Twenty-four of the thirty-two counties returned only Republican members. Of the nine counties of Ulster, the Unionists had a majority in only four—Antrim, Derry, Down and Armagh. They were in a minority in Tyrone and Fermanagh, while three of the Ulster counties, Donegal, Cavan and Monaghan, returned no Unionists at all. The *Times* reported on 17 January 1919: "The General Election in Ireland was treated by all parties as a plebiscite and admittedly Sinn Fein swept the country."

The people of Ireland as a whole had given Sinn Fein a mandate to pursue a policy of independence from the British Empire. The elected Republican members, both Sinn Fein and the Irish Nationalists, refused to sit in the Westminster Parliament and instead formed their own parliament, Dail Eireann (Assembly of Ireland). It met for the first time in the Round Room of the Dublin Mansion House on 21 January 1919. All elected members, regardless of political party, Unionists included, were invited to attend. Of the possible 105 members,[2] 33 Republicans who would have been there were in prison, most without trial since the previous 17 May. The 34 member, Pierce McCann of Tipperary East, had died in prison of the influenza pandemic then sweeping the world. Yet, despite the outcome of this democratic election, what had happened in the rest of the United Kingdom was to decide Ireland's fate.

The coalition government led by Prime Minister Lloyd George won the majority, but only with the support of the Ulster Unionists. Such support came with a price tag. In December 1919, Lloyd George proposed an Amending Act for the Home Rule Bill whereby Ireland was to become a self governing state; however, Ulster, or rather the six counties of Ulster with a Protestant majority, would not come under the control of the Dublin Parliament. They would have their own parliament based in Belfast and would still remain as part of the United Kingdom. This proposal became an act in December 1920. Thus was democracy thwarted and it was reflected in a newspaper editorial of the time: "Lord French is to-day the absolute master of Ireland. He alone, always in consultation with his Chief Secretary, will decide upon the type of government the country is to have, and it is he, rather than any member of the House of Commons, who will judge of political and administration reforms.... The programme for administration has been practically settled."[3] In this statement the people of Ireland were shown the futility of maintaining the struggle for independence within the framework of civil debate. When the forces of oppression continue to maintain themselves in power against the electoral wishes of the people, peace is broken, and a state of uncertain war has replaced it. The people of Ireland had decided their own fate through the democratic process. In their eyes Lord French represented an alien government. The first session of the Irish Parliament, the Dail, opened with Cathal Brugha presiding. He read out a message to the free nations of the world: "To the Nations of the World! Greeting. The Nation of Ireland having proclaimed her national independence, calls through her elected representatives in Parliament assembled in the Irish Capital on January

The first Dail Eireann, 1919. Thirty-six of its elected members were in prison.

21, 1919, upon every free nation to support the Irish Republic by recognizing Ireland's national status and her right to its vindication at the Peace Congress...." The clerks of the Dail for the day were appointed, and the roll call of members of the Dail was read. In response to thirty-six of these members, there came the response "Fe ghlas ag Gallaibh!" (imprisoned by the foreign enemy). The provisional constitution of the Dail was read and passed unanimously. Then with everyone present standing, the declaration of independence was read, first in Irish and then in English. When Brugha had finished, he addressed the members: "Deputies, you understand from what is asserted in this Declaration that we are now done with England. Let the world know it and those who are concerned bear it in mind." The die was cast. There was no going back.

The British government's reaction was to censor all Irish newspapers. Not to be mentioned were any references to the democratic program, the declaration of independence or the speeches of the proposer and seconder of the declaration of independence. As the Mansion House had been crowded, what was said was passed by word of mouth, and an underground press presented their words to the world. Eamon de Valera, still in prison, and one of the senior surviving Volunteer officers, was appointed head of the Dail, as Priomh-Aire, or president, with the likewise imprisoned Arthur Griffith as his deputy. On the second day Count Plunkett, father of the executed Joseph Plunkett, was appointed minister for foreign affairs. Eoin MacNeill was appointed minister for finance. Richard Mulcahy was appointed minister for national defense and Michael Collins minister for home affairs. The Dail set about creating an alternative government to take over from the British. The new government adopted a policy of resistance against Britain: first passive, then obstructive and finally active.

It had such great hopes, this Irish government, "with a Ministry of Foreign Affairs that tried in vain to get Woodrow Wilson to see it, a Ministry of Finance that exacted five or ten pounds from small shop-keepers who could ill afford it, a Ministry of Defence that tried to buy old fashioned weapons at outrageous prices from shady characters, and a Ministry of Home Affairs that established courts of justice with part-time Volunteer policemen and no gaols at all."[4]

One of its first positive actions was to secure the release of its members in prison. Collins, who had escaped arrest and in the absence of the arrested leaders had risen to prominence, broke de Valera out of Lincoln Gaol. Sean McGarry, Sean Milroy and Robert Barton were likewise rescued. On 7 March, in a face-saving gesture, the British government made a general release of its untried prisoners: Arthur Griffith, Countess Markievicz, W.T. Cosgrave, Dr. Richard Hayes, Dr. Brian Cusack and Joseph McGuinness.

On 1 April 1919, de Valera was present at the opening of the second session of the Dail. He was formally appointed president. He in his turn appointed Michael Collins as minister of finance, and Richard Mulcahy as chief of staff of the Irish Republican Army. Collins was given full power to raise a national loan "without further reference to the Dail." This clause allowed Collins to divert money to the military. Up to this point the British government had been exclusively in control of Irish revenue and taxation. If it was to have any credibility, it was essential for the Republican Government to raise a revenue. This took the form of a public loan for the campaign for international recognition and for the promotion of trade and commerce. Also included in the scope of the loan was money for the provision of a republican civil service and the establishment of arbitration courts. A land mortgage bank was established to finance the reoccupation of untenanted land. By moving thus so the Dail had become more than just a government in name only; it was becoming an alternative government.

Britain's response was to close down newspapers that reported the proceedings, or carried advertisements relating to the National Loan Scheme. The British declared that the Loan Scheme was in itself illegal, and used every means in its power to suppress it. A special government task force raided banks and checked their accounts for any trace of the loan. Yet, despite this harassment, £379,000 was raised in Ireland and almost $5 million in the United States. In the following year the Dail declared the British collection of income tax in Ireland to be illegal and ordered Irish people to refuse to pay it. The British found it impossible to take effective action against the wholesale refusal to pay. Upon the instruction of the Dail, taxes forwarded by county councils to the British Local Government Board in Dublin were now stopped. In April 1920 income tax offices in Dublin and the provinces were raided by Volunteers, and all papers and records were set on fire.

Michael Collins was appointed minister for home affairs and later minister of finance under de Valera.

The arrest of members of the Dail at 73, Harcourt St., Dublin, November 1919.

This action proved popular with all Ireland, regardless of political persuasion. Further dismantlement of the British administration occurred continually right up to the end of the War for Independence. The Dublin Custom House was raided and set on fire on 25 May 1921. All financial and other records relating to British government departments in Ireland were destroyed. Civil administration could not be maintained by the British without proper records, and, more important, without the support of the people. They now possessed neither of these prerequisites.

Another blow to the British administration was the boycotting of British law courts and the setting up of Republican courts in their place. Between 15 April and 8 June 1920, Republican courts were established in 21 of Ireland's 32 counties. These new courts provided inexpensive justice. The judges were rarely trained or qualified but had an innate sense of justice and fair play. Both solicitors and barristers put their trust in this new form of justice, and even the *Irish Times,* an avowedly Unionist newspaper, freely confessed that "the Sinn Fein Courts are steadily extending their jurisdiction and dispensing justice, even-handedly between man and man, Catholic and Protestant ... landlord and tenant."[5] A very good example of the works of the Republican courts and the attendant police force (formed in June 1919) occurred down in Munster. On 17 November 1919, two bank officials traveling by car from Millstreet to Knocknagree with £16,700 were held up by masked men at Ballydaly. The robbery was reported to the RIC, which were quick to blame it on the local Volunteers. Local commander Liam Lynch investigated the robbery. The normal procedures open to the RIC were not available to him, so he had to make use of whatever alternative resources became available. All local Volunteers were instructed to garner whatever facts or gossip they could and report back. By sifting through such evidence a group of ten men were identified as probable suspects. Warrants were issued by the Republican police for their arrest. Eight of the ten men were arrested, and put on trial on 27 April 1920. The leader of the gang and four of his accomplices confessed, revealing where they had hidden the money. As a consequence £9,208 was recovered. Seven of the prisoners were found guilty, five of whom were deported from Ireland for terms of up to 15 years. The recovered money was returned to the bank.

To further Ireland's cause, the Irish Self-Determination League was established in England and Wales as a front organization for Sinn Fein. The purpose of its many branches was multifunctional. They collected for the relief of distress in Ireland caused by British violence and fostered an Irish awareness in the immigrant population through the teaching of the Irish language, music and other cultural pursuits. Their call for self-determination for Ireland was sympathetically received by the emerging Labor Party and the Co-operative Movement. This was a sympathy that the government viewed with concern as a spread of international socialism.

Abroad, the most important mission was to establish Ireland's credentials as a nation. At the Paris Peace Conference of 1919, the Irish-American politician Frank P. Walshe interceded with President Wilson. However, the president informed Walshe that there was an agreement between the Committee of Four (the U.S.A., Britain, France and Italy) that no small nation should appear before it without the unanimous consent of the whole committee. This meant that Britain would, and did, prevent Ireland from getting a hearing. On 31 May de Valera left for America to lead a campaign of recognition there. He did not return until Christmas Eve 1920. Cathal Brugha, minister for defense, was appointed acting president in his absence.

An election poster for Arthur Griffith, then in prison.

Up until this point the Volunteers, the military wing of the Republican movement, were an autonomous organization. de Valera was priomh-aire of the Dail and president of both Sinn Fein and commander in chief of the Volunteers; but Michael Collins, the newly appointed president of the Supreme Council of the IRB, was considered by some to be the successor of Pearse as the president of the Irish Republic. Brugha recognized that there was a potential clash between the Dail and the IRB. To remove any doubt as to which was the supreme organization he suggested, on 20 August 1919, that the Volunteers should swear an oath to the elected government, the Dail. Collins and other members of the Army Executive, essentially IRB members, were opposed to the oath, maintaining that the Volunteers' oath to the Republic was sufficient. They were concerned that some day the Dail might compromise the Republican cause, as indeed it did. Brugha saw it as an attempt by the IRB to maintain

Eamon de Valera was appointed head of the Dail as priomh-aire, or president.

control over the army. The matter was discussed in the Dail, and with Arthur Griffith's support Brugha got his way. The Volunteers were required to swear an oath to the government of Ireland, thus bringing them under the Dail's control. Within the oath was the proposal that members of the Dail "would not yield a voluntary support to any pretended government authority, or power within Ireland, hostile and inimical thereto," in essence referring to the British government. Britain, alarmed that a rival government was operating in Ireland, with the support of an army, responded by declaring Dail Eireann "a dangerous association." Thereafter the Dail met in secret, and not necessarily the full Dail. Its control over the Volunteers in the process was considerably weakened, thus allowing Collins to implement his own more militant policy without recourse to the authority of the Irish government. Some form of military confrontation against the British now seemed inevitable.

3

Military Reorganization

Contrary to all expectations the Rising had lasted a week, and not all Republican garrisons had been crushed. With the order to surrender, Commandant de Valera made contact with the British military to arrange the surrender details. Unarmed, he and the volunteers marched out into Gratton Street — their white flag carried by the first-aid man — then along its length to Mount Street. Here they were met by British soldiers. One of the young Volunteers, Andy McDonnell, later revealed the following:

> The British troops who surrounded us in Mount Street did not know what to make of us. We were something unheard of before — rebels against the Empire. The officers were inclined to be friendly, if somewhat surprised that we showed no sign of fear or regret.... We were lined up under a heavy escort. Our Commandant came down the line and shook hands with every man, with tears in his eyes.
>
> Days of confinement under primitive and unorganized conditions followed. At first the Boland's garrison were housed in damp cattle stalls in the RDS grounds. After some days they were marched to Richmond Barracks ... I cannot recall ... how many different places we were brought to, but one afternoon the young lads were taken before a senior officer who told us he was taking it upon himself to release us, as he felt we were too young to realize what we were doing when we took arms against the mighty Empire.... He had no doubt we would not be led astray again, and he was sending us home to our parents and hoped that they would deal with us. We were escorted to the gate and told to go home.[1]

For the older men things were a little harder. Between 1 May and 16 June the British deported to England some 2,519 prisoners, many unconnected with the Rising. They were dispersed throughout the prisons of England and Scotland: Aylesbury, Dartmoor, Glasgow, Knutsford, Lewes, Perth, Reading, Stafford, Wakefield, Wandsworth and Woking. Some 65 of those given life sentences, including Thomas Ashe, Eamon de Valera, Eoin MacNeill, Desmond Fitzgerald, Harry Boland and Austin Stack, were sent to Dartmoor, England's harshest prison. Stafford Gaol was converted into a military prison and was guarded by soldiers. Initially the Republicans sent here were kept in isolation, one to a cell, and under a strict regime; but after a month here, and in the other prisons too, they were granted prisoner-of-war status. The cell doors were allowed to remain open, and they were permitted to socialize and use the exercise yard at will.

In June the authorities decided to centralize their prisoners and relocated them to Frongoch, near Bala, in Merionethshire, a former German prisoner-of-war camp in Wales. Frongoch was divided into two camps, North and South, based upon an old distillery building, which was converted into an infirmary. In the North Camp prisoners were housed in 35 wooden huts, 30 men to a hut. In the South Camp they were housed in the distillery grain lofts. There was a cookhouse and a barber, as well as a tailor, a shoemaker, carpenters and engineering workshops. The prison day began at 5:30 A.M., ending with a final roll call at 7:30 P.M. Sports were encouraged to dissipate excess energy, as were educational classes to occupy the mind. Those more committed to the cause radicalized the other prisoners. The Volunteer director of training, J.J. O'Connell, was made camp commandant. A quartermaster was appointed, and a Provost Marshal to ensure discipline.

Daily orders were instituted, as were drill and fatigues. Classes on tactics and strategy were taught. Of particular note was the debate over static warfare. This harked back to an address Major John MacBride made to his men before their surrender at Easter. MacBride had fought alongside the Boers in the South African War against Britain. He advocated the approach taken by Christian de Wett, the Boer commander, who used irregular troops made up of farmers who, having successfully ambushed British troops, returned home to their farms the next day. MacBride warned his men that never again should they allow themselves to be cornered in a building, surrounded by superior man and fire power. Among the avid converts to MacBride's method of warfare was Michael Collins.

At Christmas 1916 the Republican prisoners were released, as the British put it, as a gesture of reconciliation. The internees from Frongoch arrived from Wales at the North Wall on the river Liffey, Dublin. There were few people to meet them as the British authorities had concealed the time of the return to avoid demonstrations.

Raising an Army

The Irish prison camps in Britain became the universities of Republicanism, and those men released from them in 1917 were its graduates — indoctrinated and committed soldiers. They returned to Ireland to organize a new and more powerful IRA. Also at this time, February 1917, James Connolly's Irish Citizen Army was reconstituted as a separate entity. Its council appointed James O'Neill as commandant of its army. The question of the relationship to the Irish Volunteers (IRA) came up for consideration. The general feeling was that the Citizen Army should operate independently and retain its own constitution. While it shared in the belief of an independent Ireland, it found itself sometimes at odds with Sinn Fein over its socialist principles. A conference was held at which the Citizen Army was represented by O'Neill and Richard McCormack, while Cathal Brugha and Michael Collins represented the Volunteers. It was agreed that each army should retain its own status and constitution. Neither side, it was agreed, would engage in military operations without first letting the other side know. Michael Collins agreed to act as liaison between the two groups. This arrangement fell down, though, when the Citizen Army, planning a raid on Kingsbridge Station, where it was reported that there were two wagons containing military stores, discovered that the Dublin Brigade of the Irish Volunteers had got there before them. An angry O'Neill informed Collins of the situation. Collins informed O'Neill that the Dublin Brigade had not told him of their plans. As a result a direct link between the ICA and the Dublin Brigade was initiated to prevent further problems of this nature. Thereafter both armies sometimes worked on joint ventures where extra men were required.

In August 1917, Thomas Ashe, hero of Ashbourne and a senior member in the IRB, attended a meeting at the Keating Branch of the Gaelic League to further the plans for the reorganization of the Irish Volunteers. On 5 August 1917, he gave an oration to Roger Casement, at Ardfert, where he, Casement, had been arrested in the previous year. Between ten and twelve thousand people gathered to hear him. Three thousand men, many in Volunteer uniform, marched there, and there were also three hundred horsemen, five hundred cyclists and a number of pipe bands who attended. Ashe, commandant of the Dublin Brigade, was later arrested for making a seditious speech and sent to Mountjoy Prison. Denied political status, he went on hunger strike. He was force-fed, but in the process he developed pneumonia and died, on 25 September. His funeral was attended by 9,000 uniformed Volunteers. At the graveside a firing party gave a final salute. Michael Collins stepped forward to give the funeral oration. It was short and to the point: "Nothing additional remains to be said. That volley which we have just heard is the only speech which is proper to make over the grave of a dead Fenian."

Idealistic young men, mainly between the ages of eighteen and twenty-five, educated, a goodly number with university degrees, stirred by such speeches, joined the Volunteers. John Whelan, an aspiring writer who became swept up in the excitement of all things Irish, changed his name to Sean O'Faolain. In his second term at university he was approached by another young student, who invited him to join the college company of Irish Volunteers, as they were still called by many:

> Straightway my whole life changed. The university became a conspiracy. I was now both a student and a revolutionary. Never will I forget the first day I stood in a field, in a deep glen, somewhere to the southwest of the city, with a score of other raw recruits, being given my first drill by some older student, while along the two hills overlooking the glen other Volunteers stood on the lookout for police or military. Before we were dismissed our captain, Ray Kennedy, a lecturer in the Chemistry Department, spoke to us about what we were, and were there for, about the coming fight, about secrecy and loyalty. It was an autumn day of sun and shower, and just as he began to speak to us a faint, gentle sprinkling rain began to fall on us, and then the sun floated out again and sparkled on every leaf and blade of grass as if some invisible presence had passed over us with a lighted taper, binding us together not only in loyalty and in friendship but in something dearer still that I am not ashamed to call love.[2]

Such a show of strength at Ashe's funeral alarmed the British authorities. An order was issued prohibiting parades, drilling, the carrying of arms and the wearing of unauthorized uniforms in public. The response of the Volunteer leadership was to challenge this prohibition. On Sunday 21 October 1917, a series of public parades were held throughout the country. Outnumbered, the forces of law and order could only stand by and watch; and watch they did, making notes of the names and addresses of those who took part with a view to making arrests in the future. Many Volunteers were then forced to go "on the run," in order to avoid arrest.

Elsewhere, World War I entered its third year. With the collapse of the Russian army following the October Revolution of 1917 and the signing of the Brest-Litovsk Treaty, the German army on the Eastern Front was moved rapidly to the west. In April 1918, General Ludendorff launched a major attack on the Allies in the hope of destroying the British and French armies before the American Expeditionary Force entered the lines. For three weeks the British Army in France sustained an all-out assault on a front of fifty miles. The Channel ports themselves were threatened. Faced with this crisis the British government, under Lloyd George, prepared to enforce conscription in Ireland in order to raise an army of half a million men to reinforce its armies in France. The Conscription Bill came before the House for discussion. The Irish Parliamentary Party were totally opposed to it. The entire Irish Party voted against it on 16 April, but nonetheless the bill became law by 301 votes to 103. In protest the Irish Party left the House of Commons and returned to Ireland to organize resistance. A conference was held at the Mansion House in Dublin on 18 April, which all political parties, including Labor and Sinn Fein, attended to formulate a policy to oppose the act. An anti-conscription pledge was drafted to be signed in every parish in the country on the following Sunday, and on 23 April, a general strike was held everywhere in Ireland, with the exception of Belfast, in opposition to conscription. In Dublin and Cork there were massive anti–Conscription demonstrations. Ordinary people wore badges bearing the motto "Death before Conscription." The bishops of Ireland issued a joint manifesto opposing conscription. This crisis removed the last barrier against full-hearted support for Sinn Fein. The proposal to introduce conscription was perhaps an even bigger political mistake on Britain's part than the executions of 1916. The people of Ireland became united in opposition. The threat was the greatest boost the Irish Volunteers could have got. Thousands of young men flocked to join them.

The crisis abated when Ludendorff's assault was checked. On 8 August a counteroffensive was launched by the Allies. By 28 September, with the German army pushed back, Ludendorff conceded defeat. His assault had failed. With the Armistice and the end of World War I many of those Volunteers who had joined the organization as a form of protection from being forced into fighting in France drifted away. It was a blow to the Volunteer leadership, but those who remained were the men of conviction to Ireland's cause.[3]

Initially the Irish Volunteers were organized by county. Each of the thirty-two counties was a prospective brigade area. In reality, as in the case of the northeast of the country, there was but the skeleton of a brigade in some counties. The reorganization thus had to be flexible; and some brigades as time went on, due in some part to the terrain, included sections of adjoining counties within their brigade areas. Regarding structure, in theory a company comprised one hundred and twenty men — four sections and eight squads. In practice the number varied from full strength in some city and town companies to an average of thirty or thirty-five in the country. In its fulfillment as a volunteer army, officers were elected by the company by ballot: a captain, a lieutenant, and a second lieutenant. Section and squad commanders were appointed by the captain at a company council comprising the captain and his lieutenants. When there were enough companies, e.g., five to eight, a battalion was formed.

Officers met to elect a commandant, vice-commandant, adjutant and quartermaster. In similar fashion, when the battalion strengths rose to form a brigade (about nine hundred men), the

Richard Mulcahy was appointed minister for defense by the Dail and was head of the IRA.

battalion officers elected a brigade staff. Later, divisional commands were established comprising several brigades drawn from three or four combined counties. Each battalion was required to develop special services units including communications, engineering, intelligence, signals, first aid, transport and supply. Battalions formed on a town as its nucleus, built around the source of enemy strength, for instance a police or military barracks. In the country, battalions were concentrated on railway lines and bridges, rivers and bridges, and stretches of road. Emphasis on what was, or what was to become, important was decided by evolving enemy displacement. Once established, the company, battalion or brigade acted on its own initiative.

Enrolment in and service as a member of the Irish Volunteers (subsequently known as the Irish Republican Army) was entirely voluntary. It was an unpaid army, depending on the goodwill of the population for food and shelter. The Irish Republican Army was the army of the people. Discipline by and large was good, emanating from a willing submission to orders, actuated by patriotism. Later in the war, however, there were examples, particularly in the quieter areas that had played little part in the war, where Volunteers abused their position, some even resorting to brigandry.

A convention of the Irish Volunteers was held at Croke Park, Dublin, in October 1917. A central council was elected, reports were made and discussed, and decisions were reached as to future developments. While many of the delegates were thinking in terms of a nationwide military rising along the lines of Easter week, there was a new realism in the elected executive. It decided that it would not order Volunteers to take the field unless there was a considered possibility of waging a war with a reasonable expectation of success. In the meantime the Volunteers would continue to train and they would also search for arms. If it had been possible to purchase the arms and ammunition straightaway, then a more conventional textbook war might have taken place—and as in 1916, the Volunteers would again have been defeated by a vastly superior, better-trained and better-armed British army. Unable to buy arms, though curiously there are records showing that in Cork the Volunteers bought rifles and even a machine gun, from British soldiers based at Ballincollig Barracks,[4] the only recourse open to the Volunteers was to seize them from the British, in the shape of the RIC. These attacks by unarmed men on police patrols led to the development of the ambush and guerrilla warfare.

The Quality and Character of Recruits

What type of young men were attracted to the Volunteers? The answer is perhaps surprisingly summed up quite succinctly by one of their enemy, Lieutenant-General Sir H. Lawson, in a book published in 1920, entitled *A Soldier in Ireland*:

> The captains of volunteers appear to have been almost all quite young men, farmers' sons for the most part, some of them schoolmasters, most with what, for their class, must be considered a good deal of education, ignorant, however, of the world and of many things, but, as a class, transparently sincere and single-minded, idealists, highly religious for the most part, and often with an almost mystical sense of duty to their country. These men gave to the task of organizing their volunteers their best in mind and spirit. They fought against drunkenness and self-indulgence, and it is no exaggeration to say that, as a class, they represented all that was best in the countryside.

They and their volunteers were trained to discipline, they imbibed the military spirit, the sense of military honor, etc., and then, as now, they looked upon their army as one in a very real sense; an organization demanding implicit obedience and self-abnegation from rank to rank.

The Irish Republican Army seems to be particularly free from ruffians of the professional type, and the killings of police and others, sometimes under circumstances which evoke horror, were almost certainly done by members of the IRA acting under military orders — young men imbued with no personal feeling against their victims, with no crimes to their record, and probably then shedding blood for the first time in their lives....

Behind their organization there is the spirit of a nation — of a nation which is certainly not in favor of murder, but which, on the whole, sympathizes with them and believes that the members of the IRA are fighting for the cause of the Irish people.

In contrast is the description of one very much their enemy. Working out of Dublin Castle, the writer describes the Volunteers as being brutish, idealistic or gullible: "a score of Sinn Fein prisoners exercising in the Castle Yard, men who had been rounded in some raid the previous night, and were now housed in the Castle for a few hours until arrangements could be made for their transfer to an internment camp — some with lowering brows, type of that under stratum that every revolutionary movement brings to the light; some with the wild and exalted air of the fanatic; a few quiet-looking, good-tempered, country boys whose only fault, perhaps, was a spirit of adventure."[5] In this description is a British arrogance suggesting that there is something wrong with all of them in that they did not wish to be subjects of the British Empire. It is an arrogance that led, and continues to lead even in the present day, to underestimating the enemy forces.

Within the group of young men described by Lt.-Gen. Lawson, there were a sprinkling of professional soldiers with wartime experience. During World War I over 200,000 Irishmen fought in the British army. Some, like Emmett Dalton MC, Martin Doyle VC MM, and Tom Barry, perhaps the most outstanding guerrilla leader of the 20 century, returned to join the IRA. Barry describes his fellow officers in the West Cork Brigade as they were in early 1921. Most of them were very young men (with one exception). They were nothing out of the ordinary, quite typical of other Volunteer officers in their upbringing. By and large they were educated, but few had traveled outside their native county, let alone outside of Ireland. As such, they were naïve, not worldly-wise, but idealistic, brought together in their love of their native land, with a desire to free it from foreign domination. The following are those he described:

Charlie Hurley, Brigade OC

Aged 29, Charlie Hurley, promoted over the heads of many officers to take charge of the brigade, had previously held the post of vice–OC of the Bandon Battalion. "He was a remarkable man and a loveable personality," as Barry describes him. Born in Baurleigh, Kilbrittain, on March 19, 1892, he went to work at an early age in a Bandon store. While there he studied for and passed the Boy Clerks' examination and was posted to Haulbowline. Here he remained until 1915, when he was promoted and offered a place in Liverpool. This he turned down, as inevitably he would have been conscripted into the British armed forces. By this time Hurley was a member of the Irish Volunteers. Very Nationalist in outlook, he was also a member of the Gaelic League, the GAA and Sinn Fein. He returned to West

Cork and was soon involved in organizing the Volunteers. In 1918 he was arrested for being in possession of plans of the British fortifications at Bere Island. He was sentenced to five years of penal servitude, but was released under the "Cat and Mouse Act," when he and others embarked on a hunger strike. This act was originally passed against the suffragettes, whereby ill prisoners were released but could at any time be rearrested to serve out the unexpired period of the sentence. Released back into the community, he continued to organize and train the young Volunteers, urging an aggressive fighting policy. He was killed in action against the British on 19 March 1921.

Ted O'Sullivan, Brigade Vice-OC

From Western Cork, he joined the Volunteers quite early after their formation. He usually worked in the Bantry and Castletownbere Battalion area. Leading by example, he served with the Brigade Flying Column right up to the truce.

Liam Deasy, Brigade Adjutant

Aged 25, one of five brothers who joined the Volunteers, he was born at Kilmacsimon Quay, Bandon, in 1896. He himself joined the Volunteers in 1917. He was easygoing by nature but full of determination. As an adjutant he was responsible for touring the brigade area, organizing units and arranging lines of communication. Though a staff officer he was also an active member of the flying column. He died in 1974.

Sean Buckley, Brigade Intelligence Officer

Aged 46, he was born in 1874. He was the old man of the brigade when Barry met him in 1920, His hair was graying at the temples, yet despite his age he was quite fit and often marched long distances with the column, his rifle slung over his shoulder. He took part in a number of engagements. Analytical of mind, Buckley was serious by nature, but with an unexpected sense of humor to lift any moment of gloom. He was a fatherly figure towards the rest of the men, and he was always concerned for their general welfare.

Dick Barrett, Brigade Quartermaster

Aged 22, born in Hollyhill, Ballineen, in 1899, he was educated at the local National School before going on to teacher training. He became a schoolmaster and later was principal of the Gurranes National School. An organizer, as quartermaster he dealt with everything from arms, ammunition and field equipment to billeting and meals. He was captured two months before the end of the war and imprisoned. He escaped at the time of the truce and later went on to fight on the Republican side during the Civil War. He was captured and executed on 8 December 1922.

If Barry held his fellow officers in admiration, how much more so the ordinary Volunteers who fought under him. After the action at Kilmichael on 21 November 1921, in which they destroyed an Auxiliary convoy, he writes,

"It was now 1 A.M. and the scouts and sentries were inspected. When I returned half an hour later the men were all sleeping in their wet clothes on the straw covered floors. I looked at them and a thrill of pride ran through me as I thought that no army in the world could ever have more uncomplaining men. They had been practically thirty hours without food, marched twenty-six miles, were soaked through, nearly frozen on exposed rocks and had undergone a terrifying baptism of fire. Their discipline was of the finest. Compulsion or punishments were not required for this Volunteer Army; they risked their lives and uncomplainingly suffered."[6]

Training an Army

Tom Barry describes the situation regarding training that existed throughout much of the country at this time: "Desultory training of Companies proceeded irregularly. This was not satisfactory. A group of sixty or seventy men meeting for an hour once a week, with only a few rifles at most, could not be trained as efficient soldiers. One week's collective training is the minimum required to inculcate military discipline and to teach men elementary tactics. Assuming that the Brigade Staff could arrange a Company Camp for every week, it would take a year to train the whole Brigade, and by that time, of course, all the IRA would have been wiped out. Accordingly the idea of starting the training of each Company in turn was dropped and, instead, it was planned to train all Battalion Staff and Company Officers. These would then act as training officers to their own units.... The West Cork training plan envisaged the organization of five training camps of separate groups of officers, at short intervals, as an initial step."[7]

Drilling, albeit in secret, began immediately after the reorganization of the Volunteers in 1917. Growing in confidence, and seeing the support given to them at the funeral of Thomas Ashe, the Volunteers began to appear more regularly in public. The reluctance of the local authorities to confront the Volunteers, particularly in the south and southwest of Ireland, meant that drilling became a common occurrence, though in law it was still illegal. Most of the Volunteers had never held a rifle or revolver in their lives. They drilled using hurley sticks or carved wooden rifles. Hardly any of them had seen a handgrenade, let alone thrown one. Some had used shotguns, while others who had worked in quarries had used explosives. Gradually they acquired rifles, though in small numbers. It became essential that this burgeoning guerrilla army be made familiar with the weapons they were to use. Sean Moylan, later to become commandant of the 2nd (North) Cork Brigade, wrote of these early days: "Here and there was a resigned RIC man or ex-soldier familiar with the mechanism, care and use of the rifle. Selected men in each battalion were trained by these when they were available These men were given military manuals and sent round to all the Companies and a new era of military organization evolved. It is amazing now to look back on the change these rifles made on the mind of the Volunteers. Hard sinewy hands gripped them and grasped reality. Keen eyes looked over their sights and saw a vision of battle, a dream of success, a realization of this hope for freedom which remained immortal while generation after generation sacrificed and died. We were on our way."[8]

With the few available rifles and revolvers, they practiced aiming but rarely firing. Bullets were so scarce they could not be used in training. An empty shell case was inserted in the magazine or breech to prevent the abuse of the hammer action. Wooden hand grenades were carved, the same size as the Mills grenades that the British army used. They were weighted with lead to give them greater authenticity. Officers and men were taught how to throw them with some degree of accuracy, being taught how to judge distances. Maneuvers and formations were practiced in full kit. Field craft was taught — how to use the terrain to the best advantage, both for attack and withdrawal. There was so much to be learned, so much to be taught.

The Second Battalion of the Mid-Limerick Brigade regularly practiced maneuvers a few miles outside the city in the Patrickswell-Kildimo area. By and large the authorities did not interfere. This laissez faire attitude changed, though, in March 1919. At the conclusion of the exercises the Volunteers were led back into the city to the musical accompaniment of the Patrickswell Band. There was some taunting and jeering by soldiers of the British Army garrison in the city, but these were largely ignored. That evening as the band boarded their transport home some British soldiers grabbed their instruments and destroyed them. An Irish tricolor was seized and dragged through the streets. Word was sent to the Volunteers as to what was happening, and they converged on O'Connell Street in the center of the city, where they found the soldiers singing and shouting. An all-out melee ensued with liberal use of hurleys, sticks and stones. The flag was regained, and the soldiers were driven back to the safety of their garrison block. Later that night armed military and RIC accompanied by armored cars roamed the city looking for the Volunteers, who by that stage had been ordered to disperse to the safety of their own homes. Anybody caught out on the streets received a beating. The next night in open defiance the entire Volunteer battalion assembled, and armed only with hurleys marched in military formation around the city center. The authorities did not interfere, and for the moment the status quo was resumed.

Ernie O'Malley, a medical student at Trinity College, had joined the Volunteers at Christmas 1916. He became a member of F Company, First Battalion of the Dublin Brigade. In March 1918 he was summoned to appear before Dick Mulcahy, the assistant chief of staff and a former medical student himself. Mulcahy sent O'Malley to organize and instruct the Volunteers in the provinces. O'Malley recorded his efforts in his 1936 book, *On Another Man's Wound*:

> I received no guidance or instructions when sent out to organize a county or a brigade. Collins would hand me a pile of copies of the organization scheme, add some type-written notes reminding officers that their reports were long overdue; then I was left to myself. Usually I received the names and addresses of a few senior officers, the names of likely men to approach in an unorganized part of the country, and an introduction in writing from Collins in his clear legible hand.
>
> In [County] Offaly ... I paraded battalions in Tullamore; we skirmished and maneuvered through towns and the country side followed by the police. Officers were arrested and at once replaced. To save the officers I commanded the companies of a parade in turn.... In small towns I drew my gun when police asked me my name.
>
> In daytime I could now enter a town to practice quick mobilization. Shop boys, carpenters, shop owners, clerks, fell into line quickly. They practiced bayonet fighting with brush handles up and down streets; they sat on pathways or in halls to listen to my talks from the destruction of railway plant to street fighting.
>
> Men relieved each other during the day to mould lead to buck shot; gun cartridges were collected and refilled. Jewelers and locksmiths made revolver springs; they repaired weapons. Telegraphic clerks held classes with buzzers and tappers or taught Morse to signalers; harness and boot makers worked at belts and equipment, smiths and carpenters made pikes and pike

handles. Cumann na mBan sewed signaling flags and haversacks. They gathered medical supplies, made splints and packed first field dressings.... Shops were raided for cartridges and detonators, quarries for explosives."⁹

Training was inconsistent though. Some counties, particularly those in Munster were well organized by 1919, others less so. In mountainous Donegal, way up in the wild northwest of Ireland, O'Malley found a different story. Here the land was poor, the county less populated. Its brigadier was Joe Sweeney, whom O'Malley had first met at Trinity College, Dublin. He had formerly been a student at Pearse's school and fought with the St. Enda's Company in Easter week. Despite Sweeney's efforts the brigade was under strength, the Volunteers lacking commitment. So training here was begun in earnest.

Though the basics of training were learnt, engaging the enemy was something else. That needed to be taught. Tactics and basic maneuvers were often lacking. Learning them while engaged in a firefight could result in the column's being wiped out. In an ambush just outside of Ballyhahill in mid–Limerick, GHQ man Joe Good observed:

> Jackie Finn [Mid-Limerick Brigade Column OC] said he had decided to attack [an RIC patrol] on their return journey — some distance away from our village of Ballyhahill. During the ambush which subsequently took place between Glin and Ballyhahill, I saw the pathetic weakness of Our Volunteers — a weakness in military tactics and of basic instinct for sound maneuver.
>
> We had taken up our positions in a ditch. On the far side of the roadway, the river flowed. We had approached our position from a very oblique direction — and up a slight decline. Consequently, I was not aware that the ground behind us was exceedingly steep. I assumed that these Limerick Volunteers had their own proven tactics and strategy, but I noticed that most of our men were very close together (too close for my taste), so I went some distance away from them, in the direction from which the enemy would approach.
>
> The enemy party came along on bicycles. From our position in the ditch, we could not fully see their approach, nor had we a good field of fire. Only two of the enemy were allowed to ride into the ambush, or two that I could see. These were fired on and fell. There was further firing for a bit — and then silence. I was on the extreme flank and expected an order, but there was no order. Then, suddenly, one of the enemy attempted to cross the ditch immediately beside me. There was time only to turn on my back and fire at him. I presumed I had hit him, but from my position it was difficult to be certain.
>
> I tried to reload my carbine and found that I could not eject the spent cartridge case. Suddenly I heard Jackie Finn say loudly, "Where is Joe?" His call attracted my attention, and I saw that my comrades were on the move. When I turned my head I could see our attacking party creeping away up the steep hill behind us. There must have been a number of survivors among the enemy as there was firing from three or four of their rifles.
>
> Then we were running up the steep hill. I called out, "Return their fire." One of our lads immediately lay down and began to do so. I flopped down beside him, took my bolt out of my jammed carbine, and was thus able to get the cartridge case out and reload.
>
> Our return fire was sporadic and not as effective as I hoped; but I want to make it clear that these Volunteers were armed with carbines which were good enough weapons, but their ammunition did not always fit. There was Mark VI and a Mark VII issue of ammunition for those weapons by the British Government, and we very obviously had the wrong cartridges.
>
> This abortive ambush made several things clear to me: that the Volunteers in that area had received no instruction or training for guerrilla warfare; that there was no regard for lines of retreat; and that our men did not realize that they could be enfiladed, as they were.¹⁰

The by-election in County Longford in the spring of 1917 attracted young men to the Volunteers. In that April four hundred and six joined the Longford Volunteers, and two men came to the fore, IRB men Sean MacEoin and Sean Connolly. County Clare too had been successful in its recruiting, thanks to the Brennan brothers, Padraig, Michael and Austin. So much so that the county had been divided into three brigades; East, Mid and West Clare. Their activities had come to the attention of the RIC though, and in East Clare, commanded by Michael Brennan, his vice-commandant, Mauteen Devitt, and the quartermaster, Peader O'Loughlin, were on the run. Unable to remain at home, or work locally, this gave them more time to train the Volunteers in their charge. Of the East Clares O'Malley wrote:

> On Sundays we maneuvered one battalion against another, companies marched eight or nine miles to the mobilization center. Officers and men wore what uniforms and kit they had. Police and military followed us; we carried out tactical exercises whilst both our parties watched for and avoided the real enemy. The numbers gave the men more solidarity and confidence. During a practice attack I once watched an officer [Ignatius O'Neill] from Milltown Malbay, who had been in the Irish Guards, train his men to advance under cover. He carried a haversack full of clay balls and from behind belabored his men when they did not keep close to earth.
>
> I gave military books to the officers and typewritten notes, lectured to them and endeavored to make field work and study interesting. It was a difficult task. All day they worked hard at their farms or in towns; when evening came there was an added task.... In the day time Peader and I, sometimes Maurteen Devitt, worked out schemes on our maps. We studied the country very carefully, night found us far away from where we had set out that morning.[11]

Former soldier Tom Barry was appointed training officer for the West Cork Brigade. He organized training courses for its officers. In his book, *Guerilla Days in Ireland,* he describes his first course:

> As the men arrived in camp, they were detailed to sections and section commanders appointed. Their first parade was to listen to a talk on the plan of defense and security measures [should their training be interrupted by the British security forces]. The men were told to act as if they were expecting attack at any hour of the day or night, and the most detailed instructions were issued. For the next hour they practiced occupying their defense positions, aiming and trigger pressing and moving in extended order as directed. It was an unorthodox approach to training, but the circumstances necessitated the departure. After all, if an attack had come, all that really would have mattered, would have been that the men would obey orders, shoot straight and move in a proper formation. Their ability to salute or to form fours smartly would not have been a consideration.
>
> Day and night alarms were given. If men called out of bed came too slowly or made too much noise, they had to commence all over again, until eventually they leaped from bed, dressed, equipped themselves and moved silently and swiftly in proper order, to their defense positions within a period of three minutes.... These IRA officers were intelligent men and quickly realized that such a surprise was possible.
>
> From eight in the morning until six in the evening the men drilled and trained. Close order, extended order, arms drill and elementary tactics occupied the first four days. During the remaining three days more advanced movements were undertaken and special attention was given to "re-drilling." In this each officer, in turn, took command of a section and handled it for an hour or so. Attack and defense exercises were a feature of the training, and after these, at a signal, all would come together to talk over and criticize the movements. Situations were envisaged of engaging the enemy at a stated strength, moving in a certain formation, and officers were appointed, in turn, to command the column. The officers showed an extraordinary keenness on all parades, but particularly for sham battles.

At night the Column assembled from 7.30 to 9.30 P.M. in a large barn for a lecture or for written exercises. The lectures were not those which could be compiled from textbooks, since there were none which could tell this Flying Column how it could fight and continue to exist in the midst of enemy posts through the years ahead. I.R.A. policy, Flying Column tactics and security measures, ambushes, town fighting, elementary signals, map reading and blackboard problems were all considered until the men's minds held nothing but thoughts of war....

Many statements have been made by Ministers and Generals in various countries on the necessity for long periods of training before even an infantry soldier is ready for action. This is utter nonsense when applied to volunteers for guerilla warfare. After only one week of collective training, this Flying Column of intelligent and courageous fighters was fit to meet an equal number of soldiers from any regular army in the world, and hold its own in battle, if not in barrackyard ceremonial.[12]

During the truce, without fear of police or British Army interference, training courses for officers were extended to five weeks. Ernie O'Malley, then OC of the 2nd Southern Division, gives details of such a training session, held in the grounds of Galtee Castle, County Tipperary, in his book *The Singing Flame*, (19–23). The course is paraphrased below:

Total length of Course — 5 weeks.

Trainees — 70 officers from the Division's Brigade and Battalion staffs, to be divided into 8 squads.

All officers to be fully equipped with rifles, bayonets, small arms, grenades and kit.

Course Details

First two weeks devoted to training as ordinary soldiers with an emphasis on proficiency of arms. For the remaining three weeks the officers to be trained in administration, scouting, field-sketching and engineering. Practice assaults on barracks, springing ambushes, night maneuvers, the ability to maneuver various size units, the use of explosives and land mines.

Daily Timetable

6:00 a.m. — Bugle call for Parade.
Breakfast and a short rest.
Inspection of arms.
Short route march.
Cross-country run in full kit.
Open air lecture.
Extended order across country.
Reconnaissance or patrol work.
12:00 p.m. — Midday meal and a short rest.
Lectures.
Bayonet practice.
Revolver and grenade training.
Marksmanship using .22 caliber ammunition.
One and a half hours for rest and recreation.
6:00 p.m. — Tea.
Sunset — Parade in full kit (a mixture of Irish, American and English drill).
Private study for an hour or more.

The Volunteers at this early stage were still very much a part-time army. Many of their members worked full time, and gave what spare time they had to the movement. Punctuality was a problem, especially in the country, where many did not possess clocks or watches,

Untrained and unarmed, young Volunteers like these took on the might of the British Empire.

but went by stomach time — dawn equaled breakfast, noon equaled dinner, and late afternoon meant tea. Absenteeism and carelessness were also problems, as was untidiness. Lack of neatness, in clothing and equipment, was a constant source of irritation for the officers, who knew that this quality instilled discipline and pride in the men. It was all very amateurish, this part-time Irish army, but it was a beginning. Irish author Frank O'Connor takes up the story in his autobiography, *An Only Child*: "In the absence of proper uniform our Army tended to wear riding breeches, gaiters, a trench coat, and a soft hat usually pulled over one eye, and I managed to scrape up most of the essential equipment, even when I had to beg it, as I begged the pair of broken gaiters from Tom MacKernan. I conducted a complicated deal for the Ministry of Defence and bought a French rifle from a man who lived close to Cork Barrack, though when I had risked a heavy sentence by bringing it home down my trouser leg, all the time pretending I had just met with a serious accident, it turned out that there wasn't a round of ammunition in Ireland to fit it."

By the end of the war uniforms were still being improvised. Ernie O'Malley, later commandant of the Second Southern Division, described the uniform of a flying column in South Tipperary: "Some of the column wore green-gray uniforms, but most of the uniforms in the area had been captured by enemy raiding parties. Some wore their caps back to front; a few had uniform caps, one boy had a triangular forage cap, and there were hats with pinned-up sides and turned down brims. All wore riding breeches and leggings. His men had rifles, khaki slings of ammunition or leather bandoliers; some had grenades slung dangerously by their levers in their belts." Tom Barry described his own men, the Volunteers of the West Cork Brigade Flying Column, after their victory at Crossbarry:

> Although they had neither food nor rest since the previous evening they were a cocky lot. Their faces were unshaven, unwashed and graying with fatigue, but their steps were still springy, and as they came in to pass where I stood, their shoulders jerked back so that no one would assume they were tiring. Their boots and leggings were muddy, their trench-coats hung open, no collars adorned their necks and their caps when not stuck in their belts, were worn with the peak to the back or over their shoulders. Their rifles were at the trail, and some carried captured rifles slung across their backs and sets of enemy equipment as well as

their own. The center section lugged along with evident pride the captured Lewis gun and ammunition drums; the first machine-gun we ever possessed. They not only looked tough but were tough. Yet I knew them to be lighthearted youths who would normally have been happy working on their farms, or in the towns or back at their schools, had they not volunteered to fight.[13]

Of his own raggle-taggle officer's uniform O'Malley wrote:

> I had overhauled my kit and books. I carried two guns; one was a Mauser automatic.... I had a prismatic compass, prismatic binoculars around my neck, a map case, ammunition pouches and haversacks, a series of wrist straps for a fill of cartridges, a whistle, and a luminous watch. I had a book sewn together, and bound in soft leather, of selections from English training manuals with my written notes and sketches; I carried it in a waterproof case. My coat was burnt, torn and scratched. It had been darned with colored wools, patched with odd cloth, and the pockets, its most important part, were lined with moleskin. They could support the weight of notebooks, books, maps, pencils and medical supplies. I was my own base, and I looked it.

Structure

The Volunteer structure, particularly at GHQ level, underwent a series of changes both in personnel and the redefining of departments from 1914 onwards. The execution of many of the GHQ staff after the failure of the 1916 Rising introduced a new, perhaps harder, leadership. Again there was a strong IRB involvement. Particularly noteworthy was the change from the Department of Communications to that of Propaganda. Now the Republican cause had an answer through its illicit yet widely read newsletters to the British, who controlled all the organs of publicity through censorship. This was perhaps the first modern war where propaganda, both positive and negative, was to play a major part in shaping opinion both in Ireland and abroad. The GHQ structure of 1920 was as follows:

Director of Intelligence (Acting President of the Republic and Chairman of the Supreme Council of the IRB)
Michael Collins

Director of Organization	Military Chief of Staff	Quartermaster General	Director of Engineering	Director of Purchases	Director of Propaganda
Diarmuid O'Hegarty	Richard Mulcahy	Sean MacMahon	Rory O'Connor	Liam Mellowes	Piarias Beaslai
	Adjutant General Geroid O'Sullivan				

Though there was a senior army command structure, it cannot be said that the Irish army was created as the result of a clearly conceived plan. Nor can it be said that its campaigns were conducted to a clearly defined strategy. Nor indeed, that it was controlled by a general headquarters staff. The army in the field acted upon its own initiative and made its own decisions. The looseness of the Volunteer organization was to prove a source of strength during the war, in that if one area was inactive or had suffered a setback it did not affect the activities or morale of other districts. Brigade commanders, and they alone, were responsible for their brigade areas.

The Brigade

The country was divided by GHQ into brigade areas, which usually, though not always, coincided with county boundaries. In Cork in 1917, the pre–Rising Volunteer structure had survived intact and expanded. By 1919 the cork brigade, unquestionably the most active brigade in the country, had become large and unwieldy. Tomas MacCurtain, the commanding officer, taking advice, decided that it should be split into three separate brigades: First Cork — commanded by Tomas MacCurtain and situated in the center of the county extending from Youghal to the Kerry border beyond Ballyvourney and including the city of Cork; Second Cork — commanded by Liam Lynch and situated in the north of the county; Third Cork — commanded by Tom Hales and situated in the west of the county.

The brigades were each divided up into companies, and companies into battalions. In the Third (West Cork) Brigade, Volunteers were organized into a brigade of five battalions, with a sixth added in 1918.

Numerical Strength of the Companies of the Third Cork Brigade
(Brigade Commandant: Tom Hales)

First (Bandon) Battalion
(Battalion Commandant: Tom Hales)

Ballindee	35
Kilbrittain	45
Timoleague	12
Barryroe	55
Clogagh	20
Bandon	12
Innishannon	22
Crosspound	30
Kilpatrick	16
Mount Pleasant (Farnivane)	20
Newceston	35
No. of men	302

Second (Clonakilty) Battalion
(Battalion Commandant: Jim Walsh)

Clonakilty	25
Ardfield	22
Bealad	15
Kilmean	20
Lyre	18
Ahiohill	25
No. of men	125

Third (Dunmanway) Battalion
(Battalion Commandant: Con Ahern)

Dunmanway	25
Ballincarriga	30
Shanavagh	30
Ballineen	22
Kenneigh	30
Behaugh	30
Aultagh	40
Togher	36
No. of men	243

Fourth (Skibbereen) Battalion
(Battalion Commandant: J.B. O'Driscoll)

Skibbereen	30
Castlehaven	20
Myross	16
Leap	40
Bredagh	20
Lisheen	25
No. of men	151

Fifth (Bantry) Battalion
(Battalion Commandant: Michael Murray)

Bantry	50
Caheragh	20
Drumsullivan	15
Kealkil	15
Coomhola	20
Glengarriff	20
No. of men	140

Sixth (Beara) Battalion
(Battalion Commandant: Peter O'Neil)

Castletownbere	24
Bere Island	40
Rossmacowan	30
Adrigole	16
Inches	40
Ardgroom	45
Ballycrovane	36
Urhan	30
No. of men	261

Third Cork Brigade strength: 1,222 men

The Flying Column

Originally each battalion had the capability of forming a column for the purpose of ambush and attack upon police and military barracks. Based on the South African Boer War model, after such an attack the column was stood down, its Volunteer members slipping back into civilian life until the next time. Sometimes the RIC would arrest men they knew or suspected of being Volunteers. Forewarned, a number of Volunteers went on the run. In mid–1920 GHQ Dublin issued the following instruction to all IRA Brigades: "At the present time a large number of both our men and officers are on the run in different parts of the country. The most effective way of using these officers and men would seem to be by organizing them as flying columns. In this way — instead of being compelled to a haphazard and aimless course of action — they would become available as standing troops of a well trained and thoroughly reliable stamp, and their actions would be far more systematic and effective."

Instructions were to appoint flying column commanders. Their duties were outlined by GHQ:

1. To gain experience for himself and his men by planning and then carrying out simple actual operations as outlined in operation orders Nos. 1 to 7.*
2. By harassing smaller and quieter military and police stations.
3. By interrupting and pillaging stores belonging to the enemy.
4. By interrupting all communications.
5. By covering towns threatened by reprisal parties.

It was the establishment of the flying column and its use in successful ambushes that negated to a considerable degree the disproportionate figures between the overwhelming number of British forces and the Volunteers. A successful column called for strict commitment in its soldiers. They had to be the best; well trained and disciplined, but, more important, well led. These essentials Tom Barry listed, as they prevailed within the West Cork Column:

1. The command of the brigade flying column was absolute. The column commander could not be interfered with by anyone. His decisions were personal, subject to no authority whatsoever, within or outside the column. His was the responsibility, and it was he who had to take the blame for any failure. No one could share his authority and no one should share his responsibility in the event of disaster.
2. Every battalion and company in the brigade and all their resources were to be at the disposal of the flying column. Without those units of organization the flying column would be ineffective and its existence curtailed.
3. Only picked Volunteers of the IRA would be accepted for service in the flying column. Unwilling men would be a danger. All the officers of the battalions and companies were expected to spend a period on column service, but they were not

---

This was a reference to an earlier communiqué relating to assaults on buildings, ambushing and disarming police patrols, the interruption of enemy dispatches, cutting lines of communication between police and military barracks, and attacking British forces carrying out reprisals, in particular the Auxiliaries and Black and Tans.

compelled. However, any officer who shirked such service would soon be considered as unfit to continue to be an officer of the IRA.

4. The men who volunteered for the column were made aware of the strict discipline which would have to prevail. It would have to be severe. They had also to understand that mobility was one of the most essential considerations; that they would have to march long distances, eating whenever food was available, sleeping in outhouses, if no other accommodation could be secured, and generally living hard. Each man also knew that because of the odds against it, the column continually faced destruction.

5. Column officers and section commanders were appointed by the column commander, irrespective of the ranks held by the men previous to their enrolment in the column. Thus a company lieutenant might be a column section commander and thus over a battalion commandant should the lieutenant be deemed the most suitable.

Flying columns at battalion level might number anything between twenty-five and fifty Volunteers. Tipperary No. 1 Flying Column, set up in October 1920, with Dinny Lacey as commandant, had seventy men. The brigade column, drawing men from most of its battalions, might in itself be quite small, but could draw additional men from battalion columns on a rotating basis. Alternatively it could combine several battalion columns to form a brigade column of any number up to several hundred men. The only limitation were the number of arms available. The structure of the East Limerick Brigade columns, as of mid-1921, shows a degree of sophistication perhaps not associated with guerrilla armies:

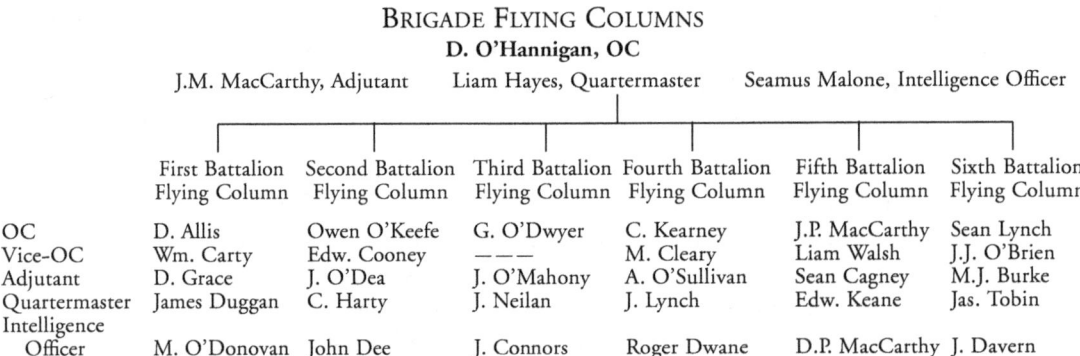

	First Battalion Flying Column	Second Battalion Flying Column	Third Battalion Flying Column	Fourth Battalion Flying Column	Fifth Battalion Flying Column	Sixth Battalion Flying Column
OC	D. Allis	Owen O'Keefe	G. O'Dwyer	C. Kearney	J.P. MacCarthy	Sean Lynch
Vice-OC	Wm. Carty	Edw. Cooney	---	M. Cleary	Liam Walsh	J.J. O'Brien
Adjutant	D. Grace	J. O'Dea	J. O'Mahony	A. O'Sullivan	Sean Cagney	M.J. Burke
Quartermaster	James Duggan	C. Harty	J. Neilan	J. Lynch	Edw. Keane	Jas. Tobin
Intelligence Officer	M. O'Donovan	John Dee	J. Connors	Roger Dwane	D.P. MacCarthy	J. Davern

In West Cork by March 1921, British forces invariably operated in mechanized units of not less than three hundred. The IRA had to respond to this by increasing the size of its brigade flying column if it wanted to take on one of these enemy units. The column was increased to one hundred and four officers and men. While all the men were equipped with rifles and revolvers, there were only forty rounds of ammunition for each rifle available. The creation of a brigade column was a necessary but potentially dangerous step in that it concentrated its best officers and men in one grouping. As weapons were drawn from the various companies, if the column was destroyed then effectively the brigade fell with them. To engage the enemy on this basis called for very special leaders, and in Tom Barry the brigade had such a man. At that time the West Corks were holding down at least five thousand

British soldiers, not to mention the various paramilitary police forces. They had no choice but to risk everything in each assault. This comes across very strongly in Barry's book, *Guerilla Days in Ireland*. The West Cork Brigade Flying Column had four officers, including a medical officer. The column was divided into seven sections of fourteen men (including the section commanders). Each section was trained to act as an individual unit in support of the column should the column be attacked in the flank or rear:

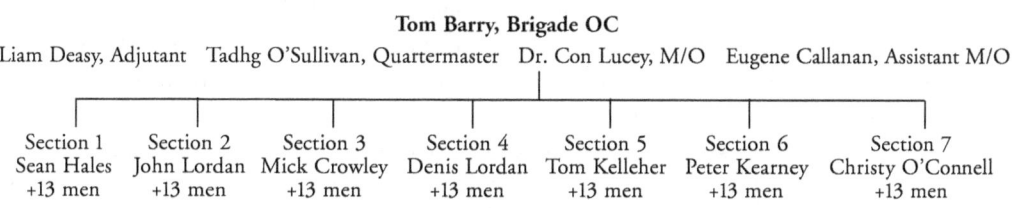

Tom Barry, Brigade OC
Liam Deasy, Adjutant   Tadhg O'Sullivan, Quartermaster   Dr. Con Lucey, M/O   Eugene Callanan, Assistant M/O

Section 1	Section 2	Section 3	Section 4	Section 5	Section 6	Section 7
Sean Hales	John Lordan	Mick Crowley	Denis Lordan	Tom Kelleher	Peter Kearney	Christy O'Connell
+13 men	+13 men	+13 men	+13 men	+13 men	+13 men	+13 men

The Column also had a bagpipe player, Flo Begley, who was assistant to the brigade adjutant.

Following meetings between the First Cork and Tipperary brigades concerning closer cooperation across county boundaries, GHQ in Dublin looked at restructuring the Volunteers into much larger groupings. Thus was created the idea of divisions and, logically, the cooperation between divisions enabling them to put a sizeable army in the field at some stage. An additional bonus to this proposal included the involvement of the less active county brigades, thus taking pressure off the Munster brigades, who had borne the brunt of the war. While a number of columns existed throughout the country by 1921, a considerable number did little more than exist. The two main causes for this were either that they operated in poor guerrilla country or the leadership was poor. Where the second was the case, GHQ removed the leadership and replaced it with one of its nominees.

A meeting was held in the North Cork Brigade area from 24 April 1921 regarding the formation of the 1st Southern Division. Delegates included Sean O'Hegarty and Florrie O'Donoghoe of Cork No. 1 Brigade, Liam Lynch and Sean Moylan of Cork No. 2 Brigade, Tom Barry and Liam Deasy of Cork No. 3 Brigade, John Joe Rice of Kerry No. 1 Brigade, and Humphrey Murphy and Andy Cooney of the Kerry No. 2 Brigade. Not represented were Kerry No. 3, Waterford No. 1, Waterford No. 2, and the West Limerick Brigades. As GHQ representative, Ernie O'Malley took the chair. He read out the GHQ document that brought the division into being. Liam Lynch was appointed its OC. The meeting being thrown open to discussion, underlying tensions between GHQ's representative and the officers in the field were aired. Prominent was the question as to why senior members of GHQ had never visited the area. There was a feeling that GHQ was out of touch as to what was going on down in Munster. Decisions were being made without consultation with the brigades fighting the war.

O'Malley did his best to answer the question, but reading between the lines in his book and Barry's book, residual resentment remained among commanders in the field. The delegates looked for assurance that the creation of divisions would extend the war into the East, North, Midlands and the hitherto Western seaboard, taking some of the pressure off the South. O'Malley was able to assure them that the Limerick City, East Limerick, South Tipperary, Mid-Tipperary and Kilkenny brigades would be formed together in just a few days, as the 2nd Southern Division, and others would follow soon after. Also vitally necessary for progressing the war, the commanders stressed, was the need for .303 ammunition, to contain the enemy during the summer months. Again O'Malley gave his assurances that all was being done to obtain arms and ammunition. With these things in place the delegates firmly believed that victory would almost certainly be achieved by them but realistically perhaps not until the spring of 1922.

Many of the officers present, and Tom Barry in particular, were of the opinion that the brigade flying column of one hundred men was the most effective in carrying out guerrilla warfare. The removal of active brigade officers, seconded to the division, would be disruptive. The division had its part to play in the final days of the war, but not at present. What Barry was concerned about was that local control, by the men on the ground who knew the shifting day-to-day situation, would be subsumed and directed by Dublin. This was why the British were failing. Their troops were acting under direct orders from their headquarters, thus denying local officers on the ground from taking the initiative under changing circumstances. Despite the reservations, the divisions were established, but they were never used in the remaining two months before the end of the war. At the time of the truce the division structure was as follows:

Irish Army Command at the Time of the Truce

- Dublin No. 1 Brigade: Commandant — Oscar Traynor.
- South Dublin Brigade: Commandant — Andrew MacDonnell.
- 1st Northern Division: Donegal (Four Brigades), Commandant — Joseph Sweeney.
- 2nd Northern Division: Tyrone and Derry (Four Brigades), Commandant Charles Daly.
- 3rd Northern Division: Belfast, Antrim and North Down (Three Brigades), Commandant — Joseph McKelvey.
- 4th Northern Division: Armagh, West and South Down, and North Louth (Three Brigades), Commandant Frank Aiken.
- 5th Northern Division: Monaghan, East Cavan and South Fermanagh, Commandant — Dan Hogan.
- 1st Eastern Division: Meath, West Meath and Kildare (Nine Brigades), Commandant — Sean Boylan.
- North Wexford Brigade: North Wexford and South Wicklow, Commandant — Joseph Cummin.
- South Wexford Brigade: Commandant — Thomas O'Sullivan.
- Carlow Brigade: Commandant — Liam Stack.
- Midland Division: Longford, Leitrim and Fermanagh, Commandant — Sean McKeon.
- First Western Division: Clare and South Galway, Commandant — Michael Brennan.
- Second Western Division: South Roscommon, South and East Mayo, North Galway, Commandant — Thomas Maguire.
- Third Western Division: North Roscommon, Sligo, part of Mayo, Commandant — Liam Pilkington.
- Fourth Western Division: North and West Mayo, parts of Sligo and Galway, Commandant — Michael Kilroy.
- First Southern: Cork, Kerry, Waterford and West Limerick (Ten Brigades), Commandant — Liam Lynch.

- Second Southern Division: Kilkenny, Limerick, and part of Tipperary (Five Brigades), Commandant — Earnan O'Malley.
- Third Southern: Leix, Offaly, and part of Tipperary (Five Brigades), Commandant — Michael McCormick.

Arming the Volunteers

Even before the outbreak of the war in 1919, the search for arms and ammunition became paramount. Weapons in small amounts were smuggled in from Britain and America. Loyalist big houses were raided in the search for guns, but as often as not the arms secured were out of date or perhaps not suited to guerrilla warfare. An obvious source of up-to-date arms, if they could be secured, were the RIC barracks up and down the country. These barracks varied in size and strength from a garrison of maybe four in some out of the way village to forty or more in a large town or city. The barracks at Eyeries in west Cork was a typical small barracks, with a sergeant and three constables. The few Volunteers at Eyeries spoke to Charlie Hurley, who commanded a company of Volunteers at nearby Castletownbere, and a plan was formed to attack the barracks. On St. Patrick's Day 1918, the Volunteers assembled at Eyeries and marched off to nearby Castletownbere where they proposed to parade around the town. As they set off, five of them slipped away and made their way back to the barracks unseen. The plan was to lie in wait until the door of the barracks was opened and then rush it. Two of the policemen, Sergeant Nugent and one of his constables, had gone off for the day to keep an eye on the Volunteers, so there were just two constables on duty. The five Volunteers had three revolvers between them: two .45 Colt revolvers each with five rounds, and a .32 revolver with two rounds of ammunition. As they approached, the door unexpectedly opened. Christy O'Connell, one of the Volunteers, takes up the story:

> At the door, I came face to face with the barrack orderly whose name, I think, was Dalton. He also saw me with my suspicious disguise, and to turn to tell the others would be fatal. I whipped out my little gun, and ordered, "Hands up!" In return, he swiftly pointed his right hand at me, and I pulled twice on the trigger. There were two dull clicks — my two rounds were duds. There was no shot from his side either — it was his finger he was pointing at me, thinking I would mistake it for a gun in the dark. Then he backed in quickly to slam the door, and I hurled myself at him with full force. There was a step down inside, and the force of the impact sent him reeling into the hallway. Again I ordered, "Hands up!" and this time he obeyed. It was with mixed feelings I stood there in the hall, holding up this giant RIC man. I can still picture him — fair complexion, broad shoulders and deep chest, a man of splendid physique — and the light from the table-lamp in the dayroom shining through the open door. I was thrilled at having taken this symbol of British imperialism, as it were, by assault, anxious that my comrades should come to my assistance and fearful every moment of getting a clatter from Cahill (the other constable) whom we expected to be there. Luckily, we learned later, he had gone out for a drink, and that was probably why Dalton had opened the door, anxious for his return before the sergeant got back.
>
> At last, my pals, sensing there was something wrong when I did not report back, came bursting in. Joe Foley and Sean O'Driscoll, with revolvers drawn, took charge of Dalton. Con O'Dwyer, Peter O'Neill and I rushed upstairs where we expected to find the arms. It was so dark now that we could not find our way round; we had no matches, and flash lamps were unknown to us at that time. Then I thought of the table-lamp in the day room, and ran

down for it. We had lost a lot of time and though Jim McCarthy and my brother, Dave, were on the look-out, the others would be in on us at any moment. With the lamp, I passed Joe, Sean, and the captive at the foot of the stairs, forgetting that I had given him a good chance of recognizing them. With the aid of the lamp, we found the rifles, took them from the racks and rushed out into the darkness while Joe and Sean covered our retreat.[14]

A few weeks after the raid on Eyeries Barracks, an unarmed band of Volunteers from the same Castltownbere Company under Captain Charlie Hurley carried out a daring attack on a party of armed soldiers. Having been notified that a group of three soldiers had left the town on foot, the Volunteers raced ahead and took up a concealed position in a narrow lane near the main road. As they approached, the three Volunteers jumped out on them and wrestled them to the ground. Two of the soldiers were carrying rifles, the third a package. They were quickly disarmed, and the captured rifles were taken away to safety.

More daring perhaps was the raid that took place on 5 June 1918 on the barracks of the Royal Engineers at Bere Island, Cork. Eugene Dunne, the intelligence officer of the Adrigole Company of the Beara Battalion, learned that there was a large quantity of guncotton stored on the island in a building some 50 yards from the engineers' barracks. Guncotton, cellulose nitrate containing a relatively large amount of nitrogen, was used as an explosive. A meeting was arranged with Con Lowney, captain of the Bere Island Volunteer Company, and it was resolved to raid the stores. The raid began at 12:30 A.M. A duplicate key was used to gain access to the stores. Inside the Volunteers found 52 boxes, each containing 56 pounds of guncotton, as well as primers and detonators. Each box was carried from the stores to the pier, a distance of 250 yards, where they were loaded aboard Volunteer Tim Moriarty's boat. With the boat loaded to capacity it was discovered that there were still six boxes remaining, as well as electric cable and one large bag of black powder. These were hidden away on the premises of John Houlihan, a local businessman, down on the pier, for later recovery. The boat was then rowed across the harbor to Bunnow where it was unloaded, and its precious cargo was taken to a prepared dump in the Adrigole area.

As early as 1917, GHQ in Dublin had set up a munitions factory in the cellar of a bicycle shop at 198, Parnell Street. By Christmas of that year they were manufacturing one hundred hand grenades a week in it. By the time of its discovery by the British, on 10 December 1920, they had reduced the explosion time from seven to three seconds. The munitions factory also began the manufacture of trench mortars. Just off Parnell Street, in Dominick Street, another munitions factory was producing detonators. Out in the country, Sean Treacy and Jerome Davin from the Third Tipperary Brigade began experiments with some of the gelignite captured in the Soloheadbeg raid of January 1919. They developed "mud bombs," a stick of gelignite molded in sticky yellow clay and ignited by a fuse. When thrown the clay stuck to buildings and roofs before exploding. Later experiments revealed that a coating of linseed oil gave even better adhesion.

An opportune moment gave the Bantry Battalion the chance to secure some arms. On the afternoon of 26 September 1918, a Fianna lad brought word to battalion commander Dan O'Mahony that two RIC constables had left Bantry on bicycles and were proceeding towards Ballylickey. One of them was armed with a .303 rifle, the other with a revolver. With eight unarmed Volunteers, O'Mahony ambushed the two policemen along the road at the bottom of Caher Hill near Donemark Bridge. It was dusk and, though unarmed, the Volunteers had the element of surprise. Bicycles and policemen tumbled to the ground as the Volunteers rushed them from ambush, and after some brief resistance, the rifle and revolver were seized and the policemen were tied up.

The RIC barracks at Eyeries was replaced by a stronger military barracks. As time went by it also revealed a weakness that the Volunteers were able to exploit. The barracks was supplied from Castletownbere by a horse-drawn wagon. It traveled between the town and village at the same time every day. The convoy was guarded by two armed soldiers in the wagon itself and two junior officers who walked a few paces behind. After two thwarted attempts, Volunteers from the Inches Column, of the Beara Battalion, four in number, armed with rifles and revolvers, finally succeeded on 28 September. As the wagon came abreast of them, at a little place called Bealnalappa, they dashed from cover and held it up. One soldier considered resisting, but quickly changed his mind upon seeing the determination of the attackers. The Volunteers got away with a Lee-Enfield rifle and an accompanying bandolier of .303 ammunition, plus a Webley revolver.

Following the Armistice of 1918 ending World War I, an American transport ship, the *Defiance*, arrived at Dublin Docks to gather up army huts and other stores left there by the United States Expeditionary Force. As the dockers began to load these stores aboard they discovered that the hold already contained cases and cases of revolvers, rifles and ammunition. The Citizen Army was informed and Seamus McGowan, responsible for acquiring arms, was smuggled in as a docker to arrange getting some of the arms ashore. The ship was heavily guarded by U.S. Marines to prevent theft and pilfering. Nevertheless the ICA and the ITGWU members succeeded, over an eight hour period, in breaking open the cases and smuggling fifty-six .45 revolvers, 2,000 rounds of revolver ammunition, 5,000 rounds of Springfield ammunition in canvas bandoliers, and other pistols. These were got past the marine guard and were hid in the little tin lavatories on the quays, later to be smuggled out of the docks. Arrangements were also made with a member of the crew to buy twenty-four .45 automatics which had been issued to the crew. These were lowered over the side in a canvas bucket to a boat waiting below. The Springfield rifles were too long to smuggle out past the guards, so were left, to the regret of the smugglers.

A party of half a dozen ICA men under the command of Captain M. Kelly carried out a daring raid for arms at Portobello Barracks. They succeeded in getting into the barracks as workmen, then smuggled rifles out through the railings to a horse and cart outside driven by ICA man Dick Corbally.

Causing maximum embarrassment to the British soldiers involved was the incident that appears in the memoirs of Major General Wimberley (memoirs now housed in the Imperial War Museum, London). At the time, May 1920, Wimberley was a captain in the Cameron Highlanders, based at Queenstown (now Cobh), County Cork: " We had to learn our job the hard way. Very soon after our arrival an unsuspecting road patrol, with their rifles stupidly clipped on to the side of their bicycles, were surrounded in a village street by a number of young men supposedly playing a game of hurley on the village green, a game akin to our own Highland Shinty. They apparently made friendly remarks and gestures, and gradually closed in on the cyclists. A few seconds later they had knocked the Jocks off their bicycles with their hurley sticks, and held up the men with revolvers. They removed the rifles' ammunition and bicycles of the soldiers, and they released them to return, under the NCO in charge, to our camp, very ashamed."

Up until this point no member of the Crown forces had been shot in the acquisition

A wanted poster for Dan Breen, who with other Tipperary men were responsible for the killing of two policemen at Soloheadbeg, thus starting the War for Independence.

of arms. This was to change in January 1919 at Soloheadbeg in County Tipperary, where it could be said the war of liberation began. Soloheadbeg is situated about two and a half miles from Tipperary town. Explosives for the local quarry were routinely taken by a horse and cart, escorted by about half a dozen fully armed men of the paramilitary Royal Irish Constabulary. A company of local Volunteers from the South Tipperary Brigade, commanded by Seamus Robinson, resolved to ambush it. The explosive they intended for grenades and demolition work. They were informed that the explosives would be conveyed on 16 January. All that cold winter day they lay in ambush along the road, but there was no sign of the cart and its escort. As darkness descended they moved off for the night. The next day they returned, and the day after that, but still there was no sign of the explosives cart. The rest of the company were dismissed, leaving just nine men, Seamus Robinson, Sean Treacy, Sean Hogan, Tim Crowe, Patrick O'Dwyer, Michael Ryan, Patrick MacCormack, Jack O'Meara and Dan Breen. Their main concern was to remain unseen. If it became known to the police that a group of strangers were hanging around the neighborhood, they would have become suspicious. Every day before daylight they made their way to the ambush site, not leaving until it was dark. On the fifth day, 21 January, the lookout spied the cart. As luck would have it there were only two guards — only two, but these men were trained in the use of arms. They would have completed a course in the effective use of hand grenades, and of course they were disciplined. "Hands up!" the Volunteers called out. In response the policemen brought their rifles to bear.

The Volunteers acted first and opened fire, killing the two men, Constables James McDonnell and Patrick O'Connell. James Godfrey, the cart driver, and Patrick Flynn, a council employee, looked on in horror. Realizing the intentions of the Volunteers, Flynn secreted thirty of the detonators about his person. The Volunteers, realizing that the alarm was now raised, seized the rifles and other police equipment, mounted the cart, and drove off at speed. Hogan, Treacy and Breen went off with the cart; the other Volunteers dispersed and made their separate ways to safety. As night drew on, the men with the cart arrived at a prearranged site and hid the dynamite. Then abandoning, the horse and cart a few miles away, they set off across country. In the distance they saw the lights of the military trucks, scouring the roads for them. After a fifteen mile walk they found shelter for the night at the cottage of an old woman sympathetic to their cause. The following day they continued on their way and on to safety. The British responded by declaring martial law in the district and began raiding houses. When Volunteer headquarters in Dublin heard of this unauthorized exploit, they made plans to get the men out of the country and away to America.

The ambushers, however, refused to go, believing that if they did their exploit would be looked upon as the act of criminals or cowards. Instead they went on the run, determined to carry on the fight. What GHQ feared most was committing this idealistic but poorly armed and poorly trained force to a conflict. Their view was that the Volunteers were more effective as a threat and they rarely sanctioned any actions. Effective preparation over a long period of time, though, often brings forgetfulness of purpose. The Volunteers out in the country, realizing that every beginning is premature, went on the offensive. The action at Soloheadbeg galvanized Volunteer headquarters into action. Planned attacks were instituted against RIC barracks all over Ireland.

The Strategy and Tactics of Guerrilla Warfare

Guerrilla armies should not necessarily be considered to be inferior to the army they are fighting against simply because they are numerically inferior in numbers and firepower. The size of the guerrilla army is determined by the nature of the terrain, the skill and motivation of the fighters, their requirements in food, supplies and shelter, the tactics used, and the need to keep their own casualties to a minimum. Any given area can absorb only so many fighters. Initially at the start of a guerrilla campaign the size of the unit is of necessity limited. The larger the group the more difficult it becomes for them to escape after an action, especially if they are inexperienced. Therefore the growth of the flying column was commensurate with experience. Sean Moylan, military commander in North Cork during the War for Independence, neatly summed up this situation: "Some have expressed surprise that the IRA campaign was not made more spectacular. By this they meant, of course, a concentration of forces and bigger battles. Such people had no conception of conditions or of the grand strategy that directed the campaign. We visualized the fight as a long one in which British ruthlessness would be more intensified the longer it continued. It was essential to keep an army in the field, its liquidation could not be contemplated."

The guerrilla army must play to its strengths, making full use of local knowledge of both the town and countryside, and how to operate within them. What to the enemy may be perceived as retreat following an attack is to the guerrilla withdrawal and survival. The fundamental principle of guerrilla fighting is never to engage the enemy unless the skirmish or ambush can be won. The very existence of the guerrilla army is a victory in itself. A byproduct of this is the frustration and demoralization of the enemy from never knowing when an attack might come. Tom Barry, in his account of the Anglo-Irish War, *Guerilla Days in Ireland,* sums up this situation: "Strange as it may seem, it was accepted in West Cork that the paramount objective of any Flying Column, in the circumstances then prevailing, should be, not to fight, but to continue to exist. The very existence of such a column of armed men, even if it never struck a blow, was a continuous challenge to the enemy and forced him to maintain large garrisons to meet the threatened onslaught on his military forces, and for the security of his civil administration. Such a column moving around must seriously affect the morale of garrisons, for one day it would surely strike...."

The element of surprise is the weapon of the guerrilla army, taking advantage of the enemy's weak points, be they military installations or personnel. The principle form of attack carried out by the IRA was the nighttime attack on RIC barracks, and the daytime ambush of police and army personnel. To take the enemy by surprise is at the root of all military teaching, and no more so than when a smaller force is fighting against a superior and better armed force. Tom Barry succinctly explained this mode of fighting: "We never laid an ambush except by the side of the road. The British were more experienced, better trained, and better shots. My Volunteers often had to go into action without having fired one shot in training so our tactics therefore were to attack at close quarters whenever possible. We always fired at the enemy from a range of 10 to 15 yards — there are no bad shots at 15 yards — at that range you couldn't miss your target."

Outright confrontation in the early stages of the war would surely have seen the annihilation of the Nationalist army, as with the Dublin Rising of 1916. The post–Rising IRA fought the war on its terms, as a mobile force, repeatedly attacking without giving any rest to the enemy. The impact of a successful ambush on both Irish and British opinion was not gauged in purely military terms alone. It had ramifications, as a consequence, to the morale of both the victors and the defeated and as a means of forming international opinion through propaganda. Guerrilla warfare is transitory, in that it is constantly evolving, though rarely to a set timetable, until the guerrilla army acquires the characteristics of a regular army in the field and is in a position to deal a final blow and achieve victory. The early stages of this model are clearly visible in the Irish war, which may be divided up into three distinct phases.

First was gaining the support of the population. In this case the IRA was an army of national liberation. The people had democratically voted for independence in the general election of 1918. This gave the army a moral right to exist. The majority of people, particularly in the south and southwest, saw it as their army and gave it their support. In the second phase, the army of liberation not only launched attacks against the police and military forces of the British, but it also attacked its lines of communications, as well as the administration and institutions of the occupying power. The IRA attacked police and army barracks, inland revenue offices, and customs and excise offices. It then went on to keep in check the enemy's attempts at rebuilding its badly shaken civil administration. The official unpublished British account of the war, *Record of the Rebellion in Ireland, 1920–1921* (vol. 4, part 3) points out that Britain's "offensive power was always hampered by endless defensive duties, such as guards and escorts ... leading to fluctuations in strength of the troops." Thus troops were diverted away from the main operation of pursuing the guerrillas. In the wake of the destruction of the British system, the Republican government set up its own alternatives to the British administration, instructing the people to boycott the British system. The IRA was also tasked with guarding and protecting the establishment of the replacement Republican institutions and the people who established and used them. Up until this point county brigades acted independently of each other and of GHQ in Dublin. But in the third phase, by the end of 1920, brigades were being formed into divisions, combining the forces from several counties and fighting to a preordained plan. The war began to develop into conventional warfare, with flying columns of brigade size probing enemy garrisoned towns with a view to bringing the garrisons to battle. With the creation of the Second Southern Division, Ernie O'Malley, its commandant, outlined his strategy for progressing the war:

> I decided to organize a divisional column of one hundred men. We would move in three parallel columns and begin in County Kerry, the area which had done least. As time went on, I knew we would have to strengthen some of our columns to close with the British columns which were beginning to move around in our area. We needed careful training in maneuver, and we would have to go into towns to look for fight. I intended that we would sleep out; that meant hay-rick covers, ground sheets and blankets. I sent word to brigades to select men for the new column. Our men in small columns could, I felt, meet the same number of men or more in the open, but as our numbers increased our officers would be more liable to be out maneuvered by the British officers. I hoped that as a result of our new action I could select some officers whom I would send to sleepy areas for organization, training and operations. I knew that action and comradeship would knit more closely the officers and men of a column, and that any later orders to them would be more promptly obeyed.

As has been said, the development of this form of warfare does not always follow a predictable and uniform progression, but as will be shown, the IRA had reached the beginning of phase three before a truce was announced.

The tactics of the war are the practical measures taken to achieve the final goal, in this case the independence of Ireland from colonial rule. For the guerrilla army the tactics are both variable and flexible, to meet the situation as it presents itself. Maneuverability is fundamental not only in attack but also in withdrawal, to avoid encirclement. Encirclement is the enemy's only way of forcing the guerrillas into a decisive battle, which because of the enemy's superior numbers would lead to the destruction of the guerrillas. The development of an exit strategy by the guerrillas not only ensured their safety, but in turn was also turned into an attacking force against elements of the advancing encirclement. This is most admirably demonstrated following the ambush at Grange, County Limerick, on 8 November 1920, and more especially at Crossbarry by the West Cork Flying Column on 19 March 1921.

Nighttime movement by a guerrilla force enables them to advance into position for an attack or ambush unseen, particularly where the danger of betrayal presents itself. In this case it was the presence of Loyalist families living in certain neighborhoods (as at Modreeny in North Tipperary). Almost without exception, this movement by night was the means adopted by the IRA. In some cases, to ensure complete security, Loyalist families were held as prisoners for the duration of the preparations and assault upon the enemy convoys.

Flexibility enables guerrillas to adapt themselves to all unexpected circumstances as opposed to the rigidity of the professional army of occupation, which will be acting under strict instructions. The surprise and sudden attack of the guerrilla can in a matter of minutes cease with its withdrawal, leaving the enemy with nothing to counterattack. The guerrilla uses the terrain not only in attack, but also in defense, preventing the enemy from physically advancing — for example across rivers or through bog-land or over mountains. By this careful selection of the terrain, superiority shifts from the encircling enemy to the defending/withdrawing guerrillas. The enemy then advances at its peril, leaving itself open to sniper fire from elements of the withdrawing guerrillas. In this way the initiative has shifted from the advancing numerically superior force to the numerically inferior defending force.

One of the weakest points of the occupying army are its rail and road communications. Lying in ambush along entrenched roads and using exploding mines along roads, with an attack on the survivors, are two of the most successful means of acquiring arms and ammunition from the enemy. This inevitably leads to a change of policy in the use of trucks, from single vehicles to convoys, and by the spacing out of convoys so that at any one time only one vehicle lies within the ambush zone. The guerrillas adapt to this by either breaking up the convoy and preventing the other vehicles from coming to the aid of the ambushed vehicle or by forcing the convoy to bunch up, both by the use of explosives or barriers in the road. By using the terrain to their advantage, the guerrillas can achieve the same results against large convoys by using larger groups, with many of the fighters in subsidiary roles, blocking and guarding secondary roads that can be used to bring in enemy reinforcements, and keeping open the lines of withdrawal.

The humane treatment of captured enemy soldiers in these attacks will show the moral superiority of the guerrilla army. Prisoners, unless they are of high status, and may be used as bargaining chips, were not be taken. Survivors were freed and the wounded cared for, provided it did not endanger the guerrillas. All of these courses, as will be shown, were practiced by the IRA. Sean Moylan (North Cork Brigade) in particular was noted for his humane treatment of prisoners, so much so that at his court-martial following capture former prisoners testified on his behalf.

Initially the terrain for assault or ambush is chosen by the guerrillas. With success and the liberating of an area, the guerrillas must push out from their comfort zone in order to confront the enemy once more, but in the sure knowledge that an exit strategy is in place whereby they can safely withdraw to the liberated area. The ground should again be favorable to the guerrillas, with care taken to avoid areas where enemy reinforcements can be quickly gathered in support of units of their army or police force under attack. If this cannot be avoided, then attacks should take place at night or should be a combination of several guerrilla groups, many acting in noncombatant, or support, roles. Alternatively these other groups should launch diversionary attacks while the primary target itself is being attacked. The object of the exercise is not only to defeat the enemy and extend the area of liberation but also to capture the ammunition expended in the assault, so that the war may continue to its intended conclusion. An intended ambush at Farranlobus, two miles from Dunmanway, County Cork, on 9 October 1920 by Tom Barry and the West Cork Flying Column illustrates this principle of careful planning and a full use of the terrain. His first consideration however is the survival of the column:

> [The Column] occupied positions on the Dunmanway-Ballineen road to attack a party of troops.... This patrol of British soldiers traveled daily from Dunmanway in a particular formation. First came about twenty cyclists, and after them, in a lorry, about twenty other soldiers. At times the cyclists would pass Farranlobus five minutes before the lorry-borne troops. On other occasions, there would be a twenty minute interval between them. Consequently it was necessary that the cyclists should be dealt with without an exchange of shots, so that the troops following would not be aware of the ambush until they drove into the position and were attacked.
>
> The attack on this party had to be arranged as follows. Three riflemen were sent four hundred yards directly behind the Column, on to the high ground, from where they could fire on an enemy attempting to come in from either flank or from the rear. Nineteen riflemen under the Column Commander, who were to attack the cyclists with fixed bayonets, were placed behind the northern ditch of the road, extending about 80 yards, the estimated length of the enemy cyclist column. At a given signal this group was to jump the ditch, and each man was to attack the nearest soldier. No shots were to be fired by the I.R.A. The remaining group of fourteen, with the Brigade OC in charge, were posted 150 yards further west, inside the same ditch at the northern side of the road. They were to attack the lorry as soon as it arrived in their midst. They were not to be diverted under any circumstances from the task, but it was hoped that the main IRA party would have dealt with the cyclists in time to aid this group.[15]

All too often, as in this case, the British troops failed to appear, though they had predictably followed the same routine on the previous six days.

Urban warfare, attacking the enemy in its very heartland, be it sabotage, assassination or attacks upon the occupying power's soldiers, is perhaps not fully appreciated for how important and dangerous it is. Small guerrilla units, rarely more that two or three but each acting under the direct orders of one controlling leader, can prove devastating. In assaults on enemy personnel, this is close-up fighting, never lasting more than two or three minutes, always taking the enemy by surprise; its weapons are the hand gun, sawn-off shot-gun and hand grenades. The speed of the action and withdrawal is essential for the attackers to escape to the refuge of a safe house. This form of assault produces anguish amongst the enemy, they never knowing when an attack may come. In cities supporting the guerrillas, reprisals following such attacks are inevitable. In cities such as Dublin, where there was a Loyalist population intermingled with its Republican neighbors, reprisals were limited for fear of killing, or at the very least antagonizing, and thereby alienating, the Loyalist population. The real importance of guerrilla warfare in Dublin during the War of Independence apart from the propaganda victory it achieved in the national and international press, was the assassination of British agents which denied vital intelligence to the Crown authorities.

4

Passive Resistance

Passive resistance is a nonviolent form of warfare. It is the refusal to accept the laws or norms of an oppressive regime. In Ireland during the period 1918 to 1921 passive resistance took several forms. In its way, it was as effective as guerrilla warfare, showing the rest of the world that the people of Ireland refused to accept British jurisdiction over their affairs.

The first mass protest was the anti-conscription campaign of 1918. The country as a whole said "no." People, politicians and the Church, all said "no" to conscription. In this as in so many other of its proposals, Britain got it badly wrong. Their intention to enforce conscription in Ireland, while postponing the establishment of Home Rule, enraged everyone. The Irish no longer trusted Britain to keep its word. Home Rule had been put off repeatedly, and yet Britain still expected Irishmen to go off and fight for "small nations." To the majority of Irish people — citizens of a "small nation" — it was incredible hypocrisy. When the proposal was presented in the House of Commons the Irish Party voted against the levying of conscription in Ireland. Nonetheless the bill was passed into law on 16 April, by 301 votes to 103. John Dillon and the Irish Party MPs left the Commons in protest, and returned home to organize opposition to the act. On 18 April, the lord mayor of Dublin convened a meeting at the Mansion House to debate the issue. In the face of this national threat all parties — the Irish Parliamentary Party, Sinn Fein and the Irish Labor Party — became as one in their opposition. There was little disagreement, and at the end of the meeting Eamon de Valera drew up the words of the Anti-Conscription Pledge: "Denying the right of the British Government to enforce compulsory service in this country, we pledge ourselves solemnly to one another to resist Conscription by the most effective means at our disposal." For international consumption the following declaration, also drawn up by de Valera, was passed unanimously by the conference:

> Taking our stand on Ireland's separate and distinct nationhood and affirming the principle of liberty that the governments of nations derive their just powers from the consent of the governed, we deny the right of the British Government or any external authority to impose compulsory military service in Ireland against the clearly expressed will of the Irish people. The passing of the Conscription Bill by the British House of Commons must be regarded as a declaration of war on the Irish nation.
>
> The alternative to accepting it as such is to surrender our liberties and to acknowledge ourselves slaves.
>
> It is in direct violation of the rights of small nationalities to self-determination, which even the Prime Minister of England — now preparing to employ naked militarism and force his Act upon Ireland — himself officially announced as an essential condition for peace at the Peace

Signing the anti–Conscription Pledge, Sunday, 21 April 1918.

Congress. The attempt to enforce it will be an unwarrantable aggression, which we call upon all Irishmen to resist by the most effective means at their disposal.

At that very moment the Catholic bishops of Ireland were holding their annual conference at Maynooth. They were expected to make some statement concerning conscription. A delegation from the Mansion House Conference, consisting of the lord mayor of Dublin, the Nationalist MPs John Dillon and T.M. Healy, William O'Brien representing the Labor movement, and Eamon de Valera of Sinn Fein, went to see them in the hope that they could persuade them to sanction resistance to conscription. In that it did not mention violence, the bishops had no qualms in accepting de Valera's motion. The bishops came out in support, declaring, "We consider that Conscription forced in this way upon Ireland is an oppressive and inhuman law which the Irish people have a right to resist by every means that are consonant with the law of God."

Days later, the Irish Trades Union Conference convened a meeting in Dublin to decide what form of protest organized Labor would take. Fifteen hundred delegates attended the congress. The unanimous decision was that a twenty-four-hour general strike should be called. The Women Workers' Union organized a march through Dublin in support, bringing the city to a halt. Gone were the days when the police could break up such a march with impunity as in 1913. The eyes of the world were upon Dublin. That Sunday, 21 April, the Anti-Conscription Pledge was signed at church doorways and in other places across Ireland by thousands of people. On 23 April a one-day general strike was held nationwide. Cities and towns, with the exception of Loyalist Belfast, came to a halt. Trains, trams and taxis did not run; banks, factories and shops closed for the day. No newspapers appeared throughout much of the country. Ships were left unloaded along the quays. People came out onto the streets in orderly protest against conscription. The British government was shocked by the response, but more so by the organization behind it. Its response was predictable: it put in place measures to replace civil rule by military command, under field marshal Lord French. His response was typical of the military mind: "Home Rule will be offered and declined, then conscription will be enforced. If they [the Government] will leave me alone I can do what is necessary. I shall notify a date before which recruits must offer themselves in various districts. If they do not come, we will fetch them."[1] What would have undoubtedly led to bloodshed, had French tried to impose conscription on Ireland, was averted when the last German offensive of World War I was checked and pushed back. Within months Germany sued for peace. The conscription crisis was over, but what a remarkable time it had been.

The shootings at Soloheadbeg in January 1919 saw a crackdown by the British government on drilling by the Irish Volunteers. The homes of known Volunteers were raided and searched, and numbers of arrests were made. In Limerick, Robert J. Byrnes, a Volunteer and prominent member of the Trades and Labor Council, was arrested when guns were found at his home. He was sentenced to twelve months hard labor, by a court-martial, on 13 January 1919. His response was to demand that he be treated as a political prisoner. This being refused, he and the other prisoners arrested at the time embarked on a policy of disobedience. This led to reprisals and beatings of the prisoners. Their boots and clothing were removed, and the leaders, including Byrnes, were handcuffed day and night and put in solitary confinement on bread and water diets. They responded by going on a hunger strike. After three weeks Byrnes was removed to the hospital in a weak condition. There he was guarded day and night by three members of the RIC. A party of the local Volunteers attempted to rescue Byrnes; but rather than see him escape, one of the policemen shot him, mortally wounding him. The policeman was himself shot dead and two other members of the guard were wounded, one fatally.

Fearing unrest, the British authorities proclaimed Limerick a military area and subject to martial law. Checkpoints were set up throughout the city, tanks and armored cars patrolled its streets. Permits to enter and leave the city had to be applied for. An office was set up where those applying for permits were vetted by the police. Name, address, physical details — height, weight, color of hair and eyes — were entered on the card. This was then duly dated and stamped. For some, the permit had to be renewed on a daily basis. This led to massive disruption and long delays.

On the morning of 13 April, the Limerick Trades & Labor Council, representing thirty-five trade unions throughout the city, met to discuss what action should be taken. A further meeting was held that evening to finalize plans. Their decision was to declare a general strike, to commence the next day. A strike committee was established and the strike, it was decided, should begin at 5:00 A.M. the next morning, 14 April. The strike committee appointed subcommittees to deal with finance, sale and distribution of food, permits, vigilance, and — as the committee was increasingly aware of their need to put across their message in the face of British censorship — a propaganda committee. Before the start of the strike the committee had printed multiple copies of a proclamation, which were posted throughout the city:

LIMERICK UNITED TRADES AND LABOR COUNCIL
PROCLAMATION

The Workers of Limerick, assembled in Council, hereby DECLARE CESSATION OF ALL WORK from five A.M. on MONDAY, FOURTEENTH OF APRIL, 1919, as a protest against the DECISION OF THE BRITISH GOVERNMENT IN COMPELLING THEM TO PROCURE PERMITS IN ORDER TO EARN THEIR DAILY BREAD.

By Order of the Strike Committee,
Mechanical Institute.

Taking over a printing works, the strike committee produced permits, proclamations, lists of food prices, their own strike money, and a news sheet, the *Daily Bulletin*. The city surrounded as it was, the British authorities thought that they could contain the "Limerick Soviet," as it came to be called, denying it any publicity. But it just so happened that the city was crowded with foreign journalists who were there to cover a proposed transatlantic flight by a Major Woods, who was supposed to land there for refueling. The strike committee fully briefed the journalists, among whom was a representative of the Associated Press of America, whose agency served 750 U.S. newspapers. Also there were representatives of a number of European newspapers. There was no way that the British authorities could censor these foreign newspapers, and in particular the American papers, as their journalists had a direct line to America through the American cable at Valentia. Limerick's response to British militarism was in all the newspapers within twenty-four hours.

The strike committee issued money in denominations of ten shilling, five shilling and one shilling notes, with the promise that if shops would honor them, the Trades & Labor Council would redeem them when the strike was over. Permits were given for the movement of perishable goods. The necessary skilled labor was provided to maintain water, gas and electric supplies to the city. Permits were issued to supply petrol for doctors' and other essential users' cars. The Food Committee ensured that food was received and distributed fairly. Distribution centers were established from which traders were supplied goods at prices for resale fixed by the committee. The opening and closing of shops was regulated, public houses were closed for the duration of the strike. Citizen police ensured that there was no looting: not one case of misbehavior was brought before the court during the strike. Both the British Army and the police withdrew from the streets.

The bishop and clergy of Limerick issued a manifesto condemning the imposition of martial law and the misery that it had brought to innocent people. Limerick Chamber of Commerce, representing the many businesses within the city, sent a strong memo to Andrew Bonar Law, leader of the Conservative Party, demanding that he bring pressure to bear in having martial law repealed. On 26 April, after twelve days of the strike, martial law was lifted and the city returned to work.

In April of the following year,

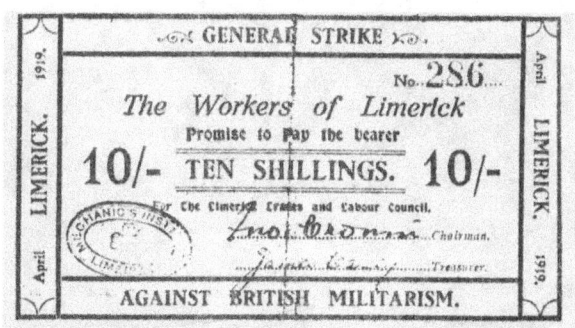

A ten shilling note issued during the Limerick General Strike, 1919.

with Britain's continuance to arrest Volunteers and members of Sinn Fein, there was a second general strike in Dublin. Republicans in jails demanded political or prisoner of war status. This being denied, on 5 April, sixty men in Mountjoy Prison in Dublin went on a hunger strike. In the days that followed, both night and day, huge crowds gathered around the prison, saying the rosary, and singing hymns and Fenian songs for the prisoners to hear. Knowing that they were not alone encouraged the prisoners in their struggle. British soldiers with bayonets fixed to their rifles patrolled the streets in numbers. RAF planes flew low overhead in an attempt at overawing the people below. But the people were not overawed. On 12 April the Irish Labor Party and the Trades Union Conference called a general strike in support of the prisoners. The response was overwhelming, Dublin came to a standstill. After three days, the prisoners, who had been on hunger strike for ten days, were offered release on parole. They refused. The government then offered them unconditional release. Their release had as much to do with pressure brought to bear in England as it had with pressure in Ireland. The British press was aware of the ill feeling towards Britain by other nations in its suppression of democracy in Ireland. Of the success of the hunger strike, the *New Statesman* (17 April 1920), a London-based weekly periodical, wrote: "In the last resort subject peoples have an argument to which there is no reply; Sinn Feiners have discovered this argument."

Having discovered the power of politically motivated industrial action, Sinn Fein and the labor movement launched a second strike in May 1920. The "Munitions of War" strike, as it became known, lasted until December. The Irish Transport Workers refused to carry armed soldiers or Black and Tans. If they boarded a train the engine driver would refuse to start. This escalated on 22 May 1920 when dockers as well as railwaymen refused to handle munitions of war. A voluntary fund of over £116,000 was raised to support men who were sacked.

The strike had a parallel with the "Hands Off Russia" campaign waged by British

Irish women protesting against the killing of innocent people during reprisals.

workers against the export of munitions to Poland. The Irish TUC hoped to get backing from the British NUR, but in this they were disappointed. The NUR prevaricated, realizing that this was a strike for political purposes and support for it would be construed as being anti–British. The Irish transport workers were thrown back on their own resources. The railway companies came under pressure from the British government, which threatened to cut their grants and subsidies, and so began suspension and dismissal of workers who refused to transport soldiers or munitions. Eventually drivers and firemen were brought in from other parts of Great Britain to replace them. This betrayal by fellow members of the same trade union led to scuffles and assaults upon the British workers, who could work only under guard, with armed soldiers riding with them on the footplate. Nonetheless, by August several smaller lines were forced to close. Only one goods train a day ran from Athlone to the west. The passenger service was suspended. Galway was completely cut off from train services. By the end of August between 900 and 1,000 railwaymen had been dismissed. With a reduced service, the railway companies were ordered to give government traffic absolute priority. By November the strike fund, even when topped up by Sinn Fein funds, had run low. There were between fifteen thousand and sixteen thousand railwaymen out of work.

The National Labor Conference held at the Mansion House in Dublin on 16 November debated continuance of the strike. There were some calls to abandon it in the face of the suffering beginning to be endured by the dismissed workers, but on the whole the meeting was for the continuance of the strike. There was genuine hardship, and figures within the Labor movement looked for an honorable way of ending the strike. The British, looking for a way to break the strike, then began arresting leading members of the Irish Labor Party and the TUC. Papers and records of the Food Committee that saw to the distribution of food throughout the country were also seized. This threw the Labor movement into disarray. The strike began to crumble. On 13 December a party of armed troops were carried on the Great Southern and Western Railway. On 21 December, with Christmas approaching, a conference held at the Mansion House voted unanimously to return to work. The strike, lasting eight months, was over.

Perhaps the greatest form of passive resistance — just ignoring the British system — was the establishment of the Republican courts. The parish court, the very basic form of justice, was presided over by a man or woman appointed by the local Sinn Fein club. They

Women protesting against the execution of Irish prisoners of war.

were ably assisted by the Republican police, men from the local Volunteer company. Then there were district courts, usually presided over by a person with some legal experience. Finally there was the highest court, the supreme court, which generally met in Dublin. By August 1920 the Republican courts were operating in twenty-seven counties of Ireland, including five counties in Ulster. After British forces broke up a number of courts, arresting the court officials, the Republican courts went underground, meeting wherever they could on as regular a basis as could be managed. Decisions arrived at using common sense, rather than hard and fast fixed legal precedents, saw even Loyalists in the South resorting to them for justice.

On 14 March 1921 six Volunteers were hanged in Mountjoy. Preceding the executions large crowds of women, including the friends and relatives of the condemned men and numbered at 20,000, gathered outside the prison walls. Prayers were said, and hymns were sung. The *Freeman's Journal* (14 March 1921) reported: "The subdued demeanour of the people, their anxious looks, and whispered talks were all indicative of the mingled feelings of sympathy and horror in which they regarded the awful tragedy at hand. Before dispersing ... the crowds outside Mountjoy Prison sang 'The Soldier's Song' and 'Wrap the Green Flag Around Me Boys.' The hangings commenced at 6 o'clock. The prisoners were executed in pairs at intervals of one hour: 6 o'clock—Thomas Whelan and Patrick Moran, 7 o'clock—Thomas O'Brien and Patrick Doyle, 8 o'clock—Francis Flood and Bernard Ryan. Moran and Whelan had been convicted of murder for their part in the shooting of the British intelligence officers in Dublin on 21 November 1920. The other four had been convicted of being involved in an ambush at Drumcondra, Dublin.

As the war progressed towards its end, in Dublin the people began reclaiming their city. The dusk to dawn curfew imposed by the British was by June 1921 being ignored. It was dangerous in that the citizens of the capital ran the risk of being shot by nervous young soldiers on nighttime patrol, but nonetheless out onto the streets they went. Up to 100 civilians each night were caught breaking the curfew. Their sheer weight in numbers overburdened the British magistrate's courts; and the magistrates, rather than sending them to prison, imposed fines, which invariably went unpaid.

Out in the countryside the people ignored British directives against giving shelter to the Volunteers. Florence O'Donaghue, on the run out in Kerry, wrote to his wife of his admiration for those who provided safe-houses: "Here the kindly sympathetic, un-effusive welcome of the true Gael awaits you; in every house, rich or poor, we meet keen intelligent minds, clean with the sunny freshness of nature. It is a never-ending source of wonder to me, and indeed pride too, to note what a splendid organization has been beaten out of this raw material in the last few years. No Kings or Princes in Europe could have been treated with the care and honor they bestowed on us."

Of these strikes and other forms of passive resistance, Robert Lynn, writing in the *Daily News* (5 July 1920) just days before the truce, observed, "So far as the mass of the people are concerned the policy of the day is not an active, but a passive policy. Their purpose is not to attack the Government, but to ignore it, and to build up a new Government quietly by its side."

5

The Intelligence War

For both sides, winning the war was dependant on good intelligence. In the post–Rising Republican structure, Eamon Duggan, a lawyer, was appointed director of information and intelligence. Learning as he went along, he operated out of the New Ireland Assurance Company offices in Bachelor's Walk, the same building used by the Dail Loan scheme. At an early stage Duggan was fortunate in obtaining the services of Detective Joseph Kavanagh of the Dublin Metropolitan Police. Through an intermediary, Thomas Gay, the librarian of the Dublin Corporation library in Capel Street, supplied Duggan with information regarding arrests, intended police raids and messages from prisoners.

Duggan was succeeded by the more proactive Michael Collins, who put the operation on a more professional basis. He co-opted Liam Tobin and Frank Thornton, part of the management team of New Ireland. Tobin was appointed deputy director of intelligence and Thornton deputy assistant director. Tom Cullen, IRA quartermaster general, was seconded to the position of assistant director. These three men, along with Frank Saurin, Charlie Dalton, Charlie Byrne and Joe Guilfoyle, ran the Intelligence Department, reporting to Collins on a daily basis.

When British intelligence discovered their whereabouts, the group being warned they moved to new premises, above Fowler's in Crow Street near Dublin Castle. Additional staff were invariably drawn from the Drumcondra-based 2nd Battalion of North Dublin. That was appropriate in that the department was mainly concerned with gathering intelligence regarding the city and its environs. Information also came in from other battalions in the city. John Harrington, who joined H Company of the 1st Battalion in 1918, was as a young doctor based at Richmond Hospital in North Brunswick Street. This proved useful, as he had access to personnel records. When the Auxiliaries were based in the North Dublin Union, their medical records were transferred to Richmond Hospital. Harrington was able to pass English addresses and other information on to the IRA battalion intelligence officer, who in his turn passed the information on to the IRA director of operations in England. This resulted in a number of Black and Tan and Auxiliary officers' houses being firebombed as reprisals for house burnings in Ireland.

IRA Intelligence Gathering in the City

With a dedicated team, intelligence was gathered and acted upon more promptly. A lot of material was freely available in various publications. The newspapers and society magazines gave details of appointments and transfers of RIC officers and their attendance at social functions. Photographs were cut out and pasted onto cards. Senior British Army Officers were traced through *Who's Who*. Notes of their addresses and clubs, their interests and other social pursuits were noted. Later their mail was intercepted. Details were kept on hotels and restaurants and sports meetings where police, army and British secret service agents gathered. Lists of Republican sympathizers were kept. People who worked in the public sector, such as maids, receptionists and porters in hotels, telephone and telegraph operators, postmen, and railway and ferry operators, all could be expected to pass on information. The provinces also sent information into Dublin through appointed brigade intelligence officers, and Dublin sent out information to them on how to proceed with intelligence they had received relevant to the country districts.

The ambition of Irish intelligence was to have at least one person working in every government department who could pass on information. Collins was particularly fortunate in discovering that people within the Crown administration were willing to pass information to him. During the war he was able to persuade a number of Dublin Castle staff to work for Irish intelligence. These were mainly junior clerks, recruited through their membership in the Gaelic Athletic Association and the Gaelic League. Collins was also successful in obtaining the services of one particular police clerk in the Detective Department of G Division, Edward (Ned) Broy. In his witness statement to the Bureau of Military History, Broy recalled that one of his duties was to buy groceries at Findlater's shop in George Street. Here he came into contact with the shop's bookkeeper, a Miss Smart. They found that they shared similar political beliefs. Having sounded him out Miss Smart asked him one day if he "would mind meeting Mick Collins? I told her I would have no hesitation whatever." Broy met Collins in January 1919 at 5, Cabra Road, the home of Michael O'Foghludha, and agreed to work for him. Broy turned out to be a very valuable spy. At first Broy's information was negated by the delay under the Duggan administration, but under Collins' more efficient regime it proved very valuable. Broy informed Collins of the intended arrest of the senior members of Sinn Fein in early 1918. They for their part chose to ignore the warning, believing that they could achieve more by being seen by the rest of the world as wrongly imprisoned political prisoners. Collins did not see it that way and avoided capture himself. So rich was the information coming in from Broy that Collins saw him directly, sometimes on a daily basis. Duggan's early recruit, Kavanagh, recruited James MacNamara, the son of a policeman as well as the confidential clerk to the assistant police commissioner in Dublin Castle. Collins' third success was in obtaining the services of Lily Mernin, a typist in the military intelligence adjutant's office in Parkgate Street. She passed on information regarding British spy reports on Volunteers, arrests and court-martials, and later names and addresses of Castle personnel, including British intelligence officers. In September 1919 Sergeant Jerry Maher of the RIC in Naas joined the intelligence team. He was clerk to the district inspector and was able to supply Collins with information about circulars from RIC headquarters as well as current codes being used. Maurice McCarthy, an RIC sergeant in Belfast, also supplied Collins with police codes.

Regarding secretarial assistance at the Castle, "Periscope," the pen name of an administrator in Dublin Castle at the time, wrote, "The ordinary Irish typist was held to be suspect, and accordingly the recruiting-ground was England, where the pressure of economy was gradually resulting in numbers being at length discarded. An attractive salary, a spice of adventure, were sufficient inducements to attract numbers of workless ladies.... 'Tudor's typists' became the rage, and the sight of large numbers in summery attire, more suited perhaps for tea at the Shelbourne or the Bonne Bouche than for office routine, trooping to the balcony when anything novel appeared in the Castle yard, lent a new flavor of romance to the scene."[1]

One of "Tudor's Typists" was Nancy O'Brien — Michael Collins' cousin. She had been working in the post office service in London and was brought over to Dublin as a cipher clerk to decode messages. It was an incredible lapse of security on the part of the British not to check her background. With her help Collins was getting some messages even before the British secret service officers for whom they were intended. Perhaps Collins' most important recruit was Detective David Neligan, who was later transferred to military intelligence. On one noted occasion Neligan arranged for Collins to secretly enter G Division's office and look at secret files.

IRA Intelligence-Led Assassination

Dick McKee, of the Dublin Brigade of Volunteers, even before Collins took over as director of intelligence, had initiated his own form of intelligence gathering. He identified police detectives and had them followed. In the back of his mind was a plan to remove them and the threat that they posed. Sinn Fein and IRB policy at the time was against assassination, no doubt on the basis that it might become reciprocal. Mick McDonnell, of the 2nd Battalion, pushed for the formation of an assassination squad, and in mid–1919 his proposal was accepted. Likely candidates for the Squad were invited to a house at 35, North Great George's Street, off Parnell Street. Initially six men were chosen with more recruited in the following months. The Squad, popularly known as the "Twelve Apostles," comprised

The "Apostles" (left to right): Joe Leonard, Joe Slattery, Joe Dolan, Geroid O'Sullivan (standing), William Stapleton and Charlie Dalton, were appointed to assassinate enemy intelligence agents.

Mick McDonnell, his brother-in-law Tom Keogh, Joe Leonard, Sean Doyle, Jim Slattery, Bill Stapleton, Pat McCrae, James Conroy, Ben Barret, Vinnie Byrne, Paddy Daly and Mick Kennedy. Nominally McKee was in charge, subject to direction from Collins. Initially the Squad was based in Oriel House, but soon moved to a builders' yard, "George Moreland Cabinet Maker," in Abbey Street. The Squad, attached to the Intelligence Department, became the first permanent body of fighting men.

The first action of this squad was the assassination of Detective Sergeant Patrick Smyth of G Division, the political section of the DMP. Smyth had in fact been warned that he would be shot unless he desisted from his overly zealous political activities. He refused. In the early days all candidates for assassination were warned and given the chance of resigning from the police. Upon Smyth's refusal, a four man squad was selected for the assassination: James Slattery, Tom Keogh, Tom Ennis and Mick Kennedy. Usually someone from Irish intelligence would accompany the Squad to identify the target. They waited for a number of days near his house in Drumcondra. On 30 July, as he approached, he was shot at by all four assassins. Smyth returned fire, and though badly wounded staggered towards his house and somehow managed to get in. Mortally wounded, though, he died a week later. In a clinical appraisal of the assassination, Slattery was to write of it: "We had .38 guns and they were too small. I thought that the minute we would fire at him he would fall, but after we hit him he ran. The four of us fired at him. Keogh and myself ran after him right to his own door and I think he fell at the door, but he got into the house. He lived for [a week]."[2] The weapons were ideal for concealment but were not heavy enough for a clean kill. Collins ensured that the men were issued .45 caliber revolvers and bullets.

Their next mission was on 13 September 1919. On the previous day there had been a police raid on Sinn Fein headquarters in Harcourt Street. The target had been Collins. He succeeded in escaping, but his would-be captor, Detective Daniel Hoey, did not. He was shot dead. Hoey had been the detective that had picked out Sean MacDiarmada for the firing squad after the failure of the Rising in 1916. In November the Squad fired at Detective Thomas Wharton near St. Stephen's Green. Wharton, though wounded, survived and retired from the force. Detective Sergeant John Barton, barely two months in G Division, investigating Wharton's attack, was himself shot dead on 30 November 1919. The following month Detective Constable Walshe, a clerk in G Division, was fired upon but escaped. In February 1920 Detective Constables Walsh[e] and Dunleavy were targeted. The two policemen returned fire, but Walshe was killed and Dunleavy was wounded. Detective Constable Henry Kells, a plainclothes G man, was killed on 14 April. A week later, on 20 April, Detective Constable Laurence Dalton, who had just been transferred to G Division, was assassinated. For its own safety G Division, was moved to Dublin Castle, but on 8 May 1920, Detective Sergeant Richard Revell was shot at seven times near his home. Though wounded he escaped. On 30 July 1920, Squad man Paddy Daly shot and killed Frank Brooke, director of the Great Southern and Eastern Railway, in his office. Brooke was a secret member of the British Military Advisory Council and an advocate of assassinating known Republicans. By the summer of 1920, the political G Division of Dublin Metropolitan Police had been effectively neutralized. The Squad were undoubtedly ruthless, but they were convinced of the rightness of what they were doing. They obeyed strict orders and killed only under order or in self-defense. They were a new breed of Volunteer, proactive rather than reactive as had been the men of 1916.

On 19 December 1919, the Squad, assisted by some Volunteers from Tipperary, attempted their most audacious plan to date, the assassination of the British general Sir John French. The ambush had been long planned but had been frustrated by French's security guard, who continually changed his routes of travel. On the 19th the squad succeeded in ambushing him in his car at Phoenix Park. He and his guards escaped, but a Volunteer, Martin Savage, was shot dead, and two DMP men were wounded.

At the end of 1919, Detective Inspector W.C. Forbes Redmond was brought in from Belfast as assistant commissioner to reorganize G Division. He brought with him his own trusted team. Not knowing Dublin, though, he sought the services of James MacNamara, one of Collins' agents within the castle. From then on he was a marked man.

The British secret service adopted a policy of trying to integrate their own agents into the very heart of the Volunteer leadership. Their first agent was John Charles Byrnes, a former soldier and grandson of an RIC district inspector. His handler was Lieutenant Ralph Isham of the Royal Engineers, an American anglophile. After World War I, Isham had been inducted into SIS to deal with Bolshevism in the British Army. Byrnes, a former sergeant major accused of fomenting unrest among the troops, was turned by Isham and reported on the socialist activities of his former comrades. With demobilization the unrest was dissipated. Isham now put forward a plan to integrate British agents into the newly emergent IRA. The plan was accepted and Byrnes was chosen as the first agent. Using the alias of Jameson, a traveling salesman for Keith Prowse & Co., a music company, Byrnes joined one of the London based Irish Self-Determination League branches. These branches were fronts for Sinn Fein. In charge of the branch was Art O'Brien, an old friend of Michael Collins.

At the time, Collins was hard-pressed to find revolvers. Byrnes told O'Brien that he could help. After further talks O'Brien contacted Collins with the good news. Believing Jameson (Byrnes) to have been fully vetted, Collins agreed to meet him in Manchester. Byrnes was able to supply the guns—.45s and .38 automatics. Through O'Brien, Collins invited Byrnes to Dublin. Byrnes added to the lure that not only could he supply arms, but he also had contacts within the British Army and could supply details of troop movements. Byrnes traveled to Dublin as John Jameson and stayed at the Granville Hotel in O'Connell Street. He was picked up and taken to a safe house in St. George's Street South, and there he met Collins once again. By supplying top secret documents related to the British Army in Ireland, Byrnes entered the fringe of IRA intelligence. Further meetings with Collins followed, but Collins was beginning to have doubts about Jameson and began making enquiries of his own. Collins fobbed off any further meetings with the British agent until these were complete. Byrnes was making reports to his handlers in London through Dublin Castle, and some of these were intercepted by Collins' agents in the Castle.

On 22 January 1920, Byrnes returned to Dublin uninvited. Liam Tobin, Collins' deputy, saw him, and Byrnes proposed that he could be even more useful if he could be appointed minister of propaganda. Collins' enquiries had revealed that Jameson was not employed by Keith Prowse and Co., and that reports sent to London through the Castle revealed details that only Jameson knew. Independent reports coming from both Broy and MacNamara convinced Collins that Jameson was a spy, and he discouraged any further meetings with him. Byrnes returned to Dublin on 28 February. All Republicans known to him were told to have nothing to do with him. Byrnes, however, managed to find a group of them, including Joe O'Reilly, Collins' personal assistant. O'Reilly agreed to arrange a meeting for him with Collins. On 2 March 1920 several Squad members arrived at Jameson's hotel to take him to Collins. They caught a tram to Glasnevin, in north Dublin. Walking down a quiet lane they confronted him with the truth and shot him twice—once in the heart and once in the head.

Detective Inspector Redmond, meanwhile, had become very proactive in his pursuit of Collins. On the night of 20 January he organized a raid on Cullenswood House, where Collins had a basement office. Richard Mulcahy and his wife were also living there. Irish intelligence chiefs Frank Thornton and Tom Cullen were only just in time to warn them. Collins ordered Redmond's execution. Redmond perhaps underestimated his enemy. He had established himself not in the safety of Dublin Castle but at the Standard Hotel in Harcourt Street, Dublin, not far from 76, Harcourt Street where Collins himself had an office. Redmond walked to work each day completely unescorted, in the belief, perhaps, that no one would suspect that a smart-suited businessman, his ensemble topped off by a bowler hat, could possibly be a high placed member of the British security service. His one concession to security was the wearing of a bulletproof vest. Knowing this, on the evening of 21 January, Squad member Joe Dolan put a bullet in his head. Soon after that Redmond's Belfast team returned home.

One month later, on 18 February, H.H. Quinlisk, from Wexford, was shot dead. He was more traitor than spy. He was an ex-soldier who had been captured by the Germans in France and joined Roger Casement's ill-fated Irish Brigade, which recruited prisoners of war. At the end of 1918 he turned up in Dublin. He was known to the Republicans, and being down on his luck he was given sums of money from the National Aid Scheme to tide him over until he found work. Quinlisk, or Quinn, the alias he was using, was eventually found a job with New Ireland Assurance, but he was always short of money. He asked again and again for funds, reminding the National Aid staff that he had done his bit for Ireland. In the end they got tired of him and appealed to Collins. Collins gave Quinlisk a one-off payment of £100 and told him to leave Dublin. Quinlisk did, and apparently lost the money at Galway Races. He returned to Dublin and was soon asking for more money. He was refused point blank, and in anger he went to the British authorities. In return for money he agreed to betray Michael Collins. Quinlisk was unfortunate in that it was Ned Broy who typed out his statement. Quinlisk asked to meet Collins and was directed to a hotel in Cork. At the time of the scheduled meeting the hotel was raided by the police. Quinlisk was then kidnapped by the Cork command of the IRA, who shot him dead on the outskirts of the city.

Private Smith, his first name now lost to history, a clerk at military intelligence under Colonel Hill Dillon, was shot in broad daylight on a crowded street in Dublin on 24 March 1920. Using the alias of Fergus Bryan Molloy, he let it be known that he could obtain arms. Blindfolded, he was taken to see Liam Tobin, where he admitted that he was a British agent but wanted to work for the Republicans. He agreed to obtain arms for the movement but wanted to speak to Collins personally. Tobin agreed and gave him an address and time. Smith reported back to the Castle, where unfortunately for him Lily Mernin typed up his report. The details were reported back to Collins, who ordered his execution.

Two days later, on 26 March, Alan Bell was killed, and with him the first British spy network closed down. Bell, a resident magistrate in Portadown in northern Ireland and a former RIC man, had been seconded to Dublin Castle to enquire into the Dail funds. He seized the books of several banks in an attempt to track down the Republican money and was responsible for a number of raids on Sinn Fein offices, resulting in the rough treatment of those arrested. In the process he confiscated over £71,000 from Sinn Fein headquarters. Not perhaps generally known was the fact that he directed the actions of Detective Inspector Forbes and was also member of a three man secret committee which had advocated the shooting of identified Volunteers. The killing of Thomas MacCurtain, the lord mayor of Cork, a short while later was the decision of this committee. For the Volunteers, it became a case of getting Bell before his committee assassins got them. On his way into work from Monkstown, on 26 March, Bell was pulled from a tram by a four-man team as the tram reached Ballsbridge; he was shot three times in the head. His death, reported in the newspapers, produced a storm of revulsion, but the readers might not have been so repulsed had they been aware of his full activities.

Most executions were the result of expediency, but the killing of Captain Lee-Wilson was pure revenge. Lee-Wilson had been present at the surrender of the Volunteers of the Easter Rising. He was particularly brutal in his treatment of the prisoners and especially the old Fenian Tom Clarke. After his surrender, Clarke was dragged to the steps of the Rotunda Hospital and there forced to strip naked in order to humiliate him. Suffering from an old wound, Clarke was slow to obey, resulting in Lee-Wilson tearing off his jacket and opening up the wound. Many of the prisoners who saw this vowed revenge. In June 1920 Lee-Wilson was tracked down to Gorey in County Wexford, where he was an RIC district inspector. On the morning of 15 June he was shot dead.

British Counterintelligence

In his 1985 book, *Secret Service*, Dr. Christopher Andrews, then a fellow and senior tutor at Corpus Christi College, Cambridge, used the description "The Irish Debacle" as his chapter heading on British intelligence in Ireland during the War for Independence. British intelligence was, he suggests, a shambles. More recent research, however, indicates that this statement is not strictly true. British intelligence, in Dublin at least, had one or two major coups.

At the outbreak of the war in 1919, the gathering of political intelligence in the capital was conducted by G Division of the Dublin Metropolitan Police. In the rest of the country it was undertaken by the Special Crimes Branch of the Royal Irish Constabulary. At the outbreak of the war Inspector Ivon Price, chief of the RIC Special Crimes Branch, was appointed head of a military Special Intelligence Branch, with the rank of major. Though he was answerable to his own commander in chief in Ireland, he was also obliged to report regularly to Vernon Kell, head of MI5, in London. A conflict of loyalties thus arose. Kell, for his part, also involved MI5 in independent initiatives in Ireland and failed to inform the other intelligence-gathering departments of his activities. There was also a small Admiralty Intelligence unit, answerable to the admiral commanding the naval base at Queenstown (Cobh), which was independent of naval intelligence based in London. With so many intelligence organizations involved there was a lot of overlapping — but little exchange of information. The commission of enquiry into the Easter Rising of 1916 rightly found that there was a failure of communication among the intelligence community.

Throughout 1917 and 1918, British intelligence looked for links between Sinn Fein and the Germans, in the process ignoring the development of the military wing of the Republican movement. Most of the leadership of Sinn Fein were arrested on the flimsiest of evidence. With the exception of de Valera, the arrested men and women believed in nonviolent resistance to British rule. Forewarned of his own intended arrest, de Valera nonetheless elected to be arrested, seeing himself in a propaganda role as a high profile political prisoner. The two men the British authorities would have gained most from by their arrests, Michael Collins and Cathal Brugha, both ardent advocates of physical force, were forewarned and escaped arrest. With the Sinn Fein leadership in prison, and not expecting opposition, the British government now prepared to introduce conscription in Ireland. They seriously underestimated opposition to such a move; people, politicians and the Roman Catholic Church all came together in opposition. There were massive demonstrations, and thousands of young men rushed to join the Irish Volunteers. Plans for imposing conscription were abandoned when the last German offensive of World War I was checked in the summer of 1918 and the enemy were forced back. In November the war ended.

The postwar general election of December 1918 saw a landslide victory in Ireland for Sinn Fein. They set up the Dail as an independent parliament of the Irish Republic. Brigadier-General Byrne, inspector general of the RIC, urged the British commander in chief in Ireland, Sir John French, to negotiate with Sinn Fein, with a view to splitting the politicians from the Irish Volunteers. French saw this as weakness on Byrne's part and sent him off on permanent leave. In January 1919 Major Ivon Price, the wartime cocoordinator of intelligence in Ireland, returned to Britain and was not replaced. Naval intelligence in Ireland was wound up, and military intelligence was severely cut back. Only the DMP's G Branch, and the RIC Special Crimes Branch remained, and these, in French's opinion, were woefully inadequate. By the end of 1919 five of the ten DMP political detectives were dead, and a number of RIC intelligence officers had also been assassinated. An unsuccessful attempt had also been made on Lord French. British intelligence in Ireland was almost nonexistent. French decided that any future secret service should be directed from London by Sir Basil Thomson, director of intelligence, MI5. The military agreed that in the future, along with the police intelligence service, all agents should be controlled by MI5, with the exception of any military agents already employed by the existing Intelligence Branch at GHQ, Dublin Castle. This exception meant that a parallel system remained. This led to duplication, an increase in expenditure, and rivalry between the two contending intelligence networks. A Belfast inspector of the RIC, W.C.F. Redmond, was appointed assistant commissioner of the DMP, with the mission of reorganizing the demoralized detective division. Detective David Neligan, Michael Collins' man in Dublin Castle, gave him details relating to Redmond. Collins sent his assistant, Frank Thornton, to Belfast to obtain a photograph of his new adversary. On 21 January 1920 Redmond was shot dead by members of the Squad. With the shooting of Redmond, G Department of the DMP ceased to have any further effect.

In April 1920 the British cabinet appointed Sir Hamar Greenwood as chief secretary in Ireland. He took over much of the work previously undertaken by Lord French, the lord lieutenant, turning French into little more than a figurehead. Under Greenwood, General Sir Nevil Macready, commissioner of the London Metropolitan Police, was appointed general officer commanding of the British Army in Ireland, and General Hugh Tudor became chief of police. Both were experienced soldiers. On 11 May 1920, upon Macready's recommendation, all Irish intelligence gathering was placed under a single director of intelligence, Colonel Ormonde de l'Epee Winter, who became known as "O." He was described by an intimate of Dublin Castle intrigue during the final years of British occupation, writing under the pen-name "Periscope":

> Passing under the archway that pierces a block of buildings the Upper Castle Yard is entered. Who is this so lightly tripping, so debonair, his breast a blaze of ribbons won with the gunners in France and other fields? It is Colonel Winter, the Chief of Intelligence. That his only training is war, that he lacks any first-hand knowledge of Secret Service methods, is irrelevant. He is a brave man, and one cannot cope with a secret society that holds life cheap without a stout heart. At first sight one would imagine him the typical colonel of light comedy — slight and small, dapper, delicate of speech, eyeglass set in eye. He is one whom men would follow even to the cannon's mouth; perhaps not the best man for his present job, but hard-working, earnest, and just.[3]

"Periscope" grossly underestimated Winter's ability. True, he was a strange choice of appointment. He was a Royal Artillery officer, lacking any experience in intelligence work prior to his appointment; but he did possess good organizational skills, and he was innovative. Winter was a slightly built, monocle-wearing forty-five-year-old First World War officer who went about his new task with a will. When he came to the job his primary source of intelligence were the RIC and DMP weekly reports. With the inability of G Division, the intelligence department of the DMP, to infiltrate the post–Rising Volunteer movement, information was scarce and largely out of date. In addition there was practically no up-to-date military intelligence either. Winter, who confined himself to security in Dublin, was faced with the prospect of starting an intelligence department virtually from scratch. His methods of obtaining information were outlined in his 1955 autobiography, *Winter's Tale*:

1. Agents obtained by local Police and through the agency of Local Centers.
2. Agents recruited in England and sent to Ireland.
3. Dublin Special Branch.
4. Persons friendly to the Police volunteering information.
5. Those persons who give information whilst under arrest or in prison, with a view to escaping the punishment of their crimes.
6. Captured documents.
7. Information from ordinary Police sources based on observation.
8. "Moutons" [infiltrators] placed either in prisons or in detention cells with rebel prisoners.
9. Listening sets.
10. Interrogation of prisoners.
11. Censorship of letter of prisoners in jail.
12. The establishment of Scotland House, London [the address to which anonymous letters were to be sent].

From the day of his arrival Winter was a marked man. Irish intelligence sources within Dublin Castle were quick to inform Collins about the new British intelligence cocoordinator. Collins ordered his execution. On his drive to Vice-Regal Lodge to present his credentials,

Winter's car was ambushed by two of the Squad, Joe McGuinness and George Nolan, in Thomas Street, Dublin. Winter escaped the ambush, but was wounded in the hand during the assault. He did not let the failed assassination bid put him off. He set to work with a will, putting his action-plan into effect.

Dealing with item 1 on his list, Winter established the Dublin District Special Intelligence Branch. It was made up of enthusiastic ex-officers. They were trained with the assistance of MI5 and given "suitable covers" to operate under in Dublin, such as shop assistants, garage hands and similar occupations. They had some successes, but with Dublin Castle heavily infiltrated by Collins' agents, many were tracked down and killed. The others left Ireland.

Winter then established a Central Raid Bureau, a combined intelligence unit designed to track down known Volunteers. By the time of the truce they had made 6,311 raids and searches in the Dublin area. In mid–October 1920 they tracked down two members of the "Soloheadbeg Gang" then living in Dublin, Sean Treacy and Daniel Breen. For a number of days the two men were followed, Breen actually confronting and facing down his pursuers. On 11 October Winter learned that the two would be spending the night at Drumcondra House, the home of Professor John Carolan. British agents and soldiers led by Major Gerald Smyth raided the house that night. "There was a crash of glass at the front of the house, and the hall door was burst open. From the stairs came the sound of rushing footsteps," Breen recalled in a colorful account[4]:

> We sprang out of bed. Simultaneously we gripped our revolvers. Fingers were groping on our door.... Crack! Crack! Two bullets came whizzing through the door. Crack! Crack! My German Mauser pistol was replying.... Bullets were flying from every direction, and our door had been pushed partly open. I blazed away on to the landing. Blood was streaming from my right thumb, but I felt no pain. I heard a thud on the landing as if somebody had fallen. [Sean Treacy's gun jammed.] I felt a sharp pain in the region of my spine.... I told him to make his escape, and that I would join him when I had fought my way through. I raked the landing with my Mauser and heard the sound of footsteps retreating down the stairs.... I dashed out of the room on to the landing, and saw a group of soldiers coming up the stairs, their electric torches pin-pointing me as a target. One bullet grazed my forehead, another passed through the fleshy portion of my thigh; two hit me in the calves of my legs and one lodged in my right lung. But I still kept my stand and fired at the raiders until the gun was empty.... I reloaded.... As I blazed into the group of soldiers there was a hurried rush for safety. They were now in retreat and I was pursuing them down the stairs. When I got to the first floor they were charging headlong into the street. I gave them a parting shot.... I rushed back to my room. At the door I tripped over two dead bodies [Major Smyth and Captain A.P. White].... Sean had made his escape.... I stepped out on to the window-sill and dropped to the roof of the conservatory.

Breen escaped. Treacy meanwhile had successfully got away. Breen was eventually rescued and taken to the Mater Hospital, where he recovered from his wounds. Professor Carolan was also brought to the hospital, where he died of his wounds, but not before making a death-bed statement that he had been shot in cold blood by one of the raiding party. The funerals of Smyth and White took place the following day. Intelligence reports indicated that Sir Hamar Greenwood, the chief secretary of Ireland, General Tudor and other senior British officers attended. Squad members were placed along the funeral procession with the intention of shooting as many prominent officers as possible, but in the end the funeral was a low key affair with no senior officers attending.

On the afternoon of 14 October, British intelligence officers tracked Sean Treacy to the "Republican Outfitters" in Talbot Street, just off O'Connell Street, Dublin. Treacy was standing by the door of the shop when two trucks filled with troops and an armored car pulled up outside. Tracy nonchalantly walked towards a bicycle to make his escape. Another Volunteer, also standing by the door, moved smartly off, only to be stopped by the soldiers who had leaped from one of the trucks. An Auxiliary Intelligence officer by the name of Francis Christian, dressed in civilian clothes, shouted, "That's not he. Here is the man we want," and pointed towards Treacy. As intelligence officer Lieutenant Price, also dressed in civilian clothes, moved towards him, Treacy pulled his gun, and shot him dead. The other intelligence man, Christian, was then fatally wounded by Treacy. A third British intelligence officer shot Treacy dead from a range of no more than five yards. As he did so, some of the troops panicked and opened up with rifles and a machine gun, killing two civilians and seriously wounded a constable of the Dublin Metropolitan Police.

Item 2 on Winter's list was to bring in British ex-officers as agents. He established a secret recruiting office in London under Major C.A. Cameron, formerly head of the British spy network in wartime Holland and Belgium. Sixty agents were sent to Ireland, though a number proved to be unsatisfactory. Those remaining were unofficially known as the "Cairo Gang," and based themselves in houses and hotels throughout the city, living quite openly, some with their wives. These men, acting upon intelligence received, used the police and army in a series of raids and ambushes against known Republicans and suspected Volunteers. On 23 September members of the Gang shot dead John Lynch in his bed in the Exchange Hotel in Dublin. Lynch, a Sinn Fein Loan organizer, may have been mistaken for Liam Lynch, the Cork IRA leader. The Castle authorities claimed that he was shot when he resisted arrest and fired at the police. It was a well-known fact in Sinn Fein circles that Lynch never carried a gun. The following month all three of the leadership of IRA intelligence, Thornton, Tobin and Cullen, were picked up on different occasions by the Gang. Tobin and Cullen were released after some intense interrogation, but Thornton was held for ten days before he too was released. Things were beginning to look up for the British intelligence service in Dublin. In his private papers now housed in the Imperial War Museum in London, Cairo Gang member Captain R.D. Jeune wrote: "In November, information was coming in well and we were beginning to get on top of the IRA, who were becoming desperate. I happened to receive information from three different sources to the effect that something was going to happen, but there was nothing definite."[5]

The arrival of these Englishmen had not gone unobserved. Their very accents, in many cases, gave them away. British intelligence officer Captain J.L. Hardy recorded in his autobiographical novel, *Never in Vain*, that for all the hope the various agents initially sent over had of remaining undetected at their Dublin addresses they "might as well have worn uniforms." At night they ventured out after curfew, a fact that did not go unnoticed by their housekeepers and hotel clerks. They had been issued with passes to allow them to do so. Jim MacNamara in the DMP was able to furnish Collins with the names of people issued with passes. Lily Mernin in her witness statement reveals that "before the 21st November 1920, it was part of my normal duties to type the names and addresses of British agents who were accommodated at private addresses and living as ordinary citizens in the city. These lists were typed weekly and amended whenever an address was changed. I passed them on each week."

By a process of elimination it was possible to narrow down the members of the Cairo Gang. From this and other information, drawn from a variety of sources, including another well-placed source in the DMP, Sergeant Mannix, who was stationed in Donnybrook, Collins and his intelligence colleagues compiled a list of their names and addresses. In some cases mail was intercepted, such as the letter from Captain F. Harper Shrove to Captain King on 2 March. Proof was presented, a list was drawn up, and a date set for their assassinations. It was Sunday, 21 November 1920, with executions synchronized for 9:00 A.M. This particular day was chosen because Dublin would be packed with supporters for the Gaelic football match between County Dublin and County Tipperary at Croke Park, and it would be easier to move about unnoticed in the crowd. The killings were to be a joint operation of the Squad and members of the Dublin Brigade, under the command of Dick McKee, divided up into eleven assassination teams. An intelligence officer was assigned to each group to search the bodies and rooms for documents.

On the Saturday evening before the operation, Dick McKee, along with senior IRA man Peader Clancy and Gaelic student Conor Clune, the nephew of Archbishop Joseph Clune of Perth, Australia, were picked up in a raid by Auxiliaries; Clune, who had no IRA connections, was arrested at Vaughan's Hotel, and McKee and Clancy at an IRA safe house in Gloucester Street by British forces and taken to Dublin Castle for interrogation. Their arrests unknown, the operation went ahead the next day as scheduled. At 9 o'clock on Sunday morning members of the Squad entered 28, Pembroke Street. The first British agents to die were Major Dowling and Captain Leonard Price. Moving from their rooms in the same house, the Squad located and killed Captain Kennlyside, Colonel Woodcock and Lt. Colonel Montgomery. The shooting of Kennlyside was particularly brutal. As Squad member Mick O'Hanlon prepared to shoot him, Kennlyside's wife tried to prevent his killing. Mick Flanagan, the leader of the group, pushed her to one side and shot the British agent in her presence. At 119, Morehampton Road, Donnybrook, members of the Squad surprised Lieutenant Donald Lewis MacClean, his brother-in-law John Caldow, and an informer, T.H. Smith. MacClean's wife was also present. McClean asked that they not be shot in front of his wife. The three were taken to the roof where they were shot by Vinnie Byrne and Sean Doyle. Caldow survived and later returned to his home in Scotland.

At 9 o'clock members of the Squad broke down the door at 92, Lower Baggot Street, the home of Captain Newbury and his wife. Hearing the noise from upstairs and suspecting what was about to happen, Newbury pushed what furniture he could into a makeshift barricade at the bedroom door. The Squad succeeded in pushing the door open, and, discovering Newbury trying to escape out of the window, Bill Stapleton and Joe Leonard opened fire and killed him. Captain George Bennett and Lieutenant Peter Ashmun Ames (an American) were killed after a short gun battle at their lodgings at 38, Upper Mount Street, off Merrion Square. Sergeant John Fitzgerald also known as Captain Fitzgerald and Captain Fitzpatrick, of the Royal Irish Constabulary, a Tipperary man, was shot twice in the head at his residence at 28, Earlsfoot Terrace. Papers picked up at his home gave details of the movements of senior IRA men.

Another unit of the Squad, eleven strong, led by Tom Keogh, entered 22, Lower Mount Street, the home of two British agents recalled from Russia. They were Lieutenant Angliss (an Irishman), also known as McMahon, and Lieutenant Peel. McMahon had been identified by one of Collins' agents in the Castle as being responsible for the killing of fund-raiser

Members of the Cairo Gang. In a synchronized action they were wiped out at 9:00 A.M. on 21 November 1920, by the "Apostles" and a unit of the Dublin Volunteers.

John Lynch. McMahon was shot dead as he reached for his revolver. Peel, hearing the disturbance, ran to his room and barricaded the door. Unable to break it down, Squad members fired more than a dozen bullets into the room. The alarm now raised, armed Auxiliaries approached the house in numbers, and the team withdrew. At 119, Baggot Street, Captain G.T. Baggalley, a member of the military court that sentenced volunteers to death, was killed by a three man team including Sean Lemass, later to become Irish Taoiseach. (Prime Minister) Captains McCormack[6] and Wilde were staying in the Gresham Hotel, Sackville Street (Upper O'Connell Street). Their assassins pretended to be British soldiers in order to gain access. As the British agents opened the door they were shot and killed. Squad members entered a guesthouse in Fitzwilliam Square looking for a Major Callaghan. Instead they found a Captain Crawford. They could have shot him instead, but they did not. He was not on their list to be killed. They gave him twenty-four hours to leave Ireland — which he did.

Two members of the Black and Tans were killed, Cadets Garniss and Morris. Colonel Jennings and Major Callaghan, residing at the Eastwood Hotel, were more lucky; they escaped death. They had spent the night at a local brothel. Two other members of the Cairo Gang, Majors Hardy and King, also escaped death, having left their accommodation in Harcourt Street before their assassins arrived. Squad leader Joe Dolan allegedly gave King's half-naked mistress a "right scourging with a sword scabbard" for her foul-mouthed utterings.

The final tally was twelve men killed, eight of whom were members of the Cairo Gang.

There were also a notorious army courts-martial officer, two policemen and an informant among the victims. The remaining members of the Cairo Gang, as well as other agents and spies, fled to the safety of Dublin Castle and were later withdrawn to England. British intelligence in Ireland was paralyzed. Of the Squad members, Frank Teeling was captured, but Collins engineered his escape soon afterwards. McKee, Clancy and Clune were later tortured and murdered by the auxiliaries in revenge. They were reportedly "shot while trying to escape." Neligan, Collins' agent in the Castle, reported that they had been tortured before death by British intelligence Officer Captain J.L. Hardy, a man with a notorious reputation for brutality towards prisoners. When their bodies were being loaded onto a truck, the officer in charge battered their faces with a torch.

Cairo Gang member Captain Jeune escaped the butchery. He had been on an operation the previous night. Telephoning the Castle to see if he was to be relieved he was informed by Adjutant Hyems, "I am sorry to say that there have been some raids by the Shinners and I am afraid that they have got some of our fellows." So it was agreed that Jeune should return to his lodgings at 28, Upper Pembroke Street, which he shared with Captain Murray: In the flat next to Murray's and mine, I saw the body of my friend "Chummy" Dowling, a grand ex-guardee, wounded three times in the war, lying full length on the floor. As he was to have relieved me he was in uniform and had obviously been shot through the heart, probably by a small Sinn Feiner because there was a bullet hole in one corner of the ceiling. In the doorway of the bathroom was Price's body. Murray had already been taken to hospital. Colonel Woodcock, commanding the 1st East Lancs, had been shot three times, but survived. Likewise Captain Keenlyside, Adjutant of the same battalion. Colonel Montgomery had been shot on the stairs, as he came up after breakfast. He died some time later.[7]

According to the official British history of the war, *Records of the Rebellion in Ireland 1920–21*, volume 2: Intelligence, "The murders of 21st November 1920 temporarily paralyzed the special branch. Several of its most efficient members were murdered and the majority of the other residents in the city were brought into the Castle and Central Hotel for safety. This centralization in the most inconvenient places possible greatly decreased the opportunities for obtaining information and for re-establishing anything in the nature of a secret service."

That afternoon a combined force of police, army and Black and Tans, led by Auxiliaries, exacted their revenge on citizens when they opened fire upon the crowds at the Gaelic football match at Croke Park. Twelve innocent people were killed, including one of the players on the field. Dozens of others were wounded. The Auxiliaries later claimed that they had been fired upon first. Brigadier General Crozier, to his credit, condemned the actions of the British forces, being informed by one of his junior officers that "the Black and Tans fired into the crowd without any provocation whatever."[8]

On 27 December 1920 British Army Military Intelligence suffered a setback when it was brought under the control of the police. This happened at a time when army intelligence was very active. Some 500 prisoners were in their hands. The transfer led to delays in communications and authorization of actions, leading to frustration and greatly hampering the army's activities. The result of the change led to the dispersal of military intelligence personnel and the complications that led from that, including the inability to identify and process prisoners quickly, leading to congestion in the city's prisons and holding cages.

Meanwhile, Winter instigated a Raid Bureau, with the mission to read and analyze all paperwork gathered up in raids by the police and military. Between August 1920 and July 1921, a total of 6,311 raids and searches were carried out in the Dublin area. Among of the more successful raids was the discovery of both Michael Collins' and Richard Mulcahy's papers. In the raid on Cullenswood House, one of the safe houses used by Michael Collins in February 1920, British Intelligence found complete rolls and addresses of 3,000 members of the Dublin (IRA) Brigade. By March the majority of the local Sinn Fein and IRA leaders had been arrested and confined in Mountjoy Prison. Also found in other raids were financial records, photographs, details of arms imports, the military newspaper, and other such matters generated by the Irish underground. These led to arrests and in some cases murders of members of the Republican movement. Some prisoners, however, were turned and began working for British intelligence. Winter alludes that he turned at least three leading IRA members, as well as a number of lower ranking Volunteers. In the raids and in the stop and search actions by British patrols, a number of the leaders of the Republican movement were picked up, including Collins himself, but they were released unrecognized. They simply did not look like "terrorists." They blended easily into their surroundings. On a trip up to Dublin to report on activities in Cork, Tom Barry remarked of the GHQ staff, "The way of life of those GHQ officers was in great contrast to that of the West Cork IRA. Dressed like business men, carrying brief or attaché cases, with their pockets full of false papers to support their disguise, they traveled freely to their 'business' offices and to keep their various appointments. To a great extent those GHQ men kept regular business hours at those offices, but after closing hours often worked late into the night at some other venue."[9]

There is a suggestion that Collins was recognized by British secret service operatives when he was picked up in 1921, but he was released. Pax O'Faolain, from Waterford, attending a meeting at GHQ in Dublin in February of 1921, was taken by Collins to a pub in Parnell Street (either Kirwan's or Maurice Collins') which backed onto Coles Lane. There they met two warders from Mountjoy Prison who had a message from Arthur Griffith, then in jail. It may have been that they were in sympathy with the Republican movement, but more probably this was an unofficial approach by the wiley assistant under secretary, Andy Cope, of Dublin Castle, in an attempt to gauge the temperature among the Sinn Fein leadership in the run-up to the truce. As a prelude to the truce, de Valera was himself arrested, then released. Seeming confirmation that there was some sort of amnesty from attack or arrest of certain members of the Republican movement and the British authorities is evidenced in the writings of Captain R.D. Jeune, a British intelligence officer working in Dublin and one of the few members of the Cairo Gang not shot on 21 November. Previously, in September 1920, he had been involved in a raid on a number of houses in Drumcondra:

> Particular attention was attached to the house of a man called O'Connor, known to us as an active Sinn Feiner. At the arranged signal I charged the door, but it did not give, so I charged again, and this time it flew open.... There was no hostile reception, however, and the search went on. While this was happening I was standing talking to Boddington, who was in charge of the raid, then a letter was brought to him, which he read and handed to me, saying: "Money for jam." It was on Dublin Castle paper and was in these words:

> "Dear Mr. O'Connor.
>   I am having the papers you require sent to you.
>   Yours Sincerely,
>   A.W. Cope."

This was distinctly interesting. Here was the Assistant Under Secretary writing to a notorious Sinn Feiner, with whom he had obviously already been in contact.

After this I made a point of trying to find out more about this individual's doings, and found that he had done some rather strange things, such as arranging for some electricians of known Sinn Fein views to come into the Castle at unusual times. Also he was one of the very few Castle officials who could safely walk about the streets of Dublin. But it was decided that no drastic action could be taken against him, as it turned out that he was a protégé of Lloyd George, who had picked him out of the Fisheries and sent him over to Ireland under Sir John Anderson in order to get a foot in the Sinn Fein camp, or, in modern parlance, to set in motion an "initiative." Later he was given a good job in the Liberal Party.[10]

British Assassination Squads

In the months leading up to the truce, an assassination squad was assembled by the British authorities in Dublin Castle. It was given a free hand to track down and kill senior members of the IRA. The Igoe Gang, as it was known, was formed by Ormonde Winter and headed by Head Constable Eugene Igoe from County Mayo. He personally selected R.I.C members drawn from different parts of Ireland for the job. They patrolled the streets of Dublin in plain clothes, anything up to eighteen in number, some walking on one side of the street, some on the other, carefully spaced out so they would not look like a group. In this way they looked for IRA targets. They differed from other British intelligence units in that they were a completely self-contained unit, not using or sharing any facilities offered by the Castle and thus eliminating any chance of IRA agents gaining intelligence. They were responsible for several deaths. Collins eventually heard about them and sent the Squad after them. The Igoe Gang were well trained policemen and never underestimated their enemy. They understood the power of terrorism as practiced by the Squad. On one occasion the Igoe Gang stopped and questioned two recognized IRA men in the street, Charlie Dalton and Thomas "Sweeney" Newall. Dalton was released, but Newall was taken into custody. In Greek Street, Newall was told to run into the road, but realizing that it was Igoe's intention to kill him — "shot while trying to escape" — Newall refused. Igoe punched him, and he fell into the road, after which Igoe fired four times, wounding him in the leg, hip and stomach. Newall was taken to the local police station, where he was beaten about the head and face, but he revealed nothing. He was then allowed to be taken to the King George V Hospital for treatment.

Now actively searching for the Igoe Gang, Ned Kelliher, an intelligence officer for the Squad, noticed that four RIC men regularly traveled up to Dublin Castle in an open Ford touring car. Then a little later they would walk down to a restaurant on Ormond Quay for a meal. Irish Intelligence became convinced that they were members of the Igoe Gang. Members of the Squad finally confronted three of the four men in Parliament Street, on the edge of Temple Bar, and shot them, killing two outright and mortally wounding the third. It transpired that they were not members of the Igoe Gang, but their shooting drove the gang back into the Castle, effectively neutralizing them. Igoe and his men left Ireland at the end of the war. Igoe was awarded a lump sum of £1,500 and a pension by the British government.

Working alongside Igoe was Captain J.L. Hardy. He was a liaison officer between

Dublin Castle and Special Branch, Scotland Yard. Hardy was responsible for tracking down Sean Treacy. He had a particularly ruthless reputation as a torturer and a murderer of Republican prisoners. Collins spoke of him as a "notorious murderer." Tony Woods, an IRA staff captain, who was arrested when the Tans raided company headquarters in Denzille Street (now Fenian Street), Dublin, records that he and five others were taken to Dublin Castle for interrogation:

> We were taken ... to Dublin Castle and herded into a small room in the Lower Yard. We were each separately interviewed by a man in RIC uniform, a fine looking man about six foot two inches tall, who, I afterwards discovered, was the famous Sergeant Igoe. Major Hardy came in, took one look at us and went out again. He, evidently, was not going to bother with us unless Igoe decided that we were important. Hardy was a slight man and walked with a limp, but he could be deadly. He had interrogated Ernie O'Malley only a few weeks before [December 1920]. He was a brave but desperate person who never spared himself or others. He was responsible for the shootings, tortures and beatings which took place in the Castle, but he reserved himself only for the most important fish which was a relief to us. Prior to Bloody Sunday, he had lived outside the Castle in a hotel in Harcourt Street, and he used to cycle in daily. Liam Tobin and Kelleher had waited for him one day near Wicklow Street, determined to get him, but through some mischance he got by, and the opportunity never presented itself again. He was a most interesting character, a born murderer; he had been a prisoner in Germany in the Great War but escaped. Shortly after he wrote a book called *I Escape;* when he left Ireland in 1922, he wrote another *Never in Vain,* which covered the situation as he saw it, here. Then he wrote another, I cannot now recall the name [*Recoil*], which dealt with the shooting of Sean Treacy in Talbot Street on the 14th October 1920. He was the one who was responsible for tracking Treacy down, and he wrote the book I would say, because he wanted to get him out of his system. It was in the form of a novel....[11]

On 5 February 1921 British intelligence officer Lance Corporal John Ryan was assassinated by a three-man ASU in a pub in Corporation Street, Dublin. Four days later two Republican activists, James Murphy and Patrick Kennedy, were arrested by Auxiliaries in Dublin. Two hours later the Dublin Metropolitan Police found the two men lying shot in Drumcondra. Kennedy was dead, and Murphy was dying. James Murphy died in Mater Hospital, Dublin, two days later. His death-bed statement that the auxiliaries had killed them led to the arrest by the British authorities of Captain W.L. King, commanding officer of F Company, Auxiliaries.

Vincent Fouvargue, a Dubliner and intelligence officer of the 3 Battalion of the Dublin Brigade, was captured by the British, and under torture turned informer, betraying the names of the men in his unit. He was put into Kilmainham Jail as a "stool pigeon" to get information from other IRA prisoners. This he succeeded in doing. When his identity became known he was given a new identity, that of Somers, and was found a home in England. His new details were passed on to Dublin Castle, where they were seen by one of Collins' agents. Fouvargue was followed to England and shot dead on a golf course just outside of London on 3 April 1921. A note was left with him, sending a message back to the Castle that they knew he was the man who betrayed his comrades. It read, "Let spies and traitors beware, IRA."

A member of the old Cairo Gang who had escaped the November assassinations, a man called Jeffries, was recalled to London and instructed to establish a new secret service section of British intelligence, to operate in Ireland. The section was established in London, where the operatives were trained, in the spring of 1921. Little more is known of this section, but by the late spring of 1921 it was achieving results. In May 1921 they discovered the premises used by the Home Affairs Department, in Moleswoth Street, as well as the new offices of Michael Collins in Mary Street. Though there were no staff there at the time of the raid, valuable papers were discovered. Ned Broy was arrested on suspicion, following the discovery of papers typed by him at the home of Eileen McGrane, a lecturer at the National University and a prominent Sinn Fein activist. Collins sent a warning to Broy's superior to destroy any evidence implicating Broy or risk being shot. The papers were lost.

On 20 June 1921 Eamon de Valera was arrested in Dublin by a patrol of the 2nd Battalion, Worcestershire Regiment, under a false name. Incriminating documents led to his removal to Portobello Barracks. Here he disclosed his real name: "Mr. de Valera, President of the Irish Republic." He was treated as an officer prisoner and given an officer's quarters. The following day he was released. Peace feelers were in progress that would lead to the truce.

Intelligence Gathering in the Country

The intelligence war fought out in Dublin, which was by no means one-sided, was eventually won by the Republicans. But for the truce, though, it could have gone either way. The British were making great strides in reestablishing their intelligence service. In the countryside, intelligence was equally important. The Republicans had an overwhelming advantage in that, by and large, they had the support of the people, who supplied them with up-to-date information. RIC intelligence on the other hand was quite often outdated, and largely uncollated in modern terms. Where the police were politically active against the Volunteers, Republican intelligence quickly acted to counter it. Regarding this, guidelines were drawn up by IRA GHQ in Dublin:

> "Aggressive" Intelligence Officers
> Do they accompany the Military in raids?
> Were they concerned in the arrest of Volunteers?
> Were they concerned in giving evidence against Volunteers?
> Were they concerned in the death of any Volunteers?
> Were they concerned in having to go "on the run?"
> Do they spy on Volunteers or Volunteers' Houses?
> Do they take part in reprisals?
> You will also give their full names and addresses with a footnote
> Showing what you think they are worth.

An early example of one who met this criteria of being an "aggressive" intelligence officers was a police officer in Thurles, County Tipperary. RIC intelligence here oversaw the arrests and imprisonment of a number of Volunteers who had been identified when drilling. Their chief intelligence officer was Detective D.I. Hunt. Orders for his assassination were agreed upon by GHQ, Dublin. Two Volunteers, Jim Stapleton and James Murphy, were given the task. On 23 June 1919, Hunt and another policeman were seen out on the street. Stapleton and Murphy approached them, and at close quarters Murphy shot Hunt dead. The other RIC men at Thurles desisted in their pursuit of the Volunteers. In another, similar, incident, RIC Detective Kelleher, a man noted for his rough treatment of IRA prisoners, was shot dead by an ASU at a pub in Granard, County Longford, on 31 October 1920.

By 1920, Republican intelligence officers were appointed at brigade, battalion and even company level. Their duties included the security of their own forces, and the gathering of information relating to the strength and movement of the British Army, RIC, Black and Tan and Auxiliaries. Following an ambush, while the Volunteers gathered up rifles and ammunition, the intelligence officer gathered up papers and documents.

Sean Gaynor, who took command of the First Tipperary Brigade in Nenagh, appointed Austin McCurtain as Intelligence Officer. In Gaynor's account, submitted to the Bureau of Military History Statements and now housed in the National Archives in Dublin, he recalled the following:

> We regarded it as imperative that we should have a day-to-day account of all movements of the Crown forces — the police out on patrol within the town or village, where the police and military went for drinks or any form of recreation, how they obtained supplies, how often outlying posts were served by convoys from supply depots, and if any particular member of the British garrison was making himself prominent because of truculent or aggressive behavior. In addition, it was thought to be most important to have lists compiled of any civilian population who might be considered hostile, especially by giving information to the police or military authorities.
>
> McCurtain carried out the organization of intelligence himself, and started by appointing an intelligence officer in each battalion and in each company area. He required each company intelligence officer to furnish a weekly report and submit a report to the brigade intelligence officer.... All intelligence officers were asked to make special efforts to try and make contact with members of the British forces who might be inclined to be friendly, with a view to getting whatever information they were prepared to impart. McCurtain was in direct contact with the Director of Intelligence, Michael Collins.... Generally speaking, very little information was obtained through members of the Crown forces. In Toomevara an RIC man named O'Brien, and another in Cloughjordan called Feeny, did give news of impending raids in their own localities.... In order to facilitate the work of the intelligence staff, systematic raids were made on the mails. Between October 1920 and the Truce scarcely a week passed without such a raid taking place in some part of the brigade area. The battalion Intelligence Officer in Roscrea made seizures at the local railway station very frequently. The mail car between Nenagh and Thurles was so often held up that it was said that the horse would stop on seeing an armed IRA man on the road!

The British initiated a spy ring in Cork, which identified prominent Republicans for assassination. Information, notably from professional and business people, was passed on to a cocoordinator who passed it on to British intelligence. In September 1920 Irish intelligence laid a trap and caught a postal clerk in the Central Post Office in Cork. He was arrested and interrogated. He confessed everything, and gave his interrogators twelve names, some of them very prominent people. One by one they were shot dead, with the exception of one of their number who fled to London.

Following one successful ambush in May 1921, the IO of the East Limerick Brigade Flying Column, Seamus Malone, discovered a number of copies of the *Weekly Intelligence Summary* issued by the GOC British Sixth Division at Cork, Major General Sir Peter Strickland, regarding the week ending 17 May 1921. The *Summary* gave a complete list of the British military and police stations in Munster, summarized the operations of the week and detailed IRA movements, activities and plans as were known, or believed to be known, to British intelligence. Details of relevant extracts were circulated to the IRA battalions affected by the British proposals. The bulletins were then sent to the director of intelligence, Michael Collins, at GHQ in Dublin to enable a general overview of the situation. The *Summary* and the other documents captured enabled Republican Intelligence to gauge just how accurate British intelligence was. It also gave warning of British intentions for the weeks to come. What was slightly disturbing was the recovery in British intelligence gathering following the IRA's successful campaign against the RIC. Also of concern were the evolving tactics of the British against the flying columns, which were bearing fruit. With this information the IRA was able to adapt to the evolving situation.

Enjoying the support of most of the people as they did, the IRA, who were drawn from their own communities, could rely on the people to supply them with information. The people warned the Volunteers of the presence of British troops in the neighborhood and provided arms dumps on their property. Support was also given by sympathetic transport workers, especially on the railways. Support too came from the post office workers and those working in government institutions. Siobhan Creedon, who worked in Mallow Post Office, County Cork, regularly supplied Liam Lynch with transcripts of dispatches and documents. She obtained valuable information regarding implementation of the proposed conscription of 1918. By 1920 many post offices had sympathetic employees willing to pass on to the Volunteers information transmitted by the RIC through the telegraph and telephone systems. At Clonmel, County Tipperary, the IRA intelligence officer Jack Sharkey recruited Mr. P.J. O'Connell, personal clerk to the postmaster in Clonmel. Through him Sharkey received a copy of every telegram which passed through the post office on its way to the RIC. These telegrams were in code, but Sharkey obtained the key to the code, so he was able to decode them and pass on the information. The codes were changed every month, but Sharkey also received the key to the code prior to its change. In one instance he received a copy of a telegram which when decoded informed him that the IRA were in possession of the present code. In the same telegram he (or the intended recipient) was advised to use the new code — which was included in the telegram. The IRA also engaged in mail van raids. On 9 March 1920 men from the Limerick City Brigade hijacked a mail van as it was driving up Davis Street in the city, on its way to the railway station. The mail was opened and checked for any intelligence, then resealed and marked "censored." As a result, that same month the West Limerick IRA killed a man for spying for the British. It was the first, but not the last, such killing in the county.

Black and Tans pose for a photographer in County Limerick. The photograph later fell into the hands of an IRA intelligence officer who identified notorious members of this group for assassination.

Perhaps the biggest intelligence coup of the First Cork

Brigade was obtaining the services of Josephine Marchmont, a typist working at the headquarters of the British Army 6 Division. She had impeccable credentials: daughter of an RIC man and widow of a British Army officer killed in 1917. She had lost the custody of her son, Reggie, to her in-laws, who had kept the child in Wales. The man who was to become her handler, Florrie O'Donghue, offered to bring the child to her if she would agree to work for him in supplying intelligence. In October 1919, with the support of Michael Collins, O'Donaghue crossed over to Wales, where he succeeded in abducting the boy from his school in Barry and reuniting him with his mother. In exchange Josephine Marchmont supplied high grade intelligence to the IRA right up to the truce. She later married O'Donaghue.

On 3 April a section from C Company, Second Battalion of the Mid-Limerick Brigade under Captain David Dundon, raided the Inland Revenue office in O'Connell Street, the city's busiest street. The staff were held up as the Volunteers ransacked the offices and filing cabinets and took away any relevant papers in sacks to awaiting getaway cars outside. That night men from D Company under the command of Battalion Commandant Joe O'Brien set fire to the customs house in Rutland Street in an attempt to destroy their records.

In late October 1920, General Prescott Dieces, a senior British Army Military Intelligence officer, was seconded to Limerick to consolidate intelligence gathering. Irish intelligence were soon made aware of his arrival. Information from Intelligence headquarters in Dublin indicated that he was a formidable foe. The order was given for his assassination. Arrangements were made to keep him under observation. It was soon revealed that his movements were irregular, specifically designed to avoid ambush. Whenever he traveled, it was in a well-protected staff car, escorted by an armored car and Crossley tenders full of armed soldiers. When he visited clubs or other institutes he was protected by plainclothes detectives, some of whom stood guard outside the premises. Nevertheless, his movements were tracked in the hope of finding a weakness. On one occasion using minimum security he visited a house in O'Connell Street, Limerick, where he stayed overnight. An ASU was activated but arrived at the house just minutes after he had left. Meanwhile Dieces was collecting and collating information. He made observations on the RIC and how the service could be made more effective, on the ways that the army operated, and notes on the capability of the IRA and of known Republican sympathizers. Within his headquarters though, a Republican infiltrator gained access to his papers. Included were details of the formation of an assassination squad to kill known Volunteers and Republican sympathizers. This was the mission that had brought him to Limerick. His assassination became imperative.

An ASU was deployed full-time in the vicinity of Dieces' headquarters at the New Barracks. After a week, on 26 November 1920, an opportunity, albeit a dangerous one, arose. An armored car, followed by two staff cars and a Crossley tender filled with armed troops, swept out of the barracks and turned into O'Connell Avenue. As instructed, the men of the ASU, under the command of Lieutenant Tim Murphy, of E Company, deployed the length of the street and opened fire with revolvers on the first staff car, the one in which Dieces usually traveled. The soldiers in the tender returned fire as the convoy continued to speed away from the ambush. Soldiers in the barracks flooded out onto the streets in an attempt to capture or kill the Republicans, who meanwhile had withdrawn through the myriad of side streets and alleyways of the city. Two staff officers in the first car were wounded, but General Dieces, traveling in the second car, escaped uninjured. Dieces returned to Dublin soon afterward. His plans to assassinate leading Republicans were put on hold.

British Counterintelligence in the Countryside

In late 1923 or early 1924, Major A.E. Percival, formerly of the Essex Regiment serving in County Cork during the war, gave two lectures concerning his time in Ireland. In these he gave the British perspective of intelligence gathering:

1. Methods of Obtaining Information.
    Owing to the secret nature of the hostile forces and the strict oath taken by them, bribes were of little use, and, although a limited amount of money was available for this purpose, I only on one occasion found any opportunity of using it. The most profitable methods were as follows:
    (i) Most important of all, an IO must move about the country and hunt for information. It will not come to him if he sits in his office all day.
    (ii) He must keep in close touch with the Loyalists — especially those who are not afraid to tell him what they know.
    This is not always an easy thing to do, as if the IRA suspected a Loyalist of giving information or being too friendly with the Crown Forces, it meant certain death to him. It was our usual practice therefore to approach their houses after dark, and very long night journeys often had to be made in order to do this.
    Captured documents were often of great value. Notebooks often contained the rolls of the local Company, list of arms and ammunition in possession, etc. The well known lord Mayor of Cork, Terence MacSwiney, was captured as the result of a letter ordering a litigant to appear at a Sinn Fein Court which fell into our hands.
    Information obtained direct from members of the IRA. This was very rare, but I had in my area an officer of one of the local Companies whom I had convicted of some small offence and sentenced to six months imprisonment. As he was the owner of a farm, he found it very inconvenient to go to prison, and so suggested that, if I would get his sentence postponed, he would give me weekly reports of the state of his Company. This I agreed to, but threatened to enforce the sentence if the reports did not come in regularly. He proved very Useful.
    Anonymous letters. These were very numerous and had to be treated with a good deal of suspicion. It was often the case of one family trying to get a bit of its own back on a neighboring family.

2. Functions of the Battalion Intelligence Officers.
    The main duties of the Battalion IO in warfare of this nature are, I think the following:
    (i) To obtain Intelligence of the nature I have indicated above.
    (ii) To submit to his CO plans for suggested operations based on the nature of intelligence in his possession.
    (iii) Identify prisoners when captured. This was one of the most difficult things in the whole campaign. The hostile leaders were seldom known by sight and they invariably gave false names.
    A number of them thus slipped through our hands after being actually captured.

As the war progressed and ambushes escalated, the British began making use of airplanes for locating flying columns on the move. They were also used for transporting communications, rather than using telephones which might be tapped. A Royal Air Force plane made a forced landing some fourteen miles from Limerick, in May 1921. The local IRA brigade column was notified and quickly rushed to the scene. There they discovered the RAF pilot and his observer attempting to burn the papers in their possession. They were stopped, and the papers were taken away for analysis. The plane was set on fire by the Volunteers, and the crew were obliged to set off on foot. The documents seized proved to be a gold mine, with details of troop movements and action requested to be taken by the administration in Dublin Castle. Included in the papers was an order to capture or kill IRA brigade commander Michael Brennan, whom intelligence indicated was at Roxborough near Limerick. Brennan was duly warned and moved his column away. In all, the East Limerick Column destroyed two forced-landing airplanes, gathering detailed enemy intelligence from both of them.

The British also used their officers as intelligence agents in the field. They would be sent out in small teams to gather information. Their mission was usually to discover where Volunteers were lodging or to discover the underground catches and arms dumps of the IRA. The officers were dropped from trucks, their clothes designed to blend in with the local community. Ernie O'Malley, commandant of the Second Southern Division, described them as brave men but their missions ill-advised, for they betrayed themselves by their very accents. In his book, *On Another Man's Wound,* he recalled the capture of such a team:

> I was working in [dug-out] 47 when a scout came to see me. Three men had been captured on the hillside; they were British officers [in civilian dress], and the Rosegreen men had them in a dug-out lower down. I met the boys who had captured them. One had a rifle and two rounds of ammunition, the other had an empty bandolier, when they saw the three men coming across the fields. The boy with the rifle halted them; the men began to run. He fired. One of the men was wounded slightly; the others came back and all three surrendered. Each had an automatic in his pocket and an identification card. Two were gunner officers from Fethard Artillery Barracks, five miles across the hill. I sent the two boys up the hill to find out where the officers had stopped and what they had been doing. Later one came back. The officers had been searching hedges; at a house on the slope, they had asked about dug-outs. They had questioned the young man of the house.
>
> I brought them up one by one. They gave me their names, ranks, the name of their commanding officer. They had been out for a walk, they said.

The following morning at dawn, the three British spies were taken out for execution: "The volley crashed sharply. The three fell to the ground; their arms twitched. The Q.M. put his revolver to each of their foreheads in turn and fired. The bodies lay still on the green grass. We stood to attention. Then slowly we went up the hill across country making for the Center. None of us spoke till we had crossed a good many fields where wind had snaked the rye grass."[12]

The British also used "deserters," men claiming that for one reason or another they did not wish to fight anymore. They gathered information from the people they met, and others who gave them shelter. Their presence soon became known to the IRA and they were picked up. Questioned, their true purpose became known, and they too faced execution as spies.

Though it is said that the majority of the people actively supported the IRA, within their midst there was a Loyalist population opposed to the Republic. There were also former British Army officers and soldiers who still felt an obligation towards the British Empire. Then there were those who betrayed the Volunteers for money. Though not organized as a spy service, their individual information passed on to the British led to the arrests and capture of a number of Volunteers. It became essential for the various IRA brigades out in the country to eliminate these spies before their flying columns were destroyed. Intelligence officers within the brigades were ordered to track them down and procure evidence of their guilt. With this in place the spies were arrested and court-martialled. The evidence was then forwarded to GHQ in Dublin where it was reexamined and the sentence confirmed or remitted. If found guilty they were generally shot. If the evidence was doubtful, then the suspect could be ordered to leave the country at once. Ill-founded and unsourced claims have been made that under the guise of killing spies the Volunteers were guilty of ethnic cleansing, of killing Protestants.[13] Evidence clearly shows this not to be case. Reading through the local newspapers of the day, of the sixteen spies executed in West Cork, nine of them were Roman Catholics.

Loyalist intelligence in West Cork was passed through a retired Lieutenant Colonel of the British Army living in Innishannon. He was the intelligence officer for Munster. The man also led raiding parties of the Essex Regiment, a regiment noted for its brutality towards prisoners. Long suspected, the retired officer was followed by Irish intelligence operatives. Every two weeks he traveled to Belfast to pass on information. Suspecting that he was under enemy observation, four RIC men were allocated to guard him around the clock. Evidence of the man acting as a spy was sent to IRA GHQ, and the order came back to execute him. Carefully watched as he was it was not until May 1921 that an opportunity presented itself. Tom Kelleher, later commandant general of the IRA 1st Southern Division, and another Volunteer heard that the spymaster was sleeping at home. The two men entered the grounds of the man's house and waited in the undergrowth. They saw him proceeding from the house to his garage cum workshop. Leaving the other Volunteer as lookout, Kelleher approached the garage. The door was slightly ajar. Kelleher walked in. The spy turned, taken aback by the presence of a well-dressed stranger with a gaberdine mackintosh folded neatly over his arm. Kelleher's handgun was low caliber. He needed to get closer to his target. Kelleher apologized for the intrusion and asked the way to Bandon, stepping closer as he did so. "Keep straight west young man," the spy directed. Kelleher took another step forward, the man not unduly alarmed by his presence. Then Kelleher withdrew his gun and at close range fired at the spy, who spun backwards and fell to the ground, dead. On hearing the shot, one of the RIC bodyguards dashed to an open window of the nearby house, and seeing Kelleher fleeing the scene, opened fire. Kelleher was wounded, but not badly, and with his companion managed to escape.

Irish Intelligence, both in the city and in the countryside, was quick to grasp the importance of information gathering, and the equal importance of denying intelligence to the enemy. Without doubt the British enjoyed some success in the intelligence war, but having lost their eyes and ears in the countryside in the shape of the RIC, they had to rebuild their intelligence network, which was not easy given that their very accents gave them away. In Dublin, when their intelligence service was virtually wiped out with the mass assassination of its officers and the deep penetration of the British administration by Irish Intelligence, their actions, but for some supplied by paid informers, ceased to be intelligence led.

6

Urban Warfare

While the Squad provided the men for political assassinations, particularly of the rival intelligence network, the Dublin brigades of Volunteers carried out the war of liberation itself in the capital. The importance of such attacks was in their propaganda value, in that they showed the world that Britain was not in control of even the most heavily patrolled city in the world, Dublin. The IRA chief of staff, Richard Mulcahy, was firmly of the view that Dublin was by far the most important military area in Ireland. IRA possession of Dublin was more important, he believed, than even the outstanding achievements of the Volunteers in the southwest. If Dublin was lost, he felt, all the other victories counted for nothing.

By late 1920, at the height of the war, British Intelligence estimates of the strength of the Dublin brigades was as follows:

1. Dublin City and Dublin County south of Dublin City:
   One brigade consisting of four city battalions and one South County battalion (6) and also
   5 Battalion, probably used as "GHQ Troops."
   Total units — 6 battalions consisting of 52 companies.
   Strength — Approximately 201 officers, 4,160 other ranks.
2. Fingal, i.e., County Dublin north of Dublin City:
   One brigade consisting of 3 battalions or 15 companies.
   Strength — Approximately 72 officers and 750 other ranks.
3. County Wicklow:
   One brigade consisting of 3 battalions or 13 companies.
   Strength — Approximately 66 officers and 650 other ranks.
   Total approximate strength — 339 officers and 5,560 other ranks.

Following the defeat of the Volunteers in the 1916 Rising, in less than eighteen months elements of the Dublin Brigade had been reformed, as is shown in their attendance at the funeral of Thomas Ashe in September 1917. Richard Mulcahy, who had fought with Ashe at Ashbourne, took over as brigade OC in 1917 and was appointed chief of staff in March 1918. There was a massive growth in recruits to the Volunteers during the conscription crisis of 1918, but this growth was to prove illusory, for when the crisis abated, many Volunteers departed. Those who remained, however, were committed wholeheartedly to the cause and strove to expand the army. Year after year the Volunteer ranks grew.

Essential now to their very existence was the acquisition of arms. While many of the rifles from the Howth gunrunning of 1914 had been lost in the Rising, many still survived in the possession of John Redmond's National Volunteers, who now returned to Ireland following the end of World War I. Other arms, perhaps surprisingly, were bought from British soldiers in Richmond Barracks at £4 per rifle. One of the earliest actions of the Dublin Volunteers occurred in March 1919, when they raided the arsenal at Collinstown Aerodrome and got away with 75 rifles and ammunition. The favored weapons of the urban guerrilla, though, were the more easily concealed handgun and the grenade. Guns were smuggled in, and a munitions factory was secretly established in the cellar of a bicycle shop at 198, Parnell Street, Dublin, to provide the Volunteers with hand grenades.

On 5 June 1919, a concert was arranged at the Mansion House in Dublin, to commemorate the birth in 1870 of the great Irish socialist, James Connolly. The Citizen Army were in attendance as stewards. The Dublin Metropolitan Police, fearing that there would be some sort of military display, were in attendance to prevent it. One of their detectives recognized Citizen Army officer James O'Shea and attempted to arrest him. Kelly, the Citizen Army officer in charge of security, went to O'Shea's aid. In the struggle that followed, O'Shea drew his revolver and fired. Several policemen and one civilian were wounded in the brief struggle before O'Shea and Kelly escaped into the crowd. Both men were then forced to go on the run. Both they and other units of the ICA later actively took part in Irish Volunteer ambushes of the Crown forces in Dublin, a fact not generally known. Tony Woods, a GHQ Staff Captain took part in some of these earliest urban actions in Dublin:

> The activities of our patrols were, at the start, rather amateurish. That is understandable, as we had no military people in our company. Most of the other companies had. Perhaps they had a more proletarian background; there were ex–British soldiers scattered among them, some 1916 Volunteers, and so on. We had nothing like that. I can remember one ambush we had on Sandford Road, between Marlborough Road and Belmont Avenue, when we attacked some tenders carrying Auxiliaries. A man McGowan, who had a long history with the North County Brigade led us. There were seven of us, some being hidden in a bank of trees that flank one side of the road, and the rest of us in the grounds of Muckross Convent. There was a major shot dead by us in one lorry. You could say it was a fair trophy for a day's outing. He was sitting in the back of a cage car, going out to a raid in Enniskerry as we heard afterwards. That caused great consternation among them and enabled us to get away. One of our lads, who received a shrapnel wound, was caught and got ten years for it. We had flung a number of grenades, when the lorries stopped, and these had proved very effective.[1]

It became evident that at some time British government officials would be targeted:

> One after the other the Chief Commissioner of the Dublin Police, The Inspector General of the Constabulary ... ceased to live abroad, and the residential portion of Dublin Castle became their homes. The gate of the Upper Castle Yard had been kept closed for some time. Now the main gate of the Lower Yard followed suit, and a permanent guard of police and military challenged all comers.... [M]ilitary officers had now been ordered to live in barracks, while those more closely connected with the defense of the Dublin District were quartered in the Castle.... On duty at the Lower Castle Yard gate are Dublin Metropolitan and Military Police, and just inside lounge a couple of Auxiliaries ready for emergencies. Bomb-catching meshwork is stretched across the archway, and a drapery of barbed wire festoons the passage ways in front of the guardroom. Twenty yards outside the Castle gate a mantrap is open, giving access to the subterranean river Poddle that runs beneath the Castle walls. A couple of Royal Engineers are below seeing that the wire entanglements across the stream have not been tampered with during the night....
>
> Over the summit of the old Castle Keep, where the Union Jack floats, peeps the cap of a watching sentry, and machine-guns are ensconced behind its parapet, a post of vantage which

> commands the Castle approaches, and gives a view over distant streets and house-tops ... great canvas screens hung from chimney-stacks and other coigns of vantage to conceal the goings and comings of motor transport in the Lower Castle Yard from prying eyes on the neighboring housetops....
>
> Be it remembered, however, that for most of the inhabitants there was little chance of recreation outside, save at the risk of a bullet or bomb, and to be cooped up in the Castle squares for weeks on end was trying not only to health but to morale.... One longs for the day when the Castle gates will open and we can walk forth again as a free man.[2]

Dublin Castle had become an administration under siege.

On 19 December 1919, members of the Dublin Brigade under Mick McDonnell, assisted by members of the Soloheadbeg Gang, of Sean Treacy, Dan Breen, Seamus Robinson and Sean Hogan, South Tipperary men on the run, carried out an audacious attack on General Lord French's armed motorcade as it approached Kelly's Corner, near the entrance to Phoenix Park, Dublin. Word had reached Collins by way of the son of a railway official that Lord French would be returning to Dublin and getting off at Ashtown Station, and from there driving up to Vice-Regal Lodge in Phoenix Park. McDonnell hurriedly organized his men, and with no motorized transport available, they cycled over to Kelly's public house at Ashtown Cross, the intended site of the ambush. The Volunteers watched as the motorcade proceeded down towards the station to collect its passengers. While in the yard of the pub, surveying the scene, McDonnell saw a large farm cart. He told Breen to turn it around, body first, and get ready to push it out onto the road to block the returning cars. Then the plan started to go wrong. DMP Constable O'Loughlin arrived to direct traffic and to ensure that the official party got through without trouble.

The dilemma was whether to seize Constable O'Loughlin, and cause a disturbance, or leave him. Meanwhile French's party had boarded the four cars and were on their way, sooner than expected. With the cars in sight McDonnell ordered the cart to be pushed out onto the road, only to discover that Breen and his men had not turned the cart and were now struggling with it. McDonnell rationalized that French would probably be sitting in the second car, and ordered his men to concentrate on that one. Suddenly a motorcycle outrider whizzed by the cart, swiftly followed by the first car in which, unexpectedly, French was traveling. Though the car was shot up, and his personal detective, Sergeant Halley, was wounded by small-arms fire, French was unhurt. As the second car approached, a hand grenade was thrown at it. The grenade burst on the backseat, and French would most certainly have been killed if he had been in the vehicle. The third car, containing French's military escort, came under intensive fire. From within, Sergeant George Rumble shot one of the attackers, Volunteer Martin Savage, in the head — just as he was about to throw a second hand grenade — and fatally wounded him. In the ambush, Dan Breen was wounded in the leg, and two armed Dublin metropolitan policemen were also wounded. French was seething at the seeming incompetence of the D. M. P. and its inability to protect him.

As attacks on the Crown forces escalated, a nighttime curfew was introduced in Dublin, following the killing of a constable on 20 February 1920, from midnight to 5:00 A.M. This was extended the next year to 8:00 P.M. till 6:00 A.M., during which time the streets were patrolled by British forces on foot and in trucks. Private J.P. Swindlehurst, Lancashire Fusiliers, stationed in Dublin at the time, recalled the situation:

> The first night passed quietly, just a few distant shots to be heard, all the city goes still at curfew which is ten o'clock. Once we heard hurrying footsteps dodging the curfew lorries, but

little else happened. Not so last night [11 January 1920], opposite our place is the newspaper office of the *Dublin Times*. At about two o'clock when the presses were going full speed ahead with the morning news, two cars drew up, and out jumped a dozen Sinn Feiners who began to shoot the place up. In about two minutes all the windows had gone, we overlooked them and could see the workmen hiding behind the machines, out of the way of flying bullets. The place is only five minutes from the barracks, and the noise of the firing brought a party of Black and Tans on the scene, the result of the fight was two killed and three wounded, one Sinn Feiner deceased and two wounded, the rest were Black and Tans. We had them laid out in our place whilst the ambulances came and cleared them to the mortuary and hospital respectively. The wounded Sinn Feiners came in for a lot of questioning from the C.I.D, they were only young men, but typically Irish.... [N]o amount of threats to shoot them brought any further news to what the CID men wanted, so they carted them off.[3]

Swindlehurst recorded another incident in his diary entry of 16 January: "Early this morning I was on sentry at the main entrance behind the iron gate, when the noise of a motor and running footsteps caused my pal and I to look out for trouble. We got it, the runner was a secret service man being pursued by Sinn Feiners in the car.

They dropped him with a fusillade of shots, when he was about two yards from the doorway. His impetuous roll, knocked us into the hall, when we were going to reply to them. In a few seconds they were gone, leaving a bomb in the roadway which failed to explode. The victim was luckily only slightly wounded, one through the leg and another through his hand. We don't know where he had been but a big party of men moved out armed to the teeth at dawn, so he must have got some information which was acted upon."[4]

British Army patrols operating during the curfew hours had strict guidelines:

1. Unauthorized persons found in the streets of Dublin City during the curfew hours are liable to arrest, but are not liable to be shot on sight unless seen to be armed.
2. Curfew patrols have the right to fire on persons acting in such a manner as to jeopardize the safety of the patrol.
3. In all cases where fire is opened it must be by order only, and strictly limited to what is necessary to effect the object in view.

During the day the British blocked off streets in surprise raids, searching and questioning all they had caught in their net. At night individual houses were targeted by British Intelligence in their search for Volunteers. Trucks would suddenly appear with searchlights blazing to light up the darkness. Houses would be broken into in search of IRA men, their doors battered in by rifle butts, and their inhabitants roughly treated. A proclamation issued by General Macready, commander-in-chief of the British forces in Ireland, decreed "that a state of armed insurrection exists; that any person taking part therein or harboring any person who has taken part therein, or procuring, inviting, aiding or abetting any person to take part therein, is guilty of levying war against His Majesty the King, and is liable on conviction of a Military Court to suffer death."

Sometimes Volunteers would be discovered and taken away to be tortured for information. Those giving them shelter fared little better. It put a strain on everyone. Ernie O'Malley recalled that when he was on the run in Dublin he stayed at a safe house that was being used by other Volunteers. He was woken in the night by screams. Two Volunteers, young lads, thought that the Black and Tans were in the house and were going to kill every-

A British raid in Sackville Street, Dublin.

body. Their nerves had gone. It had all become too much for them. Though safe houses were raided, there was never a shortage of those willing to shelter Volunteers. Operating within their own city, the Volunteers nearly always had the advantage. They knew the shortcuts that led to safety. The British authorities, lacking this detailed knowledge, were never completely in control of the streets, either by day or by night.

On the afternoon of 1 June 1920 members of the Dublin Brigade carried out a daylight raid on the sentries and guards of the King's Inns in Dublin, not far from the British military base in the North Dublin Union. The operation was led by Peader Clancy. The sentries at the gate were held up and disarmed. The remainder of the Volunteers proceeded into the building and located the guardroom, where they held up the guard. Securing the key, they unlocked the rifles from their chained racks and removed them to an awaiting Ford car, which was driven away. The haul included thirteen rifles and a Lewis machine gun. There were no casualties, and no shots were fired. On 15 July 1920 men from the Dublin Brigade entered the sorting office of the recently restored General Post Office. They held up the staff, then systematically went through the mail leaving and entering Dublin Castle. Valuable information was gained by Republican Intelligence, and Lord French had the novelty of receiving mail marked on the envelopes with "Passed by Censor, IRA."

In July 1920 the Auxiliaries arrived in Ireland to supplement the existing British forces. They were a corps d'elite of ex-officers, paid £1 a day. They were divided up into fifteen companies of one hundred men and spread throughout Ireland. Five companies, C, D, E, F, and Q, were based in Dublin. By and large they were given a free hand in their activities, and this led to beatings and murder by them. Being an officer corps. they were looked upon initially as some sort of supermen. A few well-organized ambushes by the IRA proved otherwise. It should be said, however, that the Auxiliaries were never taken for granted. They were intelligent, and for the most part brave, if sometimes brutal.

On 20 September 1920, a small team of the Dublin Volunteers attempted to hold up a British Army work detail collecting loaves from a bakery in Church Street, Dublin. The detail was escorted by armed soldiers. The intention was to surprise these men and take their rifles. In the ensuing struggle three of the soldiers were shot dead. One of the Volunteers, Kevin Barry, a medical student, was captured and subsequently hanged. On that same night, a newly promoted head constable from the training camp for Auxiliaries in Gormanston, near Balbriggan, County Dublin, was shot dead in a public house. A Black and Tan was also wounded by IRA personnel. The incident appears to have been completely unplanned. Later that night the police ransacked Balbriggan, killing two men, looting and burning four public houses, destroying a hosiery factory and damaging or destroying forty-nine houses. The attack received widespread publicity in the British and foreign press, and it became known as the Sack of Balbriggan. It caused a heated debate in the British Parliament over reprisals.

On 26 September the RIC police barracks at Trim were captured and destroyed by men of the Dublin Brigade. A very risky venture, given the close proximity of so many British garrisons in the city, it was the only case of an occupied police barracks in the Dublin District being captured. In another attack, on an armored car in Dublin, Volunteer Liam O'Connell was shot and later died. He was taken home to Glantane, near Mallow in County Cork for burial, where his eulogy was delivered by his close friend Liam Lynch, commandant of Cork No. 2 Brigade. The action increased British activity in the city, with stop and search, and prompted a number of intelligence-led house raids. On 20 December British troops discovered an IRA bomb-making factory in Dublin. Some Volunteers were arrested in the raid and imprisoned, which proved to be a serious loss to the Republicans.

Previously, on 20 October 1920, the inspirational vice-commandant of Tipperary No. 3 Brigade, Sean Treacy, was killed in a gunfight with British intelligence officers on Talbot Street, in Dublin city center. British intelligence officer Lt. Price was killed instantly by Treacy, and Francis Christian, another British officer, was fatally wounded. Treacy was shot dead from behind by a third officer. Two civilians were also shot in the crossfire.

An Active Service Unit drawn from the 2nd Battalion of the Dublin Brigade was formed, consisting of fifty men. Its type of warfare, and its armaments, were distinctly different from the flying columns in the country. These men carried revolvers and hand grenades, which were more easy to conceal as they moved around the city. The British army and the Auxiliaries, who operated in Dublin, originally patrolled on foot, but in May of 1920 it was decided that patrols of less than one officer and twenty other ranks should travel by

British soldiers seal off a street prior to an extensive search for arms and IRA men.

motor transport. The danger of overcrowding vehicles had to be guarded against and every man had to know his task in the event of attack. The soldiers traveled sitting back to back, their rifles pointing outwards towards the populace. The Volunteers had at first been hesitant about attacking the trucks for fear of civilian casualties. As circumstances became critical, the Volunteers decided on street ambushes, and attacks became more frequent as the war progressed, until they became an almost daily occurrence. Quite often three operations a day were carried out. Aungier Street, and its continuations of Wexford Street and Camden Street, on the south side of the city, became a popular ambush site because of the numerous roads and alleyways leading off, that offered a means of escape.

The 3 Battalion of the Dublin Brigade operated in the area bounded by Westmorland Street, along the south quays to the Grand Canal Basin and back as far as Baggot Street. It was densely populated. An active service unit principally made up of unemployed men was formed. They were put on permanent standby and were constantly seeking targets among the Black and Tans and Auxiliaries in Lower Mount Street, Brunswick Street, and Townsend Street. These were the arteries along which the enemy trucks traveled to and from Beggars Bush Barracks. The area was a warren of lanes and alleyways, filled with small cottages and tenements. Knowing the area well the ASU found it easy to get away after an attack. The enemy were reluctant to follow for fear of being led into a trap. Writing in August 1922, one British administrator based in Dublin Castle at the time related that "towards the close of the year 1920 the campaign of murder began to quicken still more. The streets of Dublin became the scene of butchery.... Here attackers took equal risks with attacked.... The attacker did not wear uniform, and could in a moment turn himself into a peaceful citizen; this fact gave him an unfair advantage, but at least his opponent had a possible chance."[5]

In addition to trucks the British also used armored cars. Up to December 1920 the British Army was using up to ten armored cars throughout the city: two Rolls Royces, four Austins and a few Jeffrey Quad armored cars. These early armored vehicles was beset with mechanical problems, particularly in the availability of spare parts. The Jeffrey cars were never really up to the task in hand and were soon abandoned. While excellent vehicles, the Austin cars lacked spare parts. A new armored car, the Peerless, was introduced. They were practically unstoppable.

Following the killing of a number of its intelligence officers and others on 21 November, Crown forces carried out nearly one hundred raids in a twenty-four hour period in Dublin, which led to the arrests of a number of Squad and Dublin Brigade members who had taken part in the operation to eliminate the Cairo Gang. The success was tempered in that it was not possible to identify large numbers of those arrested. Soon afterward, in an intelligence led raid, the British discovered the temporary home and office occupied by the IRA chief of staff, Richard Mulcahy. He succeeded in escaping, but left a lot of valuable papers behind. Though the Cairo Gang had been eliminated, British intelligence in the capital had not been completely destroyed.

January 1921 was a month of considerable activity in Dublin. On the 13th, British soldiers manning a checkpoint at O'Connell Bridge panicked and opened fire on a crowd of civilians, killing two and seriously wounding five. Between 15 and 17 January, British soldiers cordoned off an area bounded by Capel Street, Church Street, North King Street and the Quays, and conducted a house by house search, but with little result. Another cordon was established on 18 and 19 February in the area about Mountjoy Square, again with little result. The deduction drawn by military intelligence was that the extent of an area selected for cordoning must be searchable in twelve hours maximum; otherwise the element of surprise was lost. Many of the houses in Dublin had interlinking underground cellars and passages which permitted suspects to escape. Policy revision dictated that cordons should be restricted to smaller areas that could be searched in two or three hours.

The brigade's response was an ambush of enemy troops at Drumcondra in the north of the city. The whole thing went badly wrong though; one Volunteer was killed and five captured, of whom four were later hanged. The brigade suffered a further setback when later that month they ambushed a British patrol in Brunswick Street (Pearse Street). Two Auxiliaries and one Volunteer were killed in the firefight. To discourage further attacks on their truck patrols, the British forces began carrying Republican prisoners, with notices to that effect. This was short-lived following its report in foreign newspapers. The grenade attacks continued, but to prevent them from entering the vehicles, the British army trucks were covered in mesh. The IRA responded by attaching fishing hooks to the grenades, which would catch in the mesh and explode. Volunteer Tony Woods describes an attack in which he took part, led by Noel Lemass:

> We were patrolling a main route as usual on the chance that the right sort of target would present itself. This day, we had started off walking from Appian Way along Upper Leeson Street, turning down by the canal along the then quietly residential Mespil Road. Somebody observed tenders approaching from Baggot Street Bridge. Quickly we slipped into the front gardens of the houses, all of them had plenty of trees, shrubs and the sort of cover we needed. There were three tenders, one a caged one the other two open. Cathal Shannon, a 1916 man, flung his grenade at the caged Crossley, but it bounced off, rolling on to the road, where it exploded. They stopped at once, and there was quite a bit of shooting, as they took us on. In fact they jumped out and tried to surround us. We retreated through the gardens into Burlington Road, but they did not follow us. I think they were being cautious. They could not be sure that they would not walk into a trap if they did so. It was a tactic often used at that time, to run away while a better placed group, frequently armed with a machine gun, took them on. That was done I know in the Dardanelles, as the narrow part of Wexford Street was called.[6]

John Harrington, of H. Company, 1st Battalion, recalls another ambush:

> One action I do recall was at the corner of Dorset Street and Blessington Street, a favorite spot. There was a pub there on the corner, a short distance down in the direction of Bolton Street, with an angle porch having a substantial pillar in the very corner. I lounged behind that while other members of the company were placed strategically around. We were of course armed, and each of us carried some grenades. However there was an accidental hold up of trams near the junction, and the OC could see that there might be heavy civilian casualties if a full-spirited ambush took place. He was reluctant to miss the opportunity completely. When therefore one Crossley lorry came into view, complete with wire cages that they were equipped with to ward off grenades, Liam Grimley and the rest of us let fly, and one at least of the grenades landed right inside the lorry. In the resultant confusion we separated quickly. I retreated up Blessington Street, Berkeley Road and into Geraldine Street which is a street of small residential houses. I could see that the top of it was already cordoned off. Well now, this will just give you an idea of the spirit among the people at the time. I could see that if I proceeded with the hardware I was carrying I would be a goner. I therefore turned inside the first little porch, tapped at the door and was admitted inside. There was a hall stand there. Taking the weaponry from my pockets, I slipped them into the drawer. "There," I said, to the woman, a complete stranger to me, "I will call back for those later." Scarcely another word was exchanged as I emerged upon the street, fit now to pass through any cordon.[7]

Ernie O'Malley, who was in Dublin in February 1920, describes a third such assault in his book, *On Another Man's Wound*: "Outside Stephen's Green I saw men attack a netted lorry and an armored Lancia of troops. Eggs [hand grenades] shattered in a tearing smash, one burst above the Lancia; automatics shot quickly, rifle reply came more slowly then the rifles merged with the swaying thresh of a machine gun. The passersby ran or threw themselves on the pavement. I lay down, watching. A man flattened on his blood in the cobbled street, two soldiers lay loosely against each other in a corner of the Lancia; up the street men tried to stop the red stains on a woman's white blouse. Women beside me were moaning and praying: 'O Sacred Heart of Jesus, help us.' I ran for a lane beside the College of Surgeons and was soon in York Street." That an attack could come at any time played on the nerves of all. The constant shootings, hold-ups and raids left their mark. If a truck backfired people instinctively looked for cover or dived into doorways. Then there were the shootings and grenade attacks themselves.

The Auxiliaries carried out random murders as reprisals. On 9 February 1921, two political Republicans, James Murphy and Patrick Kennedy, were arrested by Auxiliaries in Dublin. Two hours later Dublin Metropolitan Police found the two men lying shot in Drumcondra. Kennedy was dead, but Murphy lived long enough to tell the police what had happened. Captain W.L. King, commanding officer of F Company of the Auxiliaries, was later arrested for the killings. He was tried by court-martial, but two Auxiliary officers provided an alibi for him and he was acquitted.

On 1 March an attack was made about 7:00 P.M. upon a force of RIC who were escorting some prisoners in trucks from Phoenix Park to Dublin Castle. As the convoy reached the north quay hand grenades were thrown and rifle fire opened from the other side of the river Liffey. Several civilians were wounded in the crossfire, including three children, twins Madge and Lilly Monaghan, aged twelve, and Lizzie Brennan, aged eleven. On 5 March the Volunteers staged two ambushes on British troops in North Dublin, one at Parnell Square, the other at Clontarf. Fire was exchanged, and IRA men threw hand grenades. One civilian was killed and four wounded in the crossfire. In all, the Dublin Brigade carried out 53 attacks on British forces in the city during the course of March. In the month that followed they carried out 67 attacks — more than two a day.

British troops had some success in March 1921, when they discovered an IRA munitions dump in Dublin; 15 rifles, 54 revolvers, 8 shotguns, 3,440 rounds of ammunition, 235 bombs, 814 detonators and a large quantity of explosives were seized. They had even more success on 29 April. Soldiers from the 24 Brigade raided Blackhall Place just north of the Liffey near Arbour Hill Prison and

Civilians being searched and questioned by Auxiliaries.

captured 40 men of the Active Service Unit of the 1st Battalion of the IRA's Dublin Brigade. Such a capture led to serious disruption in IRA attacks in the city.

On 14 May members of the Dublin Brigade attempted to free Sean MacEoin, imprisoned for the shooting of District Inspector McGrath of the RIC. The house where MacEoin was staying had been surrounded. He made a break for it, firing at his would-be captors and killing McGrath in the process. MacEoin escaped, but was captured a month later. His would-be rescuers stole an armored car on the North Circular Road, killing two British soldiers in the process. The car was driven into Mountjoy Prison, but the armed guards became suspicious and a firefight developed, obliging the I.R.A men to shoot their way out of the prison. Two soldiers from the Royal Marine Battalion were killed in the skirmish.

Perhaps the most remarkable event carried out by the 2nd Battalion Dublin Brigade ASU, one certainly that gained worldwide publicity, was the attack on the Customs House and the burning of its records. The records related to the financing and administration of British government departments in Ireland. The ASU, led by Tom Ennis, with the assistance of members of the Irish Citizen Army, entered the building on 25 May 1921. Further units, assisted by the Squad, acted as a covering party outside. Desperately short of ammunition, the covering party had at best five rounds for their revolvers. As the building caught fire a British armored car, manned by members of F Company, Auxiliary Division, crossed O'Connell Bridge. It came under intense fire and was also bombed, causing four casualties. It was followed by three or four armed Lancia cars, manned by Q Company of the Auxiliaries, based at the North Wall. They opened fire on the Volunteers. Hearing the firing, a party of Black and Tans who were stationed in an hotel along the quays ran towards the customs house to give support. The Volunteers opened fire on them, lobbing hand grenades too. More British reinforcements started arriving by trucks. Almost out of ammunition, and with the customs house ablaze, the Volunteers' withdrew as best they could with heavy losses. From the Volunteers viewpoint the action was a success in that the target was destroyed—but it came at a heavy cost. Inadequately armed, they lost 6 men killed, 12 wounded and some 70 men captured.[8]

The attack had been authorized by de Valera, very much as a means of drawing the world's attention to the Irish struggle. The action was supported by Brugha, in what was seen by senior Volunteer officers as an attempt by him to wrest control from Collins, and reestablish de Valera's authority. De Valera's theory of how the war should be fought was locked in a 1916 timeframe of static warfare, as indeed was Brugha's. T.P. Coogan in his biography of Collins suggests that Brugha never "seriously believed they could win the war. For him, carrying on the fight was the important thing, keeping

The burning of the custom house, Dublin, 25 May 1921.

faith with the men who had raised the standard in other generations."⁹ This theory allowed for blood sacrifices. Because of the Brugha/de Valera mindset, the Volunteers in the customs house raid were left in an exposed position for an inordinate length of time. With the loss of so many men, the Intelligence Department and the Squad were amalgamated into the Dublin Brigade, which restored overall control in Dublin to de Valera and Brugha. Patrick Daly was put in control of the new force. He records the following in his witness statement:

> We had approximately eighty men between the two units; the remainder were either prisoners, wounded or killed.... When I took over I told the men that we were having no staff officers. Every officer and NCO would be a leader in attack. The Lieutenants would not alone take orders from me, but they would look for jobs and keep the men employed. Every Tan and military lorry was fair game, but no individual shootings of civilians must take place; no man had the right to say who was a spy. Headquarters were the only people who would give an order for an execution. I kept in touch with [the] Brigade OC as well as Intelligence, and the two half–Companies worked very well, as a day never passed without some lorry being hit up, sometimes with very good effect. British dispatch riders were constantly being relieved of their motor-bicycles and dispatches. Laundries were invaded and military clothing destroyed. Provisions going to military barracks were seized. The enemy was harried in every way possible.

The IRA lost further men on 29 April 1921. Soldiers from the British 24 Brigade captured the active service unit of the 1st Battalion of the Dublin Brigade at Blackhall Place. Some forty IRA men were captured without resistance. Yet despite these very real setbacks, throughout the month of May the Dublin Volunteers carried out one hundred and seven attacks on British forces in the city.

In June the British inaugurated a new system of effective patrols in the capital (see Appendix I). Instead of the previous mass roundups of sealing certain sections of the city and searching them, they changed their tactics. Each battalion was allotted an area for patrolling. The most effective foot patrols made sudden surprise appearances by day or lay up in ambush at night. They adopted a policy of searching any suspicious looking individuals, and this soon paid dividends. It proved far more effective than the general roundups. On 20 June de Valera was arrested by a patrol of the 2nd Battalion of the Worcestershire Regiment under a false name. He was taken to Portobello Barracks, where he divulged that he was "Mr. de Valera, President of the Irish Republic." He was treated well, and the next day he was released. Previously, on 9 May, Erskine Childers had been arrested in Dublin and released a few hours later, by order of the government. The British were putting out peace feelers to, as they considered them, the more moderate Sinn Feiners.

That June through its

A dead IRA man lies on the ground following the gun battle that followed the burning of the custom house.

intelligence system, IRA general headquarters learned of the intended arrival by rail of military reinforcements from Britain, men to be sent on from Dublin to other divisions in the country. Railway lines were mined and in other cases sections of line were removed. Snipers were posted to fire on derailed trains. The theft of telegraph keys and batteries in a number of robberies had previously puzzled British intelligence; now they discovered to what use they had been put. The IRA had moved away from bombs with fuses to electronically detonated bombs with trailing wires of several hundred yards. With the losses of British personnel in these ambushes the use of troop trains was abandoned. Under revised plans troops moved on foot in extended order or traveled by motor transport. In order to protect them while in the city, British Army snipers were placed on advantageous rooftops, and motor transport through the city was provided with flanking patrols. Even airplanes over the city were used to spot potential ambushes. As a result, 14 further units passed through Dublin to the provinces, with a loss of just two wounded. The British were learning to adapt to urban guerrilla warfare.

In the month of June 1921, the Volunteers carried out ninety-three attacks on British forces in Dublin. In one daytime assault, members of the Dublin Brigade attacked the participants of a cricket match being staged in the grounds of Trinity College. One of the teams was made up of British Army officers. In the attack a woman spectator was tragically killed in the crossfire. On 3 June an ASU from the Dublin Brigade set fire to the Shell Factory, then being used as the British Army's motor repair and ordnance depot. Though the building was badly destroyed, the repair shops were saved. On 26 June, Auxiliary cadet William F.H. Hunt was shot dead in the dining room of the Mayfair Hotel in Baggot Street, and another was wounded. There is no indication that Hunt had been involved in any atrocities, and his death was a one-off exercise in terrorism, as an example to the British government that none of its personnel in Ireland were now safe. The following day it was reported in the newspapers that Lloyd George, the British prime minister, had written to President de Valera, requesting a truce. Meanwhile the war carried on.

Towards the end of June the IRA brigades in Dublin initiated a campaign of sniping at guards and patrols during curfew hours in the capital, particularly those operating around the Castle and the customs house. The truce came as a surprise to many. All sorts of actions had been planned. In Dublin itself an operation that would have eclipsed the shooting of the British intelligence officers on Bloody Sunday was about to take place. It was timed for the day that the Auxiliaries got paid. The center of the city was to be surrounded by Volunteers. Every hotel and public house frequented by the Auxiliaries was to be entered simultaneously, and any found there were to be shot. The truce came into being just days before the intended operation.

7

The Splendid Women

The Irish War for Independence was perhaps the first war of the twentieth century where women played an active role, as is seen in the chapters on passive resistance and intelligence gathering. The women taking part in the demonstrations risked been beaten by police batons; the women acting as spies risked torture and long periods of imprisonment. There were others, though, in their physical participation in pursuing the war, who risked death by hanging or the firing squad if captured. A number of strands in Irish society all came together about 1913 to produce women, who like their menfolk were prepared to take up the gun in the struggle for an independent Irish Republic.

Suffragettes

The Irish suffragettes, an offshoot of the English movement, shared the same aims as their English sisters — to secure the vote for women and achieve equality with men. The first suffrage movement in Ireland was the Dublin Women's Suffrage Association, founded in 1876 by Anna Haslam. The suffrage movement attracted well-off, educated, articulate, middle-class women to the cause. Many were from Unionist Ascendancy families, the old Anglo-Irish, who had been the backbone of British rule in Ireland. Charlotte Despard, sister of Sir John French, later lord lieutenant of Ireland; Albinia Broderick, sister of the Earl of Middleton; Madeleine ffrench-Mullen; Maud Gonne, later to marry Irish Nationalist major John McBride; Constance Gore-Booth, later Countess Markiewicz; her sister Eva Gore-Booth; and Hanna Sheehy-Skeffington, later to found the Irish Women's Franchise League in 1908, were all drawn to the suffrage movement. At first they were skeptical of the Nationalist parties, and the Nationalist parties saw votes for women as a mere sideshow to the achieving of Home Rule.

The change came in suffragette thinking with the establishment of the Irish Citizen Army. Here was a socialist movement that actually promoted equality of the sexes. Markiewicz, who had joined Sinn Fein in 1908, joined the Citizen Army, as did Madeleine ffrench-Mullen and Dr. Kathleen Lynn. Charlotte Despard moved even further to the left. Having taken up residence in Belfast, she came to support the Revolutionary Workers Group, which later became the Irish Communist Party, in their efforts to unite Catholic and Protestant workers. Helen Chenevix, a suffragette and one of the first women graduates of Trinity College, Dublin, was joint founder with Louie Bennett of the Irish Women's Suffrage Federation, which brought together the various suffrage organizations. Most of the members of the new Federation were also members of other political organizations and parties. Chenevix was a member of the Labour Party and an active trade unionist. Patricia Lynch, also with left-wing leanings, had been born in Cork but had been taken to London as a child. She was an active suffragette in England. Lynch wrote articles for the radical *Workers Dreadnought*. Suffragette leader Silvia Pankhurst asked her to report on the 1916 Rising in Dublin. This she did, and sent other articles back to England regarding Ireland's plight. This led to the suffragettes supporting the Irish cause, giving a seal of approval for Irish suffragettes to support the Nationalists.

Socialists and Trade Unionists

The aims of the Socialists included the equality of women, and so it found favor with the majority of suffragettes. The only problem was that they were socialists, and the majority of suffragettes in Ireland at that time were middle class. The notion of an independent socialist republic with power in the hands of the workers did not find favor with the more right-wing Nationalists, who saw them as ungodly Communists. Irish Marxism was a curious beast though. Most of its supporters were practicing Christians. Connolly, a Roman Catholic, received Holy Communion before his execution. The establishment of the Irish Citizen Army, again offering equality of the sexes, drew in a number of middle-class women who by their education and ability to articulate rose through the ranks to become officers. By 1916, while the Nationalists (the men that is), agreed over the establishment of an Irish republic, they only had some vague notion of expanding the franchise to women should they succeed. Under the socialist policies put forward by Connolly and Larkin, women were offered equality. They were encouraged to play an equal part and supported in that effort.

Working-class women seized this opportunity with both hands. Delia Larkin, sister of Jim Larkin, who formed the Irish Citizen Army as a protectionist force for striking workers, was a founder member of the Irish Women Workers' Union, established in 1911. In 1913 she organized support for victims of the Dublin Lock-Out. Her union was closely linked to her brother's Irish Transport and General Workers' Union and held its meetings and social events in Liberty Hall. Katie O'Connor, a printer by trade was also active in the Irish Women Workers' Union, and as a girl of just 16 she acted as a messenger between the various garrisons in the 1916 Rising. Rosie Hacket was born in Glasgow but had moved to Dublin and was an early organizer of the Irish Transport and General Workers' Union in the city. She joined the Irish Citizen Army and was also active in the 1916 Rising. Mary Galway, up in Belfast, set up the Textile Operatives Society in 1893. In 1897 she successfully led 8,000 people out on strike for better conditions. She received support from Larkins' ITGWU. The Socialists and trade unionists came together in 1916 in support of Connolly's Irish socialist republic. Connolly somehow found common ground with the Volunteers, thus bringing together the two political factions of the right and left, and with them the women of Ireland. In the Irish Declaration of Independence we can see the influence of Connolly. It begins "Irishmen and Irishwomen...."

Cumann na mBan and Inghinidhe na hEireann

The two women's groups most closely connected with Irish Nationalism are Inghinidhe na hEireann (Daughters of Ireland) and Cumann na mBan (Womens' League). Inghinidhe na hEireann, the older of the two movements, was also formed to advance women's rights, and as such drew members from the suffrage movement, including Madeleine ffrench-Mullen, a Volunteer in the Irish Citizen Army. Inghinidhe was founded in 1900 by Maude Gonne in response to the exclusion of women from the various right-wing Nationalist organizations. The Countess Markievicz, a member of Sinn Fein and an officer in the Irish Citizen army, joined Inghinidhe in 1908. So the countess, and she was not unique, we have a linking of the suffragettes with the socialists and the nationalists. Inghinidhe merged with what was to become Cumann na mBan in 1913.

The Countess Markievicz was condemned to death for her part in the Dublin Rising.

Cumann na mBan evolved out of a discussion held by a number of Nationalist women at Wynn's Hotel in Dublin. It was the bringing together of a number of like-minded women to form a women's auxiliary to act in support of the newly formed Irish Volunteers. The first meeting of the new organization was at Wynn's on 5 April 1914. Thereafter it held its meetings in Brunswick Street, before moving to 6, Harcourt Street, Dublin. It established branches throughout Ireland. The Cumann set out its aims in its Constitution: "Cumann na mBan is an independent body of Irish women pledged to work for the Irish Republic, by organizing and training the women of Ireland to take their places by the side of those who are working and fighting for its recognition." On 23 April 1916 the military council of the IRB integrated Cumann na mBan, the Irish Volunteers and the Irish Citizen Army into the Army of the Irish Republic.

The influence of the earlier pro-suffrage organization, Inghinidhe, was still felt in the new movement, as is indicated in the statement issued by Cumann in 1919: "Cumann na mBan is proud that its members rallied under the Republican flag in Easter Week, 1916, and claim that by taking their places in the firing line, and in every other way helping in the establishment of the Irish Republic, they have regained for the women of Ireland the rights that belonged to them under the old Gaelic civilization, where sex was no bar to citizenship.... [which rights] were guaranteed to them in the Republican Proclamation of Easter Week."[1] Constance Markievicz, perhaps the most famous member of Cumann na mBan, wrote about her experiences as a mem-

A Cuman na mBan brooch, the words entwined around a rifle.

ber of the Citizen Army just prior to the Rising: "On Easter Monday morning there was a great hosting of disciplined and armed men at Liberty Hall. Padraic Pearse and James Connolly addressed us and told us that from now the Volunteers and the ICA were not two forces, but the wings of the Irish Republican Army. There were a considerable number of ICA women. These were absolutely on the same footing as the men. They took part in all marches, and even in the manoeuvres that lasted all night. Moreover, Connolly made it quite clear to us that unless we took our share in the drudgery of training and preparing, we should not be allowed to take any share at all in the fight. You may judge how fit we were when I tell you that sixteen miles was the length of our last route march."[2] Connolly's women soldiers were no frail sisterhood dressing up and pretending to be soldiers — they were soldiers.

The Easter Rising, 1916

Forty Cumann na mBan members, many of them members of the ICA, went out to fight with the men on Easter Monday.[3] They were stationed in all the Volunteer strongholds, baring one — Eamon de Valera's at Boland's Mill. Whether out of chivalry or chauvinism, he refused to allow women fighters in his garrison, in defiance it may be added, of senior command. While some women did undertake nursing and domestic duties, a goodly portion of them fought alongside the men. Winifred Carney, James Connolly's secretary, entered the General Post Office with a typewriter and a Webley revolver. With the building secured, women from Cumann na mBan starting coming into the post office carrying arms from various dumps in different parts of the city. Later these women were employed as dispatch carriers, visiting practically all of the Volunteer posts and commands in the city. It was very dangerous, as they came under fire from British Army snipers. Volunteer Margaretta Keogh was shot dead outside of the South Dublin Union. Connolly was unstinting in his praise of these brave women. In one communiqué he wrote, "[A]nd in the hour of our victory let us not forget the Splendid Women who have everywhere stood by us and cheered us on. Never had man or woman a grander Cause, never was a Cause more grandly served."

Amid all the fighting, during the height of the insurrection, some women went out on scouting missions and carried dispatches from one garrison to another. Constance Markievicz, appointed as a staff lieutenant under Michael Mallin, relates that some ICA women sallied forth out of the Stephens Green stronghold and held up bread vans when the garrison ran out of food. Prior to the commencement of hostilities Markiewicz was appointed to inspect the defenses around the Green. As she recalled in her *Prison Letters*, "He [Mallin] took me round the Green and showed me how the barricading of the gates and digging trenches had begun, and he left me in charge of this work while he went to superintend the erection of barricades in the streets and arrange other work.... This work was very exciting when the fighting began. I continued round and round the Green, reporting back if anything was wanted, or tackling any sniper who was particularly objectionable." In fact, it is recorded, she actually wounded a British sniper firing from the nearby Shelbourne Hotel.

In the defense of the Green and College of Surgeons, the women soldiers suffered one casualty, Margaret Skinnider. She was a teacher by profession, born in Glasgow of Irish parents. Skinnider was a member of the Glasgow Cumann na mBan and had arrived in Ireland after smuggling in a supply of explosives. Her original duty during the Rising was as a dispatch rider between the GPO and Stephens Green. When the Stephens Green garrison withdrew into the College of Surgeons she got up onto the roof of the building and returned the fire of the British snipers in the Shelbourne. She was from all accounts an expert markswoman. In an assault on an enemy position she was wounded three times but survived and lived until 1971. Markievicz recalled of her the following: "We had only one woman casualty — Margaret Skinnider. She, like myself, was in uniform and carried an army rifle. She had enlisted as a private in the ICA. She was one of the party who went out to set fire to a house just behind Russell's Hotel. The English opened fire on them from the ground floor of a house just opposite. Poor Freddy Ryan was killed and Margaret was very badly wounded. She owes her life to William Partridge. He carried her away under fire and back to the College.... Margaret's only regret was her bad luck in being disabled so early in the day (Wednesday of Easter week) though she must have suffered terribly, but the end was nearer than we thought, for it was only a few days later that we carried her over to Vincent's Hospital, so that she would not fall wounded into the hands of the English."[4]

Markievicz later proposed taking another small mixed group of men and women soldiers to the Shelbourne Hotel, but her request was turned down by Mallin. He could not risk more casualties to his soldiers. Everyone was needed to defend the position that they had been entrusted with. Also at the Stephens Green garrison was Dr. Kathleen Lynn as medical officer, holding the rank of captain, and Madeleine ffrench-Mullen, who was in charge of the Red Cross. Mallin and Markievicz and the other defenders held out for six days. Their garrison was not captured, but under Pearse's surrender order they were obliged to give in. The British officer who took their surrender was a Captain Wheeler, a relative of Markievicz.

Elsewhere the women of the Citizen Army alongside their male comrades not only defended positions but also went on the offensive. Helena Moloney was among the soldiers led by Sean Connolly who, seeing one of the gateways of Dublin Castle unprotected, entered the yard. The shot one soldier but they were driven off by reinforcements and took up positions in their designated garrison within the City Hall and the neighboring newspaper offices opposite the Castle. Moloney was an actress with the Abbey Theatre who had fingers in a number of Nationalist pies. She was a founding member of Inghinidhe na hEireann, secretary of the Irish Women Workers' Union, and a council member of the Irish Citizen Army. While raising the tricolor on the roof of one of these offices Sean Connolly was mortally wounded. Dr. Kathleen Lynn was sent for from Stephens Green. As a captain in the ICA she nominally took charge following Connolly's death and surrendered the Volunteer force when it was overwhelmed by the British.

As the days went on the Republican cause was seen to be lost. On Friday, 28 April, at mid-day, most of the women in the GPO were evacuated. On the following day, wishing to prevent any further unnecessary loss of life, Padraig Pearse asked Elizabeth O'Farrell to act as an emissary to the British, which she agreed to do. She carried with her a note of surrender. The British Army authorities responded:

From the Commander of the Dublin Forces, to P.H. Pearse
29 April, 1.40 P.M.
   A woman has come in who says you wish to negotiate with me. I am prepared to receive you in Britain Street, at the north end of Moore Street, provided you surrender unconditionally. You will proceed up Moore Street accompanied only by the woman who bears you this note under a white flag.
   W.H.S. Lowe Brig Genl.[5]

So ended the 1916 Rising, where the women of Ireland demonstrated that they were the equal of men. The twenty-two women in the Marrowbone Lane Distillery garrison, upon its surrender, marched behind the men in ranks of four, keeping step as far as Richmond Barracks, where they were separated. The next morning the women were marched off to Kilmainham Prison. Of her fellow defenders, both men and women, the fanatical Countess Markievicz was to observe that the memory of Easter Week with its heroic dead is sacred to us who survived. Many of us could almost wish that we had died in the moment of ecstasy when, with the tri-color over our heads we went out and proclaimed the Irish Republic, and with guns in our hands tried to establish it.[6]

Over seventy women in all were made prisoners, including Constance Markievicz, Dr. Kathleen Lynn, Madeleine ffrench-Mullen, and Margaret Skinnider. Markiewicz, as a commander, was tried by court-martial, found guilty and sentenced to death. Her sentence was later commuted to penal servitude for life, and she was deported to Aylesbury Prison in England. All but twelve of the women had been released by 8 May 1916. A general amnesty of prisoners was announced by the British government in June 1917, and Markievicz and the other prisoners were released. In the general election of December 1918 Constance Markievicz became the first woman to be elected to the British Parliament. As a matter of Sinn Fein policy she refused to take her seat and sat in the Dail instead.

With the executions of Connolly and Pearse, control of the Volunteers fell to Eamon de Valera. He was totally opposed to women as fighters, and under him they were relegated to a subsidiary role to the Volunteers. However, it has to be said that some women refused to accept de Valera's strict interpretation of their role. They continued to carry arms, ammunition and dispatches, and engaged in intelligence work. The women of the Cumann obtained safe houses for men on the run, looked after the wounded, attended to the needs of prisoners and collected funds for the prisoners and their dependents. They also disrupted British recruitment drives prior to the end of World War I.

Linda Kearns, though not a member of Cumann na mBan, was a member of Sinn Fein. She acted as a courier for Michael Collins. At the height of the War for Independence she bought a car, and this she used for the transport of guns from one IRA brigade to another. In her witness statement submitted to the Bureau of Military History (entered under her married name, Mrs. Linda McWhinney), she recalled that on 20 November she transported guns captured by the Volunteers at the Cliffoney/Moneygold ambush in which three RIC men, Sergeant Perry and Constables Keon and Lafferty, had been killed and Constable Lynch mortally wounded. With her were three IRA men, Jim Devins, in command, Eugene

A Cuman na mBan protest outside Kilmainham Jail.

Gilbride and Andy Conway. At 11:30 A.M. as they drove through Sligo and back out into the countryside, they were stopped by a large party of Auxiliaries who searched the car. The arms were discovered and recognized as the arms captured at Cliffony: 10 rifles, a Webley revolver, 2 police belts, a police pouch, a haversack, 2 bandoliers, a Maxim gun belt, 328 rounds of ammunition and some automatic pistol ammunition. The four were driven back to Sligo RIC Barracks, where they were badly beaten up, Kearns included. She was then separated from the men. The Auxiliaries promised her that if she revealed where she was going and who she was going to meet, she would be released. She refused. The Auxiliaries then left, and the RIC took over: "[T]he RIC took me on again.... [A] notorious fellow ... gave me a bad time. He beat me about the head and chest and broke one of my front teeth. A real Cockney Black and Tan who was among them protested. After this, they put me in the mortuary ... and locked me up."

A few days later the four Republican prisoners were put aboard a Royal Navy destroyer and taken to Ulster, where Kearns was imprisoned in Derry Jail. On 11 March 1921 she was sentenced to ten years of penal servitude and put on board a boat for Liverpool to serve out her sentence in Waltham Prison. On 14 September 1921, she was sent back to Ireland to serve her sentence at Mountjoy Prison. From here, on 31 October, with IRA help, she, along with Miss Coyle, Miss Burke and Miss Keogh, succeeded in escaping by using a rope ladder thrown over the wall of the prison yard. During the later civil war she took the Republican side, and later joined de Valera's Fianna Fail Party. She fell out with de Valera, however, in 1936 over the party's new laws that affected women's rights regarding work. One of the "Splendid Women" had returned to her roots.

R.M. Fox, in his *History of the Irish Citizen Army*, lists the ICA women who were on active service after 1916, by which we may construe they were actually in arms, given the past history of the army.

WOMEN ON ACTIVE SERVICE AFTER 1916

Name	*Length of Service*	*Posts*
Byrne, Mrs. (Colgan)	1918–23	Barry's; Hammam
Caffrey, Mrs. (Kelly)	1918–22	
Cahill, Mrs. (Byrne)	1918–23	Hughes Hotel
Colgan, Mrs. (Phelan)	1918–23	Barry's; Hammam
Collins, Mrs. (Flinter)	1918–23	Barry's; Hammam
Creegan, Mrs. (Cahill)	1918–23	Barry's; Hammam
Crothers, Mrs. (Hunter)	1918–23	Barry's; Hammam
Cunningham, Marie	1918–23	General Service, South Co. Dublin
Douglas, Mrs. (Gethings)	1918–23	Barry's; Hammam
Gethings, Mrs.	1918–23	Barry's; Hammam
Grimley, Mrs. (Gethings)	1918–20	
Hanlon, Mrs.	1918–23	Barry's; Hammam
Kavanagh, Mrs. (Colgan)	1918–23	Barry's; Hammam
Kearney, Mrs. (Burke)	1920–23	General Service, South Co. Dublin
Lyons, Mrs. (Ashmore)	1918–23	Carlisle Buildings; Hammam
O'Curran, Mrs. Mary	1921–23	General Services South Co. Dublin
O'Shea, Molly	1918–23	Hammam
Shanahan, Lilly	1918–23	Hammam
Solan, Mrs. (Kelly)	1918–23	Hammam
Solan, Mrs. (McKay)	1918–23	Hammam

8

Guerrilla Warfare

Freedom will never come without a revolution, but I fear Irish people are too soft for that. To have a real revolution, you must have bloody-minded fierce men, who do not care a scrap for death or bloodshed. A revolution is not a job for children, or for saints and scholars. In the course of revolution, any man, woman or child who is not with you is against you. Shoot them and be damned to them. — Richard Mulcahy, Military Chief of Staff, IRA

These are the terrible words, quoted in *Survivors* by an old man who heard them spoken, the words of a man once considered to be quiet of nature. The War for Independence, a war that need not have been fought if Britain had acceded to the democratic wishes of the Irish people, lasted for two and a half years. It resulted in the deaths of 1,300 people, 1,000 of whom were civilians. This leaves a figure of just 300 combatants killed. It hardly seems enough to have forced Great Britain to the negotiating table. The truth of the matter is that it did not. The war ended because of opposition at home in Great Britain.

The Volunteers, when they embarked on war, had no overall plan dictated by GHQ, and in fact they acted independently of a centralized control until quite late in the war. The very democratic nature of the Volunteer organization, and the fragmented communications between GHQ and the brigades in the early days, meant that local groups largely acted upon their own initiative. They had moved away from the concept of a general rising throughout the country, as envisaged in the 1916 Rising. The Irish Volunteers, now increasingly known as the Irish Republican Army (IRA) adopted guerrilla warfare to achieve their ends. This change evolved in response to British activity, coupled with the need to acquire arms.

The Anglo-Irish War was a typical guerrilla war. It followed what we now perceive as a predictable pattern, which divides up into four progressive stages:

1. 1919–20: Attacks on RIC patrols in order to acquire arms and ammunition.
2. 1920–21: Attacks on RIC barracks (a) to acquire arms; (b) to capture and destroy those barracks, obliging the paramilitary police to withdraw from the area. This denied intelligence gathering by the police. It also gave the IRA the freedom to maneuver within the "captured" area and for resting its soldiers;
3. 1920–21: The establishment of flying columns. Originally brought together for individual operations against the enemy, the original company-based columns were afterwards stood down. With men forced to go on the run, they formed permanent company flying columns from June 1920 onwards. The preferred size of the column was around twenty to thirty men. For larger operations, company

columns often collaborated. This led to brigade flying columns, drawing men from the various companies, moving about, and operating within the brigade area. With the formation of divisions, notably in the south and southwest of Ireland, the various county brigade columns were brought together to form larger columns comprising several hundred experienced fighters. When fighting on its terms, this permanent small mobile army in the field was able to take on equal and superior numerical forces and defeat them.

4. 1921: Isolating the enemy. Larger flying columns drove the British from the countryside back into the towns and cities. At night these garrisoned towns were isolated from other British garrisons. The IRA then made probing assaults, often taking over these towns for several hours, opening fire on police and army barracks before withdrawing.

The final stage of winning the war, interrupted by the truce, would have been capturing of these isolated British-occupied towns and cities (the importation of arms permitting), forcing the British back on Dublin, and negotiating for peace.

Tom Barry, the most successful of the Irish guerrilla leaders.

Ernie O'Malley's literary masterpiece, On Another Man's Wound, *an account of his part in the war, became a best seller.*

British Counterinsurgency, 1919-20

The British Army for its part was faced with a form of warfare completely new to it, and for which the experience and training of its personnel in conventional warfare was of little value. Initially it attempted to fight a small war by using big-war methods, as happened later with the Americans in Vietnam. In November 1919 Lord French, the British commander in Ireland, had 34 battalions (37,259 soldiers) under his command. He believed that to subdue Ireland he would require 36 battalions. At the end of World War I, with the defeat of Germany and its allies, Lord French might have expected reinforcements; but instead the wartime army, mainly made up of conscripts, was being reduced through demobilization. Britain also had other imperial and international commitments, which precluded, temporarily, additional troops being sent to Ireland. So as an alternative French was forced to enlarge the RIC with non-Irish recruits. In creating an additional police force French had turned a military campaign into a police action. This was in line with Lloyd George's insistence that "you do not declare war on rebels," the premise being that to have used the army gave credence to the IRA as a military force, whereas by using the police, the IRA were criminalized. This meant, however, that the military became a subsidiary to the police and never got a free hand. Authority, confusingly, was divided between police and army.

Under the new regime General Tudor, as the newly appointed head of the police force, was given freedom of action. As a soldier he brought military ideas to the problem. He concentrated the police in strategic areas. Before his time barracks had been abandoned because they had small garrisons and could not be defended. Tudor reopened barracks in dangerous locations and strengthened the physical buildings and the size of the garrisons. He rearmed the police with modern rifles and issued Lewis guns and hand grenades. Tudor equipped the police with up-to-date motor transport: Lancia armored cars and Crossley tenders. As the ambush of vehicles became more pronounced a light-weight bulletproof armor, manufactured by Thorneycroft's, was fitted to vehicles, and wire-cages were fitted on top of open trucks.

The existing intelligence system was defective. It consisted of three separate, independent, organizations; the Dublin Metropolitan Police Detective Department, the Royal Irish Constabulary Crime Branch, the Dublin Military District and General Headquarters Intelligence Branches. Tudor merged the first two organizations to produce a more up-to-date intelligence system under chief of staff Colonel Ormonde Winter. The problem was not entirely resolved however as the military intelligence staff, though supplying information to the police, remained independent. Their methods of operation were at odds. The police leaned towards decentralization, leaving much to local judgment and initiative. The military preferred a centralized policy but had no experience of guerrilla warfare so was inclined towards large sweeping operations. The introduction of martial law in some parts of the country changed the balance from police to army, but the civil administration, the basic law of the land, acted as a check. So at no point did either police or army have a completely free hand, though this did not stop atrocities against the general public by both bodies.

By 1921 the regenerated Irish police force (RIC and Black and Tans) numbered 17,000. The Auxiliaries numbered 2,200, and regular British Army troops in Ireland numbered over 50,000. In addition in August 1920, the Ulster Special Constabulary was raised. This controversial force, tainted by religious bigotry, and independent from the RIC, was raised from the Ulster Defense Force. It was divided into the A Specials (a full-time force) and the B and C Specials (who were part-time) who policed Ulster, thus freeing up security forces to police other parts of Ireland.

What the British military authorities most wanted was to bring about another rising in Ireland, which, like the Dublin Rising of 1916, they could put down and destroy the IRA in the process. What they got instead was a guerrilla war. The introduction of permanent flying columns provided a force that could be destroyed if located, as opposed to the original will-o-the-wisp columns that after engaging in an action were stood down. The problem that beset the British was where a flying column came from before the action and where it went afterwards.

The British response was to send a strong force of military and paramilitary police to overwhelm the column by superior numbers and arms, in an encirclement of the locality where an action had taken place. They then gradually closed the circle to trap, with the intention of bringing the column to battle and annihilating it. Immediately after an engagement, however, the column invariably took evasive action to avoid such encirclement, marching anywhere up to fifteen miles across the fields away from the scene. The men of the local Volunteer company, who acted in a subsidiary role to the flying column digging trenches, felling trees, or providing cover against enemy reinforcements when the column was in action, then acted as scouts, taking the flying column safely out of the danger area before they themselves disbanded to return to their homes and jobs. The very large numbers of British forces employed in an encirclement mitigated against them. Coordinating such a force took time. The very terrain, chosen by the flying column, usually bog land or mountains, meant that part of the encircling force inevitably moved slower than other sections, thus allowing a gap in the encirclement that the column, if it was still in the area, could slip through.

The column was at its most vulnerable when it was being rested. Due to the numbers that made up a column, it was rare for its members to rest or eat as a whole unit. Column members were distributed over a fairly wide area when seeking food and sleeping accommodation. Such facilities had to be obtained from many widely separated houses and cottages. Thus broken up into smaller units there was always the danger of being isolated and captured by raiding parties. To a degree this problem was solved by the local Volunteer companies in whose territory they moved. They, with the assistance of the Cumann na mBan (the Women's Movement), provided accommodation and food and stood guard to protect the resting column. A designated assembly point was usually nominated for the re-forming of the column should danger present itself.

As early as 1918, Lord French, recognizing that he lacked sufficient trained troops to

Lord French (foreground left), commander in chief of British forces in Ireland.

carry out his plans, considered using aircraft to detect Volunteer units in the field. Lieutenant-General Sir Frederick Shaw carried out a feasibility study on his behalf. Shaw came up with the proposal of establishing "Entrenched Air Camps" from which the country could be policed. The effective operational radius of fighter aircraft at that time would have required the establishment of one squadron in each province. At that time this would have required the addition of three extra squadrons to the one already in Ireland. The proposal was discussed at a meeting of the military council in August 1918, where ideas on the best use of airplanes was discussed. The obvious answer was in bombing and machine-gunning from the air. The argument against this was in recognizing armed insurgents from groups of people going about their daily business. To operate this scheme the civilian population would have to be removed, as in South Africa, and placed in concentration camps. This would then have left a free-fire zone, making a target of anyone within the cleared area. Airplanes could then have been used against columns on the march, but they would have been effective only on level ground and ground without cover. To avoid such aerial attacks the guerrillas would invariably carry out marches at night. This by and large negated any superiority gained by aerial power.

Progressing the War

In Ireland the key to any successful war against the British was to remove the eyes and ears of its intelligence source — the RIC. Towards the end of 1919 the chief of staff of the Irish Republican Army, Richard Mulcahy, began summoning three regional commandants from different areas of the country every fortnight; he instructed them to select one police barracks in their area and attack it within the month. These attacks began in January 1920. So successful were they that in April 1920 the RIC were withdrawn from all rural areas, leaving great swathes of the country in Republican hands. Of the 1,299 RIC barracks throughout Ireland, 434 were abandoned. They were later burned by the Volunteers that Easter, along with 22 regional tax offices. What this showed the British was the organizational ability of the IRA. Practically no income tax was collected from then on. County councils refused to help surveyors to assess tax, and later in the cities, corporations also refused to give any information. By the summer of 1920 the IRA had successfully attacked over 351 vacated police barracks, along with 15 occupied ones. From 8 May the British began fortifying the remaining police barracks with steel shutters over windows, cutting of loopholes and laying barbed wire entanglements around the building. "Defence of Barracks Sergeants," 33 in number, were recruited to instruct the police in the defense of their barracks. They were paid £7 a week, a not insubstantial salary for a workingman in those days.

Once the police had been removed the Dail put in its own police and courts. With attacks by the IRA and their boycott by the people, there was considerable disillusionment among the members of the RIC, and this manifested itself in mass resignation. Unable to replace these men in Ireland, junior minister Walter Long proposed the recruitment of non–Irishmen into the RIC, as mentioned above. Lord French agreed that English ex-soldiers should be appointed. Recruiting offices were set up in London, Liverpool, Glasgow and Dublin in late 1919. Because of their makeshift uniform, half police and half army, this new force became known as the Black and Tans, taking their name from a local hunt in Munster.

They were paid ten shillings a day and first arrived in Ireland on 25 March 1920. In July 1920 ex–British Army officers were recruited as the Auxiliary Division of the RIC, and designated as Temporary Cadets. Though nominally part of the RIC both of these new divisions lacked the discipline of the old RIC and soon developed an odious reputation for looting, torture and murder. In his biography, *Ireland For Ever,* even their commander, Brigadier-General F.P. Crozier, admitted his horror at what was done by his men: "Never before had the R.I.C. been used so ruthlessly and at times surreptitiously, to destroy and create a new note of anguish in the country."[1]

The Restoration of Order in Ireland Act continued and extended the emergency powers created by the wartime Defence of the Realm Act (DORA), but coupled to an ill-disciplined paramilitary police force the British security policy in Ireland alienated the civilian population without suppressing IRA activity. The guerrilla tactics carried out by the Volunteers kept the British forces under a perpetual nervous strain. This type of warfare was beyond anything they had previously experienced. For the most part they were men who had fought in the trenches. Their thinking was trench-warfare thinking. The British forces, army and paramilitaries, were permanently on the back-foot; reactive rather than proactive in combat situations, save for massive encirclements, which only rarely met with any success. The security forces were always aware that an ambush could happen at any time. Their one advantage was speed through mechanized transport, but quickly realizing this, the IRA negated this advantage: "Enemy movement was prevented or restricted by continually potholing the road, digging holes in it at intervals, or by trenching and then covering the openings with soft earth so that an unsuspecting lorry would dash in. Trenches might be left open, then they had to be filled in by the British before an advance could be made. Walls were torn down and spread over a large area or piled up in cuttings where it would be more difficult to remove the stones. Heavy trees were felled across the road, barbed wire wound around them and kept in position with staples to prevent or retard the use of cross-cuts [by saws]. Our snipers delayed convoys or raiding parties; they had to get down to attempt to outflank the attackers. The enemy moved more cautiously; raiding parties increased in strength, but night raids, save in towns and villages, were less frequent."[2]

Local county councils that had given allegiance to the Dail no longer employed men to repair roads. So the British responded by rounding up men, where they could find them, to fill in the trenches and remove obstacles. British troop convoys were then equipped with small cranes, saws and ropes, to remove obstacles. The danger was that such obstacles might also conceal an ambush.

British Army Counterinsurgency, 1920-21

In April 1921 Lord French, in an interview with the *Daily Mirror,* admitted that the Volunteers were an army, "properly organized in regiment and brigade, led by disciplined officers." They had taken the initiative and were confronting the occupation forces with new and unexpected tactics to the point that those forces were now on the offensive. What was required was more robust action. This became possible with the proclaiming of martial law in parts of south and southwest Ireland, turning a policing action into a military action. Given a free hand, free from the restraints of habeas corpus, the British Army embarked on a more ruthless campaign against the IRA. Still fighting a small war with big-war methods, a major rethink was required based upon the experiences of two years of fighting the IRA. Major A.E. Percival, of the Essex Regiment, based in County Cork, drew up some proposals:

1. Training of Troops

A guerrilla war of this nature demands a very high state of training on the part of the troops. The majority of operations are carried out in small parties and a great many of them at night. Individuality in the N.C.O. and Private Soldier is, therefore of great value. In this regard the whole Army was seriously handicapped in 1920-21, as a very large proportion of the men in the ranks were youngsters of two or three years' service, or even less. The work from the Private Soldier's point of view was very arduous, as escorts were constantly being called for.

A large number of raids and searches carried out were naturally unsuccessful, and in these conditions, there was a great danger of the troops becoming tired and slack. To avoid this, we decided to try and make them interested in the proceedings which we did by means of lectures and talks on local I.R.A. celebrities etc. We also encouraged them to bring in any information they might pick up. The result was extremely good, as the troops, almost without exception, became very keen on the work and took a great interest in everything that was done.

Of course, the work there was excellent training for young troops, as they always had to be very much alert to prevent being surprised — especially when they were on sentry duty.

Their chief failing was in the lack of Musketry training they had received. In this type of warfare targets are few and fleeting. I think those who have tried it will agree that it is no easy matter to hit a single man running fast and across country, especially when you have often to run some distance yourself. Troops taking part in such warfare should have very thorough musketry training as each individual man really becomes a sniper.

2. Use of Arms Other Than Infantry

Artillery: We had no experience of it. I do not consider, however that there is any scope for the use of artillery in warfare of this nature, unless the rebels form themselves into larger bodies than they did in Ireland. As it was, there were really no targets upon which artillery could fire.

Tanks: these were too slow moving and too noisy to be of much use in the very open warfare of the South of Ireland. They might, perhaps, be useful in large cities for clearing streets, or taking on rebel strongholds such as the Four Courts.

Armored Cars: Two types of armored cars were used — the heavy and slow Peerless, and the fast Rolls Royce. Both were very useful.

- (i) The Peerless. This was used chiefly to economize manpower in escorts, etc. It was suitable to accompany three-ton lorry convoys, and also for local work, e.g., mail escort to the station, escort for officers drawing pay, ration parties, etc. It was a mistake to send Crossley cars with Peerless AC, as the reduced speed of the latter caused a heavy strain on the axles of the Crossleys.
- (ii) The Rolls Royce. The chief uses of this were:
  - (a) To escort Crossley cars or Sunbeam touring cars. In this way they were usually employed when Brigade Commanders or staff officers wanted to make a tour of the Brigade area.
  - (b) For offensive operations. They were used with great success for sudden descents on given areas in towns, or on outlying country villages, when the state of the road permitted. Owing to their speed and quiet running they were particularly suitable for this work. They carried a crew of four and were armed with a Vickers Gun. A Hotchkiss gun was often carried also, as a reserve and for use if the AC broke down.

Aeroplanes: Owing to the shortage of landing grounds these were little used. It is doubtful whether an airman can see much in a country of this nature, but he should, I think, be able to reconnoiter roads and report whether they are trenched or blocked. Also if an ambush is reported in a definite locality the RAF could be asked to make a reconnaissance of that locality.

IRA suspects rounded up by the Essex Regiment in Bandon, County Cork (courtesy the Imperial War Museum).

3. Suggested Future Tactics

As far as I know, no official book has been published on the subject of guerrilla warfare, such as we had in Ireland, but I will give my own ideas on the best tactics to be pursued should such conditions recur.

The question appears to resolve itself into the rival claims of the Block-House system, such as was adopted in South Africa, and the Mobile Column system.

The possibility of building blockhouses was often discussed in 1921, but we reckoned then that to work any block-house system, we would require a great many more troops than there were at the time in the whole of Ireland. The country is so thick and intricate that it would be impossible to stop small parties of men getting through unless the block-houses were very close together. On the other hand, if sufficient men were available, a line of temporary posts or "stops" along the edge of the area being worked by the Mobile Column, would, I think, be of great assistance, as they would restrict the area of maneuvers at the disposal of the enemy. In our area, for example, these might have been placed along the lines of the Bandon river while the mobile columns were working to the south of it.

British troops crossing a trench dug by the IRA. Such disruptions hampered the speedy movement of troops (courtesy the Imperial War Museum).

> In either case, whether blockhouses are established or not, offensive action must be taken and this can best be done with a number of mobile columns moving about the country and mutually co-operating with each other."

Lacking the men for a block-house system, the British Army formed their own flying columns to engage the Republicans in ambush and destroy them. Ernie O'Malley commented: "Enemy columns wearing civilian clothes and equipped somewhat like our columns, or in full war kit with helios [heliographs] for signaling and blood hounds for tracking, had been moving through parts of Tipperary and Kilkenny. They slept during the day, usually, and tramped into the night. Another column might try to pass itself off as one of our own from an outside area."[3]

In response to the British use of flying columns, and the use of thousands of troops in ever-larger encirclements, the IRA brigades reverted to using smaller flying columns (of about thirty men), to avoid roundups. These columns, though, could expand into larger fighting units by drawing upon men from their own brigade and other brigades, for nighttime assaults on enemy occupied towns.

The war fought by the Volunteers was originally on a county by county basis. Initially each IRA brigade operated as a separate entity. This meant that the British could not concentrate their soldiers in just one part of the country. Unfortunately for IRA headquarters, some parts of the country were not as active as others. There were two reasons for this; not every county was ideal guerrilla country, and some brigade officers were plainly unfitted for their office. As the war progressed, though, there was greater liaison between the IRA brigades, eventually leading to regional divisions consisting of several county brigades comprising several thousand men — in effect, small armies. This meant that hitherto passive counties now went on the offensive. Great swathes of the country were cleared of Crown forces. The British were forced back to the cities and towns, leaving the countryside to the IRA. In that the IRA did not physically hold ground, this is not perhaps fully understood nor appreciated until one realizes the number of RIC barracks that were captured or forced to close. At the time of the truce, the British were, due to their imperial and international commitments, unable to bring fresh troops in, and contrary to popular misconception, the Volunteers, though still lacking the heavy arms to achieve complete victory, were on the offensive in several counties.

9

1919: The War Begins

On 21 January 1919, with the killing of two policemen at Soloheadbeg in County Tipperary, the war for Irish independence began. Up until that point there was no GHQ policy on how a war should be prosecuted. The raison d'être for the Volunteers, existence was that they should exist as a threat. The action at Soloheadbeg changed all that. By the end of 1919 sixteen policemen and soldiers had died.

The War in Cork

The Volunteer situation in County Cork was typical of the pre–Soloheadbeg situation across the country. At the end of World War I they had been reorganized under the direction of Tomas MacCurtain, the brigade commandant. Twenty battalions with an average of 8 companies each, a total strength of about 8,000 men, made up the brigade. At the beginning of 1919 the brigade was split into three separate more manageable brigades under Tomas MacCurtain (No. 1), Liam Lynch (No. 2) and Tom Hales (No. 3). In April 1919 representation was made to GHQ in Dublin for arms. All they got were a few revolvers, ideal for urban terrorism but no good for guerrilla warfare. It became clear to the Cork brigades that if they were to prosecute a war of any sort, they would have to arm themselves by their own ability. Raids had already taken place in parts of Cork, particularly in the 3 (West Cork) Brigade area where rifles had been captured from the RIC. Again though, there was no GHQ policy on the acquisition of arms. Without such a lead, responsibility by default fell on each brigade. Liam Lynch, commanding No. 2 Brigade, was approached in April 1919 by Con Liddy, officer in command of Araglin Company, with a view to raiding Araglin RIC Barracks. Lynch made an inspection and obtained sanction from GHQ to go ahead. On Sunday morning, 20 April 1919, when three of the four RIC men from the barracks were at Mass, a party of seven Volunteers approached the building from the rear. When the remaining constable unlocked the door to get a pail of water from outside, he was held up by the Volunteers. Surprised, he took to his heels. The Volunteers dashed inside and cleared the barracks of all arms, ammunition, equipment and papers before escaping.

At Kilbrittain, which lay in No. 3 West Cork Brigade's area, the local RIC police station was reinforced by a further 60 to 80 British soldiers, based half a mile away at the Castle. They were linked by telephone. The two bodies acted in close conjunction, the police supplying the intelligence and the army acting upon it to virtually close down any

From such unpromising material as the lads of the Clonmult IRA Unit emerged one of the most effective guerrilla armies of the 20th century (courtesy Cork City and County Archives).

operations by the local Volunteers. Armed cycle patrols acted by day and foot patrols operated at night. Soon a regular pattern emerged, which was noted by Volunteer intelligence officers. A night patrol, usually five soldiers armed with rifles under the command of an NCO and a policeman armed with a revolver, left the Castle at dusk and proceeded towards Burren Pier. On the night of 16 June fourteen Volunteers rendezvoused at Rathclarin, along the route that the soldiers would take. Two of them were ordered to the front and rear to prevent any of the soldiers from escaping. The remaining twelve, none of them armed, were detailed to attack the Crown forces. They would have the element of surprise on their side, but if anything went wrong, they knew that they might be killed. The soldiers and police arrived at a junction in the road, and as they debated which route to take, the Volunteers pounced on them. In a short but vicious struggle the policeman and four of the soldiers were disarmed. The fifth broke free and succeeded in striking one of his attackers with the butt of his rifle before he too was overpowered. The soldiers and the policeman were tied up. The captured rifles and one revolver, along with 200 rounds and equipment, were carried off and hidden for future use. The difference between this and other ambushes was that prior to the attack at Rathclarin assaults had been mainly directed against the RIC. Now the war had stepped up a gear, and attacks were to be conducted against the British Army itself.

With the extension of guerrilla warfare against the British Army training in tactics and an exchange of information became essential. The West Cork Brigade organized a course to coincide with the annual Gaelic League Irish Course for National Teachers at Shorecliffe House, Glandore, over the week of 9–16 August 1919. GHQ in Dublin sent specialists, including Dick McKee, the director of training, and commandant of the Dublin Brigade, to instruct the class. They were taught how to conduct successful guerrilla attacks, how to prepare explosives, how to move in extended order, at the double, and while crawling, and the use of signaling, scouting and intelligence gathering. Perhaps more important, they learned confidence in their own ability to lead and train others. What came out of the training course was that the survival of the column was paramount. In an attack, provision must first and foremost be made for an evacuation of the column. Targets should be attacked only when there was a high probability of success. Any engagements with the enemy should be broken off if there was a danger of the column's being surrounded by a relieving force. Without the column there was no fighting force, and without a fighting force there could be no war.

At the end of April, prior to the training course at Glandore, Liam Lynch had gone to Dublin to put forward the case for increased activity in his area. While he received sanction to do so, and to coordinate activities with other brigades, he was instructed that there should be no casualties. Lynch came away with the impression that GHQ were not fully aware of the type of war that they were now fighting. Headquarters for their part were very aware of the negative publicity that would be engendered if police or military personnel were killed. The British propaganda machine would portray it as murder to the world, and in particular in the United States, where much support for Irish independence was drawn. Nevertheless, with the necessary sanction Lynch proposed to strike at the most powerful stronghold in his brigade area, Fermoy Barracks, in his search for arms. This was a British Army barracks, and heavily defended. Subsequent intelligence indicated that an attack on the barracks itself need not be launched. Another possibility for gaining arms had presented itself. Every Sunday an armed party of British soldiers attended a service at the nearby Wesleyan church. On Sunday morning, 7 September 1919, fourteen soldiers of the Royal Shropshire Light Infantry, with a corporal in charge, left their barracks and proceeded the half mile to the church. On that Sunday, waiting around the church were about twenty-five Volunteers. They had just six serviceable revolvers among them. The others carried short clubs concealed up their coat sleeves. Volunteer Larry Condon was in charge of the main party. The remainder were ordered to close in from the rear to prevent the British soldiers from escaping back to their barracks once the attack had begun. Three cars were provided to take away the captured arms.

Though the Fermoy Company supplied the most men, Lynch brought in capable men from other companies, including four from Mallow, five from Ballynoe and two from the Waterford Brigade. As the British soldiers approached the church Lynch blew a whistle and the Volunteers moved in. He called upon the soldiers to surrender, but they prepared to resist. Shots were exchanged, and it came to hand to hand fighting. Surprised as they were by the ambush, the soldiers fought back, but they were eventually overpowered. One soldier was killed and two injured. Lynch was himself wounded in the shoulder by a British bullet. The soldiers' rifles and ammunition pouches were seized and carried off. Within five minutes of the first shots being fired, two trucks full of British reinforcements from the barracks advanced on the town. This eventuality had been foreseen, and two roadside trees were felled to prevent the British troops from following the escaping Volunteers, who got away. The next night two hundred British soldiers and police, including soldiers from the East Kent Regiment, ran amok in the town as a reprisal, breaking windows and doors and looting and burning commercial premises. The day after that the district was proclaimed a martial area, subject to military rule.

Over in the west, the Bantry Company of Cork No. 3 Brigade carried out an audacious adventure in their search for arms. Two naval sloops regularly plied between Bantry and Bere Island, taking provisions and mail to the garrison there. They were well-manned and, it was believed, well armed with rifles and revolvers. The ships tied up at the new pier, not far from the town square, which was named in honor of Wolfe Tone, the late 18th century Republican leader. With 200 soldiers of the King's Liverpool Regiment garrisoned barely 300 yards away in the old Workhouse, and an RIC barracks of 15 men in the town, the captains of the ships felt quite safe. The local Volunteers collected sufficient information regarding the ships and their crews and the probable location of the ships' arsenals. On 15 November one of the two ships tied up at the new pier for the weekend. Most of the crew went ashore. The next evening, twelve Volunteers led by Ralph Keyes, the captain of the company, approached the sloop M.L. 171. While four remained on guard, the other eight boarded her. One of the Volunteers, Maurice Donegan, closed the forward hatch on the few sailors aboard and warned them that if they made a noise he would throw a bomb down on them. The armory was located, and the local blacksmith, Volunteer John Teahan, broke down the door with a sledgehammer. In the room were six Ross-Canadian rifles and two heavy black boxes. As the munitions were being removed an incident nearby drew attention away from the pier. A drunken man fell into Bantry Bay. While all attention was drawn towards his plight, the munitions were got away to safety. The black boxes contained four .45 revolvers, two Verey pistols and a quantity of ammunition.

As 1919 came to an end, Cork was under martial law, and there was a nighttime curfew. The names of occupants had to be posted up on the inside of the door of each house. As night fell, intelligence-led operations were carried out against known Volunteers. In west Cork in the town of Kilbrittain, these were led by an RIC police sergeant. Volunteers who were arrested were roughly treated as the result of his actions. The sergeant was identified and warned that he would be killed if he continued. He sought the protection of the British military and continued his work. To have let him continue risked the breakup of the local Volunteer column. It was decided that he must be killed. Normally he only ventured outside the barracks in company of the military. Continual observation of this intelligence officer showed that occasionally, and at irregular times, he would cross the road in the company of another RIC sergeant and go for a drink in the local public house. For sixteen nights a small party of Volunteers waited for him. On 15 December he appeared out on the street and was shot dead.

The War in Tipperary, Limerick, Waterford, Wexford and Kilkenny

In Limerick careful watch was kept by the RIC on illegal drilling by the Volunteers. Names were taken by the police, leading later to arrests. One was that of Robert Byrnes, soon to become adjutant of the Limerick City Second Battalion. On 13 January 1919, a British court-martial sentenced him to twelve months imprisonment with hard labor. In prison, he and the other arrested Volunteers demanded political status, which was denied to them. In response they went on a hunger strike. After three weeks some of the Volunteers were in a very weak state, including Byrnes, who was transferred to the Limerick Union Infirmary. To prevent him from escaping, two armed guards, Constables O'Brien and

Spillane, were instructed to stay with him. Elsewhere within the hospital were three other RIC men, Sergeant J.F. Goulden, Constables J. Tierney and J. Fitzpatrick, and a warder, John Mahoney. Despite the heavy guard, IRA commandant Peader Dunne decided to rescue Byrnes. The plan was to flood the ward with twenty-four Volunteers posing as visitors, and at the appropriate time overpower all the policemen and escape with Byrnes. Such was the scarcity of arms that only one revolver was available. Section Leader Mick Stack of E Company was put in charge of the operation. On Sunday, 6 April, the Volunteers entered the hospital singly or in twos. Outside a horse-drawn mourning coach, complete with a change of clothes for Byrnes, awaited to whisk him away. As they were prepared for such a rescue attempt, the police had orders to shoot Byrnes rather than let him escape.

Exactly at three o'clock one of the rescue party, Paddy Dawson, blew a whistle. Immediately the Volunteers rushed towards Byrnes' bed in a bid to overpower the policemen. Constable O'Brien was quick to act and drew his revolver, as did Spillane. Shots rang out. Spillane lost his revolver in the struggle, then threw himself bodily across the prisoner as others grappled with the other policemen who had run into the room. Batty shot Spillane, who was trying to strangle Byrnes. Then he shot the burly Constable O'Brien. With assistance, Byrne was helped out of the bed and towards the door of the ward. Down the steps they proceeded, only to discover that the mourning coach had been taken to the back of the hospital. As they attempted an escape on foot, they commandeered a horse and trap. Only then did they discover that in the initial shooting Byrnes had been shot. That night at 8:30 P.M. at Knocklisheen, three miles from the Workhouse Infirmary, Byrnes died of his wound. Constable O'Brien was also dead, and Constable Spillane lay in the hospital seriously wounded. Immediately the British sprang into action in a bid to capture the Volunteers. Patrols scoured the city and its environs. People were arrested and questioned. On the following day a detachment of the Scottish Horse arrived at the house at Knocklisheen and there discovered Byrnes' body. Later the body was handed over to his relatives for burial. Thousands lined the route for his funeral, as did the police and soldiers of the British Army. As the coffin passed the military guard outside William Street RIC Barracks, they presented arms in salute in respect to the dead Irish soldier. The war was still young, and there was still a place for such chivalry.

Knocklong Station

Following the ambush at Soloheadbeg in which two constables were killed, a reward of £10,000 was offered for information leading to the capture of those involved. On 12 May 1919, Sean Hogan, one of those involved, was arrested. At first the police were unsure who they had captured, but they eventually put a name to the face. As news of his capture spread, the other three wanted men, Sean Treacy, Dan Breen and Seamus Robinson, resolved to rescue him. An attack on the barracks at Thurles, where Hogan was imprisoned, was impossible; but Treacy knew that Hogan would be taken, most probably by train, to Cork, where men arrested under DORA stood trial. Plans were discussed as to where the rescue attempt could be made, and the men eventually decided on Knocklong Station. Five Volunteers from the Galbally Company, Eamonn O'Brien and his brother John Joe, Jim Scanlon, Edward Foley and Sean Lynch, agreed to help in the rescue.

On 13 May, Treacy, Breen and Robinson boarded the Dublin to Cork train at Emly, but Hogan was not aboard. They got off and made plans to meet the next train at Knocklong, due to arrive at 8:00 P.M. The plan was revised. Four of the Galbally men cycled over to Emly, where they boarded the train. Hogan was aboard, handcuffed between Sergeant Wallace and Constable Enright, both armed with revolvers. Opposite them were Constables Reilly and Ring armed with carbines. At Knocklong Station the other would-be rescuers waited. Shortly before the train arrived, the Cork to Dublin train pulled into the station. It had a carriage full of armed soldiers, and in another were a party of RIC men from Galbally, who got off there. Eventually the train moved off, barely two minutes before the Cork-bound train arrived. As it stopped, John Joe O'Brien leaped from the train and indicated that Hogan was aboard, and in which carriage. Treacy and O'Brien, revolvers in hand, boarded the train, and passing down the corridor, arrived at the carriage. They slid the door to one side and ordered the policemen to put their hands up. Sergeant Wallace and three of the constables complied, but the fourth, Constable Enright, drew his revolver and placed it at Hogan's neck. Treacy and O'Brien reacted very quickly and fired at Enright, who was killed instantly, shot through the heart. Sergeant Wallace lunged at Treacy, and a struggle ensued. Hogan, still handcuffed, lunged at Ring, who was about to join the struggle. Constable Reilly leaped on John Joe O'Brien's back. In the struggle Wallace fired at Treacy, grazing his throat. At this point Breen and Robinson arrived. Constable Reilly, who somehow got out of the carriage and onto the platform, saw Breen and opened fire. Breen was hit through one of his lungs and through his right arm, but picking up his revolver from where he had dropped it, he began firing at Reilly using his left hand. Under the furious fusillade, Reilly fell back. Hogan was rescued. He was taken to a nearby butcher's shop and his handcuffs were smashed open. With two wounded comrades, the rescued and rescuers fled the scene. Dr. Hennessy of Ballylanders attended to Breen and Treacy, who were later got away to safety.

Still desperately short of arms, a small party of men from A Company of Limerick City Battalion raided the homes of known Loyalists during the autumn and winter of 1919. They approached a house called Greene Barrys near Sheehan's Cross, only to discover that a number of British Army officers were in residence. A running fight followed, the Volunteers saved only by the officers' reluctance to follow them out into the dark for fear of ambush. No sooner had they escaped, than military forces, summoned by telephone, arrived on the scene. Republican intelligence out in the countryside was still in its infancy. A few days later B Company had more success when they held up Constables Clarke and Mulcahy of the RIC, at the junction of the Ballysimon and Patrickswell roads, and captured two carbines and ammunition. The RIC responded that night by wrecking the Thomas Ashe Sinn Fein Club at Claughaun, Pennywell.

The War in the West and Northwest

With increased Volunteer activity the local magistrates attempted to crush the revolt before it could get started. At Westport, County Mayo, resident magistrate John Milling was zealous in sending Volunteers to prison for unlawful assembly and drilling. He was warned about his activities, but continued. On 29 March 1919 he was shot dead as a warning to others. In May of that year the first Republican law court was set up at Ballinrobe, County Mayo, to replace the British system. By the end of the year resident magistrates presided over empty courts.

The War in the Irish Midlands

In April 1919, the local Volunteers in County Longford unsuccessfully attempted to disarm two RIC constables at Aughnacliffe. Two Volunteers were wounded in the attempt.

The War in the Northeast

Whereas the Volunteers in the south and west could rely upon the support of the people, great swathes of the northeast were populated by Loyalists — the same people who had raised an army to defend their link with Britain. While it is true that there was activity in South Down and South Armagh, the war waged in other provinces of the country could not by and large be waged here. The Roman Catholic population, particularly those living in Belfast enclaves surrounded by Protestant communities, were vulnerable to extreme reprisals. The focus of the Republican Volunteers in the cities was as a defense force. Nevertheless the abandonment of isolated RIC stations in late 1919 saw their destruction, as at Mountfield, County Tyrone, where the local Volunteers literally demolished it so that it could not be used again.

The Ulster Volunteer Force maintained a number of secret arms dumps throughout the province in the sure knowledge that the police would not raid them. In Dublin, Michael Collins received intelligence that one such arsenal, allegedly containing two hundred rifles and boxes of ammunition, existed in the isolated Inishowen peninsular of Donegal, a narrow neck of land commanded by the city of Derry. Ernie O'Malley, a junior officer from Volunteer GHQ in Dublin, was sent north to investigate. He was authorized to commandeer whatever support he needed from the Irish Volunteers in County Tyrone; Frank Aiken from the South Armagh Brigade was instructed to give him whatever help and assistance he required. In his autobiography, O'Malley narrates that he "attended a meeting of Ulster Volunteers in Derry hoping to get information about arms. But beyond the experience of sitting with sturdy men whom I liked and who would have given me little mercy if they found out what I really represented, I did not gain anything.... I chatted with British ex-officers."[1] Eventually he got word of the possible location of the Ulster Volunteer Force arms dump, and traveling in a convoy of cars the Irish Volunteers set off to find it. The journey proved fruitless though, and O'Malley returned to Dublin.

10

1920: The Second Year of the War

At the beginning of 1920 Lord French was given the authority to impose martial law whenever he pleased, without reference to the British cabinet in London. The army now took over the responsibility of initiating action against the "insurgents" and interning subjects under the Defence of the Realm Act 14B. French hoped that the army's increased participation in the campaign would produce quick results, but this was to prove illusory.

There was a massive roundup of Sinn Fein members and suspected Volunteers. Interned without trial in Mountjoy Prison, Dublin, these prisoners went on hungerstrike. After a time the British were compelled to release them. Throughout Ireland there were celebrations at their release. At Miltown Malbay, on 14 April, there were bonfires and rejoicing. The local RIC sergeant, a man named Hampson, called upon the British officer who commanded the fifty strong garrison of the Highland Light Infantry based there to assist him in breaking up the popular demonstration. At 9:30 that night Hampson and his men, with a detachment of soldiers, approached the celebrations. The soldiers took up kneeling or prone firing positions. Hampson ordered the dispersal of the crowd, but before they could react he fired into the crowd with his pistol. He then ordered the mixed party of soldiers and police to open fire.

In the massacre that followed, three men were shot dead and ten people were wounded, some seriously. British ex-soldiers who went to the aid of the wounded found themselves under fire. At the subsequent military enquiry, from which the public were excluded, the court found that the soldiers and police had been fired upon and had responded accordingly. A civil inquest was also held, but here the witnesses revealed that Sergeant Hampson, who had been drinking hard for several days, had fired first, the soldiers and police then fired upon the crowd. One RIC man, Constable McDonnell, who was on the patrol but who had not fired, swore that there was no violence from the crowd. Sergeant Hampson, Constables O'Connor and Keenan, Lance-Corporal McLeod, Privates Kilgon, McEwan, McLoughlin, Bunting and Adams were charged with murder without any provocation. They never stood trial. In September 1920 inquests were abolished in a number of counties, including Clare.

Volunteer GHQ in Dublin ordered the stepping up of attacks on the RIC, both their patrols and their barracks. Realizing their vulnerability, the British authorities abandoned their more isolated barracks. They concentrated their forces in the larger towns and cities and began patrolling the countryside in larger convoys, often accompanied by armored cars. The abandonment of the smaller garrisons allowed greater freedom of movement for the Volunteer flying columns in the cleared areas. The IRA attacks, as well as a boycott of the police by the people, prompted widespread resignations within the RIC, forcing the British government to recruit replacements in England. This led to the formation of the paramilitary

Auxiliaries and the infamous Black and Tans. In July 1920, British cabinet minister Winston Churchill suggested arming the UVF as a Northern Special Constabulary and using them in the south. His intention was to have a standby force if British troops in Ireland were required to return to Britain to deal with the rise of communism resulting from mass unemployment and social and industrial tensions then prevailing in Britain that threatened the very stability of the country.

The funeral of Lord Mayor Terence McSwiney passes through Cork City.

The Irish local government elections of 1920 revealed once more the democratic wish of the Irish people. Sinn Fein's results were as follows: Sinn Fein — urban councils 9, county councils 29; other parties — urban councils 2, county councils 4. Those who voted for Republican councils swore allegiance to the Dail. In response, on 29 July 1920, Dublin Castle discontinued all financial aid to these councils.

The Restoration of Order in Ireland Act brought about widespread acts of brutality on the part of the Crown forces, which resulted in a ruthless response on the part of the IRA in its dealings with the enemy, particularly the Black and Tans, who operated without a clear code of discipline, burning villages and murdering innocent civilians. During the summer of 1920, Crown forces systematically destroyed cooperative creameries, mills and bacon factories in reprisal, effectively destroying Ireland's agricultural economy. On 3 September coroners' inquests were abolished in ten counties in Ireland, and replaced by military courts of inquiry. Within the following three weeks eighteen murders of unarmed persons could be traced to Crown forces, none of whom ever faced trial for the murders. This was the price that Ireland had to pay. Terence MacSwiney, lord mayor of Cork, who succeeded Tomas MacCurtain after his murder by Crown forces, declared, "It is not those who can inflict the most, but those who can suffer the most who will conquer." Within months of his inauguration, on 12 August, MacSwiney was arrested as he presided over a meeting at the city hall. He was court-martialled on a charge of "being in possession of documents the publication of which would be likely to cause disaffection to His Majesty." He refused to accept the legality of the court, and he and the ten men arrested with him went on hunger strike in order to secure their release. On the third day of his hunger strike MacSwiney was put aboard a warship and deported to England, where he was imprisoned in Brixton Gaol, London. The prison doctor feared to force feed him in case he struggled against it and died like Thomas Ashe. On 25 October, after an incredible 61 days on his hunger strike, MacSwiney died. There was a feeling of shame in England at MacSwiney's death. Thousands of Londoners lined the route in respectful silence as his coffin, on its way back to Cork, passed through the capital's streets.

Seventeen highly placed members of Sinn Fein were murdered in October 1920 by members of the British secret service. It was revealed to Michael Collins by one of his men in Dublin

Castle that the authorities had adopted an official policy of "shooting by roster." Collins responded on 21 November by having these British agents, "The Cairo Gang," assassinated.

Politically the British sought to bring an end to the war by dividing Ireland into two states. On 11 November 1920 the Government of Ireland Act was passed in the British House of Commons. It proposed separate Home Rule parliaments for Southern Ireland and for Northern Ireland. A Council of Ireland was to be set up with members from each parliament, with a view to eventually removing the partition and reuniting the country (though the Unionists were informed that they would not be forced into a united Ireland). Both parliaments established by the act would be subject to the Westminster Parliament in London, requiring the lord lieutenant to approve all bills prepared by the two Irish parliaments. The Irish parliaments would not be allowed to make laws relating to foreign affairs, overseas trade, or the armed forces. Seeking to establish an independent republic, free of all British ties, the Dail rejected the British plan. Sinn Fein refused to attend the council.

Unable to get adequate answers to their concerns over Ireland the Labor Party instigated a commission to the country. Its findings were damning:

> There is a state of war in Ireland and what are called "outrages" and "reprisals" are but incidents in a bitter campaign. On the one hand, there are the armed forces of the Crown; on the other, the Irish Republican Army. While we wish to avoid making any general accusations against a body of men with so distinguished a record as the RIC, we feel compelled to express the opinion, based on personal observations, that a by no means negligible proportion of the Forces, as at present constituted, are men of intemperate habits and utterly unsuited to their duties....
>
> The Auxiliary Division of the RIC is recruited almost exclusively from ex-officers.... [I]n other districts which we visited they inspired terror as the authors of reprisals whose brutality and destructive effects were only equaled by the skill and forethought with which they had been planned.
>
> Several cases investigated by the Commission revealed the fact that these detachments had worked independently of, and brooked no interference from the other forces of the Crown. In view of their recent conduct, after the issue of orders forbidding all reprisals, they do not seem to recognize even the authority of Dublin Castle, and the question suggests itself—under whom do they serve?...
>
> The IRA is formidable because it is intangible.... In its present form it lives, fights and disperses. It is everywhere all the time and nowhere at any given moment. Without the support and sympathy of the vast majority of the population, it could not exist. This support is probably more generous and effective today than it has been at any previous period.
>
> So great has been the provocation by the forces of the Crown that 80 per cent of Irish men and women now regard the shooting of policemen and throwing of bombs at lorries with the same philanthropic resignation that Mr. Lloyd George displays towards arson, pillage and the shooting of civilians at night in the presence of their wives and children.

On 26 November the acting president of the Republic, Arthur Griffith, was arrested. As President de Valera was still in the United States seeking American support, Michael Collins, the head of the IRB, succeeded Griffith. In the following month, on 10 December, Lord French issued a proclamation which placed the counties of Cork, Kerry, Tipperary and Limerick under martial law. Many welcomed this in the hope that it would see an end to unofficial reprisals. On the following night, however, Cork was set ablaze by K Company of the Auxiliaries and the Black and Tans. The probable reason for this arson was an unofficial reprisal for an ambush which had taken place that evening at Dillon's Cross, some few miles outside of Cork. Much of St. Patrick Street, the principal business center of the city, was consumed in flames. Across the river the city hall was set ablaze. The Carnegie Free Library nearby was also put to the torch. The fire brigade was prevented from putting out the blazes because shots were fired at them by Black and Tans. The damage done was estimated at between two and three million pounds. English insurance companies refused to pay out claims, maintaining that the fires were malicious.

During the first six months of 1920, a total of 44 RIC men and British soldiers were killed. During the second half of the year, to the end of December, this toll rose to 171. The IRA lost 32 in the first half of the year, rising to 228 by Christmas 1920. In the first twenty days of December thirty-three civilians — men, including a seventy-three-year-old priest, Canon Magner and boys, were killed by Crown forces. In June there were twenty-four attacks against Crown forces by the IRA, rising to thirty in the following month. In August it was announced in the House of Commons that 556 RIC constables and 313 magistrates had resigned.

At the opening of 1920 three or four RIC men or half a dozen soldiers would boldly leave their barracks on patrols or to arrest someone. At the close of the year all cycle patrols had ceased, and British forces rarely ventured out in numbers of less than one hundred. Trucks, with armored cars to protect them, were used only in large convoys, and at irregular intervals. Isolated RIC/Black and Tan outposts were evacuated, and those remaining now housed three times their former numbers as of January of that year. Royal Navy personnel were brought in to establish wireless communications with the various divisional headquarters and the surviving barracks. With the war escalating the British government gave free rein to the army in the hope of putting the IRA under so much pressure that the Republicans would be forced to the negotiating table. While there were notable I.R.A, successes in 1920, there were also British successes. At Clonmult in County Cork thirteen IRA Volunteers were killed, and at Lackelly in County Tipperary seven more Volunteers died.

The War in Cork

On 2 January 1920, Carrigtwohill RIC Barracks was attacked by Cobh Company of the 4 Battalion, Cork No. 1 Brigade. The building was some eight miles from Cork, on the road to Waterford. The walls were breached by explosives, a new venture in Volunteer assault, forcing the defenders to surrender almost immediately. It was the first police barracks captured by the Republicans in the War for Independence. Arms and ammunition and other military accoutrements were taken. The policemen were then set free and ordered to march away.

On 7 January 1920, the commandant of No. 2 Cork Brigade, Liam Lynch, traveled to Dublin. He remained there for two months, discussing, with chief of staff Richard Mulcahy and Michael Collins, a strategy for the continuance of the war. Also there were Dan Breen and Sean Treacy, who both advocated a more proactive approach. As a consequence the regional brigades were given more freedom of action. The Volunteers then planned a systematic clearing of police barracks within their brigade districts.

If the RIC Barracks at Allihies could be destroyed or evacuated, then the greater part of the Beara Peninsula in west Cork would become a safe haven for wounded Volunteers or men on the run. Later it would offer respite for the flying columns, who carried the full strain of the fight every day. For these men each day was intense, exhausting and relentless. Capturing the barracks was very important. Twenty men were selected for the task, with others appointed as scouts and on outpost duty. Corney O'Sullivan was brought in from

Cork No. 1 Brigade to prepare and lay a mine. On the night of 12 February the party moved across country to Allihies. The barracks was an isolated building in the village; a stone wall enclosed a yard in front of it. The Volunteers took up positions in front and behind the barracks. The mine was placed in position at the base of the rear wall, underneath a window, and the fuse was lit. O'Sullivan, assisted by Volunteer Christy O'Connell, had barely reached the safety of the wall before there was a large explosion that created a breach about fourteen feet wide that reached from the ground to the eaves of the roof. The Volunteers called upon the police to surrender. Inside the building, however, two bracing walls were undamaged; and with this part of the barracks secure, the police decided to hold out in the hope of reinforcements arriving. They opened fire on their attackers. A two hour gun battle ensued, and with ammunition running low and the possibility of RIC reinforcements arriving, the attackers withdrew. Following this attack the RIC not only withdrew from Allihies but also from nearly all of the small barracks in the area, creating an even larger part of the peninsula that was free from Crown forces.

Aghada Company, 4 Battalion of Cork No. 1 Brigade, suffered a serious loss on 20 February. They were occupying a one-storied thatched farmhouse at Clonmult near Cobh when they were surrounded by the military. The first they knew of it was when two of their number were shot dead as they went out to the well to get some water to make tea. Inside the cottage Volunteer Jack O'Connell decided to make a dash from the house and fight it out in the open. With a rifle with a fixed bayonet, he and two other Volunteers dashed from the house, but they were cut down. The others in the house opened fire on the enemy, who responded with fierce rifle fire and then began lobbing hand grenades onto the thatched roof. The roof caught fire, and after a few minutes was blazing away. Rather than be burned to death the Volunteers inside surrendered. Patrick J. Higgins, company captain, described what happened next in his witness statement to the Bureau of Military History: "We were lined up alongside an outhouse with our hands up. The Tans came along and shot every man, with the exception of three ... who were saved from the Tans by the officer in charge of the military party. A Tan put his revolver to my mouth and fired. I felt as if I was falling through a bottomless pit. Then I thought I heard a voice saying, 'This fellow is not dead, we will finish him off.' Only for the military officer coming along, I, too, would be gone." Higgins was taken to a military hospital, where he recovered. He was tried and sentenced to death on 21 June 1921, but before the sentence could be carried out the truce came into being.

Two further barracks were attacked that month at Mount Pleasant, just north of Bandon, and Timoleague, in County Cork. The date chosen was the 27 of February. The RIC barracks at Mount Pleasant was a converted farm building with a farm shed attached the length of one side. Forty men were chosen for the attack, timed at one o'clock in the morning. The plan was to enter the shed and set a mine against the wall of the Barracks. Unfortunately the plan went awry when two fields away a shotgun was accidentally discharged. This alerted the garrison, and as the Volunteers approached, fire opened up on them. They returned the fire and threw a number of Mills grenades at the shed in the vain hope that it would catch fire. Very lights from the garrison were fired to summon help from Bandon, barely five miles away. With no chance now of capturing the building, the Volunteers withdrew in good order. That same night another party of Volunteers, forty in number and drawn from the Bandon and Clonakilty companies under the command of Sean Hales, attacked Timologue Barracks. Without a mine, they attempted to capture the barracks by pushing a burning hay cart against the door and then rushing it. But again the

RIC had been alerted, and a fierce firefight developed. Very lights were fired from the barracks, summoning help from the barracks at nearby Clonakilty. Again the Volunteers were obliged to withdraw, but again in good order. On the face of it both attacks had been failures, but within a few weeks both garrisons were evacuated. The attacks had achieved their goal, clearing an even greater area from British control.

The following month the British responded with a series of nighttime raids and "unofficial" assassinations of Volunteers and known supporters of the Republican cause. On 19 March 1920, RIC Constable Joseph Murtagh was shot dead. The following night masked men burst into the home of Thomas MacCurtain, lord mayor of Cork, prominent Sinn Fein member, and IRA brigade commander. He was shot dead in front of his wife. These assassins were later seen entering the local police barracks. District Inspector Oswald Swanzey, believed to have been the masked man who actually fired the bullet, was relocated to Ulster, where he was later assassinated on 22nd August as he left Christ Church Cathedral, Lisburn. In other raids a number of Volunteers were caught. New officers had to be found to replace those captured, and in the process one of the most active soldiers of the war, Dick Hurley, was appointed to command. An experienced soldier, he had served throughout World War I in the Australian army.

Morale within the Cork Brigades had suffered a blow with the police raids and the capture of Volunteer officers. It was decided to restore morale by stepping up the assaults on the RIC. The first target was the RIC barracks at Durrus. The barracks was situated at the head of Dunmanus Bay. Along with the barracks at Schull, they effectively controlled two peninsulas of land that thrust out into the Atlantic, denying the Volunteers freedom of movement. The barracks at Durrus was a strongly fortified stone building. It had loopholes and steel-shuttered windows for rifle fire. Surrounding it was an extensive field of barbed wire with only one entrance. Durrus had a garrison of twelve RIC men, armed with rifles, revolvers and hand grenades. It was situated just six miles away from Bantry to the north, which had a strong garrison of RIC as well as two companies of the King's Liverpool Regiment. To the east was Skibbereen with strong garrisons of both police and soldiers. Any attempt on Durrus would have to be completed before reinforcements arrived. The attack was given considerable thought. The only safe way of approaching it appeared to be from the lower building next door. Two gelignite bombs were prepared, each weighing about fourteen pounds. Again, withdrawal plans were paramount. All approach roads had to be blocked with felled trees, and guarded. Preparations were made to ambush any reinforcements coming along those roads, using a mixture of rifles and shotguns. The main attacking force was drawn from the Bantry and Durrus companies.

The assault began in the early hours of the morning of 31 March 1920. While a section of the command under the direction of Maurice Donegan positioned themselves in the loft of a stable at the front of the building, another section at the rear opened up on the barracks. The assault party gained the building to the side of the barracks, armed with their homemade bombs. They broke out through the roof of the house and climbed onto the roof of the barracks. Holes were made in the slate roof, and the vice-commandant of the battalion, Sean Lehane, lobbed his bombs down into the barracks below. The bombs exploded, but the ground floor remained intact. A three hour gun battle followed, the Volunteers calling upon the garrison to surrender. The defenders refused and sent up a number of Very lights in the hope of reinforcements arriving; but they did not come, though they must have seen

Belgooly RIC Barracks, County Cork, after an assault by the IRA. Later barracks were fortified with steel shutters and surrounded by barbed wire (courtesy the Imperial War Museum).

the lights at both Bantry and Skibbereen. The upper story of the building was now ablaze. After three hours, with daylight approaching, the Volunteers reluctantly broke off the attack, fearing that the British reinforcements might surround them.

Later that morning Durrus Barracks was abandoned. A week or so later the nearby Ballydehob Barracks were also evacuated. This left the whole peninsula free from enemy occupation. The RIC barracks at Adrigole and Eyeries in the Beara District were also evacuated. Barracks at Kenneigh, Ballygurteen, Milltown and Ballinspittle, all abandoned, were destroyed by the Volunteers. The RIC barracks at Ballineen, four or five miles west of Bandon, remained. It was an obvious target for attack. The British also recognized this and provided it with extra fortifications. The RIC based there were replaced by two platoons of the Essex Regiment. This forestalled any attempt by the Volunteers for the moment.

Nonetheless, eleven of the most vulnerable police barracks in the West Cork Brigade area had been evacuated over the previous six months, and their garrisons removed to larger stations, and blockhouses.

Over the Easter weekend of 1920, the Volunteers burned between 300 and 400 abandoned RIC barracks in rural areas and twenty-two tax offices around the country. With the attacks and destruction of the police barracks, the inevitable British raids followed, with known Volunteers and Republicans being arrested. These and the previously arrested Volunteers were eventually taken to Wormwood Scrubs Prison in London. They had been arrested, but there was no direct proof that they had carried out attacks on RIC barracks. On 21 April the prisoners staged a hunger strike. In the following month, again because there was no proof to convict them, they were all released.

On Easter Sunday, 4 April 1920, a meeting was called at the West Cork Brigade headquarters based at Laragh to discuss recent developments. Present were the brigade commandant, Tom Hales, the vice-commandant, Sean Hayes, adjutant Liam Deasy, quartermaster Pat Harte, intelligence officer Sean Buckley, acting adjutant Flor Begley and assistant adjutant Jim O'Donaghue, and brigade engineer Mick Crowley. The thrust of the discussion was that, while they had cleared certain areas of enemy barracks, they had failed to capture any arms in the process. There were still insufficient arms and ammunition to take on the British Army. While the smaller garrisons had been evacuated, military and police patrols still operated out of the major towns in most of Cork, patrolling the areas that had been evacuated. It was decided by the West Cork officers at the meeting that attacks upon these would become their next priority. Intelligence Officers from Bandon and Bantry battalion areas put forward proposals.

In Bandon, following the brigade headquarters' decision, the battalion went on the offensive once more. It was divided into three groups: Charley Hurley crossed the river Bandon in search of targets in Kilbrittain or Timologue, Jim O'Mahony led his men over to Innishannon, and Liam Deasy led his group to the Newcestown District. Hurley, with a troop of eight Volunteers, ambushed a cycling party of four RIC men at Ahawadda on the Timologue-Lislevane road. Two constables were killed and the other two surrendered. Four revolvers and some accompanying ammunition were captured. Jim O'Mahony, with five Volunteers from the Crosspound Company armed with two rifles and three shotguns, attacked another RIC cycling party at Highfort on the Upton Road. Two more policemen were killed and one wounded. Liam Deasy was not so fortunate, which was perhaps just as well, given the new commitment by the Crown forces to fight it out. He and twenty Volunteers from the Newcestown Company, poorly armed (most of them had only cudgels), had proposed to attack a nighttime cycling patrol of twenty well-armed soldiers. They remained in position from ten o'clock at night until five o'clock the next morning, but the patrol did not appear. The Newceston Company were more successful a few days later when, under Captain Dick Hurley, they ambushed a patrol of RIC men at Mount Pleasant, wounding one of them and securing their arms.

The Bantry Company (3 Cork Brigade) staged two ambushes, in June 1920, on police patrols at Snave Bridge (on the 14) and at Clonee (on the 21st). Two policemen were killed. The company's main proposal, put forward to brigade headquarters as a means of securing arms, was less violent. Ralph Keyes, its captain, suggested that a trial consignment of arms should be purchased in Britain and dispatched as a case of machinery, addressed to G.W. Biggs & Co., an important merchant in Bantry and a known Loyalist. Permission was given, and in December of that year the first case of arms arrived at Bantry Railway Station where it was diverted to the Volunteers. The Bantry Company had even more success when in April 1920 a large quantity of gelignite and 4,000 detonators were sent under a strong RIC escort from Cork to Bantry. On its arrival at Bantry the gelignite was unloaded, but for whatever reason the detonators were forgotten. The train continued on to Baltimore, where they were discovered by battalion quartermaster Michael Callaghan. They were later used with landmines to destroy enemy transport in ambushes.

As always, the British response was to stage raids on the homes of known Volunteers, looking for the missing detonators. The detonators had been safely hidden, though, in a previously prepared dump, and by this date many of those Volunteers known to the police were on the run and actively engaged in flying columns. In Bantry, following the deaths of the RIC/Black and Tans, their comrades took their revenge by murdering the invalid brother of Volunteer Michael Crowley and fire-bombing the homes of other Volunteers.

By the Spring of 1920 Volunteer activity had increased to the extent that the Loyalist *Irish Times* reported on 1 May that "the forces of the Crown are being driven back on their headquarters in Dublin by a steadily advancing enemy…. The King's government had virtually ceased to exist south of the Boyne and west of the Shannon."

Things were not perhaps as black as the *Irish Times* painted them, but its observation was the penultimate goal of the Republican army, prior to its seizure of Dublin. Ernie O'Malley decreed the following: "Soon we would have to destroy railways, the main supply artery of the garrisons. That would mean a food survey and arrangements for exchange of surplus food between areas and a closer contact between our divisional staffs and the county, city and borough councils and Dail members. The Dail unable to meet as a body, carried on its work in committees. It was not safe for them to meet as a Parliament. As we destroyed communications Dublin would be cut off from the country; we would have to build up civil control by areas, and the First and Second Southern [divisions] would act together. Liam Lynch and I had exchanged our ideas on, and our plans for the future. We saw what hardening was to come. The people of this country would have to give allegiance to it or if they wanted to support the Empire they would have to clear out and support the Empire elsewhere."[2] The British response was to bring in reinforcements. The *Freeman's Journal* reported in June of that year that Dublin quays were "jammed with tanks, armored cars, guns, motor lorries and thousands of troops, as if the port was a base of [a] formidable expeditionary force." The British Army in Ireland was now costing half of the total expenditure of the army throughout the empire. In addition was the cost of maintaining the Auxiliaries and Black and Tans.

Unlike in Britain the coast guard in Ireland, like the police, were politicized. They had access to guns and acted as a coastal police force. The Clonakilty Battalion under Dan Harte attacked Ring Coastguard Station in the search for arms. The principal building was surrounded, and fire was opened up on the windows of the first floor. Under this fire cover, two Volunteers, Jim "Spud" Murphy and John "Flyer" Nyhan rushed the door. They surprised two coastguards men who readily surrendered their rifles. They were the only two on duty that night. The other coastguards men lived in the nearby married quarters, and they had their rifles with them. The dilemma of whether to attack the quarters was quickly resolved when a series of Very rockets were set off to summon assistance. The nearest barracks at Clonakilty were barely two miles away, and as the Volunteers had failed to set up roadblocks, that assistance could arrive in a matter of minutes. The Volunteers withdrew.

Throughout County Cork a series of arrests were made. Included in the roundup were Fermoy battalion commandant Michael Fitzgerald, vice-commandant Larry Condon and company captain John Fanning. Plans were drawn up for their rescue; but bearing in mind the attempted rescue and subsequent death of Volunteer Robert J. Byrnes in Limerick in April 1919, the possibility of casualties weighed against the move. An alternative plan presented itself when Volunteer intelligence reported that some British Army officers fished on the Cork Blackwater, a noted salmon river. Lynch decided to capture them. They could be used either in an exchange of prisoners or with the threat of a reprisal, as an assurance that the Republican prisoners would not be executed. He finalized his plans, and on 26 June 1920, assisted by Sean Moylan, Patrick Clancy, George Power, and Volunteer Owen Curtin as second driver, they proceeded to the fishing hut in two cars. The latest intelligence was that General Lucas and three other soldiers — two officers and a subaltern — were there. The subaltern was arrested, then the officers were rounded up. They were taken completely by surprise and no resistance was offered. The other two officers were Colonel Danford of the Royal Artillery and Colonel Tyrell of the Royal Engineers.

The subaltern was released with a note written by Lynch for the commanding officer of the British forces at Fermoy, notifying him of the capture of the three officers, who would be treated as prisoners of war. Lucas and Danford were placed in one car with Lynch and Clancy, and Tyrell was placed in the other. They set off in the direction of Mourne Abbey, the second car some 50 yards or so behind the lead car. Avoiding Fermoy, they headed south. Two miles south of Rathcormac, Lucas and Danford held a brief conversation in Arabic, then sprang on Lynch and Clancy. In the struggle, Curtin, the driver, lost control of the car and crashed it into a roadside ditch. He was temporarily knocked out. Lynch meanwhile became involved in a struggle with Lucas, both men finishing up on the road. Clancy grabbed Danford, and a second fight ensued. By now the second car, which had gone on ahead, returned. Lynch meanwhile had overpowered Lucas and had drawn his gun. Danford was winning his struggle with Clancy. Lynch called out to Danford to surrender, warning him that he would shoot. Danford ignored the command, and Lynch fired. In the quick movement of the struggle, the bullet struck Danford in the face. With the fight now over, Lucas was permitted to give Danford first aid. Recovered, the Volunteer who had been driving the crashed car was sent into nearby Rathcormac to get a doctor for the injured British officer. The other Volunteers bundled Lucas into the other car and drove it away to the safe house of John O'Connell at Mourne Abbey. Colonel Tyrell was left to wait with Danford for the doctor. From Mourne Abbey, Lucas was transferred to Lombardstown and then to the West Limerick Brigade area, before finally being taken into the East Clare Brigade area. London Irishman Joe Good spoke to Lucas during his captivity. Good observed that

> Lucas was the traditional British officer. He appeared to be quite a simple man, apart from his military veneer which his training had given him. During our first conversation, Lucas was looking down the valley from the hill at Templeglantine. It was a very beautiful view, and from where we stood we could see a number of counties. He remarked to me, "This is a country worth fighting for." ... We continued to talk, casually but with increasing familiarity as the sun set over that landscape of the Golden Vale of County Limerick. I pointed out that we were within spitting distance of the lands confiscated by Elizabeth and handed to Spenser, and where he had retired to write his *Faerie Queene*. Lucas quoted some stanza from Spencer's poem, and then stopped abruptly — and added after a long pause, "I suppose it's high time that the natives resumed care of the Four Green Fields."
>
> This, I remember, surprised me even more: an English officer being familiar with that idea of the "Four Green Fields," the old image in Irish poetry for the four provinces of Ireland.[3]

Concerted British activity in the district forced Lucas' removal back to Limerick, where at Oola, on 30 July 1920, he succeeded in escaping from his escort and got back to his own forces. He had been a prisoner for one month. His detention had been a real propaganda coup for the IRA. For his part Lucas came to understand his enemy better. He acknowledged that they were a disciplined force with high morale. Two days earlier, on 28 July, at Oola, two British soldiers, in a search party looking for Lucas, had been killed and two wounded in an IRA ambush. On the day that General Lucas escaped, elements of the East Limerick Column under George Lennon ambushed a British Army cycling patrol of six soldiers near Buree, on the road to Kilmallock, killing one soldier in the brief firefight.

Previously, in June, there had been some minor engagements in Western Cork. In Bantry on 12 June a unit of the local IRA under Ted O'Sullivan ambushed a small party of RIC men at Anagashel on the Bantry-Glengarrif road and shot dead a constable. On the 22nd Maurice Donegan, with a five man team, attacked a patrol of five RIC men at Clonce Wood, on the Bantry-Durrus Road. One constable was killed and another wounded. At Bantry an over-officious RIC intelligence man known for his brutality was sought out and killed just outside of the British Army barracks. On that same day Maurice Donegan and a small unit of Volunteers ambushed an RIC bicycle patrol at Glengarriff, where one constable was shot dead.

On 22 June, Jack Fitzgerald, captain of the Kilbrittain Company, led an attack on the coast guard station at Howes Strand. Intelligence revealed that the recently enlarged garrison (from six to ten) were now armed. Observation revealed that on a fixed day every week three or four of the them would cross the bay by boat to visit Courtmacsherry station and collect supplies. On that particular day the Volunteers decided to attack. About three o'clock in the afternoon, a party of sixteen Volunteers commanded by Fitzgerald proceeded towards the barracks. The sentry on duty was overpowered, and the other Volunteers rushed the building. Four coastguardsmen on the ground floor, taken completely by surprise, were quickly disarmed. Two others on the floor above also surrendered when advised to do so by their disarmed comrades. Ten Ross rifles and almost 5,000 rounds of .303 ammunition were gathered up and taken away by the Volunteers.

The Skibbereen Battalion suffered a serious setback that could have ended in disaster for them. They planned an ambush against half a dozen armed policemen who traveled every week from Leap to Skibbereen to collect their pay. A request went out from battalion commandant Sam Kingston to all nine companies to supply the ambush with their best shots among their officers. Twenty-seven men were gathered together under Kingston and brigade quartermaster Pat Harte. No rifles were available, so the men were issued shotguns. In close combat the shotguns could be most effective with their scattered shot. The men were given homemade slugged cartridges to fire. On 1 July the Volunteers lay in wait along the road at Brade. As the five policemen entered the ambush they were called upon to surrender. Their response was to reach for their rifles. The Volunteers opened up on them, but at best the cartridges only spluttered. The powder from which they had been made had been stored away for two years in an old slate quarry and was now damp and useless. The cartridges also succeeded in jamming themselves in the barrels, so they could not be removed. The police responded with rapid fire. The Volunteers fell back as best they could, and not in good order. The ambush was a farce.

Two days later, Charlie Hurley had more success. With a group of eight Volunteers from the Innishannon Company he set up an ambush at Downdaniel Railway Bridge along the Innishannon to Bandon road. Four policemen had cycled down to Bandon and were expected to return later that day. Hurley had a rifle, the others had shotguns. The mixed group of police and Tans approached. They were extended along the road, so by the time the second couple arrived in the ambush position, the first two had ridden beyond it. As the second two arrived they were ambushed. One of them was wounded, and his rifle and ammunition

West Cork IRA men shot by the British. When captured, IRA men were generally shot out of hand.

were captured. The other, a Black and Tan, raced towards the railway track in a bid to escape. He was too far away for a shotgun to be of use, and Hurley was too late to fire at him before he escaped down the other side of the track and got away. The following day, 4 July, the Newcestown Company ambushed an RIC patrol near Mount Pleasant. There was an exchange of fire before both groups pulled back without casualties.

Howes Strand Coastguard Station

Early July was proving to be a mixed bag for the Volunteers. Successes were minor, no matter how hard senior command tried to dress them up for later public consumption. What was needed was a "spectacular." Charley Hurley looked again at Howes Strand Coastguard Station. Since the successful raid at the end of June, the station had been fortified. It was surrounded by barbed wire entanglements. The windows on the ground floor had been sandbagged, while those on the upper floor had been fitted with steel shutters. The only entrances were two doors at the front of the building, and they were easily defended with rifle fire from newly cut loopholes. The defensive wall at the front of the building, some thirty feet away from the station, was now in the process of being removed. As well as added fortifications the station had also increased its strength by the addition of five marines to the staff of ten coastguards. Out in the bay a British destroyer was anchored at night from 11 o'clock until dawn. It threw a powerful searchlight onto the building every hour. At dawn the destroyer slipped out to sea. This was the time that the second assault was planned for.

With the added fortifications and manpower, greater planning was needed. The attacking force comprised the Kilbrittain Company, as before, plus men from the Timologue, Bandon and Ballinadee companies — forty-two men in all. They were led by Charley Hurley. Twenty-four men in support of the main group were posted on the Kilbrittain-Ballinspittle road to delay any reinforcements that might be sent from Kinsale, Bandon or Kilbrittain. Hurley then moved the attacking group to within four hundred yards of the station and waited for dawn. At four o'clock the destroyer sailed out of the bay. Crawling on their stomachs the attackers moved towards the partially demolished wall in front of the barracks. From their number two teams of three silently made their way towards the two doors. In each group one of their number carried fourteen pound sledgehammers to batter down the doors. Charley Hurley led one team. With him was Jim Hodnett, local blacksmith, and Dennis Manning, who was to wield the hammer. Hurley and Hodnett had two revolvers each, and Mills hand grenades. In the other team were Jack Fitzgerald, Mick O'Neill and Con Lehane, likewise accoutered. A couple of blows from Manning's hammer and the door flew open. In dashed the other two, gaining possession of the floor and staircase. The other door proved more difficult, and soon the defenders opened fire. From behind the wall the Volunteers returned fire, doing their best to distract fire from the three Volunteers now caught out in the open. Meanwhile, the other three who had entered the building had reached the upper landing just as two of the defenders came out of a room. Hurley seized the initiative and demanded their surrender. There was a moment's hesitation, then they agreed. The Volunteers took their rifles and then led them into the next room where seven of their comrades were firing at the attackers outside. With revolvers leveled at the defenders, Hurley demanded their surrender. Taken completely by surprise, and seeing that the Volunteers also held grenades, they too surrendered. The prisoners were made to stand against one wall and their rifles were taken from them. Leaving Hodnett and Manning to guard them, Hurley proceeded on his own to the next room. Here he found a marine about to fire on the Volunteers outside and compelled him to surrender too. Ten prisoners were taken. Five others in different rooms were firing from the windows, unaware that the Volunteers were already in the building. Down below the other three Volunteers were still trying to break down the other door. Hurley instructed Hodnett to go downstairs and tell them to leave it and enter by the open door. As he did so, Hodnett was fired upon by another marine. He got to the bottom of the stairs just as the second door burst open. He directed the three men up to the floor above. Now with reinforcements Hurley and the others proceeded from room to room, capturing and disarming the four remaining defenders. One man remained, the commanding officer. He was located in a room at the far end of the building and was called upon to surrender. He refused. As Hurley and another Volunteer prepared to open the door and lob in a grenade, one of the captured defenders asked that he be allowed to speak to the man. Hurley agreed and the soldier reasoned with the officer, who was persuaded to surrender too. A white flag was thrust through one of the upper windows, and the Volunteers outside ceased firing. Miraculously none of the attackers or defenders were wounded, let alone killed. The captured arms amounted to fifteen service rifles and almost 10,000 rounds of .303 ammunition. The second attack on Howes Strand Coastguard Station had been a complete success.

Ballycrovane Coastguard Station

Ballycrovane Coastguard Station was perched on a cliff overlooking Coulagh Bay, and beyond it lay the Atlantic Ocean. The station consisted of four terraced houses knocked into one and surrounded by a stone wall five feet high. Isolated as it was, the view from the upper windows covered 360 degrees. Its windows were protected by recently installed shutters. Ballycrovane had a garrison of twelve marines. The station lay within the territory of the Beara Battalion of the West Cork Brigade. This brigade decided to capture it in the search for arms. Any local men approaching it would have been viewed with suspicion, so the Volunteers sought the help of Cumann na mBan, the women's wing of the Republican movement. Forming a friendship with the wife of the officer in charge, one of its members obtained a job at the station. She was able to produce an accurate detail of its internal layout and defensive capabilities. Defenses were concentrated on the three landward sides — but not on the side facing out onto the ocean. From the outer wall to the edge of the cliff was a distance of thirty yards. Climbing the almost sheer cliff at night would be suicidal. A daylight climb, with the risk of exposure, was the only way. These things considered, Liam O'Dwyer and Christy O'Connell, the two officers in charge, decided to go ahead. Exposed as they would be, and with the danger of reinforcements arriving before they could complete the mission, they asked the officers of the nearby Castletownbere Company if they could attack Castletownbere Coastguard Station at the same time, to confuse any reinforcements. After surveying its position and defenses, the company agreed to do so, and both operations were planned for midday on Sunday, 25 July 1920.

The Beara Company obtained reinforcements from Ballycrovane, Inches, Eyeries, Ardgroom and Kilcatherine companies. From this combined force, fifteen men were chosen for the actual attack, while the remainder took up defensive positions on approach roads. Of the fifteen attackers, four of them were equipped with sledgehammers to break down the doors of the station. Transport for the removal of the arms was parked just out of sight of

Wireless section of the British garrison at Bandon.

the station. At midday, the attackers started their ascent of the cliff. They were able to make use of a goat path for the first sixty feet of the climb, but after that it was a matter of searching for handholds and footholds. If they had been discovered at this stage they would all have been shot like sitting ducks. They reached the top and inched forward until they secured the protection of the seaward wall. At this point a wire-haired terrier, a pet of the garrison, caught their scent and began to bark out a warning.

Quickly the Volunteers vaulted over the wall and ran towards the station. Passing in front of the windows and heading towards the doors of the officers' quarters, they could see the marines grabbing their revolvers, ready to defend their station. One of the doors was battered open, and the Volunteers charged inside. Volunteer Liam O'Dwyer reached the kitchen, where he was confronted by the hysterical wife of one of the officers. As he rushed into the room, her husband, revolver in hand, was called upon to surrender. He pointed his gun at O'Dwyer and prepared to fire, negligent of his wife's safety. O'Dwyer fired first, over the shoulder of the woman, and wounded the marine officer, who fell to the floor, though not mortally wounded. Other Volunteers now entered the kitchen. O'Dwyer, looking through the window, saw the officer in charge, a man called Snowen, dash by in an attempt to get behind them. O'Dwyer went after him. Snowen dashed into another downstairs room, and as O'Dwyer passed a window outside, he opened fire on the Volunteer. The first shot missed, and O'Dwyer sought the shelter of the central column of the stone-constructed window. Snowen fired repeatedly at both sides of the column in the hope of hitting him. Meanwhile the other wounded officer, a man called Brown, managed to grab his revolver, and he ran into the next room to give support to Snowen. As he did so, one of the Volunteers fired a shotgun at him but missed. O'Dwyer, still outside, saw Brown, fired, and hit him. Snowen, having reloaded, continued firing on either side of the column. O'Dwyer fired blind a return shot and heard Snowen fall to the ground. Entering the room O'Dwyer saw that both men were dead.

Elsewhere the firefight continued. The marines in the upstairs room were blazing away at anything that moved. O'Dwyer called up to them to surrender, informing them that both officers were dead. A few moments later an improvised white flag appeared at the window. One marine, in a room by himself at the far end of the building, continued firing down into the yard below. Christy O'Connell, reloading from captured ammunition, climbed the stairs and at the top of them blasted away at the room. The marine agreed to surrender and threw his rifle out onto the landing. With all the captured marines herded into one room, the garrison arms were collected. They amounted to twelve rifles and 7,000 rounds of ammunition, six Webley revolvers and 50 rounds for each, bandoliers, Very pistols and other accoutrements. The garrison and its two dead officers were removed to Queenstown (Cobh). The coastguard station at Ballycrovane was abandoned and later burned down by the Volunteers to prevent its reuse.

As the fight at Ballycrovane progressed, the synchronized attack at Castletownbere Station was going to plan. It was lunchtime, and most of the six-strong garrison were off duty. The Volunteers under the command of Billy O'Neil simply walked into the station and held up the officer on duty. He was dressed in civilian clothes, and the Volunteers did not think to search him. Leaving one man on duty to guard him, the others went off in search of the armory. The captured officer engaged his captor in conversation, seemingly accepting the situation. As the Volunteer dropped his guard, the officer drew a revolver from inside his jacket and the roles were reversed. By now the others had found the arms and were preparing to leave. As they arrived back in the room to collect their comrade, the coastguard officer opened fire, wounding a number of them. Believing that the other coastguard men, or other reinforcements, had arrived, the Volunteers hastily withdrew. It was incredible naivety on the part of the Volunteers not to have searched their prisoner and incredible naivety which resulted in a number of them being wounded.

In the summer of 1920, the war was moving from the acquisition of arms to actual attacks on the Crown forces, be they police or British Army. The Republicans suffered some setbacks though, with men captured or killed. These operations against the IRA were usually intelligence-led by the few remaining RIC intelligence officers. Where this could be proven, the IRA went after those men. Without them the British authorities would be operating in the dark. On 17 July 1920, British colonel Gerald Smyth was assassinated by the IRA at the country club in Cork city. It was a reprisal for a speech he had made to the RIC encouraging reprisals against the civilian population. In sympathy, local railway workers refused to transport Smyth's body up to his hometown of Banbridge, County Down.

Another County Cork RIC man was also noted for his brutality towards prisoners. He was Sergeant Mulhern, the chief intelligence officer for the West Riding and the districts of Macroom and Millstreet who was based at Bandon, a strongly guarded town. Wherever he went he was strongly guarded, so there was little opportunity for Volunteers to ambush him. Anyone loitering would have been picked up and questioned. The only exception to the rule was when he attended Sunday Mass. He was escorted to the church, then his guard withdrew and returned to barracks. Between his entering the churchyard and opening the church door was the only opportunity to kill him. Many Volunteers, being strict Roman Catholics, cringed at the idea of killing him on holy ground. But the need to stop this man outweighed such scruples. On the 25th of July he made his way to the 8 o'clock Mass. As he reached out to open the church door a Volunteer stepped forward and shot him several times. The parish priest rushed out to offer him the last rites, but in ten minutes he was dead. There was an outcry from the Catholic church at what was perceived as a cowardly murder on sacred ground.

Two days later another RIC intelligence officer was shot dead. He was stationed at Clonakilty. Not only was he instrumental in seeing Volunteers arrested and tortured, but he had himself also fired upon unarmed civilians a few days previously. On 27 July he was followed by a party of four Volunteers, led by Jim Murphy, as he wandered through the town unescorted. As he was about to enter a greengrocer's shop in Rossa Street, two Volunteers stepped up and shot him in the head. He died the next morning.

The British authorities had the support of a minority of Loyalists in the Cork area, though it has to be said that not all Loyalists acted against the IRA. In a Volunteer operation at the end of July their activities were clearly betrayed to the occupying authorities. The Bantry Battalion prepared to ambush two military trucks at Snave Bridge, Bantry. A land mine was brought to the site by horse and cart. Just as the men were selecting suitable ambush positions, they heard the sound of military trucks approaching from another direction, the soldiers aboard firing their rifles though they were still more than a mile away. As they were so far away, the Volunteers were able to withdraw in good order, but clearly they had been tipped off as to the proposed ambush. The British soldiers of the Essex Regiment under Major Percival had a reputation for cruelty, and houses in the vicinity were burned as a reprisal for the intended ambush. Two Volunteers, Tom Hales and Pat Harte, were captured by the soldiers as the two approached a "safe" house. Both men were tortured, but not killed. One of the Volunteers, Pat Harte, was so badly beaten about the head that he never fully recovered.

At the beginning of August, brigade commanders of Cork, Kerry, Waterford and Limerick were summoned to GHQ in Dublin to discuss the progress of the war. Present at the meeting were the minister of defense, Cathal Brugha, who presided, Dick Mulcahy, chief of staff, Michael Collins, director of intelligence, and other members of GHQ staff. Brigade commanders included Terence MacSwiney (Cork No. 1), Liam Lynch (Cork No. 2), Liam Deasy (Cork No. 3), Paddy Cahill (Kerry No. 1), Dan O'Mahony (Kerry No. 2), Jeremiah O'Riordan (Kerry No. 3), Pax Whelan (Waterford West), and Father Dick MacCarthy in place of Sean Finn (West Limerick). Mulcahy began by praising the brigades present and encouraging others to emulate them. Then perhaps the comments that followed showed a complete lack of understanding of what was involved in achieving those successes that he had praised. In a schoolboyish, or perhaps naïve, sense of fair play, Mulcahy suggested that the Volunteers, when ambushing the Crown forces, should first of all call upon them to surrender. While such a policy was feasible where small cycle patrols were concerned, the war had moved on. The enemy traveled in military trucks with mounted machine guns, and quite often were accompanied by armored cars. The brigade commanders soon disabused him of the real situation, and Mulcahy agreed that they should do as they saw best. To the commanders it indicated how out of touch GHQ were, here in what they assumed was the relative safety of Dublin.

Mulcahy put forward the concept of containment of the enemy forces to their bases, thus restricting them from moving out into the countryside. He suggested that a ring two miles from the base should be formed and a further reinforcing ring four miles away. While the commanders agreed they had the manpower to institute such surrounding rings, what they lacked were the arms necessary. GHQ, they were informed, were trying to smuggle arms in from the Continent, but until that time perhaps a campaign of ambushing and town sniping could be introduced. It was frustrating to the commanders present, who knew that given the arms they could successfully prosecute the war.

In response to the escalation of violence, the British government introduced the Restoration of Order in Ireland Act, on 9 August 1920, which allowed for the internment and court-martial of civilians. This led to the arrest of a number of Volunteer officers. As a result, GHQ ordered all officers to sleep away from home and to appoint deputies to replace them in case of their arrest. This in its turn led to a number of the more active officers going on the run and joining the nascent flying columns.

The Cork No. 1 Brigade suffered a severe setback in August with the capture of almost its entire senior staff. British intelligence officers had opened mail and discovered that some brigade officers were due to meet at city hall in Cork on 12 August. At the last moment Liam Lynch, commandant of Cork No. 2 Brigade, added to the total when he made an appointment to see the lord mayor and senior brigade officer, Terence MacSwiney. As the meeting commenced at seven o'clock that evening, the British surrounded the building. Also in session within the council buildings at the time was a Dail Eireann court. There was confusion in the roundup, and in the mix-up that followed the raid a number of brigade staff were released along with the court personnel. Twelve brigade officers were detained though, including MacSwiney and Lynch. Lynch gave a false name and a Dublin address. The prisoners were held that night at the Cork Military Detention Block, and the next day they were transferred to the greater security of Cork Jail. MacSwiney suggested going on hunger strike until they were freed. Three days into the strike the prisoners, including Lynch, were released, there being no proof of their connection with the brigade. MacSwiney, though, was well known, and he remained in custody. He died on 25 October after 75 days on hunger strike.

On Sunday, 20 August 1920, a sizeable force of Volunteers drawn from the companies of Crosspound, Mount Pleasant, Kilpatrick, Newcestown, Timoleague, Clogagh, Innishannon and Ballindee lay in ambush at Brinney Bridge along the Crossbarry-Bandon road. The former police cycling patrol had now been replaced by a motorized military patrol drawn from the Essex Regiment, and the Volunteers were anxious to take it on. The ambush party was led by the Bandon Battalion commandant, Sean Hales. He had placed his men, divided into four sections, on both sides of the bridge. The road descended towards the bridge, then rose sharply, bending towards the west. They had lain in ambush for the previous two days, waiting for the military convoy; each evening as it grew dark withdrawing to safe houses. Now, on Sunday, it was half-past four in the afternoon, and it looked as if the ambush would have to be called off. Then suddenly they heard rifle fire. The party on the west side of the bridge had come under fire from units of the Essex Regiment, which attacked them in the rear. The Volunteers evacuated their position, returning fire as they did so. The pursuing forces came on, then found themselves under attack from another section of the Volunteers. In a fierce yet brief exchange of fire, Lt. Tim Fitzgerald of the Mount Pleasant Company was killed. This section of the ambush party then withdrew to the other side of the river. Victory had gone to the British, the ambushers had been ambushed. It would seem highly likely that, as they had returned to the same ambush site three days running, someone had observed them and reported their activities to the military in Bandon. It perhaps showed a certain naivety, still, on the part of the Volunteers. Rules of engagement require that there always be outfield scouts and a plan for a line of withdrawal. They had done neither.

Analysis of the summer of 1920 shows though they suffered setbacks the Volunteers of No. 3 West Cork Brigade had triumphed militarily. The attacks on RIC barracks and coast guard stations had produced important additions to their armaments, enabling them to launch larger offensives and meet the enemy on a nearly equal footing. Thirty-nine rifles had been captured in the month of July alone, bringing the total strength up to eighty-eight. Twenty-four thousand rounds of ammunition had been acquired from the enemy, bringing the total up to twenty-seven thousand rounds. Morale on the part of the Volunteers was extremely high.

A two week training course was held by the Volunteers of No. 2 Brigade in the late summer of 1920. In the discussions and briefings that accompanied the training, Lynch outlined his proposal for the establishment of a brigade column, or flying column as it is now more popularly known. This was to consist of up to thirty men drawn from the various battalions in the region and to remain as an active service unit in the field, armed and available, to take part in larger operations.

No. 3 Brigade, West Cork, were moving along similar lines towards the formation of a flying column in their area. They were fortunate in obtaining the services of Tom Barry, an ex–British Army sergeant who had served in World War I and later in Iraq. His was to become the name most associated with the guerrilla war in the countryside. Barry was appointed training officer, and in September 1920 he organized a training course at a camp established at Clonbouig. Thirty-six selected officers attended in order to learn how to fight a fast-moving guerrilla war. The course culminated in a thirty mile night march, designed to place the trainees at a preplanned ambush site, at Fanlobbus on the Bandon-Dunmanway road. Local intelligence reported that a convoy of three armed trucks passed this way each day. Barry and his students were joined by men from the local Behagh, Aultagh, Coppeen and Kenneigh companies, totaling sixty men in all. Barry positioned his men — a main attacking force and men that made up vantage scouts and a retiring party. A mine was laid at the eastern edge of the ambush site, and they waited. For whatever reason, the convoy did not travel that day. Barry knew better than to remain there for more than a day and withdrew his men to safety.

The first action of the No. 2 Brigade Column was a daylight raid on Mallow Barracks in the search for arms. The British Army barracks housed a contingent of the Seventeenth Lancers, noncommissioned officers and men commanded by one officer. Lynch was able to get two of his men, Richard Willis and John Bolster, employed there as maintenance men undertaking repairs and improvements. They supplied him with the necessary information for him to stage an assault on 28 September 1920. The night before, the Volunteers assembled in the local town hall. On the morning of the attack Willis and Bolster turned up for work as usual, accompanied by their "foreman," Volunteer Patrick McCarthy. All three had concealed revolvers.

General Liam Lynch, commander of Cork No. 2 Brigade.

The British soldiers went about their duties in the town, leaving only a small force in the barracks. At 9:30 A.M. Ernie O'Malley, a staff officer from GHQ in Dublin who had volunteered to take part in the raid, knocked on the front door of the barracks. In response the sentry inside pushed back the slide over the peephole. O'Malley informed him that he had a letter for the barrack warden. The sentry opened the door, and O'Malley rushed at him. The other Volunteers now rushed the door and gained admittance. Willis, Bolster and McCarthy, already in the building, now held up the guard. The senior NCO, Sergeant Gibbs, seeing the Volunteers, dashed towards the guardroom. One of the Volunteers ordered him to halt. He did not, and a shot was fired over his head as a warning. He continued on, and a second shot left him mortally wounded, in the doorway. The garrison were then rounded up and marched out onto the barracks square. By a prearranged signal three cars now arrived to take away the captured arms: two Hotchkiss light machine guns, 27 rifles, a revolver, Very pistols, 4,000 rounds of ammunition with bandoleers, and a quantity of bayonets and lances. The barracks was set on fire, but the flames were extinguished once the Volunteers had left. There were no Volunteer casualties. Angered at the death of their comrade, the local British military went on the rampage. Shops were looted and their windows smashed. Village men were beaten up. Two days later, on 30 September, an intended attack upon the Churchtown RIC barracks was postponed when it was learned that the RIC was aware of the intended attack. The flying column moved off to Freemount, putting distance between themselves and the barracks.

Ballydrachane

Jack O'Connell, the intelligence officer with the Newmarket Company, noted that a motorized British convoy traveled the four miles between Kanturk and Newmarket on a fairly regular basis. He approached Sean Moylan of Cork No. 1 Brigade with his observations, and suggested an ambush. Moylan, who had been present at the capture of General Lucas, agreed and approached brigade OC, Liam Lynch. Along with Ernie O'Malley from GHQ, Dublin, they inspected possible ambush sites. Along the four mile road between the two towns, they found one — perhaps not ideal but the best available. It was at Ballydrachane, a straight piece of road leading out of a sharp curve. Vehicles would have to slow down at the curve, possibly leading to bunching as they came out of it. Moylan suggested that they should take up observation positions and test the reliability of Jack O'Connell's report. They were there barely fifteen minutes when they heard the sound of approaching trucks. Two trucks containing twenty-four British soldiers drove by. They did exactly what was predicted. The three men agreed to an ambush the following week. An assault group of thirty men from the flying column, plus men from the local companies for roadblocks and outpost duties, was assembled. The outpost men were essential, given the short distance between the two enemy garrisons. If a larger force than anticipated was being transported, then these men would be called upon to defend both flanks in the case of enemy reinforcements.

At 3:00 A.M. on 6 October, the column moved off to take up their positions along the road at Ballydrachane. The men cut holes in the thick hedges that bordered the roads, and by five o'clock they were ready. In silence they watched as the early morning workers passed by unsuspectingly. Then came the children on their way to school. The hours passed, the day was cold, the ground was muddy. At eleven o'clock they heard the sound of an approaching truck. They all knew their orders. The truck entered the ambush site. It was on its own. Up ahead of it a farm cart was pushed onto the road to block its passage. Upon the order, the Volunteers opened fire. The fight was over in barely five minutes. The driver had been killed and the remainder were all wounded. The Volunteers ceased fire and called upon the soldiers to surrender, which they did. Rifles and ammunition were all gathered up and taken off. The Volunteers suffered no casualties. It was a textbook ambush, giving experience to those untried Volunteers present. Lynch marched his men off to defend Kanturk, the most likely place to suffer retribution; but nothing happened that night and the Volunteers withdrew the next morning. At the end of October the column was disbanded. Men from the various battalions then began forming their own individual columns of between 15 and 30 Volunteers, with the possibility of combining forces where a larger operation to present itself.

Newcestown

On the night of Saturday, 9 October 1920, Sean Hales, commandant of the Bandon Battalion (Cork No. 3), and fifteen of his men who had recently taken part in Tom Barry's second training course, received word that two Crossley tenders with sixteen soldiers from the Essex Regiment were raiding Newcestown, barely half a mile away. With a small number of scouts from the local Newcestown Company, Hales and his men set out to confront them. They cut across country and down onto the road that led into the village. Just as they did so, they were caught in the headlights of the departing Crossley tenders. The Volunteers scrambled over the walls on either side of the road, and as the first of the two tenders came abreast of them, they opened fire. It came to a halt about twenty yards further on. As the second tender approached, it too was fired upon. The two tenders were about one hundred and fifty yards apart. Their lights were switched off, and in the dark a firefight ensued. The British got down onto the road, and the party from the first tender tried to outflank the Volunteers. Instead of outflanking them, they broke right into their midst. A furious outbreak of firing followed before the outflankers pulled back. Then there was a silence. The two tenders burst into life once more and raced away. It was a fight that could have gone either way, and if the British had realized how few Volunteers there were, it surely would have gone their way. No casualties were reported on the Republican side. The Essex, led by Major Percival, reported two officers killed and three men wounded.

In an interview that appeared in Uinsean MacEoin's *Survivors,* Tom Kelleher, later to become commandant general, IRA, 1st Southern Division, gives his version of what happened at Newcestown. It shows the immediacy and chaos that was thrust upon the Volunteers:

> I fired the first shot in west Cork at Newcestown.... We were at the ready. Eventually the racket started. Major Percival himself came along accompanied by his troops in two lorries. They were approaching slowly. Sean Hales, who was in charge of us, rushed out, with only two sections of men, and told us to get in position.... The next order was, take cover on the right hand side of the road. Well now, the right hand side was definitely the wrong side to take cover because you were underneath the road, but if you went on the other side you would be right up over them because the fence there was very high. It was a big embankment there.... There were stacks of barley there. We lay like bundles. Next minute Con Lehane, who was a blacksmith in Bandon, asked Sean Hales, "Will we fire on the lorry?"
>
> "Hell's fire, why wouldn't we fire on it."
>
> A fellow by the name of Con Flynn of Ballinadee and I went down nearer to where the lorries were expected.

> We got within seventy yards of them and we peeped out through the hedge. It was lower here than where we were inside above, and it was more suitable. What was passing in front of us but a common little cart, two men with their legs hanging down in front and they going along slowly and the bloody big lorry right after them. The first thing that struck me was that the pair of you are in a very precarious position at the moment. The lorry could not pass, and you would walk as fast as it. I got ready. When the lorry was right opposite ... I flaked into the middle of it. That put things going. I got firing two shots before the second lorry was right up in front of us. So I emptied the rest of my gun into it. There was some of them wounded. You could not see them, it being pitch dark, but I could hear them tearing outside the fence as they tried to alight. What happened then, but that our own fellows started firing from behind stacks, they had retired to them — it was our first real fight — and I was caught between them. I ran for the first stack. Who was behind it only Sean Hales and he firing an odd shot out at the road.
>
> "Why do we not get out on the road and finish them," said I.
>
> "We might walk into a trap if we went out on the road."
>
> And I could not see the sight on the rifle, never mind take steady aim. So we continued to retreat towards the fence at the bottom of the field, each of them firing the odd shot.... [W]e were not doing it right of course, but we killed and wounded a few of them, though we did not know it. There was a Captain Richardson a great friend of Major Percival. His cap was found inside the hedge the next day, and half his brains inside it. There was not a wounded man among us, except Jackie Neill; he got a bullet through the sleeve of his coat. That was all.[4]

Tom Barry arrived later that night and arranged an ambush at the site should the soldiers of the Essex Regiment return the next morning, but they didn't. The column moved off and proceeded on to Crowhill, where they arrived later that day.

On 7 August 1920 an IRA column ambushed a six man RIC/Black and Tan foot patrol near Kildorrey, County Cork. In the fight that followed all six policemen were wounded, one fatally, Black and Tan Ernest Watkins. Six revolvers and 250 rounds of ammunition were recovered by the column. On 28 September, Volunteers from the 2nd Cork Brigade, under the command of Liam Lynch, successfully attacked the military barracks at Mallow and seized thirty-seven rifles, ammunition and mills grenades. Later that day British troops carried out reprisals for the raid, burning several houses and businesses.

In July 1920 a new battalion, Schull, had been formed in Cork No. 3 Brigade. Its commander was the twenty-one-year-old Sean Lehane, a second year student at St. Patrick's Training College, Drumcondra, Dublin. Though young, he had proved his worth in combat. While companies had operated in this region, based on other battalions, Lehane reorganized them into nine new companies, based at Lissagriffin, Goleen, Dunmanus, Gloun, Schull, Leamcon, Dunbeacon, Ballydehob and Skehanore. By October Lehane was to prove his worth as the battalion's commander. He proposed to capture the Schull RIC Barracks. Following the attacks on other barracks in the neighborhood, Schull had been fortified and its garrison strength increased. Nearby, about four hundred yards away, was a coast guard station occupied by a detachment of Royal Marines, some forty to fifty strong. Lehane's group had just one revolver and a few shotguns. Any hope of capturing the barracks depended upon good intelligence, speed, and organization.

Careful observation of the comings and goings of the garrison threw up an interesting fact that if capitalized upon would produce success. Every night at half past seven, five of the garrison left the barracks to collect mail and newspapers from the evening train at the local station. They were generally gone for half an hour. Over a period of a few weeks this activity proved to be consistent. When the party returned they gained entrance at the rear door by giving a password. This password was changed daily. The secret was to gain this password on the day of an intended assault. The Volunteers befriended a number of the garrison in their off-duty periods, and one in particular, a constable named Daly, revealed his Republican sympathies. He was all for resigning and joining the Volunteers, but he was persuaded not to. The Volunteers worked on him, and on 4 October 1920, overcoming his scruples, he gave them the password — "Kilmallock."

Everything had been prepared in advance, and with the password, the Volunteers acted that night. It was now a case of exact timing. The Volunteers got into position, having seen the constables depart for the railway station. They could not act too soon, as this would have aroused the suspicions of the men within the barracks. Almost half an hour elapsed before Lehane and Volunteer Charlie Cotter approached the barracks door. Lehane knocked on the door, and when challenged for the password, called out "Kilmallock!" Then they heard the key being turned in the lock and the safety chain being unhooked. As the door opened, Lehane, Cotter and other Volunteers dashed inside. The men inside were taken completely by surprise. They were ordered to raise their hands in surrender, then they were disarmed and locked in another room. Half an hour had elapsed between the departure and return of the other five RIC men. Timing it to perfection as they entered the barrack's compound, the Volunteers dashed out and captured them too. They were marched back into the building and locked up with their comrades. The Volunteers found thirteen rifles, twenty-six revolvers, sixty Mills grenades, thirteen hundred rounds of ammunition, and over one hundred confiscated shotguns taken from local people. These were taken away in two cars. The whole operation had been a complete success, without one shot being fired. The police and Black and Tans that comprised the garrison were marched away to Duggan's, a local hotel, where they were kept prisoner for the night. While this was being undertaken, the barracks was set on fire. It had been blazing away for fifteen minutes or so before the marines at the nearby coast guard station noticed anything. It was too far gone for them to do anything about it and was subsequently abandoned. Though the coast guard station and its marines remained, as they were not actively engaged in the war they were not seen as a threat, and so they were left alone.

Toureen

The flying column of Bandon Battalion of the 3 West Cork Brigade, numbering thirty-two men, under the leadership of Charlie Hurley, ably assisted by Tom Barry and battalion adjutant Liam Deasy, now planned the ambush of a military convoy in their district. Intelligence reported that a daily motorized convoy drove along the road from Innishannon, passing through Toureen. The Volunteers proposed stopping it by placing a mine in the road, then using massive firepower to compel the military to surrender. On Friday morning, 24 October 1920, just after four o'clock, the column proceeded across country by way of Crossbarry to Toureen, some seven and a half miles from Bandon and twelve from Cork. The mine was placed in a bend in the road, which should slow down the convoy, and the twenty-seven Irish men in the attack party took up their ambush positions along a three hundred and fifty yard section. Hurley placed scouts to watch for the convoy, with others to safeguard the withdrawal. Tom Barry commanded the western section, Liam Deasy the eastern, and Charlie Hurley had the center. The signal for the attack was to be the exploding of the mine.

At nine o'clock, the sound of approaching trucks was heard coming from Bandon. There was no explosion. The mine failed to go off. The first truck, carrying some fifteen soldiers of the Essex Regiment, came careering on towards Deasy and his men, at the far end of the ambush. They dropped down to the road and fired at the driver in an attempt to stop the truck. It continued on and away at speed. At the sound of rifle fire the second truck, some two hundred yards behind the first, slowed down. At the same time Charlie Hurley's men opened fire on the driver, and the truck swerved into a ditch. A three pound bomb made by IRA general headquarters was thrown. The bomb, which landed right in the body of the truck, failed to explode. Tom Barry's section now joined in the firefight. Within seconds four of the soldiers were dead, including the officer, Captain Dixon. Four others were wounded. The survivors called out their surrender, and raised their hands over their heads. The brief but violent fight was over.

The soldiers were disarmed, and the wounded and dead were removed to the grass verges to be tended to by their unwounded comrades. The truck was set on fire. The Volunteers retired without any casualties. They had captured fourteen rifles, fourteen hundred rounds, some Mills bombs and the officers' revolvers. The other truck had escaped. Its occupants had made no attempt to help their comrades in the following truck. Had the fifteen soldiers in the first truck stopped their vehicle five or six hundred yards further on, and gaining access to the fields returned to help their comrades, this would have created a problem for the Volunteers, though it was unlikely that it would have changed the outcome. Hurley had planned for this eventuality by placing a small flanking party in the field and these would have been reinforced within a few minutes.

With the probability of British reinforcements arriving in twenty minutes to half an hour, the column marched away south, across country towards the Bandon river opposite Kilmacsimon Quay. The column crossed the river by boat to safety. The military took their revenge that night upon the people of Bandon in assault and looting. The next day, fearing a repeat of the previous night, the column moved to the outskirts of the town to offer the people some protection. Perhaps the leaders realized that the reprisals had gone too far and the British soldiers were confined to barracks that night.

At a brigade council, held on Sunday, 31 October, the West Cork 3 Brigade, while agreeing to maintain battalion flying columns, decided to form a larger brigade flying column. Tom Barry was appointed its commander. With several hundred men in the column, it would seize the initiative from the enemy and become an attacking rather than a defensive force. As such, by taking the initiative and deciding when and where to attack, it could take on a superior enemy force and defeat it. It was decided that the column would be mobilized on Sunday, 21 November 1920. In the weeks following the brigade council, Barry and his staff visited the different battalion areas with a view to becoming more familiar with the terrain. Maps were prepared, with potential ambush sites, important roads and river crossings given particular attention. Points were marked where roadblocks could be set up and trenches cut to impede motorized enemy convoys.

On 17 November RIC sergeant James O'Donaghue was assassinated by a Volunteer ASU in White Street, Cork city. The following day three randomly selected civilians were shot dead in Cork city by masked men. It was generally believed that the perpetrators were Black and Tans, avenging O'Donaghue's death. In Dublin, following the Squad's assassinations of British intelligence men on 21 November 1920 and the subsequent retaliation in

Croke Park where 12 civilians were killed and 60 wounded, the Black and Tans went on the rampage in Millstreet, County Cork. The following night Liam Lynch and Volunteers from the local battalion flying column took up positions around the town to forestall a repeat of the previous night. As the Black and Tans ventured out, a firefight broke out in which two Black and Tans were wounded and Volunteer captain Patrick McCarthy was killed. The following night the Volunteers occupied Millstreet in force. The British remained in their barracks. At dawn Lynch withdrew his men.

In November 1920, following a brigade council, Lynch decided that the brigade column had become too large for its purpose. This appears to go against the experiences of other brigades, but each brigade had evolved differently to suit the prevailing conditions existing. The brigade was divided up into eastern and western battalions, with each battalion having its own active service unit. The reason behind this was that the British, instead of having to concentrate on one fighting force, would then have to deal with seven individual ASUs operating in seven battalion areas. These new units would be smaller, and therefore more easily hidden but still capable of harassing the enemy. They could also be swiftly summoned to act in combination with other battalion ASUs in a brigade column when the need arose.

Kilmichael

It was about this time, late November, that the Auxiliaries, a force of ex-officers of the British Army introduced into Ireland the previous June, established themselves in Munster. The first company was quartered at Inistioge in County Kilkenny, the second at Carden Castle, which after a short stay took over Macroom Castle in County Cork, under the command of Colonel Crake. They had a fearsome reputation, and Tom Barry was anxious to confront them as soon as possible, to see just how good they were. The Auxiliaries regularly traveled in mechanized convoys along the Macroom to Dunmanway road, and this was where Barry decided to engage them. Paddy O'Brien's Dunmanway Battalion formed the basis of the column, with support from Tom Donovan's Behagh Company for scouting duties. Four Volunteers from Ballinacarriga joined the ambush party. In all there were just thirty-six Volunteers, only twelve of whom had experience under fire.

At five o'clock on the morning of Sunday, 28 November, the Volunteers paraded and after a breakfast of bread, butter and tea set out on the five mile march to Kilmichael. It was dark and raining heavily. Along the way they met people going to Mass, and for their own safety, the men ordered them to return home. As daylight broke the Volunteers arrived at the ambush site: it was 8:15. The site chosen, one and a half miles south of Kilmichael, was in bleak and barren boggy countryside. It was far from ideal, with little real cover. The site was dictated by the presence of nearby British garrisons, and how quickly reinforcements could be sent to the scene. Here the north-south road turns from west to east for 150 yards before returning to its original direction. There were no ditches on either side of the road, but there were a number of scattered rocky eminences.

Barry spoke to his men, stressing the importance of the fight ahead. There could be no retreat. At the end of the day either the Auxiliaries or the column would be destroyed. He positioned his men.

The Command Post was situated at the extreme eastern end of the ambuscade and faced the oncoming trucks. It was a small narrow wall of bare stones, so loosely built that there were many transparent spaces. It jutted out onto the northern side of the road, a good enfilading position but affording little cover. Behind this little stone wall were also three picked fighters, John "Flyer" Nyhan, Clonakilty; Jim "Spud" Murphy, also of Clonakilty; and Mick O'Herlihy of Union Hall. The attack was to be opened from here, and under no circumstances whatever was any man to allow himself to be seen until the commander had started the attack.

No. 1 Section of ten riflemen was placed on the back slope of a large heather-covered rock, ten feet high, about ten yards from the command post. This rock was a few yards from the northern edge of the road. By moving up on the crest of the rock as soon as the action commenced, the section would have a good field of fire.

No. 2 Section of ten riflemen occupied a rocky eminence at the western entrance to the ambush position on the northern side of the road and about one hundred and fifty yards from No. 1 Section. Because of its actual position at the entrance, provision had to be made so that some men of this section could fire on the second truck if it had not come round the bend when the first shots were fired at the leading truck. Seven men were placed so that they could fire if the truck had come round the bend and three if it had not yet reached it. Michael McCarthy was placed in charge of this section.

No. 3 Section was divided. Stephen O'Neill, the section commander, and six riflemen occupied a chain of rocks about fifty yards south of the road. Their primary task was to prevent the Auxiliaries from obtaining fighting positions south of the road. If the Auxiliaries succeeded in doing this, it would be extremely difficult to dislodge them; but O'Neill and his men would prevent such a possibility. This section was warned of the great danger of their cross fire hitting their comrades north of the road and they were ordered to take the utmost care.

The remaining six riflemen of No. 3 Section had to be used as an insurance group. There was no guarantee the enemy would not include three, four or more trucks. Some riflemen, no matter how few, had to be ready to attack any trucks other than the first two. These men were placed sixty yards north of the ambush position, about twenty yards from the roadside. From here they could fire on a stretch of two hundred and fifty yards of the approach road.

Two unarmed scouts were posted one hundred and fifty and two hundred yards north of No. 2 Section, where they were in a position to signal the enemy approach nearly a mile away. A third, unarmed, scout was a few hundred yards south of the command post to prevent surprise from the Dunmanway direction.

Barry divided the column into two sections, taking command of one and putting Michael McCarthy in charge of the other. McCarthy and his men rolled down stones to within a couple of yards of the

Home secretary Hamar Greenwood reviewing Auxiliaries.

road and constructed a low barricade, camouflaging it with furze bushes. Volunteer Ned Young was placed southwest of the road, and Michael O'Driscoll to the north, where he had a clear view of the road and the approach of the enemy convoy. Tom Barry, with five men, positioned themselves on the other side of the road, and above them in the field behind, more Volunteers were placed. It was 9:00 A.M. At this point John Lordan, vice-OC of the Bandon Battalion, arrived. He asked if he could take part in the action. Barry agreed and placed him in No. 2 Section.

The hours passed. The overcast sky began to grow dark as evening approached. At 4:05 P.M. one of the scouts signaled the enemy's approach. In the distance the sound of trucks was heard. Then all of a sudden a pony and trap with four armed Volunteers appeared. These men should have joined the flying column on the previous Sunday, but they had not received notification in time. If they were seen by the oncoming convoy then anything might happen. Orders were shouted down to them to get off the road, and just as they turned into a nearby yard, the first of two Crossley tenders appeared in view. Barry had placed a stone in the road, with the order that when the first tender reached it, fire should be opened up.

Barry, dressed in the uniform of an IRA officer, waited in the middle of the road for the approach of the enemy patrol. Seeing him, the driver of the first truck slowed down, no doubt believing him to be an officer in the British Army. About thirty-five yards further on the truck entered the ambush site. Barry lobbed a Mills bomb into the first tender, killing or wounding everyone in it. He then blew a whistle. In the opening fusillade the driver was killed and the tender came to a halt. The second tender, about one hundred and fifty yards behind, slewed to a halt, and its driver attempted to turn it around, but in the process it became stuck at the side of the road. The Auxiliaries jumped out onto the road, and from the cover of their vehicle they opened up on the Volunteers. The fighting was intense—hand to hand. Revolvers were fired at point blank range. The Auxiliaries were shouting at each other calling for support. Now, down on the road, some of the Volunteers with bayonets fixed stabbed at their opponents. A wounded Auxiliary, whom Barry thought was dead as he passed him on the road, fired at Barry from a distance of four yards but missed. Volunteer John "Flyer" Nyhan bayoneted him. In less than five minutes all nine Auxiliaries in the first tender were dead or dying.

Barry and the men with him now moved onto the second truck to give support. A fierce firefight was under way. In single file they advanced towards it, approaching the Auxiliaries unseen. Then suddenly a cry went up from the Auxiliaries: "We surrender!" and again, "We surrender!" Still approaching, Barry saw some of the Auxiliaries actually throw down their rifles. Three Volunteers in Section 2 stood up in response, believing that it was all over. But then the Auxiliaries, drawing their revolvers, opened fire once more. Three Volunteers were hit and went down. From about twenty-five yards away, Barry, angered at this false surrender, ordered, "Rapid fire and do not stop until I tell you." Under intense fire from two directions the Auxiliaries shouted out again, "We surrender!" The Volunteers ignored the call and kept firing on them from barely ten yards away. It was all over very quickly then. Barry ordered a ceasefire. Sixteen Auxiliaries were dead, including Colonel Crake, and one mortally wounded. The eighteenth man had crawled into a boghole by the side of the road, where his body was later discovered.

Barry raced over and clambered up to the rocky height where the three Volunteers lay.

Michael McCarthy of Dunmanway and Jim Sullivan of Knockawaddra were dead. Pat Deasy, younger brother of Liam Deasy, was dying. Barry looked about him at his men. For most of them it was their first taste of combat. Some were in shock. Instructing two Volunteers to remain with young Deasey, he ordered the others to fall in down on the road. At this point he was in danger of losing his men through panic. Barry ordered them to attention. "The Flying Column came to attention," Barry records. "Some showed the strain of the ordeal through which they had passed, and a few appeared on the point of collapse because of shock. It was of supreme importance that those men should be jerked back to their former efficiency, particularly as another engagement with the British might well occur during the retirement ... then the Column commenced to drill."[5] Barry succeeded in getting them back. The Volunteers were then ordered to gather up the arms, ammunition, and whatever papers they could find. The haul amounted to eighteen rifles with 1,800 rounds, thirty revolvers and ammunition, some Mills bombs, and a sack of papers both military and personal.

Deasy was borne away, and preparations were made for the removal of the bodies of the two dead Volunteers. The trucks were set ablaze, and the Volunteers then marched away south, the rain falling once again. The importance of Kilmichael to the Volunteers who took part in the fight was that the Auxiliaries who appeared so formidable were shown to be only men, men who could be defeated by more determined men.[6]

It was well into the following day before the British investigated the ambush, and then in large numbers. Their approach was cautious, because they believed that a large force of Volunteers were within the encirclement, waiting to engage them in a major firefight. British soldiers moved off from Dunmanway, Ballineen, Bandon, Crookstown and Macroom. One unit of 250 helmeted soldiers moving out from Dunmanway to rendezvous with the other British forces at Kilmichael, passed barely two hundred yards from where the Volunteers were resting. As the soldiers moved on, the column moved off again, south to Lyre. For the next three days they zigzagged across the county, avoiding contact with the British forces. To have engaged just one of them would, because of the close proximity of the others, have invited destruction.

Four days after Kilmichael, on 2 December 1920, Liam Deasy led thirty men drawn from six companies of the Bandon Battalion (West Cork) in an ambush along the Crossbarry-Bandon road at Clashinimud. The road was used on a frequent basis by a convoy of three military trucks. Scouts reported that they had passed that morning and were expected to return that afternoon or evening. The Volunteers were in position by midday. Deasy placed them along a straight section of road, about two hundred yards in length. At either end were bends that would slow the convoy down as it negotiated them. Trees had been partially cut through, ready for felling, at a road junction a little further on, and also at a mile distant in the other direction. Deasy's ambush party was armed with fifteen rifles and twenty-one shotguns. In addition they had a supply of hand grenades. As dusk was falling the Volunteers heard the trucks approaching. The signal for the start of the attack was to be an exploding Mills bombe thrown at the first truck by Deasy. Barely three yards off, and with the pin removed, Deasy saw that there were civilians as well as soldiers aboard. Fearing that they might be prisoners or hostages, Deasy did not throw the grenade and replaced the pin. He yelled out to his men to hold fire. The trucks raced by. At the far end of the ambush zone, not having heard Deasy, the Volunteers there commenced firing. But seeing the civilians eventually, they ceased fire for fear of hitting them. The trucks did not return fire, but continued on at speed. Deasy later discovered that the civilians were Crown witnesses being carried back to Rosscarbery from Cork, where they had given evidence in the Assize Court. Two RIC men had been wounded in the brief skirmish, and a woman suffered a bullet wound in the knee.

Later that night the Essex Regiment got its own back. Two apparent deserters had been picked up by the Volunteers some weeks earlier. In exchange for a large sum of money, one of them said that his brother, a sergeant in the military barracks at Bandon, would cooperate in its capture. He wrote to his brother, who wrote back requesting to meet some officers of the Volunteers to discuss the matter. The meeting was arranged for half past eight at the top of Laurel Walk on the Dunmanway road. Three Volunteer officers, Captain John Galvin, Lieutenant Jim O'Donaghue and Section Commander Joe Begley went to meet the Essex sergeant. As they dropped down onto the Dunmanway road, a little way from Laurel Walk, they found themselves surrounded by a large force of the Essex Regiment who had been lying in wait for them. The Volunteers were badly beaten by the soldiers and then shot dead. The next morning their bodies were found, a hole from a bullet fired at close range in the center of their foreheads.

Sean Lehane of the Schull Battalion, temporarily replacing Tom Barry, organized a retaliatory action against the Essex Regiment on 8 December. The Volunteers set up an ambush along the Clonakilty-Bandon road near Gaggin. A solitary truck came along the road, but due to a misunderstanding never fully explained, the Volunteers did not open fire until it had almost passed through the ambush area. A few ragged shots were fired after the truck as it raced away. Unlike previous occasions, the truck stopped half a mile away, and the soldiers made their way back across the fields to where they had been ambushed. The Volunteers had withdrawn but the soldiers captured Volunteer Michael McLean and after torturing him, riddled his body with bullets, the whole scene being witnessed by a sixteen-year-old boy from a nearby cottage. The soldiers then set after the retiring column and eventually caught up with it. They began firing on the Volunteers, but realizing just how many there were, they made a strategic withdrawal.

In response to the attacks, martial law was extended by the British to include County Cork, the East and West Ridings, the city of cork itself, Tipperary, the North and South Ridings, the city and county of Limerick. Anyone caught with illegal arms was liable to be sentenced to death and shot. About this time the Cork brigades suffered a setback. At Convolute a small party of Volunteers were surrounded by a British column. They fought until their ammunition ran out. One Volunteer was dead, and most of the others were wounded. The survivors were taken prisoner and later executed.

On 11 December a truck of Auxiliaries was ambushed by the First Cork Brigade Flying Column near Dillons Cross. One of the Auxiliaries was killed, and several were wounded. That same day hand grenades were lobbed into a Crossley tender full of Auxiliaries as it was leaving Cork Military Barracks, by Volunteers from A Company, 1st Battalion, No. 1 Cork Brigade. Twelve Auxiliaries were wounded, one of them fatally. This incident appears to have provoked the burning of central Cork by a combination of Auxiliaries and Black and Tans that night. Fifty of the best shops in the commercial center of the city, most in Patrick Street, were burned, as well as the city hall and the Carnegie Library. At first the British authorities claimed that the IRA had set the city ablaze, but too many observers gave the lie to this. A military enquiry led by General Strickland firmly placed the blame on members of K Division of the Auxiliaries and the failure of their commanding officer to control them. A letter to the mother from one of the Auxiliaries involved was intercepted by Irish intelligence. It read as follows: "I contracted a chill on Saturday night during the burning and looting of Cork in all of which I took perforce a reluctant part. We did it all right never mind how much the well-intentioned Hamar Greenwood would excuse us. In all my life ... and in all the tales of fiction I have read I have never experienced such orgies of murder, arson and looting as I have witnessed during the past 16 days with the R.I.C. Auxiliaries. It baffles description. And we are supposed to be ex-officers and gentlemen. There are quite a number of decent fellows and likewise a lot of ruffians.... The houses in the vicinity of the ambush were set alight and from there the various parties set out on their mission of destruction. Many who witnessed similar scenes in France and Flanders say that nothing they have experienced ever compared to the punishment meted out in Cork."[7] Four days later, on the 15th of December, an Auxiliary officer named Harte killed a boy and a priest, Fr. Magner, in a seemingly motiveless assault at Dunmanway. There was an uproar at this senseless murder, but Harte was found by his superiors to be insane and was discharged from the service and never brought to trial.

Tom Barry kept up the pressure. On 19 December he conducted a successful ambush at Glencurrance. Two trucks containing eighteen soldiers were halted. In the ensuing fight two of them were killed and three injured before the remainder surrendered. The column captured eighteen rifles, five to six hundred rounds of ammunition and two dozen Mills hand grenades. The captured men were later released. The Fermoy Column followed up this ambush with one of their own. The column, under Patrick Egan, surprised a truck of British troops near Castlelyons. The driver was hit in the first volley and crashed the vehicle. The remaining soldiers scattered as best they could, but they were captured by the Volunteers and obliged to surrender their rifles and ammunition before being released.

Kilbrittain RIC Barracks was situated about fifteen miles southwest of the city of Cork. By Christmas 1920 the garrison had been replaced by Black and Tans. Strategically placed on the eastern edge of the 3 Brigade's area, it was a hindrance to communications, and its new garrison had developed a reputation for terrorizing the local populace. The Volunteer command decided to capture the barracks if possible and destroy it.

Cork City was burned by the Auxiliaries in 1920 as an unofficial reprisal.

It was an isolated building situated in the center of the village, set back about twenty feet from the road. It was strongly fortified with barred windows protected by heavy steel shutters equipped with loopholes for firing from. Each wall had a porthole from which a Mills grenade could be lobbed out onto any attackers. A strongly built porch protected the front door, and a thick barbed-wire entanglement covered the front and sides. The only way in was by storming the barracks directly from the front. It was unlikely that the front door could be opened by sledgehammer blows. The only alternative would be to use explosives. With this analysis in mind the brigade engineer, Mick Crowley, and former Royal engineer Peter Monahan prepared two mines. The operation was set for midnight on 31 December. Sixty Volunteers were mobilized from the Kilbrittain and neighboring companies. The six roads that led into Kilbrittain were blocked by fallen trees to prevent relief from arriving. As midnight approached, the mining party, in stockinged feet, skirted the barbed-wire entanglement and placed their mines along the wall on either side of the porch entrance. Then they withdrew to safety. The house immediately opposite the barracks had been taken over by riflemen, and others covered the sides and rear. A party of twelve Volunteers were close by, ready to storm the building once the wall had been breached. At midnight, Mick Crowley pushed the plunger — but nothing happened. He tried again, and again, but the mine did not explode. Inside the barracks, the Tans had become aware that an attack was in progress. They opened fire from the windows, which drew a response from the attackers. Shots were also fired at the mine in a vain attempt to blow it up. The attack had been a failure, and the Volunteers withdrew. It was a great disappointment for them.

The end of 1920 saw the 3 Cork Brigade very much on the offensive, taking the war to the enemy. Yet there was still much to do. At the beginning of the year they had just twenty-nine rifles; by the end they had one hundred and twenty. The number of revolvers rose from half a dozen to sixty. By December they had 30,000 rounds of ammunition and a supply of Mills bombs, all captured from the enemy. While some barracks had been abandoned and destroyed, leaving large areas under Republican control, some areas had been strengthened by the British. To the Volunteers these military garrisons were not seen to be as formidable as the RIC barracks. The police rather than the military had the local knowledge, and their raids were invariably intelligence-led. The military engaged in large encircling actions when they received intelligence of a flying column operating in their area. Invariably the column was informed of the presence of large British forces by the local people and managed to slip through the encirclement or, on one or two occasions, break through the encirclement before it was complete, inflicting casualties on the enemy as they did so. Liam Deasy, in his account of the 3 West Cork Brigade, gives an account of British displacements as they existed in this part of Cork at the end of 1920[8]:

British Regiment	*British Army Garrisons*	*Police and Auxiliaries*	*Barracks*
Essex	Kinsale	Auxiliaries	Macroom
	Bandon		Glengarriff
	Clonakilty		Dunmanway
	Ballineen	RIC/Black and Tans	Innishannon
King's Liverpools	Bantry		Bantry
	Skibbereen		Glengarriff
King's Own Yorkshire	Bere Island		Drimologue
Light Infantry	Furious Pier		Dunmanway
	Eyeries		

Abandoned or Destroyed RIC Barracks

Mount Pleasant	Ballydehob	Allihies
Ballinspittle	Goleen	Eyeries
Timoleague	Kilcrohane	Ballineen
Baltimore	Schull	Inchigeela
Castletownsend	Durrus	Kilmurry
Union Hall	Adrigole	Farran

By the end of 1920, a total of 182 policemen (including Auxiliaries and Black and Tans) and 50 soldiers had been killed by the IRA throughout Ireland and 256 wounded. Between the period of 1 January 1919 to 18 October 1920, it was revealed in the House of Commons, the lower house of the British Parliament, that 492 RIC barracks had been evacuated and 64 courthouses had been destroyed. British writ no longer ruled in the greater part of Ireland. In the West Cork Brigade area 41 of the enemy were killed to the Volunteers' loss of just five killed in action. Seventy-six rifles, forty-four revolvers, and a large amount of ammunition and explosives as well as hand grenades and other equipment were captured by the flying column.

The War in Tipperary, Limerick, Waterford, Wexford and Kilkenny

In the copies of the witness statements given to the Bureau of Military History that are now housed in the National Library in Dublin is an account given by Paddy Kinnane of an assault on Drumbane RIC Barracks, County Tipperary. The attack took place on 18 January 1920:

> The barracks itself was a one-storied building, originally used as a concert and dance hall, which had been taken over by the R.I.C. for use as a barracks. Our original idea was to hold the garrison within the barracks with rifle and shotgun fire, and to force them to surrender by setting fire to the roof. Later we were advised that a more effective way of capturing the barracks would be to blow in the gable end wall.... Selected men from the Upperchurch and Drumbane companies were chosen to take part in the attack, and units from the other companies were put on outpost duty on the roads leading to the village. Our arms consisted principally of shotguns, with a few rifles, and either two or three service rifles.
>
> When we got to the assembly point near Drumbane, some of the local Volunteers reported that two or three members of the R.I.C. garrison were gone out on patrol. A small party of our men ... followed the patrol, captured two of the three R.I.C. men, and held them prisoners while the attack was on. We experienced no difficulty in surrounding the barracks, or in placing the charge of gelignite against the gable wall. Everything so far was done without a sound. Our first reverse came with the explosion of the gelignite. It failed to breach or destroy the gable wall, but split it to such an extent that, through the cracked wall, we could see the light inside the barracks. We felt so confident that the gelignite would demolish the wall and make easy our task of capturing the barracks that we had abandoned the idea of setting it on fire, and had no materials with us to put this alternative plan into operation.
>
> It was, however, then too late for regrets, and after a short exchange of fire and after the R.I.C. had fired several Verey [sic] lights for assistance, it was decided to call off the attack. In addition to the patrol, another R.I.C. man was captured on his way back to the barracks, just before the explosion took place. He was unarmed; we kept him a prisoner until about an hour after the abandonment, when we left him in a farmer's hay barn about a mile from Drumbane.

In Limerick, the Volunteers in the city embarked on a number of small but rewarding attacks on the police and army in order to acquire arms. On 1 February 1920, a British soldier of Irish descent, Private Quinn, was wounded, in O'Connell Avenue, and his revolver taken. On 22 February Sergeant Wellwood of the RIC was seriously wounded as he emerged from the William Street Barracks. Constable Murphy was wounded in Thomas Street on 10 March, and Sergeant Conroy of the RIC was seriously wounded on 18 March. In all cases arms were seized. That same March the Kilkenny IRA attacked the RIC barracks at Hugginstown. An incendiary bomb was dropped into the building through a hole knocked in the roof. In the subsequent explosion when the ammunition caught fire, Constable Thomas Ryan was killed. A firefight continued for some time, but with little chance of securing the barracks' immediate surrender, and with the approach of dawn bringing with it the strong probability of British Army reinforcements, the Volunteers retired without loss. The barracks was subsequently abandoned.

Ballylanders

Ballylanders RIC Barracks, County Limerick, stood on one corner of a crossroads, butting onto the road to Kilfane. Strongly built of stone, with steel shutters across its windows and surrounded by eight-foot high barbed-wire entanglements, it dominated the village that gave it its name. The front of the building faced onto a large open square devoid of any cover. For some days the Volunteers from the Galtee Battalion studied it with a view to its destruction. Its one weakness was that it was a duplex. The building adjoining it was the local dispensary.

On the night of 27 April 1920, some thirty Volunteers from the East Limerick Brigade assisted by men from the local Battalion, under acting OC Tomas Malone (whose nom de guerre was Sean Ford), approached the town. Roadblocks about a mile from the town were established and manned. Twenty-five Volunteers from the brigade entered the town and took up their preplanned positions. A small group broke into the dispensary next door, and climbing the stairs, Malone and Volunteer Ned Toibin got out onto the roof, where they set about smashing the slate roof of the barracks. Battalion vice-commandant J. McCarthy placed the remainder of the men in the buildings surrounding the barracks on three sides. As the first slates were broken, these men opened fire on the barracks. The police returned fire, and launched Very rockets to summon help. As the men on the roof edged forward to drop inflammatory material into the hole to set the building alight, some policemen below directed their fire at the gap, preventing the attackers from getting any closer. A well lobbed hand grenade through the gap silenced this brief defense. Paraffin was poured into the hole and a flaming torch was dropped in. The upper storey burst into flames, sending tongues of fire shooting up through the hole in the roof.

Meanwhile, the firefight below, at almost point-blank range, continued in earnest. By pressing home their attack the Volunteers prevented the garrison from quenching the flames. Soon the whole upper storey was ablaze and threatening to crash down onto the floor below. The rate of fire from the defenders slackened, then it ceased. A makeshift white flag was pushed out of one of the lower windows. The garrison had surrendered. With reassurances that they would not be killed, the five-strong garrison, none of whom had been wounded, left the building. The Volunteers had one man wounded, Sean Meade, but not fatally. The garrison was ransacked for weapons. Nine rifles, pistols, hand grenades and ammunition were recovered. As the roof fell in, the barracks completely destroyed, the column moved off in orderly fashion.

Towards the end of April, C Company of the Mid-Limerick Battalion audaciously planned an ambush on the RIC right in the heart of the county town. An evening patrol regularly proceeded down Clare Street each night. The men taking part in the ambush were on the point of taking up positions when suddenly trucks of troops descended upon the area. Clearly they were acting upon intelligence. The IRA commandant retired his men in a carefully planned withdrawal. They retired with their arms to the nearby canal where boats were waiting to ferry them to the other side. This crossing was fortunate because the trucks of troops were just part of a larger encirclement. Now safe, the Volunteers discovered that military cordons had secured the bridges over the canal. That night the British scoured the city for the ambush party, then long gone.

The South Tipperary Brigade of Volunteers were led by Seamus Robinson, with Sean Treacy as vice-commandant. The brigade area extended from east Limerick to the border with County Kilkenny beyond Carrick-on-Suir. Its southern border was the Knockmealdown, Monavullagh and Comeragh mountains. Its northern boundary was the hills beyond Hollyford, extending to the Plain of the Golden Vale and the Slieveardagh hills beyond Killenhaule. Opposing the Volunteers were the strong military barracks at Tipperary (containing 1,000 troops), Cahir, Cashel and Fethard. There were also smaller military and RIC barracks dotted throughout the brigade area. The Tipperary Town Battalion of the brigade at the start of 1920 had just ten rifles and thirty shotguns. The British in Tipperary Town, army and RIC combined, were reckoned to have had eleven hundred and fifty rifles and revolvers. Yet, despite this glaring disparity, by the spring of 1921 the Volunteers were on the offensive and the British on the defensive. The key to this dramatic about-face was the removal of the eyes and ears of British intelligence — the RIC.

In early May 1920, Robinson and Treacy, accompanied by Ernie O'Malley from GHQ, Dublin, surveyed the brigade area for likely targets in the acquisition of arms. The RIC barracks at Hollyford stood out. It commanded a pass in this hilly part of the country. The capture and destruction of the barracks would answer a twofold problem: the gaining of arms and the ease of access by the Volunteers in future actions. The barracks was a long and high two-storied, white-washed building. Its many windows were protected by steel shutters, and loopholes had been cut in the walls. The gable end of the barracks near the road had an upper window and loopholes on the ground floor. Estimations indicated that the ground floor was six feet higher than the ground outside. Across the road from the barracks was a stone wall which would give some protection in an attack on the building. The three men approached the local company captain, Jim Gorman, an Irish-Australian who had returned to Ireland at the end of World War I, for his opinion. The four men agreed that the gable end might be breached by a mine. The local Volunteer company had acquired some gelignite as well as blasting powder, so the attempt was feasible. Lacking the necessary expertise in making large bombs, however, they changed their minds and decided to launch an attack through the roof of the building. This necessitated at least two Volunteers clambering up ladders and breaking through the slates before petrol could be poured in and ignited.

Before anything could be attempted, O'Malley insisted upon an exit strategy. From his maps with police and army barracks marked, and additional information contained in a notebook as to the strength of these barracks, O'Malley worked out that there were four barracks from which relief could be sent, all within a radius of nine miles. Roads therefore needed to be blockaded to prevent any surprise attacks. Improvised bombs were prepared for the assault on Hollyford, including hand grenades and blast bombs to blow the slates off the barracks' roof. On the night of 11 May the operation began. At 11 o'clock trees were felled across roads and stone barricades were erected across others. Sean Treacy and Ernie O'Malley volunteered to go up onto the roof. Silently they approached the barracks and climbed the ladders. Buckets of petrol and paraffin were passed up to them, the Volunteers working in stocking feet to avoid making a noise. Up on the roof the two officers began breaking slates with hammers and poured the petrol in. At this the garrison was alerted and opened fire at the Volunteers across the road behind the small stone wall. Up on the roof Treacy and O'Malley dropped lighted turfs into the holes they had made. In addition, bombs were flung down, and soon the upper storey of the barracks was ablaze. Treacy and O'Malley, now badly singed in the blaze, made a hasty retreat from the roof. The firefight below intensified; but as the lower part of the barracks did not catch alight, the RIC defenders were able to make a brave defense of their barracks. Dawn broke as the shooting continued, but with it the probability of relief now arriving, the order was reluctantly given for the Volunteers to withdraw.

Kilmallock

Kilmallock in County Limerick, one of the strongest RIC posts, was strategically placed at a bridging point over the river Maigue. As such, it was guarded by a not insubstantial RIC barracks housing eighteen Auxiliary policemen. Its capture would provide arms and ammunition, and its destruction would give unrestricted access for the East Limerick Column. Considerable planning was undertaken, and reinforcements were drawn from Volunteer columns from County Cork, County Tipperary and east Clare. Approximately sixty Volunteers were assembled on the night of 28 May. Thirty of them were assigned to the actual assault, the remainder to man various barricades and outposts, particularly along the roads to Tipperary, Limerick and Buttevant, where British reinforcements might be expected to arrive. The barracks was set back from the road and fronted by a small lawn. Defensively it was strong, built of solid masonry, steel-shuttered, loopholed and surrounded by barbed-wire entanglements. Its one weakness was the building next to it, a business premise named Carroll's which rose above it. There was a slight gap between the two buildings. The Volunteers taking part in the assault were divided up into smaller groups. Tomas Malone with Edmond Tobin and P. Hannigan were assigned Carroll's. Facing the barracks from different sides were Clery's Hotel, the Provincial Bank and O'Herlihy's shop, all of which were broken into and occupied.

Shortly after midnight a heavy iron weight was lobbed onto the roof of the barracks from the skylight of Carrol's by the Volunteers there. It crashed through the slates, creating a gaping hole in the roof. Amidst the fierce firefight that then ensued, a series of what were later to be known as Molotov cocktails — bottles filled with petrol and a burning rag in the neck — were thrown into the hole in the roof. Though initially taken unaware, the police put up a stout resistance, accurately returning fire. Up on the roof of Carrol's a hand grenade was lobbed into the hole in the barracks roof, which started a conflagration. By 2:00 A.M. the upper part of the barracks was blazing furiously, threatening to send the upper floor crashing down on the defenders. The order was given to ceasefire, and the Volunteers called upon the garrison to surrender. The policemen responded with a furious fusillade, and the fight continued. More Molotov cocktails were thrown into the hole in the roof and at the front of the building. As dawn broke the defenders moved out of the main building into an outhouse at the back as the upper floor came crashing down onto their former position. At this point the Volunteers across the road moved forward, firing as they did so. Volunteer Liam Scully was killed as he advanced, the only IRA casualty of the assault. With full daylight, the last of their ammunition spent and with the expectation of heavy army and police reinforcements arriving, the attackers withdrew in good order. The barracks had been completely destroyed, along with all its store of ammunition. Sergeant O'Sullivan and five policemen had found refuge in a specially constructed small room at the rear of the building. Police losses were never published, but they would appear to have been one constable killed and two seriously wounded. Another account suggests that perhaps eight policemen were suffocated or burned. The barracks was abandoned and future patrols of the area were conducted in daylight hours from Tipperary and Limerick.

Following the funeral of Liam Scully at Templeglatine, Commandant Clancy and the OC of the East Limerick Brigade, Donncadha O'Hannigan, traveled back to Tankardstown, where they stayed overnight and continued their journey on to Kilmallock and their final destination at Cush the following morning. Fully armed, they had avoided British garrisoned towns and had succeeded in traveling thirty miles without incident. Most of the journey had been in daylight hours. It occurred to them that if *they* had done it, there was no reason why a larger number of men, organized and equipped as a mobile active service unit, could not do likewise. Thus was conceived the permanent flying column — the maintenance in the field of a swift-moving body of armed men, able to strike at the enemy where and when a suitable opportunity arose. The two men formed the East Limerick Flying Column with O'Hannigan as OC. The original Column consisted of just twelve men, nine of whom are known by name: Commandant O'Hannigan, Vice Commandant P. O'Donnell, Commandant Tadhg Crowley, Volunteers Quane, David Clancy (brother of Commandant P. Clancy), Tom Murphy, David Tobin, Seamus Finn (later promoted to lieutenant), and Tom Howard. From then until the truce they averaged at least one major engagement against the enemy each month. The column operated out of the Fifth Galtee Battalion area. They engaged the enemy at Ballinahinch, Emly, Bruree, Kildare, Cross of the Tree (Knocklong), Grange, Glenacurrane, Dromkeen, Kilfinane, Shraherla, Lackelly and Annacarty.

Emly

At Emly on 13 July, the new flying column engaged a detachment of eight soldiers from the Lincolnshire Regiment, accompanied by two RIC men, a sergeant and a constable. The column had just five rifles, one Winchester rifle (with seventy rounds of rifle ammunition), three shotguns and three revolvers. The soldiers were stretched along the road for one hundred yards, which prevented a concentration of fire on the part of the Volunteers. The engagement lasted three and a half hours, and the Volunteers had all but exhausted their ammunition when the British soldiers surrendered. One of their number had been wounded. The soldiers were taken prisoner and were stripped of nine rifles and 650 rounds of ammunition. Upon the request of their officer, O'Hannigan wrote a note for him to the effect that he and his men had been surrounded and attacked. They had fought well, but they had been outmaneuvered and compelled to surrender. This letter was subsequently published in the *Irish Independent,* along with a note from the British officer that they had been "courteously treated by our captors and we owe them our lives." The Volunteers had gained the moral high ground by their treatment of their prisoners. This was not the image that the British government wished to see portrayed of its enemies, and further such notes, if written, were ordered not to be published. Reports of the East Limerick Flying Column's successes were forwarded to volunteer headquarters in Dublin, inducing them to order the setting up of similar columns in all brigade areas.

Drangon on the Tipperary-Kilkenny border had a small RIC barracks. Its capture and destruction would expand Republican held territory. Vice-Commandant Sean Treacy of the South Tipperary Brigade, in conjunction with the West Kilkenny Flying Column, resolved to capture it in a nighttime assault. The plan was to smash through the roof and set the barracks alight, forcing the garrison to surrender. On the night of 7 June a forward party of four Volunteers led by Ernie O'Malley began a reconnaissance of the village. As they moved towards the barracks they were challenged by a police patrol. A brief firefight ensued, with both parties firing as they withdrew to safety. Hearing the shooting the main body of Volunteers, led by Treacy, advanced on the village. Hand grenades were thrown by the police as they withdrew to the seeming safety of the barracks. Hot in pursuit, a party of the Volunteers rushed into the one-storey house adjacent to the barracks as the others engaged the police in a gunfight. Entering into the house the Volunteers climbed the stairs to the roof, which they broke open. From here they threw mud bombs (half sticks of gelignite wrapped in sticky clay which adhered to surfaces) onto the roof of the barracks. The bombs exploded, creating holes in the roof. Petrol was poured in and ignited by burning rags. The roof and upper storey of the barracks was soon ablaze. Ammunition in the upper room started to explode. From the room below a policeman called out to the attackers, telling them that they wanted to talk. Their fear was that the Volunteers would kill them if they surrendered. The Volunteers reassured them that they would be treated honorably, and a policeman pushed a white shirt tied to a rifle out of one of the barrack windows and they surrendered. Upon orders the Volunteers ceased firing. The police and one Black and Tan came out of the building with their hands raised. The prisoners' names were taken and they were warned that if they were captured again they would be shot. They were then stripped of arms bandoleers and ordered to march away. As this was going on the other Volunteers entered the burning building and removed a number of carbines and long Lee-Enfields, as well as boxes of ammunition, hand grenades and whatever official papers they could find.

North Tipperary Brigade were in action on 26 June 1920. It was their first attack on an RIC barracks. The brigade OC was Frank McGrath, a prominent local sportsman and Gaelic Leaguer. Two hundred men were involved in the attack on Borriscane Barracks, and arms and munitions were supplied by Dublin GHQ. The attack lasted for two hours; the barracks were set on fire, and surrender seemed inevitable. At that point McGrath called off the attack without explanation and withdrew his men. The failure to complete the assault left a bitter taste in the mouths of a number of his junior officers, particularly as the RIC men abandoned the barracks less than half an hour after the attackers had withdrawn. Backed up by GHQ staff liaison officer Ernie O'Malley, McGrath's junior officers complained to GHQ about his lack of leadership. An enquiry led to McGrath's dismissal and his replacement by a more active officer, Sean Gaynor.

On 9 July, Captain P. O'Donnell of the East Limerick Column led a group of fifteen Volunteers (men who had just recently gone on the run) in an ambush on an RIC bicycle patrol at Ballinahinch. The police were taken completely by surprise, and after a few warning shots from the Volunteers, they surrendered. There were no casualties on either side, and the Volunteers gained four rifles and ammunition. West Limerick, due to the flatness of its terrain, was not ideal guerrilla country. Nevertheless the men of West Limerick did engage with the enemy, but not always with a satisfactory outcome. During that summer of 1920 they suffered two setbacks due to a lack of proper organization. Word reached the local Volunteers that a police cycling patrol of a sergeant and five constables, armed with carbines and revolvers, had arrived at Tournafulla from Abbeyfeale. It was decided to ambush them on their return journey. The police left earlier than expected, and reached the ambush position before all of the Volunteers had got into position. Only two men were prepared, and with a rifle and shotgun they opened fire on the police, hoping to hold them up until the others arrived. The police hurriedly dismounted and returned fire, getting the better of the two Republicans, whom they drove off. Having successfully repulsed their attackers, they got back on their bicycles and continued back to their barracks. On a second occasion the Volunteers learned that a detachment of eight RIC men regularly patrolled along the road between Foynes and Glin. An IRA unit under Sean Finn lay in wait to ambush them. The policemen rode into the ambush completely unawares. The Volunteers opened up on them and mortally wounded one of their number, Constable Fahy. The RIC held their nerve though and returned fire. Maneuvering for position they gained higher ground and the advantage. It was only with difficulty that the IRA unit extricated itself and retired in some sort of order.

During July 1920, Tipperary's Soloheadbeg Company heard that a military mail truck, preceded by a motorcyclist, regularly traveled along the Tipperary to Limerick road. Sean Treacy, the company commandant, decided to ambush it. A regular pattern was discerned, and Treacy chose an ambush site. The company had recently acquired a number of Martini-Henry rifles, and this presented an ideal opportunity to test them out in an engagement. More or less at the appointed time the sound of a truck's engine was heard approaching. There was no motorcycle. The truck entered the ambush site and was fired upon. Almost at once a second British truck filled with troops arrived. They quickly scrambled from their vehicle and joined the fight. To their horror, after firing one round, the ambushers discovered that the ejectors of their Martini rifles failed to eject the empty cases. The probable cause was the use of incorrect ammunition. With no choice but to break off the assault and withdraw, Treacy, with rapid fire from his parabellum, kept the soldiers pinned down as they did so. Despite the failure of the ambush, two British soldiers were killed and three wounded.

That same July, South Tipperary's flying column, led by Dinny Lacey, carried out two successful ambushes. The first was at Thomastown, where six British soldiers were killed. At the Glen of Aherlow four members of the hated Black and Tans were killed. On 16 August British forces burned buildings in Templemore as a reprisal for recent IRA actions in the area. Towards the end of that month, the newly established East Limerick Flying Column, in pursuit of further action, reached the Bruree area. Quite unexpectedly they came across a military cycle patrol. There was a brief firefight before the patrol withdrew under covering fire towards Bruree. With the column in hot pursuit, some of the soldiers took refuge in a cottage, while the others fled and left their comrades to their fate. Knowing the cottage to be occupied, the column was reluctant to attack it for fear of killing the owners, known Republican sympathizers. The column withdrew in orderly fashion towards the Cork-Limerick border. Crossing the county border the column linked up with sections of the Glanworth and Ballindangon (County Cork) Volunteers. Upon intelligence, the reinforced column took up an ambush site on the edge of Kildorrey Town and there intercepted an RIC patrol, mainly consisting of Black and Tans. After engaging in what was described as a sharp fight, the RIC patrol, eight in number and most of them wounded, surrendered. Gathering up the captured weapons and ammunition, the column moved deeper into County Cork.

In the autumn of 1920 plans were made by the West Limerick Flying Column to ambush the Black and Tans based at Abbeyfeale. They had developed a somewhat bad reputation for brutality. In particular the IRA wished to kill a Black and Tan by the name of Huckerby, who while at the nearby Shanagolden Barracks had murdered an old man called Reidy in cold blood. One September night the West Limerick Flying Column, thirty strong, took up an ambush position on the outskirts of Abbeyfeale. They had nine rifles and some revolvers. The others were armed with shotguns. There were a dozen or so Black and Tans at Abbeyfeale, and they usually patrolled near enough at full strength. They all had carbines and revolvers and carried hand grenades. All ex-soldiers, they presented a formidable presence. However, a close contact ambush would negate any advantage the Tans had. An ambush site was found along the road to Mountmahon. But while the ambushers awaited final orders the cycle patrol approached and, hearing voices, silently dismounted and approached. As the patrol looked over the hedge into the fields, they were seen by members of the column, who opened fire. Constable Mahony was mortally wounded. In the prolonged firefight that followed, five more Tans were wounded before they managed to extricate themselves and escape. The column withdrew in good order to Athea, six miles away. In revenge, the sought-after Huckerby, who had escaped the ambush uninjured, shot dead two young men named Harnett and Healy.

On 18 October two Irish Volunteer brothers, Ned and Frank Dwyer, were killed by British forces in Bansha, County Tipperary. In north Tipperary, at Kilcommon Cross, Volunteers ambushed British troops, killing four and wounding three. The Volunteers in County Wexford had suffered a severe setback a week earlier on 12 October. Five of their number were killed and five seriously injured when explosives they were preparing accidentally went off in a house at St. Kearns, Saltmills.

The Tipperary Flying Column went into action for the first time on 28 October 1920. Tadgh Crowe's account of the action is recorded in the witness statements of the Bureau of Military History:

> About 9 A.M. that morning we prepared and occupied a position to ambush a tender of Black and Tans from Golden, but a lorry conveying about twenty soldiers to the rifle range in Tipperary arrived and we ambushed that instead. My recollection is that the lorry slowed up and then stopped before it came into the ambush position proper, with the result that some of our men had to crawl behind the wall to get a position nearer to the lorry.
>
> Meanwhile, the soldiers were dismounting and taking cover and we had lost the element of surprise. The military officer in charge of the party either wore Armour or bore a charmed life. He was firing from the bonnet of the lorry and Jim O'Gorman lobbed the only grenade we possessed over the wall and quite close to the lorry, but it failed to explode. Ned O'Reilly and O'Gorman — both crack shots — fired at him from the road but, as far as I could see, without effect.
>
> The firing lasted, I would say, for eight or ten minutes. One of our men, Michael Fitz-

A British military patrol driving through an Irish town (courtesy the National Library of Ireland).

patrick, received a serious wound in his thigh and had to be helped away. He was our only casualty. Lacy [the flying column commandant] then decided to break off the engagement. As the ambush position was on the main Cashel-Tipperary road there was a grave danger of further enemy forces arriving, and the Column, with the exception of two men who were assisting Michael Fitzpatrick, withdrew.

At the start of 1920 the Waterford Brigade began attacking police barracks throughout the county. As a result the smaller ones were evacuated and the garrisons moved to larger police stations in the major towns. Stradbally was attacked, as was Ardmore (twice), Ballinamoult, Kilmanahan and others. The flying column of West Waterford ambushed a British Army convoy at Piltown (Kinsalabeg) in County Waterford on 1 November 1920. Two soldiers were killed, six wounded and thirty captured. With them was RIC constable Maurice Prendeville, the intelligence officer leading the raid. Fearing for his life he promised to leave the RIC, but he later went back on his word. He was tracked down as a consequence and a month later was shot dead at the Youghal Bridge. The other captured soldiers were disarmed but were later released unharmed. A second ambush that day, on reinforcements arriving from Tramore, went badly wrong. The column was seriously outnumbered and two Volunteers were killed and two more wounded before the column made an orderly withdrawal. That same day unsuccessful attacks were carried out on the RIC barracks and Marine Station at Ardmore, County Waterford. The column was also engaged in clashes at Durrow Station, which lasted nearly the whole day, and at Ballyvoyle.

Grange

The ambush at Grange, County Limerick, on the morning of 8 November, was a textbook guerrilla action, with attention paid not only to the assault, but also to a controlled withdrawal. Information had been received of an unvarying set routine involving two trucks of British troops that traveled each morning between Limerick and Bruff. Tomas Malone, commander of the East Limerick Flying Column, decided to ambush the convoy, with the aid of the local company. The ambush site was carefully chosen, given the approach of the enemy. The column itself was positioned on the west side of the road behind a high wall; a platform of planks raised on barrels was provided as a fire-step, giving the attackers a height advantage. The majority of the men from the local battalion were placed on the opposite side of the road. Two farm carts lashed together by a ladder were ready to be pushed out onto the road to act as a roadblock. To the east of the road was the projected line of withdrawal for the guerrillas. It provided good cover should the column be faced with unexpected British reinforcements. The western side of the road was bogland, traversed by a stream. While this area would hinder British reinforcements from advancing through it, there was little protection, save for a few scattered trees, should reinforcements attack from the rear. South, beyond the stream, the road turned sharply westward. Measures to counter the arrival of British reinforcements from this direction were prepared. A mile to the south an outpost was established to intercept any reinforcements from the British garrison at Bruff, three miles away. A mile to the north of the ambush site a second party of Volunteers were positioned to intercept any reinforcements from Fedamore or Hospital.

By 5:00 A.M. the thirty-strong flying column was in position. Several hours passed before the outpost scouts signaled the approach of the trucks, traveling from Bruff to Limerick. It was 11:00 A.M. Unbeknownst to the ambushing party, a motorized convoy of eight trucks accompanied by two armored cars was approaching from the opposite direction. As the first of the intended trucks entered the ambush position it was fired on, and hand grenades were thrown. The second truck entered the zone and it too was attacked. Hearing the gunfire and explosives, the British convoy coming from the other direction halted around the bend from the ambush site. On a height above the attackers and out of their sight, the troops dismounted and advanced on foot. Meanwhile, at the ambush site the mobile barricade was pushed across the road to prevent the two trucks from reversing. This also prevented the reinforcements down the road from advancing by truck to relieve their comrades.

The dismounted British troops, outnumbering the Volunteers, came on through the bogs towards the stream, in effect outflanking the rear of those men in the column based along the high wall on the western side of the road. The British opened fire on the Volunteers with rifles, machine guns and rifle grenades. The Volunteers on the eastern side of the road were unable to help their comrades, and retreat by the Volunteers on the western side of the road would leave them open to disaster. Malone decided to counterattack as a preliminary to a withdrawal. Half the column, under Malone, advanced towards the stream to engage the British. The other half were ordered forward to a grove of trees just to the northwest of the original ambush site. With both sections in place, Malone's group at the stream opened heavy fire on the advancing yet exposed British soldiers. Without adequate cover the British troops withdrew to their trucks. As they did so, Malone took the opportunity of withdrawing his men at the stream, covered by the Volunteers in the grove. Both sections linked up north of the original ambush site and withdrew eastwards along the preplanned line of withdrawal. The Volunteers had two men wounded but not fatally. British losses were not disclosed but must have been fairly heavy, especially among the soldiers traveling in the ambushed trucks — perhaps eight to ten. In their dispersed cross-country withdrawal a section of the column encountered a convoy of two troop-carrying trucks. There was a brief exchange of fire before both sides retired that left one Volunteer, John O'Riordan, fatally wounded. The British force made no attempt to follow them, fearing a further ambush.

Lisnagaul

A Bureau of Military History statement by Volunteer Paul Merrigan recalls an action by the 1st Tipperary Flying Column on 13 November at Lisnagaul:

> [E]ight of us from the Mount Bruis company billeted with the Column near Lisnagaul. We had been selected beforehand to assist in the ambush. It was also the second or third attempt by the Column to ambush this particular party of R.I.C. and Black and Tans on their way to Bansha.
>
> The position was at a bend in the road about three miles from Bansha and about the same distance from the village of Church-road. We occupied it at about 9 A.M. My position was with the main party, and I was armed with a service rifle. About 3 P.M., a scout signaled the approach of the police party. As the tender on which they were traveling came into position, there were several shouts of "halt," but as I saw it the driver appeared to put on speed. Lacey blew a single blast on his whistle, which was the signal to open fire. The driver was killed in the first volley, and the tender hit the ditch, but it had also cleared, or partly cleared, the bend of the road. Those of the police who were not killed in the first volley got cover under the tender, and replied to our fire. The firing continued, I would say, for about eight or ten minutes, until the police shouted that they were surrendering. The firing ceased, and four policemen who surrendered were wounded.... When we got out on the road we found three others dead. One policeman had escaped, and succeeded in getting away. The arms, which we collected as a result of this ambush, were ten rifles (police carbine type), seven revolvers, all stamped "RIC," some slings of ammunition, a box of ammunition and some grenades which were on the tender. Finally, the tender itself was set on fire after the dead bodies of the police had been removed from it.

On 21 November three men from the West Waterford Flying Column were recognized driving past Walsh's Hotel in Cappoquin while carrying out a reconnaissance. In an exchange of fire RIC constable Isaac Rea was mortally wounded. Less than a week later, on 27 November, three Volunteers from the West Waterford Flying Column returned to Cappoquin and in a brief exchange of fire killed another RIC man, Constable Maurice Quirk.

On 10 December 1920, the East Limerick Column prepared an ambush near Knocklong. As the enemy vehicles entered the site it proved to be a much larger convoy than had been expected. The ambushers were greatly outnumbered, forcing them to retreat in haste. There appears to have been a suggestion of panic in the Volunteer ranks, but this was steadied by the courage of a British ex-soldier called Johnny Riordan. He covered their withdrawal. As he himself withdrew he was shot and mortally wounded. The Black and Tans failed to pursue the withdrawing column, and Riordan was rescued by one of his comrades who came back to help him. Riordan was carried off, but he had lost too much blood. Despite the ministrations of a friendly doctor Riordan died.

Glencurrane

At Glenacurrane, County Limerick, on 17 December, the East Limerick Flying Column, under the command of Donncadha O'Hannigan, attacked and defeated a motorized convoy carrying mail from Fermoy to Tipperary. Four British soldiers were killed and the rest captured. Rifles, ammunition and hand grenades were also captured before the trucks were set on fire. The mail was taken away for scrutiny by the brigade's intelligence officers. The civilian mail, after being censored, was reposted. Included in the haul was a box of medals to be issued to military personnel for "Gallant Conduct in Ireland." The attack had come about when word reached the East Limerick Flying Column that the British were using the main Limerick to Tipperary road, between Fermoy and Tipperary, for the shipment of mail and supplies on a fairly regular basis. Very early on the morning of the 17 December, the column moved down from the Galtee Mountains and proceeded across country to rendezvous with Commandant David Barry and his Cork Volunteers at Glenacurrane. Commandants Barry, from Cork, and Tom Malone, of the East Limerick Column, placed their men in ambush. A tree was partially cut through in readiness for felling across the road as a blockade. Malone, who had led the attack at Grange the previous November, had expected a much larger convoy, so he had sought reinforcements from the men of Cork, making it the strongest force ever assembled in the county for a single operation. The Cork Volunteers brought with them a Hotchkiss machine gun. Just prior to the attack a number of civilians passing along the road were made prisoners for their own good, including a Church of Ireland minister.

The Volunteer outpost signaled the approach of the convoy. It consisted of two trucks carrying twenty soldiers of the Lincolnshire Regiment, based at Tipperary, and a Sunbeam touring car. As the convoy approached the ambush area the tree was felled to block the road. The ambushers opened fire in flank and rear, thus preventing them from reversing. It was a short firefight, the Lincolns having been taken completely by surprise. Several of the soldiers were wounded, four fatally. When it was all over the Church of Ireland minister was summoned to attend to the dying men. The Volunteers seized all the captured rifles, some boxes of grenades, and about 300 rounds of ammunition. The wounded soldiers were taken to a cottage about a mile away at Athnaslinga, where their wounds were treated. The column then withdrew to billets in the Glenroe and Tully areas, and the Cork unit returned home. As Christmas approached the column was stood down and the Volunteers were given a few days leave to spend with family and friends.

On the 20th of December, the West Kilkenny Flying Column ambushed a joint army and police patrol at Nine-Mile-House, between Clonmel and Kilkenny. British reinforcements came under attack twice. In all, eight soldiers and an RIC sergeant were killed, and several of the Crown forces were wounded. The Volunteers suffered no casualties and withdrew from the scene to be stood down for Christmas.

Like an end of term report, London-Irishman Joe Good, who had been sent down to Limerick by GHQ, Dublin, was to report: "It soon became clear to me that open war was in full progress. All the Volunteers that I was to see there carried arms openly, and they seemed in very real possession of many towns and villages. Many of the R.I.C. barracks had fallen, and I could feel that it wouldn't be too long before [West Limerick Brigadier Garret MacAuliffe] and his men would make their move on the city of Limerick itself.... The regular British Army was, to an amazing extent, stalemated, non-combatants, leaving, as it were, a clear field of fire between the Volunteers and the local police or RIC forces."[9]

On St. Stephen's feast day, 26 December, a dance was arranged by the local branch of Cumann na mBan to raise money for the East Limerick Brigade to purchase arms. The venue was Caherguillamore House, half a mile from Holycross on the road between Bruff and Fedamore. Elaborate arrangements were made to keep the venue secret, given that Volunteers from the brigade would be attending. Those wishing to go to the dance were notified to proceed to a specified place where they were then directed on to a second location, where eventually they were given the ultimate destination. In this way it was believed that the dance could be enjoyed without police interference. Unfortunately the location was betrayed to the police, for financial gain, by a member of the East Limerick Brigade.

The dance started at nine o'clock that night. Sentries were posted around the house as a safety measure. There were about one hundred women at the dance, and about one hundred and forty men, including most of the brigade. Shortly before two o'clock in the morning, while the party was in full swing, trucks containing three hundred RIC men and Black and Tans from Bruff and Limerick arrived at the house. They entered the grounds, and after surrounding it they advanced on Caherguillamore House. A shot was heard, then after a few seconds a second and a third shot. A constable from Bruff had been shot by one of the sentries, who was himself killed by another policeman. A second sentry was also shot. Sometime earlier Martin Conway, a Volunteer captain, and two other Volunteers, Nicholas Dwyer and John Gerard, had gone out to inspect the sentries. They were out near the Cahir road when a delayed truck of Tans arrived. Exposed as they were in the truck's headlights, the three men made a run for it. The policemen fired on them. Conway was wounded but dragged himself away, pursued in his escape by a small group of Tans. About four miles away from the house they caught up with him and killed him. O'Dwyer and Gerard, though also wounded, succeeded in making good their escapes.

The element of surprise now gone, the Tans opened fire on the house with rifle and machine-gun fire. Inside Caherguillamore House the order was given: "Wanted men, make your escape!" Some did succeed, but by then the enemy were already in the house. The enemy burst into the ballroom and ordered everybody to put up their hands, and roughly separated the men and women. A Cumann na mBan woman was slapped across the face and a revolver was placed to her head when she protested at the violence towards the men prisoners. The men were beaten up by the police as they were questioned. Recognized Volunteers were led away to Limerick Gaol for further interrogation. Five Volunteers were killed in the action — Edward Moloney, Henry Wade, Daniel Sheehan, John Quinlan (lieutenant) and Martin Conway (captain). Of the male prisoners, fifty-eight were recognized as Volunteers and were sentenced to ten years' imprisonment. On Tuesday, 28 December, the mail car from Limerick to Bruff was waylaid by a party of Volunteers. Going through the letters the identity of the man who had betrayed them was discovered. By then he was far away and never traced.

The War in Kerry and Clare

The war in Kerry and Clare was a vicious little war marked out more by reprisal and murder by the paramilitary police of the occupying power than by ambushes as in other counties. In April 1920 a joint patrol of the RIC and the Highland Light Infantry fired into an unarmed crowd in Miltown Malbay. They were celebrating the release of Republican prisoners imprisoned for illegal drilling. Three men were killed and nine wounded. The county coroner found nine soldiers and a policeman guilty of murder and served warrants on them. No action was taken by the British, and the men accused of murder were moved away from the district.

Brosna

At the start of June, the Kerry Column, with the aid of men from the West Limerick Column, planned the capture of Brosna RIC barracks, which was a remote police station in the midst of bogs and hills, ideal guerrilla country. It stood in the village, at the southeast corner of the square, beside the cemetery. Possibly through the work of an informer, although it was never ascertained, the military heard of the IRA's intention and, lying in wait, surprised and captured the men, many of whom were unarmed, as they made their way to Brosna village.

Realizing that the British would not be expecting another attack on Brosna quite so soon, the Kerry IRA decided to attack it just a few days later on the 5th of June. Again they requested the aid of the West Limerick Column. Mossie Harnett, in charge of sixteen Limerick Volunteers all armed with captured carbines and rifles, met up with T.M. O'Connor and Dan McCarthy and their men that evening at a field across the river from Brosna. As night descended the Volunteers made their way to their appointed positions facing the barracks. It was an ill-conceived venture; no mines were available to blow open a door or bring down a wall, nor any provision made for breaking open the roof and setting a fire. As the final Volunteers moved into position the defenders within the barracks became aware of their presence and began firing at the moving shadows. The Volunteers responded, and hand grenades were thrown at the barracks roof in an attempt to smash it open but with little success. The attack lasted all night. The RIC vainly sent up Very lights begging for assistance that never came. Dawn broke, and the assault continued. The morning wore on, and with little chance of capturing the barracks and with every reason to suspect that a heavily armed military reinforcement was now on its way, the Volunteers retired section by section in good order. The two columns disbanded, and the Limerick men made their way home. Some of the West Limerick men, seven or eight in number, acting as outlying scouts for the attack on the barracks, now came under attack themselves by part of the relieving force. That morning, nine policemen from the nearby Abbeyfeale RIC Barracks, having seen the Very lights the night before, made their way to the relief of their comrades by a little back road, or boreen, known as Betty's Road. They discovered the Volunteers and opened up on them. As they left the barracks at Abbeyfeale, the police had been observed by a member of the Abbeyfeale Volunteer Company. Hastily rounding up as many Volunteers as could be found, and under the command of James Collins, they set off in pursuit of the policemen. Armed only with shotguns, the Volunteers, just four in number, in turn surprised the police, seriously wounding Constable Martin and slightly wounding others. Returning rapid fire, the police retreated to their barracks, allowing the scouting party to escape.

In an assault upon the RIC barracks at Rathmore, County Kerry on the night of 11 July 1920, Alexander Will, from Forfar in Scotland, became the first Black and Tan to die in the war. Two days later, on the 13th, two RIC men were killed in an ambush in Dingle.

Rineen (or Drummin)

The staff of the Ennistymon Battalion, Mid-Clare Brigade, were made aware that a Crossley tender of RIC and Black and Tans regularly traveled between Ennistymon and

Miltown Malbay twice weekly. Ignatius O'Neill, a former Irish guardsman and now commandant of the Ennistymon Column, decided to attack it. An inspection of possible ambush sites along the route came down in favor of a stretch of road at Rineen, or Drummin, as it was also known. The site chosen was alongside the track of the narrow-gauge West Clare Railway. Here the railway ran alongside yet steeply above the road. This offered a height advantage for the attackers. Behind it the ground rose in a series of hills that was an ideal line of withdrawal should a retreat be forced upon them. The ambush site was chosen because there was a sudden curve in the road, which meant vehicles would have to slow down to negotiate the bend. This was to be the start of the ambush zone. Shotgun men, it was decided, would be placed down here at ground level, right next to the road. If there was more than one vehicle then some of the riflemen up on the railway embankment would have to protect these men. Across the road on an elevated level O'Neill decided to place more riflemen. Scouts were to be deployed, and the local Moy Volunteers were appointed to keep clear the lines of withdrawal should the column come under attack.

At 4:00 A.M. on the morning of 22 September 1920, the Volunteers started off for the ambush site. They passed Liscannor on the opposite side of the bay without incident. There was a garrison of Royal Marines based there in the coastguard station, and their close proximity to the ambush site had to be taken into account. Arriving at the ambush position the Volunteers were allocated their ambush sites and again briefed by their officers. Then everyone was ready, and they waited. Their armament, apart from the previously mentioned shotguns, consisted of rifles (six had been captured previously in July from a military patrol in Ennistymon), a few carbines taken from the RIC, and two hand grenades in the possession of Peter Vaughan, an American ex-soldier who had experience of grenades from his time in France during World War I. From the railway embankment, some forty feet above the road, the scouts now surveyed the surrounding ground, looking for the enemy tender. As they waited a train approached, and everyone took cover. The train passed by, then all was quiet once more. Down on the road carts passed, their drivers oblivious of the men who waited.

At last the word came that three cars were approaching. The first car entered the ambush site, and fire was withheld until the two other vehicles entered the fire-zone. On the first car went and was away. There were no other cars. The signal had been misinterpreted. All they could do, once the mistake had been investigated, was wait for the return of the vehicle. A scout, John Clune, was sent off to Milltown to discover when the car might return. Later that day he reported back, and the Volunteers prepared themselves. In the distance a Crossley tender was sighted, even before its engine could be heard. The truck entered the ambush site and the shotgun men opened fire at it from close range. The driver and most of the occupants were killed instantly, and the Crossley slewed to a halt with its dead. A lone survivor leaped from the tender on the far side of the road. He ran some five hundred yards before he too was shot dead. There was to be little mercy for the Black and Tans. The six paramilitaries were dead. Five rifles, one revolver, and three thousand rounds of ammunition were captured, as were bandoliers and other pieces of equipment.

The largely inexperienced Volunteers now crowded down onto the road. The men responsible for protecting the withdrawal also left their posts, thus exposing everyone to danger. None of the approach roads had been blocked, and there was the danger of British reinforcements advancing from Liscannor, Ennistymon, Ennis and Kilrush. Volunteer Dan Kennelly, ex–British Army and former RIC man, was alive to the danger and shouted at the men to get back to their posts. As the Volunteers began returning to the hillside, a truck was heard coming along the road. It contained a relieving force of soldiers of the British Army. The truck came to a halt as the driver saw the abandoned tender. The soldiers leaped from their vehicle and ran up the railway embankment to gain a height advantage. As they did so, they saw the Volunteers withdrawing up the hills beyond. They opened up on the retreating Volunteers with rifle and machine-gun fire. Now a second British Army truck arrived, and the soldiers joined their comrades in pursuit of the fleeing IRA men. The Volunteers were now outnumbered and outgunned. The British fired at random as they climbed the hills, but this proved ineffectual. The Volunteers gained the hills and found some protection. The British advantage was now lost. The soldiers continued racing after the retreating men, but the Irishmen were more used to the hilly terrain. The British lacked their stamina. Having gained the hills, what now became the Volunteer rearguard (including the ex–British Army men, O'Neill and Kennelly) now turned retreat into attack. They picked off the leading pursuers as they struggled to climb the hills. Then they sought out the enemy machine gunner and apparently shot him dead. After some time the machine gun opened up again with long bursts as someone else took over. The rearguard concentrated their fire on it, and again it became silent. Then the rearguard began to move off in pursuit of the remainder of the column, which they rejoined. The British did not pursue them any further. O'Neill had been wounded in the thigh but was able to walk with assistance. Volunteer Michael Curtin was also wounded but not badly. When they caught up with the column, the wounded men were carried to a nearby house, and a doctor was sent for. They were then carried across the hills and away to safety. The column's inexperience had nearly cost them dearly.

A British account of the ambush and its aftermath, drawn up by the RIC, appears in Ernie O'Malley's *Raids and Rallies*:

> At 11 o'clock in the morning, an NCO in Ennistymon was told that a police car was to be ambushed that day. He went straight to the military barracks and reported. A party of troops from the garrison was dispatched along the Miltown Malbay road, with instructions to examine likely positions for ambushes. Shortly after passing Lahinch shots were heard ahead. The party pushed on and came into touch with the rebels as the latter were scattering inland.
>
> The troops came under fire from both flanks, and the driver of the motor car was wounded. A Lewis gun was brought into action and a few minutes later a second small party of troops came up in support, whereupon the rebels scattered and fled. The rebels took skilful advantage of cover behind banks, whins and hedges.
>
> The troops now came back to the road, and at a point where the road is about 25 yards from the railway line, they found the bodies of the victims and the wrecked car. There were signs of a regular bivouac which had clearly been occupied from before dawn. Hats was strewn about and there were a few haversacks and coats as well as meat tins. Empty rifle and shotgun cartridges, and also sharp-nosed bullets whereof the points had been carefully filed, converted them into dum-dum bullets were found. The original wounds caused by the dum-dum bullets were bad enough, but the bodies showed that after the men had fallen the criminals fired at their victims at short range with shotguns. The evidence of this bestiality was undisputable. Search was made for the body of the missing constable, but it was not found until the next morning. The wounded man had managed to crawl nearly 400 yards, but as the tracks showed, he had been hunted down and butchered in cold blood.
>
> During the fight the rebels fired from two houses, and it is certain that not only were the occupants fully aware of the ambush, but also deliberately refrained from giving any notice, as they certainly could have done. However, they did not get off scot-free for their houses

were set on fire and burned to the ground. There were other people who could have given warning and did not do so, and who are therefore accessories to the murder. Two trains passed within six to ten feet of the ambush, every detail of which must have been visible from the line. The guard and driver of the train must have known of the ambush, and it is impossible that some of the station officials at Miltown Malbay should not have been informed. It is worth noting that a priest wearing what appears to be military medals was reported to have formed one of the ambush party.[10]

It is a curious account of the ambush by the police and Black and Tans, and it includes black propaganda for domestic consumption. The nearby houses, which played no part in the ambush, were burned by the Black and Tans; and in the absence of Volunteer prisoners, the local populace, innocent of what had happened, suffered at their hands. The curious reference to a priest wearing military medals having taken part in the ambush is very strange. It may be that an eyewitness thought that this is what he saw, or perhaps the British authorities had deliberately set out to blacken the name of local Roman Catholic priests.

Later that day resident magistrate Lendrum, an over-zealous magistrate who had sent Volunteers to prison for drilling, was dragged from his car at a level crossing near Doonbeg, taken to a nearby beach and shot dead. That night the Black and Tans took their revenge. Six civilians were killed and twenty-six building were burned, including the town halls of Lahinch and Ennistymon. On 26 September Black and Tans burned the village of Kilkee, County Clare. On 13 December, two Volunteer officers, Michael MacNamara and William Shanahan, were abducted and shot by the Black and Tans in Clare. Their bodies were later discovered near Kilkee on 19 December.

The 31st of October 1920 was one of the bloodiest days of the war in Kerry. Ten people died that day in a series of tit-for-tat murders. Two RIC constables were shot dead in Abbeydorney by IRA men. Two more were killed a little later, and two were wounded in nearby Ballyduff. The Black and Tans responded by burning the creamery in Ballyduff in reprisal and shooting and bayoneting a civilian, James Houlahan. That night two Black and Tans were shot dead by Volunteers in Killorglin, and two more were wounded in Dingle. The Tans descended on Killorglin, burning the Sinn Fein Hall, the Temperance Hall, a garage and the home of a local Sinn Fein activist. A civilian was shot and later died of his injuries. The IRA responded by kidnapping two RIC men in Tralee, County Kerry. It is believed that they were murdered and their bodies were hidden. Police violence broke out in Tralee as they unsuccessfully searched for their kidnapped colleagues. The following day the Black and Tans burned the county hall in Tralee. Riding around the town in trucks, they fired shots at people going to Mass. Local man John Conway was shot dead. Shops and businesses were ordered to remain closed by the Tans until the 9th of November. On 2 November the Black and Tans shot dead local Volunteer Tommy Wall, in Tralee. They returned on the 4th of November and burned the businesses of known Sinn Fein supporters in the town.

On 12 November 1920, two Volunteers were themselves ambushed and killed in a gunfight against superior odds in Ballymacelligott, not far from Tralee. This incident was used in a British propaganda film to show that Britain was winning the war against the terrorists. A faked film, indicating that a major battle had taken place, was shown on Pathe News. One particular scene depicted a Black and Tan and an Auxiliary searching a civilian suspect. In the background, lying on the road, is a supposed dead Volunteer. The shoes the civilian is wearing are curiously similar to the shoes being worn by the searchers. The road in Tralee where the search is being conducted, according to the film, was identified by many who saw the newsreel in cinemas in Dublin as being the Vico Road, Dalkey, just south of Dun Laoghaire, County Dublin. The British still had a lot to learn about propaganda. On Christmas Day 1920, a patrol of Auxiliaries under the command of Major B.A. McKinnon murdered two civilians that they came across on the outskirts of Tralee. McKinnon then ordered their houses to be burnt.

The War in the West and Northwest

The first successful attack on a police barracks in Sligo took place in June 1920. The period up to then had been fairly quiet as regards Volunteer activity. On 26 July men from the West Sligo Column successfully attacked a small RIC bicycle patrol at Ballyrush, securing the men as prisoners and taking their rifles, revolvers and ammunition off in triumph.

A still from a British propaganda film showing the aftermath of the "Battle of Tralee," 12 November 1920. The photograph in reality shows the Vico road, Dalkey, Co. Dublin, a view recognized by many Dubliners.

The Volunteer organization in County Clare was driven by factionalism. This perhaps explains why so little was achieved. It was not until the summer of 1920 that brigade OC Sean Corcoran stamped his authority on the county. On 29 June 1920, during an IRA ambush at Ballina, northern County Mayo, an RIC man was killed and one wounded.

On 19 July a cycling patrol of four RIC men was ambushed near Taum, County Galway. Two of the policemen were killed; the other two surrendered, and after being disarmed, were released unharmed. A hue and cry was raised and the police and military searched the surrounding area for the attackers. Failing to find them the police and Black and Tans rioted in Taum, firing their guns at shop windows and throwing grenades in the streets. They burned the town hall and a drapery warehouse. Suspected Republican sympathizers were beaten up and threatened with death.

In North Mayo in July of 1920, the RIC were twice ambushed. In one ambush on the 29th of the month, one RIC man was killed and one wounded, at Ballina. In August the North Mayo Volunteers were assisted by the West Sligo companies in the capture and burning of Enniscrone Coastguard Station, County Sligo. They secured explosives, arms and ammunition in the process.

The East Mayo Column under Sean Corcoran and Sean Walsh (captain of the Bohala

Company) captured the RIC barracks at Ballyvarey, on 22 August 1920. Arms and ammunition were secured in this successful operation. This was to prove to be the only barracks captured by the Mayo men, though. Nonetheless, the British, fearing further raids, closed a number of the smaller outlying barracks, thus clearing areas that were then taken over by the Republicans.

Volunteers ambushed an RIC cycling patrol at Ballyrush, County Sligo, on 26 July. Overpowering the policemen, they disarmed them. The police were later released unharmed. That same month the South Sligo Column, under its OC Frank Carty, carried out an ambush at Chaffpool, some three miles from Tubbercurry, killing RIC district inspector Brady and wounding two others. The RIC responded by taking reprisals against Tubbercurry. On 25 October, three RIC men were killed and three wounded in an ambush at Moneygold, County Sligo, on the Grange to Cliffony road. Later, three Volunteers and their Cumann na mBan driver, Linda Kearns, were arrested and imprisoned for the killings.

On 14 November Father Michael Griffin, a priest at St. Joseph's Church, Galway, was taken away by "persons unknown." He never returned. His disappearance was reported to the police the following day. On 17 November the MP for Belfast (Falls), Joseph Devlin, stood up in the House of Commons and accused the British security forces of kidnapping Fr. Griffin. The body of Fr. Griffin was found the next day in a shallow grave in a bog near Barna, outside Galway City. It subsequently emerged that he had been kidnapped by the Black and Tans and murdered for his Republican sympathies.

The Irish Midlands

County Longford Volunteers, under the leadership of Sean MacEoin, carried out an assault on the RIC barracks at Drumlish on 6 January 1920. The attack was abandoned when the mine they were using to blow a hole in the wall of the barracks failed to go off. Following the burning of evacuated RIC barracks in April, an attack by the North Longford Column on Ballinamuck Police barracks led to its abandonment, too.

In February 1920, the Monaghan Brigade Flying Column under the command of Eoin Duffy launched a successful assault against the RIC barracks at Ballytrain. With their capture of arms and ammunition, more was perhaps expected from them; but this was Loyalist territory, and attacks had to be aborted when it was suspected that spies had given away their positions.

The South Kildare (or 5 Battalion of the Kildare) Brigade under Captains John Hayden (A Company), Joseph Maher (B Company) and Patrick Cosgrove (C Company) attacked Luggacurran RIC Barracks on the night of 20 April 1920. The building was set ablaze, causing its destruction. One Volunteer, John Byrne, was killed in the assault, dying from fatal burns as the roof caved in as he tried to retrieve ammunition from the building.

The County Longford Column raided the British Army barracks at Longford Town and Ballymahon on 18 August 1920 in a search for arms. In their assault on the Upper Military Barracks in Longford Town, Sean MacEoin, its commandant, was assisted by a deserter called Jordy, who provided details of the barracks. Sean Connolly successfully raided the Ballymahon Barracks, getting away with ten rifles, four revolvers, twelve grenades and much-needed ammunition.

On 10 September Irish Volunteer Patrick Gill was shot dead by the Black and Tans in

Drumsna, County Leitrim. Four days later, on the 14, James Connolly of Unshinnagh, Kinlough, was shot dead by the Black and Tans in front of his own house. On 23 September two RIC men were killed in an ambush by units of the East Mayo and South Sligo Volunteer brigades. The ambush was at Ratra near Frenchpark, County Roscommon. One Volunteer was killed before the attackers withdrew. His body was mutilated by the Black and Tans before being dragged behind a truck through the streets of Ballaghderren. Two days later, on 25 September, Volunteers from the East Mayo Brigade hijacked a train. As it steamed past the Black and Tans barracks at Ballaghderren they opened up a furious fire, taking the Crown forces completely by surprise. A number of Tans were reported wounded, but none fatally. The following month, on 12 October, the East Mayo Brigade killed four Black and Tans in an ambush at Ballinderry.

In September 1920 the County Meath Volunteers assaulted and captured the RIC barracks at Trim. They got away with a substantial amount of arms and ammunition. In response, on 27 September, the Black and Tans burned the town center in reprisal.

On 31 October an RIC district inspector by the name of Kelleher was shot dead in the bar of the Greville Arms in Granard. The next day at Ballinalee, also in County Longford, an RIC constable called Cooney was also killed. On 5 November, the Black and Tans looted and burned the village of Granard as a reprisal. On the following day, as news reached them that the village of Ballinalee was to be raided by a combined force of Auxiliaries and Black and Tans, Sean MacEoin and twenty men from his North Longford Flying Column went to its defense. A motorized convoy of eleven trucks carrying the avenging Tans was halted and drawn into a firefight. As many as twenty of the Auxiliaries and Black and Tans were reputedly killed, and a number were wounded. No official figure was given by the British authorities. After a two and a half hour gun battle the British retreated, believing that they were facing a much larger enemy force. The IRA column remained in the village for a week, safeguarding the people.

Two Volunteers were killed by British forces at Ardee, County Louth on 30 November 1920.

The Northeast

The war in Ulster was fought in the counties that had sizeable Roman Catholic/Nationalist populations — South Down, South Armagh, Monaghan, Fermanagh and Donegal. It was only in the summer of 1920 that the war, in a sectarian form, broke out in Belfast and Derry, with terrible consequences in tit-for-tat murders. The war here was different. It was sectarian, hence the use of the terms Roman Catholic and Protestant, rather than Nationalist/Republican and Loyalist/Unionist. Employment, or the lack of it, was also an underlying factor, in that Catholics were perceived as having taken Protestant jobs.

In the latter part of the winter of 1919-20, the Volunteers went on the offensive with attacks on RIC barracks in Ulster. There were also urban hit and run attacks on the Crown forces in Newry. As elsewhere in Ireland, isolated barracks were abandoned by the British and then later burned by the IRA. In the northeast, garrison attacks began in February 1920. Back in Ulster once more, Ernie O'Malley took part in the attack on Balltrain Barracks in County Monaghan. The assault was led by brigade commandant Eoin O'Duffy in the first successful capture of a barracks during the War for Independence. A gelignite bomb was used to breach a hole in the wall. The garrison, using an improvised white flag, surrendered. Nine rifles, several revolvers, hand grenades and ammunition were seized. The barracks was evacuated and later destroyed.

On the night of 9 May a column of two hundred Volunteers under the command of Frank Aiken attacked the RIC barracks at Newtownhamilton, County Armagh, and completely destroyed it. Most of Aiken's men were deployed to prevent reinforcements from coming to its relief. As so often in these cases, relief was not sent until the following morning, the British troops fearing a nighttime ambush. A mine was used in the attack to breach the barracks wall and the barracks was set ablaze. There was a brief firefight, but with no hope of relief the six policemen inside finally surrendered. Arms, ammunition, hand grenades and police papers were seized before the building was engulfed in fire. The following month the Armagh Brigade was again in action. RIC sergeant Tim Holland and a civilian, Peter McReesh, were killed in a brief but bloody fight with the Volunteers near Cullyhanna in south Armagh, on 6 June 1920. Ten days later, on the 16, a strong Volunteer force launched an attack on the RIC barracks at Cookstown, County Tyrone. In the assault Volunteer Patrick Loughrane was killed.

In the council elections of January 1920, the Nationalists took control of Derry City and appointed a Catholic mayor. Under Lloyd George's intended Partition of Ireland, Derry was included in Protestant Northern Ireland. The success of the Nationalists came as a severe blow to the Unionists. Tensions simmered until 12 July, the day that commemorates the victory of Protestant King William III over Catholic King James II at the Battle of the Boyne. On that day in 1920 Sir Edward Carson delivered a speech inciting action. His words were taken up by other extremists, and on 19 July armed mobs invaded the Catholic quarter of the city in an orgy of destruction and mayhem. For four nights the rioting continued. British troops on the scene did not interfere to stop the attacks. Nineteen people were killed and over fifty people were wounded, the majority being Roman Catholics. The few members of the IRA in the city did the best they could to defend the Nationalist community, but in so doing they came under attack themselves from the British Army.

On 21 July Loyalists forced over 7,000 Roman Catholics and left-wing Protestants from their jobs at Harland and Wolff's shipyards in Belfast. Sectarian rioting broke out as a result in both Belfast and Derry. Both Catholics and Protestants were driven from their homes. Upwards of forty people were killed in Derry and twenty-two in Belfast.

On 22 August 1920, RIC detective Swanzey was shot dead by an assassination squad from Cork as he was leaving church in Lisburn, County Antrim. Swanzey had been named as a murderer by the coroner in the inquest on Cork mayor Thomas MacCurtain. A sectarian mob attacked the Catholic district of Lisburn in retaliation for his death, burning houses and attacking Catholics. In Belfast there were further attacks on Catholic areas in the city. Some thirty-three people were killed in a ten day orgy of revenge.

On 6 December 1920, Frank Aiken, with a flying column of reputedly three hundred Volunteers, attacked the RIC barracks at Camlough, County Armagh. The greater part of the force positioned themselves along roads by which relieving enemy forces were expected to arrive. The defenders, just six RIC men, held out for several hours. A relieving motorized convoy of troops from Newry was ambushed with losses. With reports of the approach of British forces arriving from several other directions, the column retired in good order. Later that morning, in reprisals carried out by the sectarian Ulster Special Constabulary (men formerly members of the UVF), a number of buildings in the village of Camlough were burned. The Roman Catholic school at nearby Aghdavoyle was shot up by the Black and Tans, the children forced to dive for cover beneath their desks. The day after, Frank Aiken's home and the homes of ten of his relatives were burned.

Following the Partition Act of December 1920, attacks on Catholics in Derry and Belfast were begun again by armed UVF men in an attempt at what we know today as "ethnic cleansing" to create "A Protestant State for a Protestant People." The IRA drafted in to defend the Catholic minority succeeded in driving the Protestant gunmen out. The British Army in the two cities, up until then merely observers, now invaded the Nationalist districts of these two cities and engaged in firefights with the IRA. In the following days twenty-eight people were killed in Derry and fifty-five wounded, the majority of them non-combatants. Terror erupted in Belfast in an anti–Catholic pogrom. Firms in Belfast forced employees to take an oath of allegiance to the king. Those who refused were sacked and driven from the premises. Catholics were driven out of mixed religious areas of the city, and members of the UVF daily sniped into Catholic areas of the city. The British Army was unable — or unwilling — to take action. Martial law could have been proclaimed to stop armed Loyalists from attacking civilians, but it was not.

11

1921: The Last Year of the War

At the opening of 1921 the Dail was recognized by many, both in Ireland and abroad, as not only the de facto but also the de jure functioning Irish parliament, democratically elected by the Irish people. Any British claim on authority to rule Ireland was based on the presence of nearly 60,000 soldiers (costing the British authorities £1,300,000 per month) and 15,000 Auxiliaries and Black and Tans, as well as the regular police force, to shore up that authority. In January the counties of Wexford, Waterford, Kilkenny and Clare were placed under martial law. Habeas corpus, the very basis of English democracy, was suspended.

On 9 February at Drumcondra, a suburb of Dublin, two young men, Patrick Kennedy and James Murphy, were murdered by the Auxiliaries. They had been arrested earlier that day and taken to Dublin Castle for interrogation. About midnight they were driven out into the countryside by an Auxiliary called King and two other cadets. In the morning the youths were found in a field in Drumcondra. Kennedy was dead, Murphy was dying. Before dying, Murphy revealed what had happened. They had been made to stand against a wall. Buckets were put on their heads, and they were then shot. The Auxiliaries were identified, and according to their nominal superior, General Crozier, they demanded to speak to a highly placed government official. The three Auxiliaries threatened that unless they were released from custody and reinstated in their former positions, they would give evidence concerning the sanctioned murders that they and others had carried out. The administration, "paralyzed with fear of exposure," as Crozier described it, acquitted the three men and reinstated them. Late at night on 6 March, two men wearing goggles, with their coat collars turned up and hats pulled down, entered the home of the former mayor of Limerick, Michael O'Callaghan, and shot him dead where he stood at the foot of the stairs. That same night, at about half past one in the morning, the then current mayor of Limerick, George Clancy, was also murdered in his home.

Reports of such atrocities in Ireland tarnished Britain's reputation both at home and abroad. Murders such as these — and there were many of them — internment without trial, and the burning and pulling down of houses as reprisals showed that Britain's moral right to rule Ireland had become untenable. During the early months of 1921 there was widespread revulsion at Britain's reprisal policy. What might have been tolerated in Iraq, India or Africa was unacceptable in Ireland, whose people were still considered to be British. Following the demolition of several houses in Middleton, County Cork, the *Daily Mail* (1 January 1921) reported: "This is of course martial law. It is legal and disciplined. It is we must believe, necessary. But it is horrible."

On 19 February, former Prime Minister Herbert Asquith speaking in London declared, "I say deliberately that never in the lifetime of the oldest amongst us has Britain sunk so low in the moral scale of nations.... [T]hings are being done in Ireland which would disgrace the blackest annals of the lowest despotism in Europe." His sentiments were echoed by Sir John Simon, speaking in Sunderland: "A system of vengeance has been established in Ireland, and after what had happened there, I beg to hear no more about what the Germans did in Belgium." That arch-organ of right-wing Britain, the *Times,* shared this view on 29th January 1921: "Deeds have unquestionably have been done in Ireland which have lastingly disgraced the name of Britain."

On 6 April in the House of Lords the Archbishop of Canterbury pleaded "with the Government to arrange, if possible, a genuine truce, with a view to a deliberate effort after an agreed solution to the Irish difficulty.... The present policy is causing grave unrest throughout the Empire, and exposing us to misunderstanding and the hostile criticism even of the most friendly of other nations of the world." There was also growing pressure from America for Britain to reach some sort of agreement with Sinn Fein. For their part the British were relying on the forthcoming Government of Ireland Act, coupled to a general election, which would give the proposed southern government some degree of home rule, thereby ending the war, yet keeping Ireland within the Empire. The Sinn Fein government, while agreeing to put up candidates to prove its legitimacy, made known its position: the time for Home Rule was past — they wanted independence, they wanted a Republic. Sinn Fein stated that its members would not sit in the new British-sponsored Southern Ireland Parliament. They would continue to meet as An Dail.

The general election, to bring the Southern Ireland government into being, was held in May 1921. In every constituency where Sinn Fein stood — except one, County Donegal, where a Unionist stood but later withdrew — Sinn Fein was elected unopposed. The *Times* of London, in no way sympathetic to the Republican cause, reported on 14 May 1921: "The result is a sweeping victory for Sinn Fein and a virtually unanimous repudiation of the Government of Ireland Act."

Trinity College, Dublin, a center of Unionism in a sea of Republicanism — a "rotten borough" that disproportionately returned four members of Parliament — predictably returned four Unionists: Messrs. Thrift, Alton, Fitzgibbon and Sir James Craig. Nonetheless, with these four exceptions Sinn Fein won 124 seats out of a total of 128.

The war continued. Between May and July 1921 more than 160 British soldiers and policemen were killed by the IRA. This was well over 25 percent of all British casualties since the start of the war in 1919. With the formation of IRA divisions — the combining together of several county flying columns to form what was essentially an army in the field — the war took on a new dimension. Potentially, on their terms, trained and armed, these divisions were capable of taking on equal-sized, and sometimes larger, British forces and destroying them. By 1921 the IRA had successfully pinned down large numbers of British soldiers and police and cleared large areas of the country. British troops and paramilitary police scarcely dared to leave their barracks except in parties of several hundred. After the British Army's last major effort to encircle and destroy the Cork brigades in June 1921, they retreated back to their barracks. In response the IRA began making probing attacks upon the larger British garrison towns and cities, particularly in the province of Munster. Bandon itself, heavily garrisoned by soldiers and police, was entered eight times by armed columns of the IRA. In Munster IRA active strength was reckoned to be about 900, operating in flying columns. In County Cork there were about 1,800 Volunteers available, though not fully committed to the war. They had over 1,200 guns, and plans were afoot to import several thousand rifles, machine guns and ammunition from the Continent.

In other parts of the country the British forces were enjoying some measure of success. Irish guerrilla leaders in less active parts of the country became concerned over sustaining a campaign over the summer months. The unusually dry weather permitted British armored trucks to travel over the mountain roads and through the bog lands favored by the guerrillas. The lengthening summer days gave the British more time to prepare and execute encirclements, giving the flying columns little respite. Such is the nature of guerrilla warfare, though, that the flying columns could just melt away and re-form when conditions better suited them. Nonetheless, by the time of the truce nearly five thousand Republicans (not all of them soldiers) were in internment camps, and one thousand five hundred were serving terms of penal servitude. Despite this during the week ending 25 June 1921, the IRA carried out fifty-two attacks against British forces throughout Ireland.

Although the British military declared that, given sufficient troops, they could destroy the IRA, the reality was that due to industrial unrest at home and imperial and international commitments abroad the British government was unable to put more troops into Ireland. With deaths reported weekly, recruitment into the Auxiliaries and Black and Tans slowed down. By 1921 recruitment into the Auxiliaries alone had dropped by 50 percent in England. The war had reached a stalemate. People of influence in war-weary Britain, sickened by the atrocities carried out in their name and the return of dead and wounded soldiers and police, demanded a settlement to the problem.

Unaware of the rising tide of opposition in Britain to the war, the Volunteers out in the country had little choice but to fight on. It became imperative that they acquire more guns and ammunition and bring more men into the fight. Without the guns and men there was the real possibility that they would not be able to continue the war. If a truce was to come they had to be seen to be in a position of strength. At the beginning of 1921 a senior IRA man from Cork, Mick Leahy, was sent to Genoa, Italy, to organize the purchase and shipment of arms to Ireland. The arms were to include machine guns, rifles, handguns and ammunition. Myross Strand near Glandore Harbour on the southwest coast of Cork was the intended landing place. Transport was in readiness and arms dumps were prepared. For whatever reason, the money which had been allocated for the purchase never arrived in Italy. The reason was open to much speculation, including the fact that a truce was in the offing and that Michael Collins postponed the purchase as a show of good will. This seems unlikely given the fact that even during the truce he was organizing a continuation of the war in the northeast, sending both experienced fighters and arms up to Ulster. There is a strong probability that MI6 discovered the plan and Britain brought pressure to bear on the Italian government. This setback aside, other attempts were being made to acquire arms from Germany. Charlie McGuinness, the skipper of the *Sancta Maria*, brought in arms from Hamburg aboard the ship following the truce but prior to the treaty, in November 1921, and another shipload of arms was brought in aboard the *Frieda*. So though the Republicans were having to slow down operations due to lack of arms and ammunition, plans were underway to rectify this situation.

While they waited, the IRA resorted to burnings and destruction as methods of attack. A policy of counter reprisals on a nationwide scale was adopted. The burning of the houses of Unionists known to be active supporters of the British administration in Ireland was begun, to counter the burning and destruction of Irish Republican properties. Approval for such burnings had to be agreed upon by Republican GHQ, who issued a caveat: "[F]or the purpose of such reprisals no persons shall be regarded as enemies of Ireland, whether they may be described locally as Unionist, Orangemen, etc., unless they are actively anti–Irish in their actions." Such a statement flies in the face of some modern-day revisionist historians, who have erroneously claimed that the IRA embarked on a process of ethnic cleansing of Protestant men and women.

The War in Cork

At the opening of January 1921 the senior officers of the three Cork brigades met at Donoughmore to undertake a review of the situation and to share information. All three brigades had developed along similar lines of engaging the enemy, both police and army in ambushes and acquiring additional arms by raids on barracks.

Early on the morning of 15 January, just before dawn and with snow falling, Sean Moylan, commandant of the Cork No. 2 Battalion Column, lay in ambush with his men along the road just outside the town of Rockchapel. Fairs and markets had been prohibited by the British, so the local farmers gathered at unofficial sites to buy and sell cattle. These fairs were declared illegal, and British troops hearing of them went out to break them up. Such a fair was being held just outside Rockchapel, and it was almost certain that the British would hear of it. So Moylan and his men were waiting for them to appear. They found an ideal ambush site. A Humber car had been in an accident about two miles west of Newmarket. It was still there several days later. Any British convoy driving along the road was bound to investigate it. A messenger arrived to inform them that four trucks of soldiers at Newmarket were about to set out. A further messenger brought news that the British had hostages aboard their trucks to prevent an ambush. Moylan explained the situation to the men with him, giving orders that they should not open fire unless he blew his whistle. They heard the approaching trucks, four of them as expected but all of them containing hostages. When the British sighted the abandoned car they slowed down. Two drove slowly past it. The third drew up to investigate. The last truck was twenty yards behind. Each truck was in a perfect ambush position. From the ambush site Moylan could see that the hostages were handcuffed. They could not escape, even if they had half a chance. The convoy moved off. The Volunteers waited all day for their return, but as before there were still hostages aboard the enemy trucks. Moylan let them pass through.

At midnight on that same day, the Third Battalion of Cork No. 2 lay in ambush at Shinanagh. Intelligence indicated that a motorized convoy of cars passed by weekly in the early hours, between Limerick and Buttevant. At the ambush site the Volunteers trenched the road. Earlier than expected a motor car was heard along the road. As it approached, the Volunteers, not yet in position, saw that it contained British soldiers. The few Volunteers down on the road opened fire at the car. Its driver accelerated away at speed, but he could not fully clear the entrenchment. The car's rear wheels struck the far side of the trench, and the vehicle toppled backwards into the hole. The driver had the presence of mind to turn off the lights, and in the darkness, returning fire as they did so, he and his companions escaped. The ambushers retrieved the guns and ammunition left behind, but in addition they found a bag containing files and dispatches from the British intelligence officer in Limerick to the IO in Buttevant. By the following day the documents were on their way to Michael Collins by way of the Mallow to Dublin mail train.

Kilbrittain RIC Barracks was looked at again. The failure to capture it on New Year's Eve had been due to a defective mine. Since then the defensive barbed-wire entanglements had been added to, so that they stretched outwards halfway into the road. The height was increased to four feet. A large tree at the rear of the barracks was cut down to remove any potential cover for would-be attackers. That aside, it was still the same barracks and could be attacked in the same way — if a way could be devised to explode the mine. Sure in his mind that it could be, the Kilbrittain Company captain, Jackie O'Neill, decided to attack it again on the night of 15 January. The Kilbrittain Company made up the body of the attackers, with support from Ballinadee, Ballinspittle and Timologue companies. The explosive charge now had a fuse attached. As before, two Volunteers in stockinged feet carried the mine up the path and laid it along the wall near the doorway. The fuse was lit and they retired to safety. As they did so the police became aware of what was going on and sent up Very lights to summon aid. By the illumination of the lights the police opened fire on the Volunteers. Again the mine failed to explode. Return fire from the Volunteers in the house across the road gave their comrades some cover as they retreated across an exposed one hundred and fifty yards under intensive fire. Surprisingly, all got away without injury.

Activated by the attack early the next morning, troops of the Essex Regiment engaged in a series of raids in the neighborhood. They surprised a unit of fourteen Volunteers of the Bandon Battalion led by Sean Hales, at Quarry's Cross, seven miles north of Bandon. Fire was exchanged, and with the failure of the Essex troops to push home the advantage the Volunteers carried out a successful rearguard action and got safely away. Operating in what they perceived as Republican territory, the Volunteers had become complacent in their precautions and almost paid the price.

On the morning of 18 January Charlie Hurley, OC of the West Cork Brigade, training officer Tom Barry, and adjutant Liam Deasy reviewed the flying column. It numbered seventy Volunteers, including some new men. They were all armed with rifles, but they had only fifty rounds apiece. For two days the men were occupied with training and exercises. On the morning of the twenty-second, they moved into an ambush position at Mawbeg, along the main road from Bandon to Ballineen. Intelligence reports revealed that a motorized convoy of five trucks of the Essex Regiment regularly traveled along the road most mornings. On the previous night a spy had been court-martialled and found guilty by the IRA. That morning at eight o'clock near the ambush site the spy was executed and his body left along

Members of the West Mayo Brigade Flying Column. Column commander Michael Kilroy is standing far left.

the road. Passersby saw the body and read the notice attached to him—"Shot by the IRA, Spies and Informers Beware"—before they proceeded on their way, unaware of the presence of the column. Though the authorities must have been informed of the body, no one came to investigate. At half past three that afternoon, the column withdrew.

Bandon

Instead of waiting for British troops and police to fall into an ambush, the 3rd Cork Brigade now felt confident enough to take the battle to the enemy. Units of the Bandon and neighboring companies under the command of Tom Barry, resolved to attack the occupying forces in Bandon Town itself. The Essex Regiment, noted for their brutality, had a garrison in Bandon. There was also a strongly fortified RIC barracks. It was decided to attack both simultaneously. On the night of Sunday, 23 January, Charlie Hurley led his section of eighteen Volunteers across the river to take up positions in front of the military barracks. Tom Barry circled the town on the south and brought his section of sixteen men up to the corner of Shannon Street, where the army barracks was situated. Liam Deasy and his twelve men proceeded along Market Street to Main Street, Bandon, the site of the RIC barracks. The plan was to induce the enemy to leave their barracks at the sound of gunfire, thus exposing them to the ambush parties.

At midnight Miah O'Neill of the Kilbrittain Company silently walked through the barbed wire entanglement surrounding the military barracks and laid a mine with a percussion cap against the gate of the barracks. The intention was that when the gate was opened the force of it opening would detonate the bomb. The Volunteers opened up on the two barracks; and though the defenders returned fire, they had no intention of leaving the safety of their fortress and exposing themselves to enemy fire. The assault on the two barracks continued for two hours before the Volunteers, after retrieving the mine, were forced to retire when ammunition ran low, with the loss of one man, Dan O'Reilly. Though a disappointment, the action was a psychological victory for the Volunteers, as the British, with superior numbers of men and arms, as well as armored cars, refused to come out and fight. Satisfying too was the fact that no reinforcements from nearby garrison towns would risk coming to the aid of their comrades for fear of being ambushed.

Tom Barry analyzed the result of the attack. In this perhaps we have the model for a good guerrilla leader, in that he does analyze his successes and his failures, in order to learn from the experience:

(a) The Brigade Column had carried out an attack which would not be contemplated some months before. The occupation of the main enemy garrison town of West Cork for four hours, and the close quarter attack on all three barracks by seventy riflemen against seven hundred and fifty heavily armed enemy troops, was an assurance that the IRA Column was both capable and confident.

(b) There would be a heightening of morale all over the West Cork IRA Brigade. Our supporters in the town would not feel unprotected, waverers would come out on our side and British loyalists would think twice before acting against us or disobey the decrees of the Government of the Irish Republic.

(c) The enemy were perturbed at the effrontery of the IRA at this attempt to engage them in their main fortress. The attack pointed the way for many other visits by large or small units of the IRA and kept the garrisons on their toes during the nights. Those troops who were either attacked or sniped by night were not capable of the strenuous work of operating over a countryside the following day. This was the beginning of a harassing campaign in Bandon, which told heavily towards the end as it wore down the nerves of the enemy and shook his morale. Bandon was their main nerve center and every blow struck there was worth two in any other West Cork town."[11]

That the British forces had failed to leave the safety of their barracks at night suggested that another attempt should be made to capture the RIC barracks at nearby Innishannon. An earlier attempt had been made in the previous August, but the accidental discharge of a shotgun had alerted the garrison, and the attack came to nothing. A fresh attempt was planned for the night of Tuesday, 25 January 1921. Its success depended on successfully blowing open a hole in the building. For support a party of eighteen Volunteers were selected to cover the main road from Bandon, just in case relief should be sent. Another strong party under Charlie Hurley lined the Kilpatrick to Innishannon road at Brinney. A third group of twenty-two men, under Tom Barry and Liam Deasy, formed the assault party against the barracks. With every man in place, a three-man party under Deasy approached the barracks with their mine. It was laid in front of the door, and the Volunteers retired to safety with the connecting cable. The plunger was pushed down — but the mine again failed to explode. Nevertheless the Volunteers opened up on the fortified barracks, and fire was returned. The garrison sent up a number of Very lights as a signal to Bandon that they were under attack, but no one came to their aid.

With no hope of storming the barracks four riflemen were left to fire intermittently at the building while the remainder of the column withdrew towards Brinney to link up with Charlie Hurley and his men. Here it was hoped that they might ambush a relieving party. Though they waited into the morning, no one came to relieve Innishannon Barracks. The column withdrew. Failure of the mine to explode again proved a severe disappointment to Barry and his men. If they could get that right, and knowing that the British would not send out reinforcements for fear of ambush, then a new RIC barracks could virtually be attacked and destroyed every day, subject to the availability of dynamite for the mine. Without the explosion, rifle fire on its own was simply a waste of ammunition. Barry blamed himself for the failure of the mine in that he as brigade training officer should have gone to GHQ himself or sent some other officer to learn about explosives. On the night of the 28th two sections of the flying column reentered Bandon and fired upon the various British barracks. This was intended as a harassing action aimed at alarming the enemy and preventing them from resting. After a time the Volunteers withdrew in good order.

A combined RIC/British Army patrol. Note the hostage (white arrow) in the front vehicle (courtesy the National Library of Ireland).

Elsewhere in County Cork the events leading on from 28 January 1921 were the subject of considerable controversy. The First Cork Brigade planned an ambush along the Macroom-Cork road at Dripsey, ten miles west of Cork City. The British authorities were warned of the intended assault, by a Mrs. Lindsay of Coachford, a Loyalist friend of General Strickland. As a consequence the column was itself ambushed in a pincer movement. Thanks to the use of outlying scouts fifty men of the column escaped, but one Volunteer was killed, five were wounded and five captured. In accordance with martial law six of the captured men were sentenced to death. Evidence led to the fact that it was Mrs. J.M. Lindsay of Leemount House, Coachford, who had betrayed the column with the assistance of her chauffeur, a man by the name of Clarke. The two were arrested by the IRA, and word was sent to the British that they would die if the captured IRA men were executed. The Volunteers, Thomas O'Brien, John Lyons, Daniel Callaghan, Patrick Mahony, Timothy McCarthy and John Allen, were executed by firing squad on 28 February. The old lady and her chauffeur were likewise killed, without, it should be said, the sanction of GHQ. The British press poured odium onto the heads of a cowardly IRA who had murdered a woman. In truth, though, the British authorities could have agreed to leniency, but they needed a martyr. That same night several British soldiers were shot throughout the city as a reprisal.

At the end of January a flying column of the Second Cork Brigade under Liam Lynch conducted an ambush along the road west of Newmarket. They took up positions shortly before 6:00 A.M. It was a cold but dry day. The ambush position was not perhaps the best, but Lynch believed this would allay the suspicions of the Black and Tans. An elaborate withdrawal strategy was prepared if things went wrong. A few days previously they had let four trucks pass when they noticed that hostages were being carried. But on this day when two cars approached there were no signs of hostages. The first car slewed to a halt when its driver noticed a trench cut into the road. The second car also stopped. As they did so the Volunteers opened fire. The Tans abandoned the cars and took shelter behind a fence and returned fire. After some time Lynch blew a whistle, and the Volunteers stopped firing. Lynch called upon the British to surrender. Their response was a renewal of rifle fire. The Volunteers replied in kind. After some further time in which two of the Tans were killed and most of the others were wounded, the Black and Tans surrendered. Their arms were gathered up and loaded aboard one of the cars, which was driven away by the Volunteers. The wounded were put into the other car and allowed to drive away. As a precaution to slow down any pursuit, a number of trees were felled across a number of roads, confusing the British as to which way the Volunteers had withdrawn.

Burgatia House

The Third West Cork Brigade Flying Column moved from Newceston and crossed the river Bandon at Clonakilty in order to attack the RIC barracks at Rosscarbery. On Tuesday, 1 February, the column occupied Burgatia House, home to a Loyalist family, a mile or so from Rosscarbery. The family were made prisoner, though treated well. Final preparations were planned by the Volunteers and explosives were prepared for a mine. Wednesday morning the postman from Rosscarbery arrived with the letters. Arriving unexpectedly, he saw what was going on. Discovered by the Volunteers, he was promptly arrested. The dilemma now facing the Volunteers was what to do with the postman. If they kept him prisoner, suspicions would be aroused, and at the very least someone would be sent to find him. At worst the post office might notify the police. Naively perhaps, the Volunteers agreed to release him if he gave his word of honor that he would not betray them. He agreed and was released. As an ex-serviceman in the British Army, he went directly to the police and told them what was going on. By four o'clock that afternoon, with all preparations made for the attack, the Volunteers were waiting for dark before they set off. Then word was received from a sentry that a strong force of RIC and Black and Tans were attempting to surround the house. The Volunteer officer commanding, Tom Barry, detailed various sections to take up positions to prevent the enemy from closing. A detail under James Murphy was instructed to hold a line between the sea and Burgatia House to enable an orderly withdrawal, and possibly to allow an attack on the enemy's flank.

Meanwhile, the RIC and Tans, outnumbering their enemy, opened fire from the road, smashing windows in the house. Upon Barry's orders the Volunteers withheld their fire. Cautiously the British force moved forward. One group in particular advanced further ahead than the others. Barry had hoped to lure them all into a fire zone before giving the order to open fire, but this group were now close to the house. Barry gave the order, and the thirty men within the house opened fire. Some of the enemy were killed or wounded in the fusillade before the others took to their heels and ran back down to the road. The main body of the Black and Tans then maneuvered for position to attack the house. Murphy's detail now found themselves on the point of being outflanked and moved off to higher ground where they regained the initiative once more. From here they opened up on the exposed attackers, forcing them to withdraw. The withdrawal allowed the Volunteers within the house and immediate grounds to withdraw themselves. These were sound tactics, for while it was possible for the Volunteers to have seized the initiative, strong British reinforcements could be summoned from Clonakilty, barely six miles away, and with Burgatia House situated on a peninsula, the Volunteers would have been trapped and wiped out. The first rule of guerrilla warfare is survival, and it was the rule applied in this situation. The column retired eastwards in perfect order. Later that night Tom Barry and three other Volunteers returned to Burgatia House, now abandoned temporarily by the family and servants, and put it to the torch. Then they proceeded into Rosscarbery where they shot up the RIC barracks. Not knowing the strength of their attackers the RIC returned fire but did not venture out.

On 4 February, the RIC and Black and Tans and a strong contingent of soldiers from Bandon began an encirclement of the area, converging on the town land of Maryborough between Kilbrittain and Timologue. The RIC had strong intelligence that Volunteers were resting there. The column, however, was just outside the encirclement. Having rested, they fell in behind the encircling British soldiers and advanced a few miles behind them as they moved forward. In the encircling movement the Crown forces gradually closed in on the area. All men between sixteen and sixty were ordered to be arrested and brought to Kilbrittain village. Volunteer Paddy Crowley, who was within the encirclement, was shot dead while trying to fight his way out. All the other Volunteers, not part of the flying column, within the encirclement escaped. The arrested civilian prisoners were questioned by the police, and forced to demolish two houses of known Volunteers before being released.

On the night of 8 February, shortly before ten o'clock, fifty-five Volunteers of the Third Cork Brigade's flying column approached the town of Skibereen, a town not completely committed to the Republican cause. Forty-three riflemen took up ambush positions about half a mile from the town. Twelve of the guerrillas led by the flying column commander moved into the center of the town looking to make contact with enemy patrols. They probed the outer streets, moving towards the army and Black and Tans' barracks, but found only three unarmed off-duty soldiers from the King's Liverpool Regiment. They were smartly arrested by the Volunteers and taken off to Caheragh, where they were well treated and given a meal. Their good treatment had much to do with their commanding officer, Colonel Hudson, an honorable man who had given strict orders to his men on the treatment of IRA prisoners. The following day the two privates were provided with a horse and trap and taken back to Skibereen. Colonel Hudson publicly expressed his gratitude for the humane treatment to his men in the local newspaper.

Meanwhile, the two enemy barracks in the town were fired upon, then the Volunteers withdrew to the corner of Ilen Street and Bridge Street, hoping to induce the Crown forces to come out after them. The street lamps were shot away, and in the darkness the Volunteers waited. Among the civilians caught up in the episode were members of the Skibereen District Council. Recognized for who they were, part of a weak and vacillating group of men, they were lectured on their lack of commitment to the Republican cause. One of the Volunteers suggested that to prove his loyalty to the Republic their spokesman should stand on an empty porter barrel at the corner and sing the Republican national anthem, "The Soldiers' Song." This he did to the amusement of all, his pomposity burst and he hating every moment. Then he and his fellow councilors were sent on their way. For two hours the Volunteers remained in the town, occasionally firing at the enemy barracks, but they were unable to draw the enemy out. Final volleys were fired, and the Volunteers withdrew back to the main ambush position. In the town the Crown forces must have known that the Volunteers had withdrawn, but they refused to leave their barracks in pursuit, fearing a nighttime ambush.

Leaving Skibereen, the Third Brigade Flying Column retired to Caheragh, and from there they marched over to Barnagaoite on the southern slopes of Mount Kid. They rested for two days and prepared a mine for an intended attack upon Drimoleague RIC Barracks. The mine was much larger than those used on previous unsuccessful occasions. An earlier reconnaissance of the barracks had shown that its barbed-wire entanglements reached almost to the roof. An attack upon it would prove a challenge. Still very unskilled in explosives work, the Volunteers believed that it was necessary for the mine to actually touch the building to be effective. As such, a cradle apparatus of two eighteen-foot beams was constructed so that the bomb could touch the wall above the wire entanglement. At seven o'clock on the evening of Friday, 11 February, the column, seventy in number, moved off towards the barracks. At Dromore they collected a further eighteen Volunteers who were to act as scouts and ensure that a point of withdrawal was secure. From the main body, a section of men were ordered to hold the road to Aughavill, to prevent reinforcements arriving from Bantry. The other men worked their way unseen to their appointed places.

At midnight the assault began. The mine was placed against the upper wall, but in the process the noise alerted the garrison within. There was a violent explosion as the mine went off, but little damage was done to the barracks wall. Most of the impact was deflected away from it. The Volunteers opened up on the barracks in a desultory fashion, but in truth the whole thing was a waste of time and ammunition, given that the barracks was still intact. After half an hour they withdrew. The British announced one casualty in the action, a Sergeant Bransfield, who was wounded. The following morning after a few hours rest, the column continued on. At Nowen Hill, on the way to Kealkil, they observed a military convoy of four trucks of Auxiliaries approaching. The Volunteers took up defensive positions and awaited their arrival, determined to give them battle. It was evident that the Auxiliaries had seen them but were perhaps unsure of how many Volunteers there were. The trucks halted, and after a few minutes by their discussion occupants, they withdrew, as the decision was against confronting the Volunteers.

To avoid ambushes the British began moving their troops, when possible, by rail. Liam Deasy, while traveling by train from Cork to Kinsale, was horrified to see a party of twenty armed Auxiliaries board the train at Bandon. At first he thought that they were going to search the train, and he thought of how he might escape. But then they all sat down in the carriage next to his as passengers. At Desert Station three Volunteers, in what would have been recognized as Volunteer uniforms, trench coats and leggings, waited for the train. Deasy beckoned them to his carriage, and the three boarded the train. After Deasy explained the situation he and the three men made plans for how they would fight their way out of the situation should they be discovered. But to their relief, the Auxiliaries got off at Dunmanway Station and marched away, leaving the Volunteers to continue their journey in peace.

Drishanebeg

C.J. Meaney, commandant of the Millstreet Battalion (Cork No. 2), put forward a proposal to ambush a troop-carrying train that passed regularly through their area. Liam Lynch was invited in to give his opinion. The two men analyzed the situation and came up with a plan. The line near Drishanebeg, one mile east of Millstreet Station, was selected for the ambush. Here a high embankment made it possible for riflemen lying on either side of the track to have a clear field of fire without endangering their comrades on the other side of the track. The next problem was how to stop the train at the ambush site. After a number of suggestions it was decided that two armed Volunteers would climb up onto the footplate and order the driver to stop at the designated ambush site. At half past six on the evening of 11th February, with everything planned, the Volunteer column moved into position.

A Volunteer traveled aboard the train to ascertain where the British troops were. At Rathcoole the Volunteer signaled to two others, who climbed into the cab and ordered the driver to stop at the designated ambush spot, indicated by a lighted bicycle lamp on the line. The train came to a halt. Burning torches were thrown down into the cutting, illuminating the train's passengers. A whistle was blown, and the troops were called upon to surrender. They opened up in response with rifle fire at discernible targets. Fire was returned, and for fifteen minutes an intense firefight raged. The more experienced of the British soldiers leaped from the train and sought shelter beneath its coaches, returning fire. The situation was quite bad for the British. They were isolated and surrounded, fired upon from both sides of the track. The Volunteer leader ordered a cease-fire, and the soldiers were called upon again to surrender. With one man dead and a number of them wounded, they surrendered. Fifteen rifles and seven hundred rounds of ammunition were gathered up and taken away. There were no casualties among the Volunteers.

Lieutenant Clarke, the officer in charge of the Auxiliaries in the ambush, later gave his version of what happened. In deference to the British class system, he traveled alone in the first class carriage. When the attack occurred, the NCO, Sergeant Boxold, took command of the troops. Clarke in his account endeavors to show himself in a good light, while exaggerating the number of the enemy and blaming others for his lack of leadership:

On the evening of the 11th January 1921[the correct date was 11 February] I was in charge of a party of 4 other ranks traveling from Buttevant to Killarney. At Mallow I picked up another 10 men of the same Regiment, and I took charge of the whole party. The train left Mallow at about 20 minutes to seven. The Sergeant placed the men in two carriages.

I gave orders to the Sergeant to detail men to keep a look-out in the carriages. There were 8 men in one carriage, and 7 in the other. There were three coaches on the train — my men were in the leading coach.

No directions were given to us by the Railway officials as to what carriages we were to occupy. I got into a first-class carriage in the next coach.

The train proceeded on its way, and we stopped at Banteer. At Banteer a lot of men, whom I took to be Cattle Drovers, got out of the train. A few people got into the train at Banteer.

I did not get out of the carriage at Banteer. I looked out of the window — I saw nothing to arouse my suspicion.

The train next stopped at Rathcoole. I did not get out of the train here. I looked out of the window and I noticed a good many people on the platform. There were so many for the size of the Station that I became suspicious. I drew my revolver and laid it under a newspaper on the seat. I was alone in the carriage at the time, and I was afraid the train might be fired on whilst we were leaving the Station. Altogether I saw only 4 or 5 men who were opposite my carriage and moving towards the station exit. I think they were the Cattle Drovers I saw board the train at Mallow. Why I was suspicious was because they were opposite my window and close together. I saw no people on the platform when we drew into the Station. I did not notice the movements of any of the Railway officials at Rathcoole. I did not notice anything peculiar on the train leaving Rathcoole.

About 10 minutes after leaving Rathcoole I heard the brakes go on and the train began to slow up. I dropped the window and had a look out on the left hand side of the train as it was moving forward. I saw a small bonfire on the left-hand side of the track. The train then pulled up dead. Immediately fire was opened on my carriage — I heard no shouting.

When I looked out of the carriage I saw two groups of men on the embankment; one group of men opposite my carriage, and the other group of men were opposite the carriage in which my party were. They were on the same level as the carriages. I saw flashes and heard the reports as they fired into the carriages. I was looking out on the left-hand side, but we were also being fired on from the right-hand side of the embankment as I noticed the bullets striking the floor from that direction.

I had my revolver in my hand — I fired at the men on the left-hand side who were opposite my carriage. When I had emptied my revolver I ducked down in order to re-load. While I was doing so I heard shouts of "come out the military" also "come out and fight" and "put up your hands."

When I had re-loaded my revolver I opened the left-hand door of the carriage and jumped on the track.

During the whole of this period we were being fired on.

The men opposite my carriage made a rush at me. There were about half a dozen men opposite my carriage when I jumped out. They were not more than about 3 or 4 yards away from me. I fired 5 rounds at these — I am unable to say if I hit any of them; they fell back from me.

I then dived right underneath the train and got to the other side where I saw other civilians. They fired at me. I got underneath the train and tried to make my way to the men's carriages which were about 30 yards distance from my carriage. While I was underneath the train I reloaded my revolver again.

When I was underneath the coach in which the men's carriages were I saw some of them on the track with their hands up and the Attacking Party were disarming those on the Railway Track and pulling the others out of the carriages. This all happened on the left hand side of the train. I was able to see this by reason of the fact there was a bonfire and the Attacking Party carried Flash Lamps and they also had a Railway Lamp. There were shots being fired at the men while they were disarmed. I remained underneath the carriage.

The Attacking Party after disarming the men and taking their equipment, began to search for me. I heard the attacking party asking the men where was the officer. The Attacking Party searched the top of the train and the carriages but were unable to find me. They used Flash Lamps and the Guard's Lamp.

I started to crawl back to the rear of the train as my wish was to get out into the open country. When I got towards the end of the train I saw that some of the attacking Party were drawn across the line. I then got back underneath the second coach. I climbed on to the Axle and hid myself there. The Attacking Party during this time were rushing about looking for me. I heard a man, whom I took to be the leader, shout "get the officer." I heard the men being ordered to get back into the carriages.

I heard all the doors being closed by the Attacking Party. I heard them say to the guard "get on now," and the train started. As the train started and the Axle revolved I fell off. I seized the Cross Bar of the brake which is just behind the Axle and pulled myself up half laying and half sat there. I then found out that I had been wounded in the leg. I was unable to make myself heard at Millstreet where the train pulled up owing to the excitement and fuss that there was there — I was feeling very weak and was tangled up and required help to get out. At Rathmore I managed to extricate myself from the position which I was in and I was helped up to the platform by a policeman.

At Rathmore I went and found out what had happened to my men. I also saw the Engine Driver. He then told me that as the train left Rathcoole at the far end of the platform two men jumped on to the Engine — he told me they were armed with revolvers and had given him orders to proceed until he was stopped by them. I then gave orders to the Driver to proceed direct to Killarney as fast as he could and not to stop at Headford Junction where, in the normal course of events, he should have stopped. He complied with my order.

I estimate the numbers of the Attacking Party were at least 100. I saw two men of the Attacking Party in a Military Uniform which I took to be the uniform of the IRA as it was darkish green. I saw 4 or 5 of the Attacking Party were in Service Dress Khaki. Most of the party were armed with Rifles and Revolvers. I could not identify any of them.

The demeanor of the guard during the whole attack struck me as being completely unconcerned and I could hear him talking to the attacking Party. When he was told to proceed they called him by his Christian name: also the demeanor of the Engine Driver at Rathmore was very unconcerned, as he did not seem to be at all excited considering what he had been through.

I think the name the Attacking Party called the Guard was "Walter." I did not hear any of the rest of the conversation between him and the Attackers. I did not speak to the Guard at all.

As we had not been detailed to the Carriages by the Railway Officials, and as the rebels were in two parties opposite my men's carriages and my own carriage, when the train pulled up dead at Rathcoole I presumed that they must have telephoned up the line our position in the train.

I have never received any instructions or orders re disposing my men when traveling by train at Stations when the train is halted. When I crawled from under the train on the right side I was again fired at by the rebels from that side. I saw about half a dozen Civilians jump out of the train on to the track with their hands up. I heard the Rebels shout at them to get back into their carriages which they did.

When I was under the train I was able to see what I have already stated from the lights in the compartments and the bonfire on the line.

The following casualties were inflicted on the party under my charge:

Sergt. Boxold	Killed.
Pte. Hollyhome	Died of wounds.
Pte. Sutton	G.S.W. left shoulder and several minor wounds.
Pte. Lloyd	G.S.W. Hand, Arm and Side.
Pte. Hodge	Wrist and Side.
Lt. Clarke (myself)	G.S.W. through the thigh.[12]

February proved a black month for the Cork Volunteers. In the first half of the month forty-one Volunteers were killed in combat and ten were executed after capture. On 15 February the Cork No. 2 Column suffered a serious setback when it was itself ambushed. Intelligence reports supplied by Siobhan Creedon had indicated that senior British Army officers were planning to hold a conference in Cork that day. The indications were that several would be traveling in small convoys to the meeting along either the Fermoy or Mallow road into Cork. With two days' prior notice the column selected its ambush site. On the morning of the 15th the column was in position. Outlying scouts were positioned and an exit route was established. As the Volunteers waited they heard gunfire to the northeast of their flank. Two truck loads of troops and Tans had got behind them and were attacking their protected escape route. The British force was equipped with machine guns that soon made short work of resistance. The Volunteers were forced to withdraw as best they could under extreme fire. In the process they lost three men killed, one mortally wounded, and eight men captured. Following a drumhead court-martial two of the captured Volunteers were executed.

Upton Station

That same day, 15 February, men from No. 3 Brigade, West Cork, also suffered a severe setback when they sought to emulate the action at Drishanebeg. Cork No. 1 Brigade's intelligence officer, Florence O'Donaghue, contacted the No. 3 Brigade to inform them that a small party of British soldiers estimated at between twelve and fifteen would be traveling on the half past nine train that morning from Cork to Bantry. Brigade commander Charlie Hurley, weighing up the risks entailed to civilian passengers and conjecturing that the military would all travel together in one carriage, thought an assault would be successful. The site chosen for the ambush was Upton Station. There was no time to mobilize the battalion column, so Hurley took what men were available, fourteen Volunteers in all. They arrived at Upton Station with minutes to spare before the train pulled in. Closed in the mid–1960s, Upton back in the 1920s was a typical country station, with a stationmaster's office, a ticket office, waiting rooms and toilets, all on one side of the track, with a goods yard and store on the other.

Familiar as he was with the station, Hurley quickly placed his men in strategic positions. Pat O'Sullivan and John Butler were stationed at the toilets, with a .45 revolver and rifle respectively. Flor Begley and Sean Phelan, both with Colt automatics, were in the waiting room. Paddy O'Leary took up a position at the wicket gate at the end of the platform, and Sean Hartnett was placed at the gable end of the signal box, a little way down the line. Both of these men were armed with rifles. Hurley himself took up a position on the footbridge, armed with a "Peter the Painter" automatic with stock. On the other side of the track were placed Batt Falvey and Neilus Begley at the goods office, Denis Desmond and Dan O'Mahony behind a low wall nearby, Paddy Coakley at an upstairs window of a pub which backed onto the railway line, and Tom Kelleher and Denis Doolan behind a wall at the entrance to the goods yard. A party of local Volunteers for scouting and protection duties were posted outside in the neighborhood of the station.

Unbeknownst to the Volunteers at Upton, a party of fifty soldiers had boarded the train further down the line at the Kinsale Junction and mixed among the civilian travelers. A Volunteer, seeing this and knowing of the intended ambush, cycled for all he was worth to get to Upton before the train arrived. He arrived two minutes too late. As the train pulled into the station the attackers opened fire on the coach that the fifteen troops were traveling in. The troops returned fire, and the fifty troops in the other coaches also opened fire. As the soldiers poured out onto the platform Charlie Hurley, up on the bridge, saw that his men were greatly outnumbered. He shouted down to the platforms for them to withdraw. As he did so he attracted the attention of the British soldiers and was shot in the face, the bullet entering one cheek and emerging from the other. In his endeavors to get off the exposed bridge, he jumped down, spraining an ankle as he did so. Pat O'Sullivan was mortally wounded in the firefight, as was Sean Phelan. O'Leary, Butler and Hartnet managed to escape, though Hartnett was wounded. Batt Falvey, on the other side of the track, was shot through the head and died instantly. Denis Doolan carried a wounded Dan O'Mahony away on his back for almost half a mile. Tom Kellerher went to the assistance of Hurley and got him away too. An unspecified number of British soldiers were wounded in the ambush. Six civilians were killed and five wounded in the cross fire. The British claimed that they had been attacked by a flying column of one hundred or so rebels. This little exaggeration aside, It was a salutary lesson to the Volunteers and a propaganda as well as a military victory for the British.

The Cork IRA had suffered another setback on the previous day. The column had prepared an ambush position at Mourne Abbey, which was betrayed by an informer, Dan Shields. They were surrounded by British troops who opened fire on them from behind. Five Volunteers were killed and four more wounded and subsequently taken prisoner. Two of the wounded were later executed.

Throughout the remainder of February 1921 the Cork Volunteers continued to harass the enemy despite their setbacks. Sniping continued most nights on the three remaining RIC barracks in the Bandon area—Bandon, Kilbrittain and Innishannon—in an attempt to break the nerve of those under fire. Trenches were cut along all main and leading by-roads, to impede enemy transport. On 15 February the bridge over the Bandon River above Kinsale was blocked. The main bridge on the Bandon-Kilbrittain road was demolished, and the back roads between Bandon and Kilbrittain were trenched. On the night of 16 February a party of Volunteers concentrating on trenching an intersecting road at Crushnalanive Cross were attacked as they worked. One, at least, of the party should have been acting as a lookout but that person probably left off guard duties to help with the digging. All four of them were mortally wounded. Cork No. 1 Brigade also suffered losses. A column of the Donoughmore Battalion was surprised at Dripsey. Five members were captured. One subsequently died of his injuries, the other four were executed. Despite these losses, throughout the three days of the 16th, 17th and 18th February, the IRA created seventy-three breaches in road and rail, preventing the Crown forces from traveling. Only the main Cork Bandon and South Coast Railway remained undamaged, as it was the main supply line for the people of West Cork. All branch lines leading off. however, were put out of service.

The Middleton Battalion of the IRA was practically wiped out at Clonmult on 20 February. Five men were killed. Seven were shot after surrendering. Two taken prisoner were later executed. In the 2nd Cork Brigade area, the Mallow Battalion Column was defeated at Mourneabbey on 15 February. Five Volunteers were killed and two others who were captured were later executed. On 20 February the 1st Cork Brigade suffered a major loss at Clonmult in East Cork. Twelve Volunteers were killed after the house they were staying at was surrounded and captured by a mixed party of soldiers and Auxiliaries. The British alleged a false IRA surrender, leading to the wounding of some British troops and in turn led to the killing of all the Volunteers in the house. Brigade intelligence were convinced that an informer had told the British and this conviction led to a number of executions of suspected spies and informers. In response to the deaths of its members, the 1st Brigade went on the offensive. On 25 February, the column, under Dan "Sandow" O'Donovan, ambushed a large British motorized convoy at Coolavokig in County Cork. Three Auxiliaries, including Major Grant, were killed and eight soldiers wounded. As reinforcements arrived the Volunteers made an orderly withdrawal.

Further victories were necessary to restore morale among the Volunteers of County Cork. In West Cork, Tom Barry sought to restore it with an assault on the town of Bandon. He particularly wanted to engage the Essex Regiment, which had a bad reputation for brutality and the murder of captured Volunteers. In his book, *Guerilla Days in Ireland*, Barry names eleven officers and Volunteers of the West Cork Brigade that the regiment had murdered. In the early hours of 22 February the flying column of forty-four, divided into three sections, approached the town. The main body of thirty guerrillas entered the town by the Cork road, with the intention of locating the patrol of forty-four soldiers who paraded around the town after curfew. Simultaneously the two other sections of seven men each, nearly all of whom carried revolvers and rifles, entered the town from different directions. One section under Barry entered the town from the north. The other, under Vice-Commandant John Lordan, entered by the Dunmanway road. After a brief forward reconnaissance on his own, Barry returned to his section, temporarily commanded by Mick Crowley, and instructed him to bring up the men to the previously arranged ambush position.

As they talked, they heard sound of tramping feet and English voices not far off. There was no time to turn and run for cover. All Barry and Crowley could do was to take them by surprise as they turned into the street. There were five Black and Tans, two on the pavement and three walking along the road, all of them with guns in hand, as was standard procedure. The two Republicans opened fire on them. Two fell to the ground mortally wounded. A third ran to the darkened side of the road and fled. The fourth turned back in the direction they had come and likewise fled back to the barracks as the first shot was fired. The fifth, who was shouting in panic, dropped to the ground. He evidently thought about firing back but lost his nerve. Getting to his feet, he ran off. Foolishly Barry chased after him in sheer hatred, as he himself indicated. The Tan, with revolver in hand, just fled. Barry followed in hot pursuit. He gained on him until he eventually managed to grab him by the shoulder. The man screamed in terror and, wrenching free, dived into a small shop nearby. Barry chased after him through the rooms of the shop. In the kitchen he cornered the Englishman. Although the Tan still had his revolver in his hand, it was Barry who fired first. The man fell to the ground dead, and to be sure he was dead Barry fired at him again.

Lordan's group meanwhile encountered three Black and Tans and opened fire, killing two outright. The third made a dash up the road but was intercepted by the other party of Volunteers and likewise killed. A further two British soldiers were killed. A naval wireless operator who surrendered was taken prisoner but later released unharmed. Though they must have been aware of the presence of the Volunteers in the town, there was no British response from either the police or the army. Barry withdrew his men. Rendezvousing with the main group, Barry discovered that they had encountered four soldiers from the Essex Regiment. Two were shot dead, the others fled back to their barracks. Volunteer morale had been restored. After six weeks in the field in all weathers, often hungry and always cold and wet, the brigade flying column was stood down.

The following day Barry attended a brigade meeting to plan how to further the war. The West Cork Brigade had successfully cleared the area west of Bandon. If it was to meet the enemy then it was necessary for the flying column to move out of what had been ideal guerrilla country, but not into a terrain unfamiliar to them. The Kinsale-Bandon area was chosen, but it was not without its difficulties. The River Bandon sealed off any safe retreat westward into Republican territory. After careful analysis it was agreed that the only safe way of escape, should it be needed, was a narrow corridor to the east leading into the 1st Cork Brigade area. Only with a safe withdrawal route decided upon could the 3rd West Corks begin to think of how to take on the enemy in numbers.

In the new designated area they knew that they would be facing larger enemy numbers than previously. The brigade column needed to expand accordingly. Engagements could last for a couple of hours, so ammunition had to be increased exponentially from forty or fifty rounds up to one hundred rounds. Thanks to raids and ambushes this was now possible. Given a successful import of one thousand rounds of .303 ammunition from Cork, marked as "hardware," the problem of ammunition had been solved temporarily. Increase in manpower for the brigade flying column was to be drawn from battalions in the area that the column would be operating in. Only now with the logistics in place did the brigade commanders begin to look at suitable targets. Ideas presented for discussion included a major engagement somewhere along the Bandon-Kinsale road, where motorized convoys of the enemy were known to operate, and an attack on the RIC barracks at Rosscarbery, where it was hoped British relief forces could be drawn in and dealt a major blow.

Tureengariff

On 28 February, Sean Moylan and his 2nd Cork Brigade Column ambushed a motorized Black and Tan patrol at Tureengariff. Two days earlier, the two cars of Black and Tans, equipped with a Lewis gun, had passed through Kingwilliamstown, heading towards Tralee, the British headquarters in County Kerry. As it was late the cars were not expected to return until the following day. Moylan decided to ambush them upon their return. By five o'clock the next morning the Volunteers were at the selected ambush site, some two miles outside of Kingwilliamstown. A trench was dug across the road, and the men took up their ambush positions. The day was wet, with a thick fog. They waited until nighttime but the Black and Tans did not return that day. With a small party of men left on guard, Moylan withdrew the main body for a few hours' rest. At six o'clock the next morning the column, consisting of eleven men plus local men from the Kanturk Battalion armed with shotguns in support to defend the flanks, was in position again. The fog had lifted, it was a clear bright day. Shortly after noon the two cars were seen in the distance. Moylan had arranged his men in a semicircle, bisected by the road itself. Tom McNamara, Dan Vaughan, and Johnny Jones were on the northern side; Denis Galvin, Sean Healy, Liam Moylan, Con Morley, Tom Herlihy, local company captain David McAuliffe and Con Finucane were on the south side. Sean Moylan himself was positioned at the center. The ambush party had ten rifles and a parabellum.

The cars came around the bend of the road at speed, but the driver of the first, seeing the entrenchment, braked hard and came skidding to a halt. The second car did likewise. The Volunteers now opened fire. The Tans leaped from their cars, seeking any available cover, and returned fire. After a few minutes Moylan blew his whistle, and in the silence that followed he called upon the enemy to surrender. They responded with a fusillade of bullets, and the Irishmen opened up once more in response. Following a firefight of several minutes, Moylan again blew his whistle and called upon the Tans once more to surrender. This time they did, throwing down their rifles. The Volunteers discovered that practically every man was wounded. Two of them, including the leader, General Holmes, were dead. The fight over, the Volunteers gathered up the enemies' rifles, automatic shotgun, revolvers, grenades, ammunition and other equipment and loaded them aboard one of the cars, which was driven off. The wounds of the enemy paramilitaries were attended to, and they were placed in the other car, which was allowed to be driven away. Then the Column, which had suffered no casualties, moved off.

The British countered a few days later with a well-planned swoop of the area using the combined forces from Cork, Ballincollig, Buttevant, Fermoy and Kanturk. Using armored cars and trucks, the troops were armed with mortars and machine guns. The plan was to drive the guerrilla army onto the converging British Army units. Lynch received intelligence of the operation the day before and moved most of the flying column out of the area. Nonetheless some Volunteers were caught up in the encirclement and fought their way out. Five other Volunteers were caught. They were lined up in a field where they were told to run for their lives. Three of them were shot down as they ran and later bayoneted to death. They were Volunteers Waters, Kiely and Herlihy. Volunteers Morgan and Maloney, though wounded, escaped. Lynch's immediate response was to instigate a major campaign of road trenching to limit the ability of the Crown forces to move as quickly as they had done in their last operation. Just sufficient space was left at the side of the road to permit the passage of a horse and cart, the usual means of transport for the local community. Then he looked at further ambushes.

Clonbannin

From intelligence reports Sean Moylan, OC of the North Cork Flying Column, discovered that General Strickland, GOC of the British forces in Munster, had embarked on an inspection tour. He resolved to ambush Strickland and his party. Knowing that this enemy general would be escorted by a large contingent of police and soldiers, he called in reinforcements from the Charleville, Newmarket and Millstreet battalions. Later, riflemen from Kerry were to join them. The site chosen was along the main road west of Banteer at a place called Clonbannin. Marching off at three o'clock in the morning of 5 March, the Volunteers were in their ambush positions by six. It was a beautiful clear morning. In addition to the riflemen, the column had a Hotchkiss gun and half a dozen land mines. The electronically detonated mines were placed along the road under Moylan's supervision. At seven o'clock, Moylan checked the positions and made sure everyone knew what he had to do. Then they waited.

At ten o'clock one of the outer scouts signaled that the British were coming. Along the road from the east came three wire-covered trucks. As they approached, the Volunteers could hear an accordion being played and the sound of singing. It was not Strickland's convoy. The Volunteers watched as the trucks passed by a little to the west of the ambush position. Noon came and went; the Volunteers waited patiently. At a quarter past two the signaler brought news that a British convoy was approaching from the west, the direction that they believed Strickland would come from. The first truck breasted the hill, followed by two other vehicles. Next came an armored car, followed by three trucks. They were spaced out over a distance of half a mile along the road. In laying his mines Moylan had taken this into account. His principal target was the armored car. As it passed over the mine Moylan pressed the switch on the battery, but it shorted. By now the first truck had arrived at the forward ambush position, and the Volunteers opened fire upon it. It slewed to a halt. As the armored car came abreast of them another section opened up on it with the Hotchkiss gun. A lucky shot went through the narrow slit in front, wounding the driver. The car likewise came to a halt. The other trucks slewed to a halt and a firefight broke out. Due to their careful positioning the advantage lay with the Volunteers.

The fighting continued until dusk, but by now the Volunteers were running low on ammunition. They could not close with the enemy because of the deadly fire from the heavy Maxim machine gun in the armored car. Maurice O'Brien, commandant of the Charleville section, attempted to outflank the enemy on their right, while Moylan attempted the same on the left; but the Maxim commanded the whole position. Moylan checked his watch; it was half past five. What he feared now was the arrival of British reinforcements from Kanturk and Newmarket. As the fight continued, two sections were ordered to take up positions to deal with any reinforcements that might arrive. In fact a truck full of troops had left Newmarket, but, hitting a fence, the truck had overturned. The British at Kanturk did not leave their barracks until dark and then in large numbers. Meanwhile, the Volunteers now very low on ammunition, Moylan ordered a withdrawal.

The various sections moved off in several directions, a small covering party ensuring their safe retreat. As Moylan and his section crossed the fields at Dernagree, they saw a large party of men approaching. At first they thought it was another section of Volunteers and slowed down so that they could catch them up. Then suddenly the other men opened fire. They were British reinforcements. Returning fire, the IRA men moved off in extended formation, luckily suffering no casualties. It was now dark. The British did not pursue them beyond the field boundary, no doubt fearing an ambush. Later that night Moylan and his flying column met up with members of the local company, who informed them that a British general had been killed. It was not Strickland but Brigadier General Hanway Robert Cummins, the officer in charge of the British troops in Buttevant and Ballyvonaire. He and three other soldiers had been killed when their armored car broke down and they were exposed to IRA fire. The Volunteers rested for the night at Kiskeam, moving on the following day.

Five days later informer Dan Shields, of the Kanturk Battalion, betrayed the position of a section of the 2nd (North Cork) Brigade Column at Nadd, on 10 March. Three Volunteers were killed in the British ambush. The Volunteers quickly discovered that Shields had betrayed his former comrades when an RIC sergeant based at Kanturk told the son of an old friend, Volunteer Martin McGrath. Sheltered in one or another RIC barracks, though, Shields escaped retribution and was relocated in England.

Crossbarry

On 19 March 1921 the West Cork Flying Column of 104 officers and men under Commandant Tom Barry outfought 1,200 British troops at Crossbarry, County Cork. They succeeded in breaking through an encirclement designed to trap and destroy them. In the process they inflicted heavy casualties on the enemy, destroying British Army vehicles and capturing a large quantity of arms and ammunition. It was a textbook guerrilla operation, including a tactical withdrawal.

The site for an intended ambush was chosen by Barry and brigade adjutant Liam Deasy. It was at Shippool opposite the old castle of Dun-na-long, two miles from Innishannon and seven miles from Kinsale and it was planned for St. Patrick's Day, 17 March. The column raised for this engagement was the largest raised to date, consisting of over one hundred Volunteers. Flor Begley was invited by Deasy to bring along his war pipes and to play them during the battle to inspire the men. At midnight on Wednesday, 16 March, one hundred and two Volunteers marched off towards Shippool, which they reached before dawn. They took up their designated places and waited amidst showers of sleet and rain. During the course of the day two local families supplied them with buckets of tea and bread and butter. The Volunteers waited, and waited, but the multiple convoy of Essex soldiers that traveled that road every day never reached them. They had set out as scheduled, and traveled just over a mile when they halted. It would appear that information was received by them that the IRA were somewhere up ahead, waiting in ambush They turned around and returned to Kinsale.

Sometime later Liam Deasy learned the supposed reason for their return to barracks: they were celebrating St. Patrick's Day as a "Peace Day." The lie was given to this explanation when, as evening drew on and the column having withdrawn from the ambush site, they heard the approach of a British reconnaissance airplane, flying low, searching for them. Hearing its engine some miles off, the Volunteers hid along hedgerows and ditches and watched as it flew on. Unseen, they continued on their way to Skough, near Innishannon. Barry realized that this reconnaissance aircraft was the prelude to another large-scale encirclement. With the Innishannon Company standing guard the column got some rest. The next day the column moved off again. Barry and Deasy were concerned about a large-scale British operation against the column. Reports came in that there was little British activity, which was ominous. Special care was taken as the Column moved off northwards and across the main roads between Cork and Bandon, in the hope of moving outside of an encirclement. Tom Kelleher's section of fourteen men acted as the advance guard. Early the next morning, at 1:00 A.M. the column arrived at Ballyhandle and set up headquarters at the home of John O'Leary, whose son Paddy was captain of the Upton Company of Volunteers.

Unbeknownst to the Volunteers as they arrived at Ballyhandle, the British encirclement operation was getting under way. Some 400 soldiers left from Cork, 200 left from Ballincollig, 300 left from Kinsale and 350 more left from Bandon. Later in this time co-coordinated operation 120 Auxiliaries left from Macroom, and later more troops left from Clonakilty. They proceeded to four points approximately four miles north-northeast, south-southeast and west of Crossbarry. There they dismounted and formed up in columns. While half of their number then proceeded on foot, the remainder reboarded their trucks and continued slowly after the foot patrols. It was intended that the motorized soldiers could then be quickly rushed to any point where contact was made with the flying column. The British were acting upon reliable information. One of Paddy O'Leary's officers, who had acted as backup at the debacle at Upton Station, had been captured. Tortured by the Essex Regiment, he revealed the probable whereabouts of the column.

Just before 2:30 A.M. Mick Crowley and Tom Kelleher informed Barry that lights had been seen and truck engines heard some miles to the west. Barry ordered the assembly of the column. Ten minutes later a report came of enemy movement to the east. At 2:50 A.M. dogs were heard barking away to the south . The occasional glare of headlights was seen through gaps in the trees and hedges. Barry had little choice. He suspected that the enemy might well outnumber them by more than ten to one. He decided that he and his men should retire and attempt to evade a fight, but he realized that it probably would come to a fight. If it did, then with only forty rounds for each man, the fight would have to be short and at close quarters. Observing the approach of the enemy Barry calculated that the British force approaching from the west would reach them before the others. He decided to confront this side of the encirclement, destroy it, gather up what arms and ammunition he could, and then withdraw through its weakest point, north-northwest. At 3:00 A.M. Barry addressed the column, explaining the situation to them. Each section was given its orders, which had to be strictly obeyed if they were to win. At 3:30 the column moved off towards Crossbarry. Deasy was familiar with the terrain and suggested a possible ambush site. Local company captain Tom Kellerher agreed with Deasy's choice. The decision was made to set up an ambush along the road at Harold's and Beasley's houses at Crossbarry. That morning at four o'clock, the column marched off, bound for Crossbarry with Kelleher leading the advance guard. They reached their destination by half past four.

By half past five that morning all seven sections were in position, five along the road and two others placed well back to cover the Volunteers' flank and rear. Each unit prepared earthworks where they were lacking existing cover. The sections were as follows (according to Tom Barry's plan):

Section No. 1: Laneway and Harold's house, under the command of Sean Hales.
Section No. 2: Beasley's house, under the command of John Lordan.
Section No. 3: Beasley's garden, under the command of Mick Crowley.
Section No. 4: Between the mined road and Crossbarry Bridge, under the command of Denis Lordan.
Section No. 5: Protecting the rear of the column near Ballyhandle Castle and covering the left flank, under the command of Tom Kellerher.[13]
Section No. 6: The field fence from Beasley's garden to the mine position, under the command of Peter Kearney.
Section No. 7: The right flank covering the Bandon Road, under the command of Christy O'Connell.

The ambush site extended for six hundred yards to accommodate a convoy of up to six trucks. Some of the positions along the road were barely three yards away, and this, if properly cocoordinated, would give the attackers an overwhelming element of surprise with their opening salvo. Two mines were placed along the road, one to the east, where the trucks were expected to come from, and one to the west, which was to be set off if British troops went anywhere near it. Under no circumstances were any Volunteers to show themselves before the action began. The plan was to let the entire British force move into the ambush site, and as they reached the eastern mine it would be set off, indicating the start of the battle.

At half past six the sound of rifle and revolver fire was heard about a mile away behind them, indicating the presence of the British. Unbeknownst to the Volunteers at that time, Charlie Hurley, convalescing after the Upton Station disaster, had been surprised by a foraging party of soldiers from the Essex Regiment. In an attempt to shoot his way out, he was killed. There was a hurried conference amongst the senior Volunteer officers. With the enemy behind them and approaching from the west, contingency plans for withdrawal were updated. Barry was on the point of moving the eastern sections led by Kearney, Denis Lordan and Kelleher when suddenly they all heard the sound of trucks approaching along the road. It was a convoy of eight trucks, three in front traveling in close formation comprising two trucks and a Crossley tender, and the remaining five some distance behind. They were carrying soldiers from the Essex Regiment plus a few Black and Tans. It was 8:00 A.M. They came roaring along the road.

Completely against orders, shots rang out from sections one and two. Apparently a Volunteer had been seen by the soldiers in the first truck before it reached the mine, and the convoy began to slow down. As the first truck braked, John Lordan ordered his section to open fire on it, as it was now abreast of their position. In the close proximity of the withering fire, many of the soldiers were killed in the first burst of fire. Those who survived jumped down from the trucks and sought shelter behind their vehicles and returned fire. Volunteers on the other side of the road made short work of them, and in less than twenty minutes they were all dead or mortally wounded. Amidst the gunfire Flor Begley played his warpipes, giving encouragement to the Volunteers. A young Volunteer, Ned White of Newceston, had been a prisoner aboard the first truck. Somehow, miraculously in all the fire, he leaped from the truck and gained the safety of the Volunteers' ranks. In what could have been a British victory, instead of disembarking the troops from the other trucks and outflanking the guerrillas the other trucks turned and retreated towards Innishannon.

At section three under Mick Crowley, soldiers from the third truck were running away in disorder towards the railway line. Believing that they intended to regroup, six Volunteers under Barry crossed the road in pursuit of them. The Volunteers opened up on the fleeing men, wounding and killing a number of them before the remainder reached the railway embankment and escaped without any thought of regrouping. The six rejoined Crowley's section, now in fierce action against the soldiers of the second truck. As the section gained the upper hand, rifle fire broke out on the left rear as British reinforcements from the Hampshire Regiment joined battle. Section five under Tom Kelleher, about four hundred yards to their rear, had come under fire. This was serious, because Kelleher's section was protecting the line of withdrawal. Five men from Peter Kearney's section were ordered over to help Kelleher's men. It was important that they prevent the enemy from securing the Skeenahaine height, thus giving the soldiers an overwhelming advantage. This little battle within a battle was probably key to the Volunteers' success.

With the fight down on the road almost over Barry and Deasy agreed on how to divide up the column to fall back on Skeenahaine to meet a strong enemy attack now coming from the northeast. All the enemy arms from the trucks was now gathered up, including a Lewis gun with ten pans of ammunition, twelve rifles and a large amount of .303 ammunition. It was a quarter past eight. Sections one, two and three were led off up a narrow lane, or boreen, into the fields beyond Harold's house. They met up with Christy O'Connell's section seven, who were now given the task of organizing the withdrawal. The Volunteers gained the advantageous Skeenahaine height, and from there they had a complete view of everything that was happening. Over near Crossbarry Bridge sections four and six were involved in a heavy firefight as British troops attempted a pincer movement. To the east a party of between twenty and thirty British soldiers in extended formation were advancing at the double with the intention of cutting off the two Volunteer sections at the bridge. Their intention was to cross the fields and get down onto the road that ran from Crossbarry to Begley's Forge, thus taking the Volunteers in the flank. Observing this, Deasey ordered sixty men to line the fence nearby and open up independent fire. This drove the enemy back to the house at Killeen's farm, where they had started from. Sections four and six meanwhile were hard pressed. A number of Volunteers lay dead or wounded. One of them was Peter Monaghan, the engineer who had designed the as-yet unexploded mine. As he fell his arm struck the plunger, which blew up the mine. In the surprise and confusion of the explosion, Lordan succeeded in withdrawing his men out of the encircling British troops. Tom Kelleher, whose section gave Lordan and his men covering fire in their withdrawal, sent a number of his men to occupy the ruins of Ballyhandle Castle, with instructions not to fire until the now advancing enemy was close. Their orders were to pick off the officer leading the British advance.

The advancing soldiers had split into two groups, the main group that Kelleher engaged and a flanking group hoping to gain the advantage of the castle ruins. At this point Kelleher was joined by eight seasoned Volunteer soldiers who succeeded in checking the advance of the main group. The flanking group of soldiers, moving towards the castle ruins, were about twenty yards away when the Volunteers within the ruins opened fire, killing the officer. Others were wounded, and the remainder broke, retreating in disorder. Kelleher was able to withdraw his men in good order. The British had been repulsed on three fronts. If there was more to come then it was essential for the Volunteers to regroup on more favorable terrain. Their line of withdrawal was northwards, and Raheen Hill, two miles distant, became their objective. Sean Deasy was given command of the main unit of seventy men. His orders were to seize and hold the hill. Barry brought up the rearguard of twenty-five men, together with four wounded Volunteers. He was convinced that there were more British reinforcements out there, but where?

Barry and Deasy later learned that thirty-four trucks had been seen entering the area. With a maximum of twelve men per truck, this amounted to between four hundred and five hundred men. Only later did they learn that the Auxiliaries at Macroom, who were intended to take part in the encirclement, had misinterpreted the orders and were delayed. Barry arrived at the hill with his men fifteen minutes after Deasy. They rested there for a short time, and then under the guidance of local Volunteer Tom Kelleher they were led outside the ring of enemy activity. As they were moving off the hill they espied Auxiliaries away to the north and east of their position. It was difficult to say how many there were, but the Volunteers, low on ammunition, were anxious to avoid another prolonged engagement. Barry gave orders for Mick Crowley, Peter Kearney and Jim Doyle to engage the Auxiliaries while the column withdrew to Rearour Bridge. The column moved off north-northwest and on to Raheen. This small detail found themselves an ambush site and waited for the Auxiliaries. As the Auxiliaries entered the field next to theirs, the Volunteers opened fire on them, deliberately targeting the officers. The commanding officer and his subordinate were killed in the first volley. The others panicked and fled, perhaps believing that they were facing a much larger party.

The column meanwhile had turned westward and through Crowhill. For five miles it continued in its march in a southwesterly direction before turning west once more and on to Gurranereigh, crossing fields and avoiding roads where possible. At Crowhill the right flanking section had seen a motorized convoy of Auxiliaries on the road below and opened fire upon them. The return fire was desultory, the Auxiliaries deciding against pursuing their attackers across the fields. At Rerour this same flanking section was fired upon from a distance. The only casualties were two goats grazing nearby in a field. Moving away on a slight parallel course, the flanking section did not bother to return fire. The British soldiers did not pursue the column, which continued on its way. The three Volunteers, acting as a rearguard, rejoined their comrades before they had got to Rearour Bridge. The column then proceeded on, crossing the River Brinney. At three o'clock that afternoon they sat down to a meal provided by the local people. Barry's flying column had encountered a better-trained, more numerous and far better armed force and ha dwon. The British lost up to thirty killed and wounded; the IRA lost six.

That evening the column received news of Charlie Hurley's death. Recovering from the wounds he had received at Upton, Hurley was resting at Forde's of Ballymurphy. Shortly before 6:30 A.M. he was woken by British soldiers battering in the front door of the house with their rifle butts. He warned the family of the house to remain where they were for their own safety. Dressed only in shirt and trousers, with revolver in hand, Hurley descended the stairs and confronted the soldiers, who were now in the kitchen. He opened fire on them. They returned fire and retreated out through the front door. Hurley then made a dash for the rear door. He rushed out into the yard, where he was confronted by a dozen Essex soldiers who shot him dead.

On the appropriately named Spy Wednesday, 23 March 1921, just before Easter Sunday, a group of young IRA men from C Company, 1st Cork Brigade, were betrayed by a neighbor of their host. The six young men, all local, were Jeremiah O'Mullane, Daniel Crowley, Thomas Dennehy, Michael O'Sullivan, Daniel Murphy and William Deasy. They were sleeping in the barn of a man named O'Keefe. At four o'clock in the morning a large party of Black and Tans surrounded the hamlet of Kerry Pike, which lies on the Blarney road about two miles from Clogheen Church. A number from this group then went directly to the O'Keefe house and battered down the door. The house was thoroughly searched but to little effect. Then they proceeded to the outhouses, where the Volunteers were discovered. They were ordered to their feet and lined up and searched. The Volunteers were led outside and ordered to run for their lives. As they did so they were all shot down. The neighbor who betrayed them had previously been a Volunteer himself in a West Cork Flying Column which he betrayed. The traitor was given a new identity in England.

In the days following Crossbarry, Liam Lynch, commandant of the Second Cork Brigade, now proposed molding the brigades adjoining his own into one single Southern Division, in order to coordinate major attacks on the British forces. Lynch also advocated extending the war in previously inactive counties by putting men from the southern brigades into those counties. At a conference of senior officers, two alternative proposals were drawn up to be presented to Volunteer GHQ in Dublin. Both proposals relied on GHQ's taking a more active role in guerrilla warfare in the countryside:

(a) An unarmed Flying Column consisting of 20 men from each Brigade, to be formed into a new Flying Column, to be armed by GHQ, and to be sent into inactive areas.
(b) That the six Brigades represented between them, arm one Flying Column for similar action. GHQ to be responsible for their quartering and rations. This Column to operate in previously inactive areas.

GHQ agreed to extending the fighting as per the proposals presented. They also agreed to the formation of a Southern Division, comprising the three brigades of Cork, Kerry, West Limerick and West Waterford. Liam Lynch, an IRB man, was appointed commander of the division, in charge of 30,000 officers and men. Also discussed were the lessons learned from recent actions, which were analyzed and information shared. One point in particular that came up was the vital necessity of a rearguard, especially as a means of protecting a column from an enemy encirclement. Equally important was its use as an offensive force, attacking the enemy while the main body withdrew from an action. This was the lesson taken from Crossbarry. As a consequence, new tactics evolved in the war against the British.

Rosscarbery

Following the successful fight at Crossbarry, attention now turned to the RIC barracks at Rosscarbery. If it could be captured and destroyed then a great swathe of southern Cork would fall into Republican hands. The flying column under Tom Barry had increased in size to the extent that it attracted local attention as it moved about the county. In order to confuse British Intelligence, it moved in a series of zigzag marches to disguise its true intent. By 22 March 1921, the column, consisting of seventy riflemen, had camped but a few miles short of its target. Meanwhile, at Bantry a mine containing one hundred pounds of explosive, to be used at Rosscarbery, was prepared by a new recruit to the Volunteers, Captain McCarthy, a former British Army engineer officer home on leave from India. In addition a number of crude but effective stick grenades were made of gelignite together with a detonator and time fuse placed in coffee tins packed with scrap metal and clay. Torches of broomstick handles wrapped in old sacking were also prepared, to be later dowsed in paraffin or petrol and set alight.

But first, information came in that the British had reserved a number of railway carriages for 23 March on a train traveling between Clonakilty and Skibbereen. Early that Wednesday morning the column was in position, some five miles from Clonakilty, prepared to ambush it. As they waited news arrived that instead the troops had left Clonakilty by road. It had all been a clever ruse.

On the night of 30 March, the column moved on Rosscarbery. Volunteer companies in the area began felling trees to block roads and cut trenches across others. The main body of the column was placed on the roads leading from Skibbereen, Dunmanway and Clonakilty, where any British reinforcements might be expected to come from. Ten specially selected officers and men were formed into a storming party. Each man in the attacking party was issued with a rifle and one hundred rounds of ammunition, a revolver and accompanying ammunition, and improvised stick grenades. A second group of ten riflemen prepared to follow up with burning torches. A third group of twelve riflemen positioned themselves north and east of the barracks to prevent the garrison from emerging from the back or side. A fourth group of eleven riflemen were held in reserve. Defending the barracks were a head constable, two sergeants and nineteen constables, mainly Black and Tans. The stone building was strongly fortified. There were metal shutters over the windows and barbed wire entanglements all round the building save for a narrow pathway from the front gate. The IRA company intelligence officer, Tom Moloney, having carefully studied the barracks and its garrison, revealed that the gate was usually locked at night — but not always. More worrying, perhaps, Moloney revealed, was that a hatch had been constructed in the roof. Through it, as training exercises revealed, a machine gun could quickly be brought out, producing a killing field in a ninety degree angle of the front of the building.

It was Barry who wriggling forward on his stomach, approached the gate to the barracks. It was latched but not locked. As silently as possible he opened it and pushed the gate open. There was no sign of activity from within. Barry remained at the gate. The bomb, in a wooden case, weighed about eighty pounds. Volunteers Jack Corkery, Peter Kearney, Tom Kelleher and Christy O'Connell raised it up onto their shoulders. Denis Lordan lit the two fuses, and the four Volunteers swiftly moved down the path to the barracks door. Having laid the mine they withdrew in single file, fearful of becoming entangled in the barbed wire. There was an enormous explosion which brought down a wall above the doorway, and a number of steel shutters were blown off. Amidst the dust and debris the attacking party ran towards the barracks, only to discover that the rubble had effectively formed a wall, preventing an entry. None of the garrison had been injured, and through the hole created they opened fire on their attackers. Shots were fired in return by the attackers at the exposed windows and through the gap.

Con Connolly and four riflemen were ordered across the road to occupy the upstairs windows of a house opposite. Their orders were to fire at the upper windows of the barracks and particularly to prevent the machine gun from being brought out onto the roof. A Mills grenade lobbed into the barracks momentarily reduced the return fire, but others came to take the place of the wounded Tans. A burning torch was thrown towards the gap, illuminating the enemy within. They responded by lobbing a Mills bomb back. Seeing it in time, the Volunteers dropped flat on the ground and it exploded harmlessly. The Mills bombs had a five second delay, which gave the Volunteers ample time to take cover. Barry later pointed out that if the Tans, after removing the pins, had waited two seconds before throwing them, there would have been serious casualties among the ranks of the Volunteers.

A fierce firefight ensued, with bombs being thrown by both sides. Very lights were sent up, imploring for reinforcements. It took the best part of two hours to drive the enemy from the ground floor to the floor above. Two of the defenders were dead, Sergeant Shea and Constable Bowles. Gaining entrance to the ground floor the Volunteers set the room afire hoping to bring down the ceiling above. Down the staircase the Tans kept up a steady fire, keeping the Volunteers at bay. As the room above caught fire the defenders were driven back into one of the top-storey rooms. Four hours had elapsed. The building was ablaze. The Volunteers could not get through the flames, nor could the defenders get down the stairs. From inside, the firing subsided, then ceased. The Tans threw their arms and ammunition down into the burning rooms below to prevent them from being captured. Then an improvised white flag appeared at an upstairs window, and it was all over. The defenders surrendered. They lowered their wounded down from a back window, then climbed out themselves. Nine were wounded, some badly, including Head Constable Neary. As bombs and ammunition began to explode within the building, the roof fell in. Rosscarbery Barracks had been destroyed.

There were no casualties among the Volunteers, neither killed nor wounded. As dawn approached the Volunteers withdrew in good order. They marched off to the west to mislead any pursuit, then proceeded north for five miles and there rested. Later news reached them that British reinforcements were converging on Rosscarbery, from Bandon, Clonakilty and Dunmanway. Due to the obstructions created along the roads the previous night, their progress was slow. None of the British forces passed within four miles of where the Volunteers were billeted. The next day the column continued on to the Newceston area and Bealnablath. On 3 April the column was broken up into smaller units, and the men proceeded back to their own battalion areas. Rosscarbery Barracks was a strategic base for the British Army in the area. Its destruction resulted in the Cork Volunteers having an area of roughly 270 square miles free from the enemy to use as a safe haven, to train men and to allow Volunteers to rest and recoup.

In the late spring of 1921 the British began using cavalry in numbers during its roundups. Horses had the advantage of being able to go where armored vehicles and trucks could not — across hedges and ditches and through fields. Ernie O'Malley records one such venture. He and a fellow Volunteer riding in a horse and cart along a road in West Cork, heading towards Fermoy, spied a group of horses about a mile away. Using his field glasses O'Malley discovered that there was a group of ten riders coming in his direction. His driver indicated that there were some men from the local Volunteer company nearby. Unfortunately they had broken up into smaller units earlier that day, and there were only three available to assist O'Malley in the ambush that he planned. At this point the Volunteers discovered that the ten horsemen were part of a much larger group of cavalry, all headed in their direction. It was part of an extensive roundup, with more soldiers approaching on foot from a different direction. The horsemen were moving at speed. To engage them might well leave the Volunteers trapped in the encirclement. O'Malley ordered a hasty withdrawal before the noose closed on them.

The group met up with Liam Lynch and his flying column on Claragh Mountain near Millstreet. Lynch gave them details of the roundup, in which he himself was nearly captured. It turned out that a new Volunteer, an British Army ex-soldier had absented himself from the column. His absence was not noted for some time. The man had made his way to Buttevant Army Camp, where he gave details of the column's location. Just before dawn the next morning, fifty trucks of troops plus soldiers on horseback had attempted an encirclement. Lynch, who had made a cottage his temporary headquarters, was nearly caught when a group of soldiers approached the building. Fortunately for him outlying pickets saw them in time and opened fire. Lynch, in just shirt and trousers, grabbed up his papers and ran from the building. In the brief firefight that followed, three Volunteers were killed and two taken prisoner. The assembled column, fighting a rearguard action, withdrew to safety up in the mountains. Fortunately for them another large party of British troops advancing towards them were delayed when they encountered road blockages and trenches. The column escaped through the narrowing gap.

By April the British left their bases only to conduct large-scale roundups. They would advance from three or four towns and converge on designated regions, combing them in the hope of making contact with a guerrilla column. Often forewarned through their intelligence system, the columns evaded encirclement and destroyed bridges and roads before and behind the encircling British forces.

A second regional Southern Division conference was held at Kippaugh near Millstreet, County Cork, from April 24 to April 26, 1921. It was presided over by Ernie O'Malley, representing GHQ. By the spring of 1921, GHQ in Dublin was well aware of the growing resistance among most stratas of English society to the sending of more troops to Ireland. There was a growing state of revulsion at the repression and cruelty practiced against Ireland. With this view so prevalent Volunteer GHQ pushed for more effort in driving the Crown forces back to Dublin. A policy was advocated of sending experienced officers and flying columns into less active areas to both extend the war and stretch the existing Crown forces. This, it was hoped, would force the enemy to evacuate some districts to meet the new emergencies. The policy was eagerly endorsed by the senior officers present. At the conference measures were also drawn up to deal with Britain's policy of executing prisoners and burning supporters' houses. It was agreed that the British authorities should be informed that if the shooting of captured Volunteers persisted, then the IRA would seize and execute British personnel. Accordingly, Liam Lynch wrote to the senior British officer, Major General E.P. Strickland, to inform him of the decision. Regarding the burning of houses, if this continued, Lynch wrote, then Loyalist houses would be burned in reprisal. The Volunteer officers present were in favor of extending the war, but it was revealed that despite the many raids and ambushes the three Cork Brigades still had less than 300 rifles among them. The men were acting on a rotation service basis. O'Malley informed them that GHQ were attempting to import arms from Italy. Negotiations were under way for the purchase of 20,000 rifles and 500 machine guns, plus 500,000 rounds of ammunition.

On 4 May 1921, a combined force of Cork No. 2 and Kerry No. 2 brigades ambushed a party of Auxiliaries near the village of Rathmore. Eight of the enemy were killed and their arms and ammunition were captured. That night the British responded by burning five farmhouses in the vicinity as a reprisal. As a show of strength, at 3:00 P.M. on 14 May, the Volunteers carried out simultaneous assaults on all British garrisons within the newly created division. By the end of the month the Volunteers had complete control of the hill districts and small villages of County Cork. The British held the main towns. Nighttime raids by the British ceased for fear of ambush. During daylight hours the Black and Tans and Auxiliaries moved around the county in ever larger convoys, but at this stage they were no longer in complete control of the areas that they patrolled.

Over the next few weeks Liam Lynch, commander of the First Southern Division, moved his headquarters to the more centrally placed Coolea District, a fairly isolated region of Muskerry in the Derrynasaggart Mountains. Lynch visited all the brigade areas to encourage his men and to review the expansion of the war. He met with battalion and column commanders to discuss leadership, organization, coordination, training, intelligence, security and the availability of arms and explosives for flying columns. The flying column, it was agreed by all, was the most effective formation for fighting a guerrilla war if it could act with speed and surprise. Shared knowledge and practical experience agreed that the column should have advanced and rear guards. They should not advance into territory that had not first been scouted for the presence of the enemy. Above all, continual Volunteer activity was essential. This meant disrupting enemy activity, be it cutting trenches in roads or nighttime sniping to break the nerve of the enemy by making anxious as to when the next attack might occur. From a practical point of view, in order to feed and clothe his men, Lynch introduced a levy based on the existing poor law system, money which the British were no longer able to collect. Thus everybody paid according to their means. This included the Loyalist population, who, if they refused, had goods distrained.

In May 1921, the British adopted a scheme of deploying men in a similar fashion to the IRA flying columns. Ten or twenty soldiers, usually commanded by a senior NCO, would be driven to a particular location where they would disembark and then proceed across country to a designated rendezvous where they would be picked up again. This deployment played havoc with Republican communications and led to the capture of individual Volunteers. On 8 May, Volunteer Willie Brandsfield of the First Cork Brigade was shot dead in Carrigtouhilby by soldiers of the Cameron Highlanders acting in this manner.

The 10th of May saw the culmination of the "Bicycle War." British intelligence rightly assumed that in the absence of sufficient cars at their disposal, the Volunteers were using bicycles as a means of transport to pass on information and orders. So raiding parties, apart from looking for Volunteers, were also instructed to seize all bicycles in their areas. At first Volunteer brigade commanders looked at this behavior with curiosity, but as more and more bikes were seized and fewer were available for Volunteer messengers, they acted. In the next two days, Volunteers in pairs or threes collected up all the remaining bicycles and hid them. It was a minor war within a war, but on such things victories and defeats turn. That morning the British launched a six day offensive in North Cork. British troops, Auxiliaries and Black and Tans took part in an enormous encirclement. Three Volunteers, Paddy and Dan O'Brien (cousins of Tom Barry) and John O'Regan, got caught up in it. O'Regan was badly wounded in a shoot-out, and Dan O'Brien was captured. Paddy O'Brien succeeded in shooting his way out. Dan O'Brien was court-martialled before a drumhead court and shot by firing squad on 16 May.

On 14 May the West Cork Brigade instigated an attack on the ten British garrisons within its district, both police and military, with the exception of the Schull Coast Guard Station, which, though manned by Royal Marines, had always been inactive throughout the war. At the appointed hour of 3:00 P.M., the attacks, over an extended area of about eighty miles, were begun. Approaching Castletownbere, battalion OC Liam Dwyer, Volunteers Peter O'Neill and Christy O'Connell and others had a brief skirmish with a British patrol, who having fired a few rounds, retired back to the town. As the garrison was alerted, the element of surprise was gone. Successful attacks were carried out in Bandon, Innishannon, Kilbrittain, Courtmacsherry, Clonakilty, Dunmanway, Drimoleague and Furious Pier near Rossmacowan. At Furious Piers an IRA unit under Michael O'Sullivan attacked a patrol of the KOSB Regiment. Four British soldiers were killed (Privates Hunter, McCullen, Chalmers and Edwards) and two wounded. Just outside of Bantry, battalion commandant Tom Ward and his men were fired upon by eight Black and Tans. Returning fire, the Tans retired rapidly with casualties. Near Skibbereen, an IRA unit under Battalion Commandant Con Connolly, shot dead Constable McLean and seriously wounded Constable Cooper of the Black and Tans. At Drimoleague Captain Daniel O'Driscoll's unit attacked a party of Black and Tans, forcing them to scurry back to their barracks. At Clonakilty a party of riflemen under battalion commandant Jim Hurley and Vice-Commandant Tim O'Donaghue entered the town searching the streets and public houses for any sign of the enemy. Failing to find any they moved on to the Black and Tan barracks at McCurtain Hill and the nearby British Army barracks, where they opened fire on the building, then withdrew a short way off hoping to draw the enemy out. Though the Volunteers remained in the town for over an hour, the enemy did not venture out. Hurley and his men then retired. At Kilbrittain an IRA unit of riflemen under company captain Jackie O'Neill fired on a party of Black and Tans, wounding two of them. At Innishannon, battalion adjutant Jim O'Mahony, Captain Jack Corkery and two other Volunteers shot and killed a Black and Tan named Kenna as he emerged from the barracks.

Dunmanway

The attack on Dunmanway was carried out at midday on the fourteenth. One hundred and twenty Volunteers under Ted O'Sullivan and Paddy O'Brien were involved. Volunteer intelligence had noticed over a period of weeks that a Crossley tender carrying a number of Auxiliaries arrived in the square at Dunmanway every Saturday at noon. Over the next hour the men would do some shopping then visit one of the local pubs. They were based at the local workhouse, a mile to the east of the town, a garrison of one hundred men. The RIC barracks was situated about one hundred yards from the square and consisted of twenty policemen and Black and Tans. The Volunteers were divided into two sections who approached the town from two different directions. The first section, under vice OC Ted O'Sullivan, consisted of eighteen men armed with rifles and shotguns. The second section, under battalion adjutant Paddy O'Brien, consisted of twenty-one men similarly armed. The remainder, sixty in number, took up positions around the town to prevent any British reinforcements arriving and to secure a safe withdrawal for those taking part in the action. Twenty-one Volunteers acted as messengers and scouts, linking up with the various sections.

As the Angelus bell rang at twelve o'clock, the Volunteers took up their positions within the town. They waited, but there was no sign of the Crossley tender and its passengers. At a quarter past twelve two armed policemen emerged from their barracks and proceeded towards the square. They appeared to sense that something was wrong and reached for their revolvers. Seeing them, the Volunteers in the square opened fire. The policemen dived for cover, then hastily made their escape back to the police barracks. Hearing the firing in the town the Volunteers on protection duty felled the partly sawn trees to block all roads into the town. They were not sure whether the tender had arrived by another route, but their duty was now to prevent Auxiliary reinforcements from approaching the town square. Within the town itself the police, secure in their fortified blockhouse, took no further part in the incident. Curiously, neither did the one hundred strong Auxiliary unit based at the old workhouse. Having effectively captured the town, the Volunteers found themselves without an enemy to fight. They withdrew in orderly fashion. It was a hollow victory, but it gave tremendous encouragement to the local people.

The attack on Bandon at 3:00 P.M. that same day was a curious affair. It was meant as a hit and run raid right in the heart of a strong British military stronghold. Its intention was to unnerve rather than to kill the enemy. It was designed to show that the IRA could attack at will. Tom Barry, Sean Lehane, Peter Kearney, Mick Crowley, John Lordan and Bill O'Sullivan were the Volunteers involved. A Model T Ford car, taken from the Essex Regiment, was fitted with a Lewis machinegun. The intention was to drive into the town and shootup the military barracks, garrisoned by the Essex Regiment, before moving on to the Devonshire Hotel on the other side of the square and open up on the Black and Tans who had set up a barracks there. On the appointed the day the car with its six Volunteers approached the barracks. In a field adjoining the grammar school they saw a group of soldiers of the Essex Regiment who in turn saw them but just stood and looked at them. The Volunteers opened up with machine-gun and rifle fire. Strange, the soldiers who were armed did not return fire. The element of surprise now gone, the accelerator of the car was pushed hard to the floor and the Model T sped off and away. Four miles outside the town the car was set on fire, and Barry and his men proceeded across country to Newceston. One Essex soldier was killed and seven (including some Black and Tans) were wounded.

Other attacks in Limerick, Kerry No. 1 and the Cork No. 1 brigade areas, were also cocoordinated for 3:00 P.M. on 14 May. The West Limerick men killed a Constable Bridges and wounded another Black and Tan at Drumcollogher. A unit from Kerry No.1 killed Head Constable Benson at Tralee. In Cork City the city battalions shot up the many enemy garrisons. Black and Tan constables Creighton and Ryle were killed and Constables Hayes and Brackwell were wounded. The East Cork men killed Sergeant Coleman and Constables Comyn and Thomas, and wounded Constable McDonald of the Black and Tans. A Royal Artillery Gunner was shot dead at East Ferry. The Volunteers of the North Cork Brigade suffered a serious loss when their OC, Sean Moylan, was caught up in the British roundup that followed the next day. Recognized by an RIC man, he was put on trial and sentenced to death. He was reprieved and spent the rest of the war interned on Spike Island, until the truce.

The Kealkil-Keimineigh-Ballingeary Encirclement

In late May 1921, the West Cork Brigade sought to take on O Company of the Auxiliaries, based at Dunmanway. The site chosen was at Gloundaw, midway between Dunmanway and Drimoleague. It was a good ambush site, and the entire one hundred riflemen of the brigade flying column, plus twenty shotgun men from the local companies, were assembled. The enemy were expected to number about one hundred and fifty men. In order to induce the Auxiliaries to come out, local company captain Daniel O'Driscoll and a few men shot a Black and Tan near his barracks. All day the Volunteers waited, but the Auxiliaries did not come. That evening the IRA men retired. The next morning, the 27th of May, news reached the guerrillas that there were large troop movements away to the east. There was also activity at Bantry, Skibbereen, Clonakilty, Dunmanway and Bandon barracks. A huge roundup was being planned. Barry sent out scouts to probe the extent of the approaching enemy from the east. They reported back that it was too great a converging force for the Volunteers to break out in that direction. The day after, it was confirmed that thousands of enemy troops were sweeping in from north Cork, in a line that extended from Ballyvourney to Macroom. From Macroom to Clonakilty another line of troops was also on the move. The fourth side of this box-like roundup was the Atlantic Ocean, where the Royal Navy patrolled. Hopes of escaping northwesterly into Kerry were dashed when later that night a report came in that British troops now held a line between Kenmare, Kilgarvan and Headford. The British forces were supported by field artillery. In overall command was General Strickland, whose mission was to locate and annihilate the column.

The British, Barry's scouts learned, were stopping and starting, by which Barry was able to deduce that they were acting according to a master plan detailing the movement and timing of each unit. Field commanders had no power to deviate from the plan, nor to exercise initiative. In its favor it enabled the other units to know exactly where everyone else was, at an exact time. This mitigated against what we now call "friendly fire." But this starting and stopping allowed corridors to be created through which the guerrillas could slip. Analyzing the approaches of these three lines of troops, Barry deduced the completed encircling triangle. It was thorough but slow moving. By sending out mobile reconnaissance units, distanced five or six miles apart, the British would have stood a better chance of locating, making contact with, and engaging the flying column. Further troops could then have been rushed by motorized convoys to the site. However, this did not happen.

By the fourth evening the column was maneuvering and probing for a gap between the British lines. It was forced southwest towards Ouvane Bridge on the main Bantry-Glengarriff road which skirts Bantry Bay. After a mile and a half they turned off the road and moved north to the Valley of Coomhola. With the local company standing guard, the column rested for the night. The next morning Barry sent out scouts in all directions. Later that day they reported that the British had used artillery against the slopes of Sheehy Mountain, hoping to flush out the flying column. Word then arrived that the navy had landed marines in Bantry Bay. The triangle was almost complete. The column was assembled and began a march northwards along the hilly road that led to the Kerry border. The plan was to cross the treacherous boggy land that formed the plateau of the mountain country between the old Kerry road and Gougane Barra during the hours of darkness. This was the gap the British had left. The Volunteers had the service of a local guide who had tied together a number of ropes, which the IRA men held onto. With instructions to follow in his footsteps and not to move off the path he had selected, the column set off. In the pitch black the march continued. Sometimes the Volunteers sank into the bog up to their knees. On either side of this narrow path were deep water-filled holes in which a man could easily drown before help could be given. Eventually, after an exhausting march, the Volunteers emerged at the top of Deepvalley Desmond. From there they slithered and slid down the mountainside to the level ground of Gougane Barra. They were now well beyond the encirclement. For one whole day they waited. Then news reached them that the British, having unsuccessfully completed their operation, were moving out. They had failed to capture even one active Volunteer. Now rested, the flying column followed after the British line as it moved east once more. The British returned to their barracks, never venturing out again in any numbers into the West Cork Brigade area.

The First Cork Brigade carried out a bomb attack on Bandsmen of the Hampshire Regiment at Youghal on 31 May. Seven of the soldiers were killed and more than twenty wounded. Because of the youth of some of those killed there was a mixed outcry in the British press, some calling for vengeance, while others called for the end of the war before anymore young men were killed. England, like Ireland, was war-weary.

On 1 June a cycle patrol of Auxiliaries was ambushed between Castlemaine and Milltown, by Kerry No. 1 Brigade under Tadh Brosnan. Six Auxiliaries were killed and five wounded in the attack. Again arms and ammunition were captured. Between the 4th and 14th of June the British Army and police in the district conducted an extensive encirclement of the area bordered by Kilgarven, Rathmore, Millstreet, Ballyvourney and Dunmanway. Several thousand troops with trucks, armored cars and aircraft were involved in a bid to locate and destroy the flying column. Liam Lynch intercepted the order from General Strickland to his commanders and acted accordingly to evade the encirclement. Entrenched roads and destroyed bridges greatly hampered the British vehicles, reducing the speed of the operation. While the British halted for the night, the column chose that time to escape through the encirclement. As with Barry, not one of Lynch's Volunteers nor any arms were captured.

Rathcoole

On 16 June a combined force of one hundred and forty Volunteers drawn from Millstreet, Kanturk, Charleville and Mallow columns attacked four vehicles of Auxiliaries at Rathcoole, between Millstreet and Banteer. The ambush party of sixty-five were armed with rifles and a Hotchkiss machine gun. Outlying Volunteers covering the line of withdrawal were issued with shotguns. Land mines were exploded under three of the vehicles, killing two Auxiliaries and wounding four. After a fierce gun battle the Auxiliaries managed to extricate themselves, but they abandoned in the process 1,350 rounds of ammunition. They suffered losses of twelve men killed and four wounded. Lieutenant W.E. Crossey, commanding the Auxiliaries, presented the following report of the ambush to his immediate superior, General Strickland:

> Report on ambush of "L" Coy: by armed rebels at Rathcool Co. Cork
> On the 16th instant
>
> It is my painful duty to report the facts concerning the above ambush, in which this unit was trapped on the above mentioned date. At 19.00 hours a convoy was at Banteer station, in order to meet a party returning from Cork, a batch of recruits and the "runner" returning from Dublin. The convoy consisted of 2 open Crossley tenders, 1 armored Crossley and 1 armored Lancia with 25 personnel of the company. While on column of route the armored Lancia was leading.
>
> The convoy left Banteer and when about four miles from Banteer and half a mile from Rathcool bridge, it stopped. A reconnoitering party (acting on previous information) left the

tenders and proceeded to skirmish the immediate vicinity of the road, to a depth of 400 yards on the left and right flanks. Nothing of importance or of a suspicious character was discovered during the operation. After this, the convoy proceeded over Rathcool bridge on its homeward journey.

When about, approximately half a mile beyond the bridge, previously referred to and on the Millstreet side of it, the ambush was first encountered. Here, I might point out for your information, in this ambush, the rebels had adopted an entirely new method of attack. Namely they allowed the 1st: 2nd: and 3rd cars to proceed and then exploded an electronically controlled land mine underneath the rear car. Almost simultaneously with the mining of the rear car, the second leading car was blown up. The leading car (the armored Lancia) being blown up last of all. The occupants of this vehicle (including myself) on hearing the explosions in the rear were practically blown out of it, when the last mine of all was fired, i.e. after the car had been turned round, in order to go to the assistance of the rest of the convoy.

Therefore it will be easily seen that the only car to escape being mined was the third in column of route. I may say that these mines were timed and fired with the utmost precision. As soon as the mines had been fired, a heavy and concentrated fire was opened up by the insurgents, along a front of $3/4$ to 1 mile in length.

The fire was notably heaviest, from the direction of the thickly wooded hills on our left. A fairly concentrated fire was also opened up from the railway embankment on our right. The range when the attack first commenced, was between two and three hundred yards and gradually increased to about 700 when the fight ended. I should roughly estimate, that the strength of the attackers was about 300. From the foregoing it will be easily seen that my party, badly shaken as it was by the explosions, was at a very grave disadvantage. The rebels occupied a position of great natural strength and it was utterly impossible to locate them.

I believe that the rebels sustained severe casualties, judging from screams and groans heard coming from their direction. I cannot speak too highly of the way in which my party behaved, outmaneuvered as they were by twelve to one; not overlooking the fact that at the commencement of the action, the occupants of each car had to fight as detached groups, until such time as they were able to concentrate. During the whole of the engagement, the discipline of the cadets was perfect. There not being the slightest sign of panic or nerves as might easily have occurred, owing to the sudden nature of the onslaught.

As soon as I considered it feasible, I sent to Millstreet for reinforcements. D.I.3. F. Scott being the first to go on this errand and the first to arrive at his destination some five miles distant. I cannot, find words sufficient, to express my appreciation of his hazardous task. He was single handed and under rebel fire for about a mile of his journey and finally arrived in Millstreet without a single round of ammunition, having expended it all on his journey.

This officer gave the alarm and reinforcements were immediately dispatched. Five other members of my party were successful also in getting through to Millstreet, but arrived after D.I. Scott. The reinforcements that were dispatched came along at the double. Some in a ford car and others commandeered jaunting cars. Unfortunately these were delayed by reason of three trees, which had been felled across the roadway just outside Millstreet, by the insurgents. A small number of the reinforcements were left at these barriers and the rest proceeded to the scene of the ambush on foot. By the time these had arrived, the rebels (already beaten back) had broken off the fight, which lasted for two hours, the attack itself commenced at about 19.30 hours and ceasing at about 21.45 hours.

Wireless messages were sent out from the billet for assistance and with the utmost dispatch "J" Company responded to our signals arriving at the scene of the ambush at 00.30 hours on the 17th inst., from Macroom. This unit with the CO. (D.I.I. Williams) in charge did everything possible to assist and help us. After an inspection I found to my regret and sorrow that Cadets Boyd W.A.H. and Shorter F.E. had been killed. Also that S/Ldr; Taylor OC sustained three wounds. With regards to M.T. which sustained considerable damage, I found that of the four vehicles that were in the convoy, two, the armored Crossley and the Lancia are severely damaged.

In passing, I may state that the Armour plate protecting the engine of this car, was discovered 40 yards away; having been flung that distance by the concussion, that this unit has not suffered the loss of any arms whatsoever, or ammunition, with the exception of the ammunition expended during the engagement. In closing I may state, that I consider the way in which the cadets under my charge behaved, is worthy of the highest tradition of the Royal Irish Constabulary.

Millstreet,	(Sgd.) W.E. Crossey, Lieut., &
Co. Cork	1st B.D.L. Commanding "L" Coy.
17/6/21	Aux. Div. RIC.[14]

The capture and execution of Volunteer prisoners by the British continued despite the threat of reprisals. On 21 June 1921, with the threat of execution hanging over a number of Volunteers in Cork, the IRA took a number of prominent hostages from the Loyalist community, including Lord Bandon, lieutenant of the county. General Strickland, the British OC in Cork, was informed of the fact and of the intention of the Volunteers to execute them if the imprisoned Volunteers were executed. Influence was no doubt brought to bear, and it was announced that the Volunteer prisoners would not be executed. Furthermore, the policy of shooting prisoners would be discontinued. Bandon and his fellow Loyalist prisoners were released. Castle Barnard, the residence of Lord Bandon, was set ablaze and this changed British policy regarding the burning of Volunteers' homes.

On the 23rd and 24th of June, in what appeared to be an intelligence-led mission, a large-scale swoop of the area around Millstreet in North Cork was launched by the British, using 8,000 troops. Upon their own admission the encirclement was too ambitious. In their encirclement they were greatly hampered by I.R.A entrenched roads that rendered motorized transport ineffective and led to long marches which threw out the timing for the encirclement. Liam Lynch, commandant of the 1st Southern Division, and senior members of his staff who were within the encirclement succeeded in breaking through and escaping.

One of the most daring raids of the war carried out by the Volunteers was the raid on Fastnet Rock, just off the coast of southeastern Cork. Intelligence reports indicated that the British had stored large quantities of explosive material in the lighthouse, due to its remoteness. The Fastnet Lighthouse is three and a half miles southwest of the nearest land at Cape Clear Island and ten miles from the mainland. Because of this distance from the shore it was not felt that the lighthouse was under any threat, and consequently it was not armed in any way. The raid was the idea of Richard Collins, captain of the Goleen Company and lighthouse keeper at Fastnet between 1912 and 1918. John Regan, battalion commander of Schull, took command. At the best of times Fastnet Rock is dangerous, with its heavy swells. To make the landing in the dark, which is what was proposed, called for nerve and good seamanship. The plan involved Regan piloting the boat, then jumping from its heaving deck onto the slippery wet rock.

The first attempt had to be abandoned owing to the severity of the weather, but on 29 June, the twenty-four foot *Maire Cait*, with her raiding party of twelve, set sail. In the distance the British destroyer H.M.S. *Truro*, which patrolled the coast from the Old Head of Kinsale to Bantry Bay, hove into view, her searchlights scanning sea and shore. The *Maire Cait* veered off to avoid the searchlight, and when the ship had moved on, she set in a course for the rock. The Volunteers knew that they had between two and three hours to complete their mission before the destroyer returned. Shortly after midnight the boat approached the rock. There was no jetty, only a large rock with an iron ring attached. With a rope tied around his waist, John O'Regan stood in the prow of the heaving boat. As it rose on a wave he leaped ashore. He looped the rope through the ring and hauled the *Maire Cait* in. As the others scrambled ashore, O'Regan proceeded to the two-ton steel door of the lighthouse. It was not locked. Entering, O'Regan ascended the spiral stairway to the room where the lighthouse keeper was on duty. He offered no resistance. Allowing sufficient guncotton for forty-eight hours of fog, all the remaining explosive was taken: seventeen boxes of guncotton, three boxes of detonators and primers. The prize was lowered down onto the *Maire Cait* by the lighthouse derrick, and with the wireless set smashed, the Volunteers departed. Their haul was unloaded ashore and safely dumped for use later.

In the month leading up to the truce, greater efforts were proposed by Britain to destroy the fighting capability of the Volunteers in County Cork. The West Cork Brigade, being informed, destroyed a number of buildings in their area intended by the British to house up to two thousand reinforcing troops. Numbered among those buildings were the strongly built workhouses. The British had turned out the inmates of Clonakilty and Dunmanway and fortified those. Proposed workhouses to be occupied included Bandon, Skibbereen, and Schull. In the early hours of the morning of 23 June these buildings were vacated and destroyed by the IRA. At Bandon the existing British garrisons, only a few hundred yards away from the burning workhouse, refused to send out troops for fear of ambush. With the workhouse well ablaze, the Volunteers fired a few desultory shots in derision at the garrisons, then withdrew.

Though there were no more major clashes, the column kept up the harassment. To hinder communications, telegraph and telephone equipment was destroyed at Glandore, Union Hall, Leap, Castletownshend and other post offices. Telegraph poles were cut down and roads were trenched to prevent British motorized convoys from traveling. Enemy garrisons were repeatedly sniped at, and Bandon, the town most likely to fall had the truce broken down, was entered eight times by soldiers of the IRA. The last real action of the war occurred on 26 June. The Column, having been temporarily stood down, discovered that between one hundred and twenty and one hundred and fifty Auxiliaries had descended on Rosscarbery. There were just thirty-three members of the column remaining. The column was divided into three sections of eleven men and marched to within four hundred yards of

The bodies of four British soldiers killed on 10 July 1921, only hours before the truce came into effect (courtesy the Imperial War Museum).

the town. Here they separated to approach the town from three directions. Those approaching from the west made contact with a group of Auxiliaries, who fell back before them, perhaps not realizing how few they were. The main body of the Auxiliaries took up positions in a number of houses to await the arrival of the IRA. Individual firefights took place, a number of the British paramilitaries being wounded. With daylight approaching the Volunteers withdrew to the edge of the town and set up ambush positions should the Auxiliaries pursue them. The British for their part also withdrew. The IRA suffered one casualty, Volunteer Dan Mahony who was wounded in the leg.

On 10 July, the day before the truce began, elements from the West Cork Flying Column made a desultory attack on the Inishannon Barracks. It was more for nuisance value than a full-scale assault. To have had any success both roads leading to it would have had to be blocked and guarded to prevent a relieving force from arriving to help the garrison. Tom Barry was there. A few rounds were fired, and the Volunteers withdrew. Later that night, at 8:00 P.M., in Cork, four young British soldiers were taken prisoner by Volunteers. The official report submitted to GHQ Dublin recounts the action: "At 8.00 P.M. we held up four soldiers and searched them, but found no arms. We took them to a field in our area where they were executed before 9.00 P.M." At two o'clock on the morning of the 11th their bodies were found. Barely ten hours later the truce came into effect. One of the young soldiers, it was said, had gone into a shop to buy sweets.

The War on Tipperary, Limerick, Waterford, Wexford and Kilkenny

Martial law was declared in Waterford on 5 January 1921. Two days later, on 7 January, two IRA flying columns led by George Lennon and Paddy Paul attempted to draw British forces into an ambush by feigning an attack on the Tramore Barracks. The relieving force was confronted at Pickardstown. There was a furious firefight that left two Volunteers dead, Thomas O'Brien and Michael McGrath, before the British managed to extricate themselves and withdraw with losses. What appears to be a distorted account of this assault is told second hand by Major General Stone some eighty-two years after the event, in 2003. His version appears in William Sheehan's *British Voices:*

> Usually when one of the police barracks in my area were shot up — or had just a few shots fired at it which was a trick of the IRA to get the Army out and ambush them on the way out ... a friend of mine [Captain Valentine] ... was stationed at Waterford and the Tramore Police Barracks had shots fired at it, and he was in mufti but the subaltern in charge of the party to go out was just new from Sandhurst and so he thought he'd better go with the party. And so off they went and they were ambushed on the way and it was the young subaltern's Crossley that was ambushed.
>
> But this officer in mufti found out where the firing was coming from. It was coming from a hedge overlooking the road. His vehicle wasn't ambushed. And he went along that hedge — using his revolver as a humane killer — and killed about a dozen of them. They were so busy firing on the road they didn't realize what was happening.
>
> And the IRA put up a memorial to the twelve who were killed in the Tramore ambush at the spot where the ambush took place. And this happened in 1921."[15]

That same month the eighteen-man West Limerick Column ambushed a troop-carrying train at Barrygone, County Limerick. Information was received that a mixed detail of RIC and Black and Tans would be traveling the following morning by train from Foynes to Limerick. It was arranged for a Volunteer to travel aboard the train and discover first of all if the enemy were aboard, and if so its strength. He would signal the numbers from his carriage window by waving his cap as the train approached the ambush position. Another Volunteer, Con Boyle, would then walk along the track waving a red flag to halt the train. On the day of the ambush as the train approached, the number of policemen aboard was signaled, and Boyle waved his flag to bring the train to a halt. The train stopped in the ambush position. From the rocky embankments on both sides of the track the Volunteers opened up on the carriage containing the policemen. While the passengers in the other carriages dived to the floor, the RIC returned fire. Realizing that they were pinned down, and with little chance of survival, one Black and Tan very bravely jumped down from the carriage. Even though under heavy fire, he managed to reach the engine and forced the driver and fireman to restart the train. Though they had a number of wounded men, none of the policemen were mortally so, and due to the heroism of their comrade they succeeded in escaping down the line.

Dromkeen

On 3 February 1921 the East Limerick Column, assisted by men from the Mid-Limerick Column under Commandant Dick O'Connell, ambushed a motorized RIC and Black and Tan convoy driving from Cahirconlish to Pallasgreen, at Dromkeen in County Limerick. Eleven policemen were killed and one mortally wounded.

At the opening of 1921 the East Limerick and Mid-Limerick brigades considered a joint operation against the RIC/Black and Tan barracks at Pallas. The inter-brigade boundary ran close by, and the garrison at Pallas operated in both of the brigade areas. Whether by good luck or intelligence, the Tans had located and captured the arms dump of the Mid-Limerick Brigade earlier that year. Having been deprived of these weapons, and in view of the strongly defended barracks, an assault was no longer possible. John Purcell, intelligence officer of the Mid-Limerick Column, came up with an alternative plan. By continued observation he discovered that a large part of the garrison regularly traveled in a convoy of trucks to Fedamore, eleven miles away, and returned later that day. They made the journey on the first Thursday in the month, and Purcell discovered the time and route taken. An examination of the route identified a particular part of the road ideal for the ambush, a stretch some three miles from Pallas, at Dromkeen. After a bend in the road, it ran straight for about 300 yards, slightly downhill, to a fork. Due to the angle of the fork, any barricades erected could not be seen until the vehicles actually entered that section of the road. A house at the bend at the top of the incline afforded observation of both the approaching convoy and the entire ambush position. A ruined house at the fork in the road gave good views up to Dromkeen House, halfway up into the ambush site. This stretch of the road was sufficiently long to ensure that all the convoy vehicles would be in position before the attack was launched. The position was also capable of being sealed off at the rear to prevent any vehicles from reversing out of the ambush area once the assault had been launched. It was decided to ambush the convoy on its return journey. This would enable the Volunteers to gauge its strength on the outward journey. It would also permit the column to withdraw under the cover of darkness. As a joint operation by the East and Mid-Limerick columns under Donnachadha O'Hannigan, OC of the East Limerick Column, the ambush was planned for the first Thursday in February.

On the morning of the attack, under the cover of darkness and the rain falling steadily, the column, forty riflemen strong, moved up to within a mile of the ambush site. Scouts were sent forward. They observed two trucks carrying about twenty RIC and Black and Tans, with a district inspector in charge, heading towards Fedamore. As the weather cleared the column moved up to the ambush site, and the men took up their designated positions. With the exception of Dromkeen House, all houses and barns along the ambush site were occupied by Volunteers. A farmhouse on the southern fork, just outside the ambush site, was used to detain passersby — a half dozen, in fact. Up the hill on the western side of the site, at the house which commanded a view of the road from Fedamore and in the other direction down to the roads to Pallas, a column of Volunteers, including Captain D. Guerin, Captain Sean Stapleton and Volunteer M. Meade from the East Limerick Brigade, waited. Their orders were to prevent a withdrawal by the enemy. The command post was established in the ruined house at the road junction. It was occupied by O'Hannigan, J.M. McCarthy, commandant of the Mid-Limerick Column, and a few Volunteers. Small detachments were placed at intervals on both sides of the boundary walls that lined the straight stretch of road, with more men at the fork in the road where barricades were erected. The main body of the Mid-Limerick Column was placed on the northern side of the road and included the commander of that column, Dick O'Connell, as well as Sean Carroll, James Horan, Johnny Vaughan, Joe Ryan and Ned Punch. Other Mid-Limerick men, under Jimmy Humphreys, occupied the barn on the other side of the road, using the stacked hay to give them a height advantage. Other fire positions on the southern side of the road and at the barricades were manned by East Limerick Volunteers. The barricades were made from farm carts. A line of withdrawal, should it become necessary, was provided by an armed party of the local Volunteers. In addition a number of scouts were placed over a wide area to signal the approach of an enemy relieving force.

Shortly after midday everything was in place. At 1:00 P.M. the approach of two trucks was signaled. The first appeared around the bend and began the gentle descent to the fork in the road. Barely fifty yards behind, the second truck followed. As the first truck approached the fork in the road, fire was opened up on it. On it continued towards the ruined house. Its driver attempted to take the left hand turn; but seeing the roadblock, he veered to the right. Here he was faced by the other roadblock, and having put his foot down to escape the ambush was unable — or unwilling — to stop. He struck the cart and adjoining fence, bringing the vehicle to a halt. From the front seats of the truck, a policeman and his superior officer, the local district inspector, both dressed in civilian clothes, leaped down onto the road and succeeded in reaching the nearby field. From there they made their escape, leaving their comrades to their fate. Of the remaining RIC men from the first vehicle, just three in number, one was mortally wounded and two slightly wounded. As the two leaped from the truck to take cover they were hit again, this time fatally. In the second vehicle were eight RIC and Black and Tan men. As it arrived a little beyond midway in the ambush area, the Volunteers opened up on it. The truck slewed to a halt and the police leaped from the vehicle. Some were hit as they did so and were killed outright. Another was mortally wounded and died three days later. Two regular RIC men managed to crawl beneath the truck and return fire. Five Volunteers leaped over the wall and, lying down in the road, opened up on the two policemen at close range, killing both. In the ambush eight Black and Tans and three RIC men were killed. The Volunteers suffered one man wounded: Liam

Hayes, his hand shattered by a bullet. Thirteen rifles and five hundred rounds of ammunition was gathered up, and the Volunteers withdrew in good order. By nightfall they were twelve miles away from the ambush site.

While reconnoitering in Kilkenny City, with a view to an ambush, two Volunteers were killed, and two wounded in a shoot-out in Friary Street, on 21 February. An ambush occurred at Durrow Railway Station, County Waterford, on 3 March. A train of jurors to be used in cases against IRA prisoners was attacked. While local jurors might find the prisoners not guilty, these jurors, who were in the main Loyalists, could be relied upon to give the right verdict. There was a brief but furious firefight between the unit of Waterford Column led by George Lennon and the British soldiers aboard the train. Two British soldiers were killed and several people were wounded, including members of the traveling jurors. A firefight took place between a unit of the Kilkenny Brigade and a party of Black and Tans at Garrykerin House on the Clonmel to Kilkenny Road on 12 March. Though the house where they were billeted was surrounded, the Volunteers succeeded in shooting their way out, killing one Black and Tan constable in the brief action.

Burgery

Lennon was again in action with the West Waterford Column on the night of 18–19 March. Under the command of Pax Whelan, with George Plunkett from GHQ as an observer, the column ambushed a mixed convoy of police and soldiers. The convoy from Dungarvan consisted of twelve soldiers riding in a truck preceded by a motor car which contained Captain Thomas in command, with Lt. Griffith and Sergeant Hickey of the RIC (whose job was to identify prisoners) and two other soldiers. The convoy was returning from Clonea, on the Ballyvoile road, where they had arrested a man named Murphy. On their return they had made a detour to return by way of Cloncoskraine, where a small military unit were based. They left there at eleven o'clock that night. The car led the way, with the truck containing the prisoner following. Knowing that they would return to Dungarvan, Whelan split the column into two groups to cover the eventuality that they might return by way of the old Cork road.

The main body of Volunteers lay in wait at the Burgery on the Waterford to Dungarven road, just where the road turns off to go to Lacken Hill, about a mile northeast of the town. The road was well-lined with trees and hawthorn and privet hedges. The car was allowed to pass, but as the truck arrived at the ambush site, fire was opened up on it. In the first fusillade the petrol tank was pierced, and the truck came to a halt. The soldiers jumped down and secured what cover they could. A fierce firefight then ensued. The car, having driven some distance from the ambush site, now came to a halt, and its occupants dismounted. Lt. Griffith was ordered to take the car and summon reinforcements. Captain Thomas and the others cautiously returned to the ambush site, hoping to gain some advantage. Within a few minutes of Lt. Griffith's return to Dungarven, four cars accompanied by trucks of armed soldiers, including a machine-gun party, set off to the ambush site. From the barracks at Dungarven Very lights were sent up summoning reinforcements from the Royal Marines stationed at Ballinacourty.

Captain Thomas, Sergeant Hickey and the two soldiers were themselves ambushed by a smaller group of Volunteers acting as the rearguard to the main column. Called upon to surrender, they did so and were taken to a nearby house under guard. Sergeant Hickey, upon whose intelligence the British relied, was separated from them and taken up a little side lane, where he was executed.

At the main ambush site the fighting continued, with the soldiers withdrawing under heavy fire into the nearby field, where they were able to escape. With the arrival of the reinforcements from Dungarven the fight intensified. As dawn approached, and low on ammunition, Whelan withdrew the column, leaving just a few Volunteers to cover their withdrawal, occasionally firing at the rifle flashes of the enemy. Gradually the shooting died away. Abandoned by his guards, Captain Thomas and his two men then rejoined the reinforcements. At daylight a horse was brought up to drag the truck away. As this was going on an Auxiliary by the name of Redman was mortally wounded by a sniper, John Fitzgerald. He in his turn was shot dead by another British soldier. Patrick Keating, another Volunteer from the column, went to Fitzgerald's aid. He too was shot, but he managed to escape. Keating died of his wound later that day. Sergeant Michael Hickey's body was found two days later on the little lane that leads to Knockateemore. Fixed to his tunic when his body was discovered was a note which declared that he was a police spy. A Roman Catholic, he was buried in an unmarked grave in the parish churchyard.

Confined to Limerick City, unless they ventured forth during military encirclements, the Black and Tans roamed the streets, engaging in acts of brutality against the local people. At night, following a 9:00 P.M. curfew, they raided houses of known Republican supporters. Due to the limited numbers of arms available to the city battalion, and the scarcity of suitable ammunition, a large-scale action against the Black and Tans was not possible. However it was decided that each company, or groups of companies, would go on the offensive in a series of nighttime operations to actively search out and engage the enemy. On Friday, 8 April, ten Volunteers from C Company initiated the new campaign. They patrolled around their company area, but failed to make contact with any British forces until they were returning to the Irishtown District of the city. They came upon six men of the RIC armed with carbines and revolvers who had emerged from a public house at the junction of John Street, Broad Street and Mungret Street. As it was too late to initiate an ambush, the Volunteers launched a direct assault. Battalion commandant Dundon threw a Mills grenade at the policemen, and the other Volunteers opened a barrage of revolver fire. Two policemen were badly wounded in the explosion; the others fled towards their barracks, a hundred yards away, firing back at the Volunteers as they did so.

That same night A Company, divided into two sections, patrolled their company area. One section came across an armed Black and Tan, Constable Wiggins, at the junction of Church Street and Palmerstown, close to the RIC barracks. He was shot dead. Meanwhile, some members of C Company, Commandant Dundon and Volunteers Downey and McGrath, now cut off from their intended line of retreat by British troops who had flooded out of their barracks in pursuit of the Volunteers, entered an unoccupied house to hide. The British troops were led by an ex-soldier, now a civilian, who had seen which way the Volunteers had withdrawn. From the upstairs window of the house Dundon observed all this. The three remained there until it was safe, then made good their escape. Known Republican houses were raided by the mixed British forces of police and soldiers. Doors were kicked in, the houses were ransacked and the inhabitants were beaten up. The next day a curfew was announced. All citizens of Limerick had to be indoors by two o'clock that afternoon. By two o'clock the streets were deserted. Soldiers in steel helmets and with bayonets fixed and rifles at the ready emerged from their barracks. With them were engineers in white overalls. In trucks, with Lancia cars and armored cars in support, they proceeded to designated houses, the homes of known Volunteers and Sinn Fein members, and blew them up.

Ballyhahill

On the face of it the action at Ballyhahill was no more than a skirmish, but its outcome had dire consequences for the West Limerick Volunteer Brigade. At the opening of 1921 the British forces, police and military, had begun a period of retrenchment, moving out of towns like Newcastlewest and Rathkeale, concentrating their forces in the larger cities. From cities such as Limerick they sent out large patrols in Crossley tenders, often accompanied by armored cars. A predictability of movement developed, and the West Limerick Flying Column decided to take advantage of it. During February a plan was developed and submitted to GHQ by its OC, Sean Finn, with the recommendation that neighboring columns be seconded for the action. GHQ agreed, and offered either the North Cork Column or the East Limerick Column. Finn chose his fellow Limerick men, and Donncadh O'Hannigan set out with his men to rendezvous with Finn's column. The amalgamated column comprised fifty well-armed Volunteers, complete with a horse drawn cart carrying mines and other explosives. Such an IRA column would have been unthinkable back in 1920, but in 1921 vast areas of south and southwestern Ireland had been cleared, or vacated by British forces. The column passed by two big military encampments at Mountbrown and Smithfield with a degree of near contempt, realizing that it was unlikely that they would be confronted. Arriving at Athea, the men were billeted in farmhouses in the district to await the intended operation.

O'Hannigan's march across county and his linking up with Finn's column had not gone unnoticed. A huge round up was planned by the British, concentrating on Athea. Shortly before midnight on Easter Saturday word arrived from Newcastlewest that the British were on the move from four different directions, Newcastlewest, Rathkeale, Limerick and Listowel. Commandant Finn sent out runners to bring the Volunteers in, to rendezvous at Direen Cross. Barely had the columns been assembled when the rumble of motor vehicles was heard. As sleet began to fall, Finn and O'Hannigan moved their men off to higher ground above Knocknagonna school and prepared for an assault by the British forces. There they stood to arms, the sound of enemy vehicles all around. Gradually the sound of vehicles got less and less, until there was silence. Morning came, and with it the news that the British had moved off. They had gone right by the two columns, not knowing that they were there. Then there came news that an armored car appeared to have broken down along the road at Black Heights. It was guarded by a small number of soldiers. Finn and O'Hannigan decided to attack and, they hoped, capture the car. The terrain was very open, with little cover. In open formation the Volunteers advanced towards the British party. Then suddenly the forward scouts signaled the return of a large motorized force, complete with armored cars. The two columns were caught out in the open. Dropping to the ground, they successfully withdrew without being noticed by the numerically superior British force. They returned to the high ground and waited once more; but the British, having regained their armored car, themselves withdrew. That night the columns marched off towards Ballyhahill, where they were billeted over a fairly large area.

The next day, at about four o'clock in the afternoon, three of O'Hannigan's East Limerick men wandered down to a nearby house where they had been told there lived a man who could repair their boots. They had barely arrived before they heard the approach of a mechanized convoy. As they got to the doorway the enemy was almost upon them. Unarmed, they made a dash towards their billet where their rifles had been left. Fire was opened up on them, and within seconds they were besieged by about forty members of the British forces. Brigade commandant Finn and East limerick Column commandant O'Hannigan, together with Volunteers Seamus Finn and Jim Colbert, heard the firing, and realizing what was probably happening, rushed towards the sound of the firing. The main bodies of both flying columns were dispersed and billeted some distance away. Finn could only hope that they too would hear the shooting and come to the assistance of their comrades. Vice-Commandant Garrett McAuliffe of the West Limerick Column and four or five other Volunteers were told that firing had been heard over in the direction of Ballyhahill. They gathered up their arms and proceeded towards the village but heard no sound of firing.

Nevertheless, McAuliffe sent runners to assemble the West Limerick Column. The situation was explained to them, and in open formation they advanced upon Ballyhahill village. As they progressed they came upon the assembled East Limerick Column doing likewise. Scouts were sent on in advance to find out what was happening. They returned with the news that there had been a firefight, and Commandant Quinn had been killed. The survivors of the fight came in and gave details of what had happened. The three Volunteers who had been attacked had fled back to their billet, and almost immediately it had been surrounded on three sides. A fierce exchange of fire had followed. Finn, O'Hannigan and the other Volunteers with them soon arrived at the besieged house and took up positions on the fourth side of the house, preventing the British from completely encircling it. One of the relieving Volunteers blew a whistle, alerting the besieged men that help was at hand. Under covering fire these men were able to escape from the house on the fourth side and join their comrades. Fighting a rearguard action they moved off, speedily followed by the enemy. Elements of the British force, using one of their Crossley tenders, succeeded in driving off and managed to get behind the retreating Volunteers and cut them off. A fierce fight now ensued, Volunteer Quane was shot through the neck. Rather than leave him, his comrades grabbed him and led him off. The firefight continued as the Volunteers withdrew, all the while hoping that the flying columns would hear the shooting and come to their aid. The battle continued for over two hours. Brigadier Finn fell mortally wounded. The Volunteers were short of ammunition. Of the seven Republicans involved, one was dead, one was seriously wounded. Eighteen-year-old Volunteer Seamus Finn of the East Limerick Column informed his OC that he was out of ammunition. O'Hannigan gave him the desperate order to recover the rifle of his dead commandant. The opposing forces were barely thirty yards apart and blazing away at each other, and the dead man lay between them. The four remaining Volunteers opened up with a furious fusillade of fire to cover him, as the young Finn dashed out and, remarkably, retrieved both the rifle and ammunition.

The fight continued. Then the Volunteers noticed that a strong party of RIC men who had got behind them were advancing. The Republicans turned to face this new threat and ran at them, firing as they did so. Somewhat taken aback, the policemen halted, giving the Volunteers the opportunity of reaching a fairly high fence. Screened from the enemy, they dashed along the fence and made for the added security of a rath (a circular enclosure surrounded by an earth wall). Then almost miraculously a fog crept up from the shores of the Shannon and covered both attackers and attacked. The Volunteers waited, but the British did not advance. As the fog cleared only the Volunteers remained. The British had withdrawn. For his bravery young Finn was promoted to the rank of first lieutenant for conspicuous bravery on the field of battle.

The surviving Volunteers came upon the approaching scouts and were taken away to safety. With the possibility of the British returning in numbers the two flying columns took up a defensive position in and around the village and waited. At three o'clock the next morning, with no sign of another British attempt at encirclement, the columns moved off. They marched into east Limerick where the terrain was more suitable to guerrilla warfare.

On 19 March 1921, the Waterford Column was in action at the Burgery. The fight started about midnight and continued on until 9:00 A.M. the following morning. The British soldiers, led by a captain, surrendered to the IRA and were freed. An RIC intelligence officer with them was shot.

In April 1921, the Third Tipperary Brigade intelligence officer became aware that a convoy of British troops regularly used the road between Cloghen and Cahir every Wednesday morning. After a discussion it was decided that the brigade flying column would attack it on Wednesday, 22 April. At 5:00 A.M. the column was in position. The convoy usually passed by at 10:00 A.M. The hours passed and the convoy failed to arrive. At 1:00 P.M. Dan Breen and Con Maloney, who had hoped to take part in the ambush, reluctantly left and returned to brigade headquarters. They had been gone barely half an hour when the convoy was heard approaching. As it entered the ambush site the soldiers were called upon to surrender. In response they opened fire. A short exchange of fire resulted in one soldier being killed and two wounded before the remainder of the patrol surrendered. The soldiers were disarmed then set at liberty. Their vehicle was set on fire. The column set off, then to their surprise as they arrived at Curraghcooney, a car rounded the corner and almost ploughed into them. The car was halted. Its driver was District Inspector Gilbert Potter of the RIC at Cahir. He was taken prisoner, and following an unsuccessful trade-off, he was shot on 27 April following the hanging of Volunteer Thomas Trainor in Dublin. As a reprisal the British blew up ten farmhouses in South Tipperary.

On Saturday, 25 April, Volunteers from C and E companies of the Limerick City Battalion, under Commandants Dundon and Paddy Barry respectively, went on the offensive. Tracking down a number of Black and Tans drinking in Hickey's public house, they lobbed grenades at them. Constable Redfern was seriously injured in the attack. The Volunteers got away without casualties. The Black and Tans responded, as inevitably they would, by attacking Republican clubs and pubs. The following day, Sunday the 24th, news reached brigade headquarters in Limerick that a twenty-strong RIC patrol, armed with carbines and revolvers, had proceeded down the Shannon at Plassy. The brigade adjutant summoned Volunteers from B and C companies with a view to ambushing the Black and Tans on their return. The problem facing the Volunteers was that the enemy patrol could return by any of three routes: by Plassy bank, over the Black Bridge, or by the main Dublin road by walking through the woods. The difference between each return route was one mile. Reluctant as he was to divide his forces, the adjutant nonetheless wanted revenge on the Tans for what they had done.

A patrol from B Company under Captain Troy took up a position at Corbally. A mixed patrol of B Company and C Company men under J. Kelly, OC of C Company, covered the canal route, and the brigade adjutant and four Volunteers took up a position over the railway bridge at Singland, astride the Limerick Road. Scouts on bicycles sent out to trace the policemen reported that they were returning along the Limerick Road. The party on the railway bridge soon sighted the returning enemy. As the police were about to pass beneath the bridge the Volunteers lobbed bombs down upon them. While one or two fell down injured by the explosives, the other policemen scattered along both sides of the road, seeking what cover was available. The IRA opened fire on the Tans, and they returned fire. Such had been the haste in arranging the ambush that the Volunteers had only a few rounds of ammunition, and having used them up they were forced to retire to safety. In theory the bombs should have killed or wounded most of the enemy, but in reality they were practically useless. They were a newly manufactured type of hand grenade issued by GHQ in Dublin, now being used for the first time. While they produced lots of noise, they failed to splinter to any great degree. Mills hand grenades, the type issued to the British Army, would have wiped out the patrol.

On 29 April 1921, the West Waterford Brigade Flying Column, under the command of George Lennon, ambushed a troop-carrying train at the Ballylynch Level crossing. In the hour-long fight two soldiers were killed, and one Volunteer was wounded. On 10 June the Volunteers suffered a humiliating defeat. When surrounded after an abortive ambush at Piltown, they were forced to surrender.

In the spring of 1921, Ernie O'Malley, the newly appointed OC of the Second Southern Division, convened a meeting of his brigade officers drawn from the counties of Limerick, Tipperary and Kilkenny. The division area had been swamped with British troops and Auxiliaries in an all-out attempt to destroy the IRA. Prior to the meeting both the brigadier of Mid-Limerick, and the vice-commandant of East Limerick had in a combined force engaged the enemy in furious firefights. The columns had ambushed British troops near Lackelly, but suffered heavy casualties in the fight. The columns were themselves ambushed a further three times as they retreated during a five and a half hour running fight.

The British claimed that between five and fourteen Volunteers had been killed and up to thirty wounded. The IRA admitted to six Volunteers being killed in action, whom they named. Two Volunteers were taken prisoner, tried by court-martial and summarily shot. Sean Wall, brigadier of East Limerick, was shot dead in an ambush on his way to the meeting with O'Malley. The situation had become critical for the Volunteers. O'Malley proposed to reverse the situation by seizing the initiative and taking the war back to the enemy by positive appointments to his staff. Con Maloney, a very active officer, was appointed division adjutant, and the ever resourceful Dan Breen its quartermaster. Of all his brigades O'Malley knew that South Tipperary would take the lead in the new campaign. It was the strongest and best organized. In comparison to them the others appeared more hesitant in engaging the enemy. By mixing the Brigades, by drawing men from each to form an overall flying column, he hoped to foster a more positive attitude in his men.

Having spent some six weeks campaigning in the east, the West Limerick Flying Column returned home to the Athea District. At a brigade council meeting, held at Woodcock Hill near Ballinaleena, a British ex-soldier suspected of spying was tried and found guilty and sentenced to be shot. While on the way to the place of execution the prisoner and his escort came upon a patrol of British soldiers from Ballyvonare camp. The British challenged the Republicans, then opened fire. Second Lieutenant Michael O'Shea was seriously wounded, as was Volunteer Patrick Benson. In the confusion the condemned man succeeded in escaping towards the British soldiers and freedom. The other few members of the intended firing squad fled. The two wounded Volunteers were taken by truck to Charleville. O'Shea died of his wound, Benson was held prisoner until the truce.

During the spring of 1921 the war in Limerick developed into a series of cruel tit-for-tat killings and reprisals. The mayor of Limerick, George Clancey, a former mayor, Michael O'Callaghan, and Volunteer Joseph O'Donahue, were murdered in their homes on the night of 6 March 1921, during curfew. British Military intelligence officer George Nathan, assisted by Auxiliaries from G Company, were responsible. None of them were ever brought to trial. In late April 1921, District Inspector Potter of the RIC was captured in an ambush by Dinny Lacey's South Tipperary Flying Column. He was offered in exchange for Thomas Traynor, a Dublin Volunteer under sentence of death. The British, not wishing to lose face, offered to allow four other IRA prisoners to "escape" from an internment camp in exchange. The Irish refused. Trayner was hanged on 26 April. Potter was shot in response. As a reprisal for Potter's death, seventeen houses in South Tipperary were blown up by the military. The following month Paddy Maloney, brother of Con and adjutant of the Tipperary Division, was killed in a Black and Tan ambush while fighting with Sean Duffey's Tipperary Battalion. Discovering his identity, the Tans burned his father's house and chemist shop in Tipperary.

In April 1921 Ernie O'Malley linked up with Liam Lynch so that the two divisions, his own Second Southern and Lynch's First Southern, could cooperate in a series of coco-ordinated attacks on a certain day. To O'Malley's bitter disappointment his flying column was the only one in his division that carried out an assault in conjunction with the First Southern. That evening O'Malley met up with the brigade vice-commandant, Dinny Lacey, and his column of thirty-five men. Sharp words were apparently exchanged O'Malley indicates without actually saying so. He describes Lacy as being "stubborn, in anger a white temper paled his face and his voice stuttered or came in a swifter rush." Lacy pointed out that he and his men had patrolled through south Tipperary but had failed to make contact with the enemy. Whether this was through sheer bad luck, uncertainty of the enemy's movements or faulty intelligence, it was not his fault, he maintained. O'Malley suggested that Lacy should take his men into the towns, if the British would not come out. Reacting to this slight, Lacy proposed an attack on Tipperary Town. O'Malley agreed to go with them. Contacting the Tipperary Battalion commandant, O'Malley discovered the strength of the military evening patrol and the movements of the Black and Tans. The next night at dusk, half the column, reinforced by local men, moved across the fields towards the town. Their target were the Black and Tans, who when not on duty frequented the town's public houses and hotel bars. A machine-gun section was positioned to cover the column's retirement. As they approached the town the advance guard made prisoners of anyone they found and sent them back to the reserve for their own safety. Suddenly the advanced guard came across a man who, seeing them, took to his heels and escaped. One of the Volunteers recognized him as a suspected police informer. The Tans, and the army too, would as a consequence be on their guard. With the element of surprise gone, and the danger of a possible ambush, O'Malley ordered a withdrawal. He perhaps came to appreciate the difficulty that Lacy sometimes faced. What perhaps was important about this probing action was that the Volunteers were actively taking the war to the enemy, broaching the supposed strong garrison towns held by the enemy.

On 1 May 1921, a unit of the Mid-Limerick Flying Column, with men from the East and West columns, under the command of Liam Forde, brigade OC, and Sean Carroll, column commandant, were about to take up an ambush position at Shraharla, on the border with the North Cork, when they were unexpectedly confronted by an armored car and four Crossley tenders carrying a mixed group of soldiers and Black and Tans. The confrontation was purely accidental; but the British, catching the Volunteers out in the open, reacted quicker. They opened fire with a machine gun and rifles, killing Captain Paddy Starr, Captain James Horan and Volunteer Tim Hennessy. Patrick Casey was wounded and taken prisoner. He was executed the following morning. Fighting a rearguard action the column retreated across the fields, pursued by the British. Throughout the day and into the next, the ragged battle continued. An advanced scouting group preceded the column, a rearguard keeping the enemy at bay while the main body moved off. During the night the column escaped. The British were unwilling to pursue, for fear of walking into an ambush. The following morning the advanced scouts were surprised by a company of the Sherwood Foresters Regiment at Lackelly near Knocklong. Four Volunteers were killed before the main body of the column arrived. They succeeded in driving the Sherwood Foresters off, following a fierce firefight, and succeeded in capturing all of their transport. After stripping it of ammunition, they set it ablaze.

On 14 May, in what was seen as a ruthless move, Volunteers in Tipperary under the command of Sean Gaynor ambushed and assassinated an RIC detective inspector, Harry Briggs. A Miss Barrington, a local Loyalist who was traveling in the car beside him, also died in the shooting. Her death appears to have been accidental. She was sitting inside the car alongside Briggs, but was not recognized as a woman because of her military-style riding habit. The shots allegedly were fired by Paddy Ryan, from the North Tipperary Brigade, whose family home had been burned by Briggs' order and his father carried around on motorized convoys as a hostage.

That May a flying column from the Third Battalion of the West Limerick Brigade occupied the town of Dromcollogher and ambushed an RIC patrol, killing one and wounding several others. Later that night after the Volunteers had withdrawn the Black and Tans took their revenge on the inhabitants of the town, smashing widows, breaking down doors and burning several houses as a reprisal. On 22 May, men of the Limerick Brigade Flying Column, with Bob deCourcy, divisional engineer of the Second Southern Division, laid a mine at Canters Bridge after discovering that a party of Auxiliaries would be traveling by a special train that day. The train was saved by a pilot engine which preceded the train. It exploded the mine laid on the track, bringing down the bridge.

Previously, in March 1921, the West Limerick Flying Column made plans to ambush a patrol of the Abbeyfeale RIC at Meenahela. The operation had to be aborted when, as the Volunteers lay in ambush, a motorized column of over one hundred of the enemy descended upon the locality. With insufficient men or arms to take on the new arrivals, the Column was obliged to withdraw. Still determined to attack the Abbeyfeale policemen, and realizing that such a thing might happen again, the West Limerick men sought the assistance of the North Cork Flying Column in their assault. Meanwhile a psychological war was waged, with the Volunteers putting up notices all around the town ordering the Black and

Tans (RIC) to leave Ireland immediately. Whenever the Tans came across such notices they tore them down.

With the arrival of the Cork men an ambush was prepared along a steep road half a mile out of the town that the police patrolled on a regular basis. The two columns took up their positions at dawn, with outlying scouts, and a withdrawal strategy planned. The RIC men were seen to leave the barracks and start on their patrol, tearing down notices as they proceeded. Returning via the Newcastlewest road they approached the ambush point, but for some reason they stopped a few hundred yards short and turned back. They returned to barracks and did not venture forth again that day. The columns remained in position until midnight before withdrawing. Over the next few days the RIC men did not leave their barracks. Following a Brigade meeting it was decided that the only way to engage them was to enter the town and shoot up the barracks. On the morning of 5 June the Volunteers entered the town shortly after dawn and took up positions in houses surrounding the square in which the barracks were located.

A number of the Volunteers, removing their boots, silently approached the barracks and posted on the door of the barracks itself a notice for the Black and Tans to quit Ireland. At six o'clock the door was opened and the notice discovered. It was torn down, and the door was closed once more. Half an hour later the door opened and the police moved out in extended order. About a dozen of them entered the square. They moved off, but discovering another notice affixed to a telegraph pole, they halted. As one of their number moved forward to tear it down, fire was opened up on them. Constable Jolly was killed instantly, and a number of other policemen were wounded. The remainder broke and fled back into the barracks. The weapons that had been dropped by the dead and wounded policemen were gathered up. The Volunteers fired a few pointless rounds at the barracks, but getting no response made an orderly withdrawal. Sometime later the RIC men came out of their barracks and cautiously proceeded towards the edge of the town, where they let off a few rounds before returning.

In Limerick, with its summertime ten o'clock curfew, the IRA intelligence officer of the city battalion was made aware that shortly after the curfew, a Crossley tender under the command of a British intelligence officer regularly swept out of the New Barracks each night at the same time, in order to pick up stragglers caught out after curfew. The Volunteers resolved to ambush it. An added incentive was that the enemy intelligence officer was reputedly involved in the murder of the mayor and ex-mayor of Limerick. Two problems faced the IRA men: they could not take up ambush positions until the streets were cleared, and the tender left the barracks on the dot of the curfew hour. Minutes later the streets would be filled by curfew patrols. The ambush had to take place in a very narrow time frame, and the Volunteers had to escape. As they knew the route the Crossley tender would take, they decided to ambush it with rifle and revolver fire near Pennywell, near the junction of the Dublin road bordering onto the canal, and Plassy, where boats would be held in readiness to take the attackers across the River Shannon into Clare. The site chosen was a gateway screened by houses and facing a blank wall of the Good Shepherd Convent. On the night of 18 June a small party from B Company under the command of Captain P. Troy took up positions. The curfew chimes were heard, and almost immediately they heard the approach of the Crossley tender. As it swept by, the Volunteers opened fire using rifles and revolvers. The British lieutenant and another soldier were wounded in the brief action. The Volunteers made an orderly retreat. It was all over in less than two minutes. The Lieutenant was later taken prisoner by the Volunteers and was shot dead in the streets of Cork while attempting to escape from custody.

Modreeny

The North Tipperary Flying Column was in action on Friday, 3 June 1921. The column of just twenty-three Volunteers, divided up into three sections, ambushed a combined convoy of military and police at Modreeny, between Borriskane and Cloughjordan. The enemy convoy consisted of cyclists, four cars and a military truck, the whole numbering forty men as opposed to the expected thirteen. Despite the disparity in numbers the Volunteers had the advantage of surprise. Four RIC men were recorded killed, and fourteen other members of the convoy were wounded. There were no Volunteer casualties.

On the night of Thursday, 2 June, the column of just fifteen men, led by Jack Collison, with brigade OC Sean Gaynor in attendance, was joined by eight shotgun men from Cloughjordan. Very early on the following morning they moved towards Modreeny, their intention to ambush an RIC patrol as it traveled towards the assize at Cloughjordan. This part of Tipperary had been settled by Cromwellian soldiers in the second half of the 17th century, and a number of the local farmers thereabouts were Loyalists. Hence special care had to be taken. At dawn the Volunteers arrived at the site, a double bend in the road three miles equidistant from Borriscane and Cloughjordan. In a field away from the site the two officers explained the plan of attack to the men. Ranges of fire were estimated, and each rifleman was given a succession of probable targets. Then the Volunteers were divided into three sections and moved into their ambush positions. From previous observations they knew that the police bicycle patrol would be strung out in twos, about twenty yards apart, perhaps extending over a distance of two hundred yards. The exact ambush site was the stretch of straight road between the two bends. It was long enough to contain the whole cycle patrol.

From a barn about twenty yards in from the road on the southern end of the ambush site, with views of both bends in the road, Gaynor and Collison had a clear view of the entire ambush site. Across the road from the barn, with a view up the road, they placed five shotgun men under the command of section leader Sean Glennon. To the west of the barn, with Volunteer Paddy O'Brien in command, Paddy Kennedy, Paddy Daly, Paddy Nolan and his brother Jimmy covered the upper curve in the road, about one hundred yards away from the road. On the far side of the road at the northern curve in the road, six further riflemen were placed. To the east on slightly rising ground, about one hundred yards away, a solitary rifleman, Dinny Whelan, who was an excellent shot, was placed to deal with any of the enemy who might scramble over the hedge. Way up to the north of the ambush zone was an observer and a signaler who had a view of over five hundred yards and who, by the use of flags, would give notice of the approach of the patrol. The Volunteers, knowing their duties and the duties of the other units, now settled down to wait.

The morning wore on. A young lad wandering across the fields came upon the Volunteers near the barn. He was questioned by Paddy O'Brien and Jack Collison, who told him to go and fetch his father. As the father came out across the field he was recognized by one of the local Volunteers, who informed Gaynor that he was an ex–British Army soldier. Coming up to the IRA officers, the ex-soldier thought that they were Auxiliaries, dressed as they were in trench coats and Sam Brownes, and greeted them warmly. Collison wore a well-trimmed moustache, and this probably also fixed it in his mind that they were Auxiliaries. He gave them a warning that an IRA column had been seen locally. Affecting an English accent, Gaynor questioned him about the local IRA. He answered them freely, and they were surprised at how much he knew about them without actually having seen them. Collinson asked him why he didn't pass on this information to the RIC. He said that he did. He regularly met the Cloughjordan sergeant every Saturday in the snug (private room) of Nora Ryan's pub and told him all that he had learned in the previous week. He told them all about his spying for the British. When they were satisfied that they had enough, the IRA officers told him who they were. Then the man became scared and begged for mercy. He was taken away to a hayrick behind the barn. They had decided to shoot him but then had second thoughts, fearing that the sound of gunfire might give their position away. So they sat him down and told him not to move. They would deal with him later.

The sun rose higher into the sky. Collison wished that he had more men. Ideally he would have liked to have outposts, men who could give them protection if British reinforcements arrived as they fought it out with the ambushed enemy. Way off in the distance some of the Volunteers heard the sound of trucks. They looked towards the signaler. By arm movements he indicated the approach of the enemy. As they watched, his arms indicated that twelve cyclists, four motor cars and a truck were approaching. The mathematics indicated that the British patrol numbered between forty and forty-five men. The Volunteers were hopelessly outnumbered — and outgunned. Deliberations were quickly held as to whether they should abandon the attack and let the convoy pass by unmolested. Strung out as it was the convoy would extend beyond the ambush zone. There was the danger that the British might outflank them. The men, however, elected that the attack should continue, and they would trust that surprise might even up the odds.

Collison selected Tim Gleeson to go with him to take up a new position to counter any outflanking move. The plan changed slightly now to allow the cyclists in front to pass beyond the bend in order to allow the first car to enter the ambush site before they opened fire. The cyclists entered the zone, slightly bunched up, thus compressing the convoy. The car, filled with Black and Tans, took the corner and O'Brien blew his whistle. The shotgun men opened fire with a concentrated volley. The car came to a halt, now with dead and wounded inside. The car blocked the road, preventing the other vehicles from overtaking. Paddy O'Brien and his riflemen fired at the leading cyclists. The six Volunteer riflemen across the road opened fire. The enemy vehicles came to a halt, but the truck remained outside of the ambush zone. At the outbreak of fire its passengers, between twelve and sixteen soldiers, leaped from the vehicle and scrambled for the shelter of the nearby hedge. They began to return fire with rifles and a machine gun. The driver of the truck, by a series of maneuvers, was able to turn the vehicle round and then set off at speed to summon reinforcements. The British, unaware of the true size of their enemy, took up a defensive role in a holding position until reinforcements arrived.

The Volunteers at the northern edge of the ambush site had accounted for the first six police cyclists and the leading car. Meanwhile, along the road, the soldiers from the truck attempted to outflank the Volunteers; but Collison and Gleeson drove them off with rapid fire. The soldiers responded by firing rifle grenades; but as they failed to find the range, these passed harmlessly over the lane behind the barn. The six men at the first road bend now came under concentrated fire. They fell back towards the northeast to prevent being outflanked. From this new site they could no longer control the straight stretch of road, and this allowed the RIC and military to concentrate their fire-power. The machine gun had fallen silent, either by mechanical stoppage or the death of the gunner. This allowed the Volunteers to shift positions. With the withdrawal of the six men at the bend this left only Dinny Whelan to prevent an outflanking move by the Crown forces. This prevented an attempt by the British to maneuver up the road. The positions of the shotgun men was identified; and the British, by the use of concentrated fire, were able to prevent these men from taking any further part in the fight without endangering themselves.

Collison and O'Brien, with the real threat of reinforcements arriving at any minute, now had to put evacuation plans into effect. There had been no blocking or trenching of roads, nor had telegraph wires been cut. O'Brien ordered a withdrawal. Enemy rifles and ammunition had been gathered up from those killed or wounded at the southern bend, and now by full use of the terrain the Volunteers moved out. As the IRA slipped away in groups the British continued firing at their former positions. At Killeraune Bog two of the three IRA sections met up and continued on to Knockshegouna Hill, where they met up with the third section. Here they waited until dark before breaking through the British encirclement. British casualties included four dead, confirmed by the British, and fourteen wounded (though the British only admitted to five). The Volunteers gained four rifles.

In all the excitement the spy behind the barn escaped execution. As the shooting started he hid himself in the hayrick and remained there. When it ceased he came out of hiding and was nearly killed by some of the Black and Tans who believed him to be one of their attackers. Luckily he was recognized by a policeman, and he and his son were taken into protective custody.

The North Tipperary Brigade were again in action in late June 1921. On the 25th an attack was planned on the RIC barracks at Borrisokane. Hearing of this, O'Malley traveled north. With him were men from the South and Mid-Tipperary brigades to assist in the assault. He arrived to find that the attack had been cancelled by the brigadier. As a member of headquarters staff, O'Malley took charge and ordered that the operation should go ahead the next day. The next night, the 26th of June, the attack went ahead with O'Malley leading, it is claimed, two hundred men. A fair proportion of the men were placed guarding the roads along which RIC and British Army reinforcements might be expected to come. An elaborate system of signaling was arranged, with burning sods of turf to indicate from which direction the enemy relief was coming and in what strength. With everything in place, a unit from the attacking party, including O'Malley, gained entrance, unobserved, to the house next door to the barracks. From there the Volunteers gained access to the barracks roof, which they set alight. As the roof fell in, attackers and defenders wildly exchanged shots through the roof. The defenders, thirty-five in number, returned fire. Jim Gorman from the South Tipperary Brigade was wounded by a bullet in the ensuing firefight, and O'Malley was wounded by grenade splinters. The defenders retired to a bomb-proof shelter within the barracks to await relief. Just as they should have been pressing home the attack, inexperienced units of the North Tipperary Column panicked and fled, declaring that soldiers were advancing in large numbers. This was untrue; but Sean Treacy, who had taken command, was unable to stop their flight. Gathering up the wounded, Treacy organized an orderly withdrawal of those Volunteers remaining. Though the attack was unsuccessful the building was so badly damaged that it was evacuated the following day.

Previously, on 25 June, an RIC foot patrol was fired on in Patrick Street, Limerick. On the 27th men from D Company, City Second Battalion, Limerick, under the command of Captain M. Danford and Lieutenant Edward Doran, attacked an RIC patrol in Nicholas Street, in the city, close to Mary Street Barracks. In the exchange of fire Dan Gallagher, section commander, was wounded. The police suffered some casualties, but none were fatal.

In June 1921, the West Limerick Flying Column, with the assistance of the North Cork Column, planned an ambush of a motorized convoy of four trucks and a car, carrying a mixed party of sixty soldiers and police. The convoy operated between Abbeyfeale and Newcastlewest. Volunteers Larry Harnett and Dennis Collins of the North Cork Brigade prepared mines for the ambush. Early in June forty men from the North Cork Column rendezvoused with the West Limerick Column, and after finalizing plans they moved into the ambush site at Barnagh on the night before.

Eight mines were laid along the road, and scouts were posted on the hillside to watch. As they did so the mines were wired up for a distance of a hundred yards. But as they worked the sound of vehicles was heard, and before anything could be done the trucks and the car dashed through the ambush site and were away. No one opened fire because they were waiting for the mines to explode as a signal for the start of the attack. As the Volunteers had not been seen, they decided to remain and attack the convoy on its return. The convoy, though, returned by a different route that evening. The Volunteers remained in place for three days, but as no convoys traveled along the road they withdrew. The reason why there were no more convoys was because the truce had been proclaimed.

Despite the fact that the Anglo-Irish Treaty had been signed on 6 December 1921 and ratified, albeit by a narrow approval in the Dail, on 7 January 1922, the war in Kilkenny continued. A column drawn from Dungarvan, under the command of county liaison officer George Lennon, ambushed a military convoy at Dunkitt consisting of three Crossley tenders and a Lancia armored car. The car was commandeered, and all the arms and ammunition were taken. The column was preparing for the next war.

The War in Kerry and Clare

The Kerry Brigade Column attacked a troop-carrying train from Mallow, which was halted at Headford Junction, near Killarney on 21 March 1921. The fierce firefight lasted for some time. Reports of the number of British soldiers killed vary from seven to twenty, with twelve wounded. Two Volunteers were killed as were three civilians caught up in the crossfire. Later that day three Volunteers were killed in an ambush by British soldiers at Lipole, County Kerry. Over the next two months there were a number of terrorist killings. Some were of strategic importance, while others indicated the depth of bestiality that both sides had been reduced to.

On 15 April Major McKinnon, the Auxiliary officer responsible for the murder of two civilians on Christmas Day 1920, was himself shot dead by the IRA at the Tralee Golf Course. Also killed about this time was eighty-year-old Thomas Sullivan, an informer for the British. On 4 May, with irrefutable proof of his activities, the IRA took him out and shot him dead. His body was left at the side of the road near Rathmore. A note of why he was shot was fixed to the body. Then the Volunteers waited in ambush. A patrol of RIC men came upon the body and immediately came under fire. Eight policemen were killed or later died of their wounds. Five houses and a creamery were burned by the British as a reprisal. On 9 May an IRA unit shot two RIC men near Castleisland as the two men returned home from Mass. One was killed outright and the other wounded. His life was saved when his wife, who was accompanying him, covered him with her body. Following the burning of the RIC barracks at Listowel, a patrol of Black and Tans traveling from Listowel towards Athea on 12 May arrested three young men they met along the road at Gortaglanna. They decided to execute them in revenge. One of the prisoners broke away and dashed for freedom, and though wounded, escaped. The other two were shot dead.

Elements of the Kerry Brigade Flying Column ambushed an RIC bicycle patrol on 1 June near Castlemaine. A district inspector and three constables were killed in the initial outbreak of firing. A sergeant who was wounded later died. A firefight took place at Castleisland, nine days later, on 10 June. Five Volunteers were shot dead in the incident. Four British soldiers were also killed and three wounded. With the constant fear of ambush, paramilitary police and British Army soldiers lived on their nerves. In County Clare in April 1921 a group of Auxiliaries mistook for IRA men, a group of off-duty RIC constables, in plainclothes, who were having a drink in a hotel in Castleconnell. Without warning, the Auxiliaries opened fire on them. Two RIC men, one Auxiliary, and the hotel landlord were killed in the gunfight before the mistake was realized.

At Ballyvaughan, on 21 May, the West Clare Flying Column ambushed ten members of the 8th Royal Marine Regiment, which was under the command of a sergeant. At least two marines were killed and two wounded. On the 23rd of the same month they ambushed

A combined British Army/RIC patrol under ambush in County Clare (courtesy the Imperial War Museum).

an RIC patrol at Glenwood between Sixmilebridge and Broadfoot. Six RIC men were killed, including a district inspector. Two other policemen were wounded. The column captured ten rifles. There is a curious disparity, though between the arms gained in these two skirmishes and the list of arms held by them submitted to chief of staff Richard Mulcahy on 1 October 1921:

Arms Holdings in County Clare (West Clare Brigade)

	Quantity of Weapons	Quantity of Ammunition
Rifles: Short-Magazine Lee Enfield .303	8	275
"Howth" Mauser (single shot) .9 mm	2	9
Mauser 9 magazine) .765	2	140
Miniature .22 in	2	100
Shot guns: double-barreled	24	1,500
single-barreled	36	
Revolvers: .45 caliber	48	279
Automatics ditto (Colt)	3	48
Parabellums (short)	2	11

Source: Mulcahy Papers A/II/26

On 1 June 1921, five RIC men were killed in an ambush near Castlemaine, County Kerry, and finally, with the truce so close to hand, four British soldiers were killed and three wounded on 10 July near Castleisland.

The War in the West and Northwest

In January 1921 the Galway Flying Column ambushed members of D Company of the Auxiliaries, at Kilroe, County Galway. Six Auxiliaries were wounded but none were killed. The ambush was in response to a number of nighttime murders of local councilors and Sinn Fein members committed by the Auxiliaries. Up in the northwest of Ireland, at Mountcharles, Donegal, Constable Satchwell was killed in an ambush on 1 March. In response suspected Republican houses were burned and Mary Hanley, an innocent bystander, was shot dead. RIC constable Hughes was shot dead in Donegal that same night, presumably in retaliation.

Mr. John O'Brien, chairman of the Charleville District Council, was also shot dead that same night. At about 8:30 P.M., in response to a knock on his door, he opened it to be confronted by two Black and Tans. One of them shot him, mortally wounding him; the other lobbed a hand grenade into the house. O'Brien's wife, who was upstairs, heard the explosion and rushed down to find her husband. A maid was sent for help. A priest and a doctor arrived, accompanied by the head constable and a military officer. Before dying at 4 o'clock the next morning, O'Brien gave a statement regarding his killers, who were never identified.

On 4 March 1921, the South Leitrim Brigade ambushed a motorized Black and Tan convoy at Sheermore, near Carrick on Shannon. A captain in the Bedfordshire Regiment was killed and a number of Tans were wounded. In revenge the Black and Tans ran amok in Carrick, burning and looting. Business premises, including the offices of the *Leitrim Observer*, were destroyed.

Kilfall

On 7 March 1921, the South Mayo Flying Column, under the command of Tom Maguire, surrounded a British Army patrol at Kilfall, between Ballinrobe and Castlebar, forcing it to surrender and give up its arms. The patrol was then released unharmed. Maguire's account of the ambush appears in Uinsean MacEoin's book, *Survivors*:

We planned an attack on the road between Ballinrobe and Castlebar for the 7th March 1921, at a place called Kilfall. We had information that a British party came that way on Mondays. Now it was very bad ambush country, with little or no cover. As well as that it was market day in Ballinrobe, so we could not block the road. Then again, if we did block the road and nothing came along, it being the only spot where we had a chance of doing anything — it was finished. Anyway, we decided to have a rattle at them.

I picked three of my best marksmen to bring down the driver of the lorry. If you had him, you had the rest of them copped. Of course, you would be into the middle of it yourself, because once a fight was started you could not run away from it. So, initial surprise and advantage was of paramount importance. My first marksman anyway, was Martin Conroy from Gortnacoille near Srah in the Tourmakeady district. The first time that I encountered him was after I had been appointed OC. I went up to see the Srah company. I had a chat with the men first — they were assembled in a field, and I then addressed the commander; "Ask them to fall in." As they did so, this one backed away, a slight little man, he withdrew to one side. I spoke to the OC "Who is he? What is he doing here?"

"He is a Volunteer, and a reliable man, but he will not stand into a line to drill. He is a man you can rely on."

In the meantime I had got to know Martin better. He was very fond of fowling along the Partrys, an excellent shot. So I chose him as the one to pick off the driver. To make sure however, I placed three men, Martin, then another, then another.

Having placed them, I went back over each. "Now are you quite sure you will get your man?" Martin did not have to take a bird off the wing that day, and he knew it. "I am quite sure," said he, "I'd get him if he was snipe."

The man in charge of the British party was Capt. Chatfield; he had as his second in command a man from the north of Ireland, Lieut. Craig. They were regularly drilled for dealing with an ambush, alighting from the vehicle, taking cover and returning fire. They were well drilled and were no easy cop. On this occasion, they were taken so much by surprise that only three soldiers and Craig succeeded in getting out. I had two fellows a little to the rear to cover the backs of the vehicles. One of these was a most reliable Volunteer; he never missed a drill or a parade or anything like that. I had not picked him in my original selection. I noticed then that he was very hurt about this. The second fellow was a good hefty lad. He had been in the RIC but came out and brought a supply of Mills bombs with him. These I placed at the rear.

The leading lorry appeared and with that my marksmen's shots rang out. The fight was on with a few short bursts, and the ex-RIC man, I could see was busy throwing little grenades. But he must not have known how to remove the pin because they were rolling down the road like pebbles and not exploding. At long last, I saw my other men taking aim and firing. We had cartridges loaded up with buckshot and only a weak charge, so that they could be very wounding at close quarters. Immediately they felt this, four of the enemy turned tail and fled up the road. We let them go. The others lay down, at the same time throwing their weapons away from them. They surrendered. Rushing out upon the road, I reached the lorry. There was a young soldier there, apparently dead, with his head hanging over the side. When he felt someone near him he looked up nervously. He was bleeding from the face. Opening the eyelids he gazed at me with anxious brown eyes, and I returned the stare, but I did nothing more except to tell him to drop everything he had and step out.

We had an ex-Irish Guards man with us that day, a man by the name of Michael Costello.

Picking up one of our unexploded grenades, I saw him pull the pin out. "What are you doing with that," said I.

"I am going to lob it into the middle of the bastards."

"Now, none of that," said I, holding his hand. Reluctantly he held his thumb upon the spring.

"You don't know the ... as long as I do."

I succeeded in taking the grenade from him.[16]

On the night of 16 March, County Galway Volunteers from the West Connemara Column, under their OC commandant McDonnell, attacked the RIC barracks at Clifden, County Galway. Two RIC constables were killed in the assault. The column then withdrew to the Maam Valley, where they ambushed British reinforcements sent out from Munterowan and Screebe to find them. The Black and Tans responded by burning a number of buildings in Clifden in reprisal.

On the night of 22 March three officers of the West Mayo Column, Michael Kilroy, Brodie Malone and Joe Ring, were walking along the road to Derrynakillew near Clady, looking for an ambush site, when looking behind them they noticed four RIC men on bicycles approaching. As the Volunteers were dressed in trench coats and leggings, the police must have suspected who they were. The policemen dismounted and walked towards them. As they approached, the IRA men now facing them, a gun battle began. Though fewer in number, one of the Volunteers had a Parabellum, and within a short period three of four policemen, Constables Maguire, Love and Creedon, were wounded and the fourth, Sergeant Coughlan, was dead. Four Webley revolvers were captured.

On 24 March a bomb was thrown from the Red Bridge at a group of about eighteen RIC men as they were proceeding up Altmount Street, in Westport, Mayo. A number of them were injured. The ASU, consisting of Tom Ketterick, Joe Baker and Brodie Malone, got safely away. That night, reprisals took place throughout the county.

Volunteer officer Sean Corcoran, who had organized the East Mayo Volunteers back in 1917, was killed by British troops at Ballyhaunis, County Mayo, on 1 April 1921.

Tourmakeady

On 3 May the South Mayo Flying Column under Tom Maguire combined with the East Mayo Column in an ambush on an RIC/Black and Tan motorized convoy at Tourmakeady. Six policemen were killed in the initial assault.

Men from the various Volunteer companies met near the scattered village of Tourmakeady early on the morning of the 3rd of May. There were close to sixty men. The target was a convoy of two trucks and a touring car. Intelligence reported that they would travel spaced out at intervals of about three hundred yards. Maguire divided his men into more or less three equal sections, each to deal with a designated vehicle. One group under Michael O'Brien, brigade adjutant, was placed at the green to the north of the village. Tom Maguire took command in the center of the village, taking over the post office, while Paddy May commanded a section two hundred yards further down the road near the entrance to Drumbane House. The people who lived in the extended village of Tourmakeady were rounded up, and for their own safety they were placed in an end house under guard.

A scout reported the approach of two enemy vehicles, a car and a Crossley tender, from Ballinrobe. The convoy was led by the scout car. It drove into the ambush site as far as Drumbane gateway, where Paddy May and his section were waiting. They opened fire, and the driver was killed instantly. The car crashed through a gateway, and the other policemen piled out of the car and a firefight began. At the sound of firing the Crossley tender following halted between the first and second IRA positions. The other two sections opened up on it. Some men from O'Brien's section went to the assistance of their comrades, attacking the occupants of the car, and within minutes all the policemen were dead or mortally wounded. Arms and ammunition was quickly gathered up from the dead men. The remaining police in the tender were under the command of a head constable, who organized them in gathering up their wounded and fighting a rearguard action as they sought the safety of a nearby hotel. Safe inside they knew that they could hold out until reinforcements arrived. The nearby police station at Derrypark, their destination, was bound to have heard the shooting and would contact the barracks at Ballinrobe, which would send reinforcements.

The spacing of the two vehicles had saved the police in the tender from annihilation. To organize an attack on the hotel would take time. O'Brien's plan had fallen apart. He was counting on complete surprise to capture both vehicles and their cargo of arms and ammunition. It should have been all over in a matter of a few minutes. No provision had been made to delay reinforcements by felling trees or cutting trenches along the road. It now became essential to withdraw his men before the expected reinforcements arrived. As they made an orderly withdrawal from the village, some of the policemen in the hotel dashed down the road to the post office and telegraphed for assistance. The policemen in Derrypark had also appealed for help. O'Brien and his men made for the Partry Mountains. British reinforcements, reputedly over 600 in number, were soon on the scene and began a pursuit of the Volunteers, guided by an airplane. Caught up in an encirclement, and almost surrounded by British forces, the combined columns succeeded in breaking out of the containment following a heavy firefight; and as darkness fell, they escaped. Tom Maguire was badly wounded and Adjutant Michael O'Brien, was killed. British casualties killed or wounded, though not revealed, appear to have been high. Of the four constables in the car, Constables O'Regan, and Oakes (Black and Tan) were killed and Sergeant John Regan died of his wounds. Constable Flynn, the fourth occupant of the Ford car, was wounded. Constable Power, riding in the Crossley tender, was killed and Constable Morrow was badly wounded in the arm, warranting its later amputation. In the British pursuit of the Volunteers over the mountains, Lieutenant Ibberson, who led the pursuit, was wounded. Other pursuers, it is claimed, were also wounded, but no names have been revealed. The official Republican account of this action appeared in the *Irish Bulletin*, 30 May 1921:

> At Tourmakeady, County Mayo, on May 3rd , a party of sixty officers and men of the South Mayo Brigade, IRA, engaged an enemy patrol traveling in two motor trucks. After an action lasting thirty minutes four of the enemy were killed and four wounded, one mortally. The remainder of the patrol took refuge in a neighboring hotel, and the Republicans after an unsuccessful effort to dislodge them, withdrew. Having dismissed half of his force, the Republican Officer Commanding retired with thirty men to the neighboring hills were the column rested. An hour later the outposts reported the advance of large parties of British troops. It was then about 2.30 P.M. Scouts were sent out to ascertain the enemy's numbers. They reported that the party first sighted consisted of twenty-four trucks of soldiers and that this force had been distributed to the South. South-East and South-West of the Republican position, the Officer Commanding ordered a retreat towards the North. Using the natural cover to great advantage, the Republican forces had traversed a distance of four or five miles

when the advanced guard sighted a large party of British troops holding the line of their retreat. The British immediately opened fire with Lewis guns. It was then 4 P.M.—six hours before nightfall. The OC ordered his men to take cover, and after consultation with them, decided that the column though now obviously surrounded by over-whelming forces, would not surrender on any terms. The British forces kept up a continuous fire on the republican position, which was replied to only at long intervals. The Irish troops had little ammunition and used it in concentrated fire whenever the enemy attempted a forward movement. These tactics had the desired effect. For six hours the exchange of fire continued, but the enemy never attempted to close in. When darkness came the Republican forces decided to break through the cordon, which at nightfall was greatly weakened by the withdrawal of the main body of the British troops. Although Very lights were thrown up frequently by the remaining troops, the Irish party succeeded in passing through the British lines and escaping, carrying with them two of their number who were wounded. The total Republican casualties in these actions were one killed, two wounded and two captured. Enemy casualties in the fight on the hills as observed by the Officer Commanding were one officer and one constable killed and one officer and two soldiers wounded. It is believed the enemy suffered many more casualties. A short time after the Republican column had broken through the enemy's position two flying columns of the West Mayo Brigade, IRA, arrived in the district. They had come many miles by forced marches in order to relieve the invested columns. Their assistance was, however, not needed.

Following the ambush at Tourmakeady the two RIC posts at Derrypark and Kinnury were abandoned, thus extending IRA influence over this mountainous region.

On 6 May 1921, the West Mayo Brigade prepared an ambush at the Big Wall, Islandeady, between Westport and Castlebar. The RIC patrol turned off the main road before the ambush site, their intention to arrest Michael Staunton, a Republican court judge. Returning back to the main road the police came upon five Volunteers entrenching the road. Two were killed outright, two captured and the fifth escaped but was later killed in a separate incident.

A unit of the Galway Volunteer Brigade ambushed a car as it left Ballyturin House on 15 May 1921. Two army officers were shot dead along with an RIC district inspector and his wife. Also in the car was Margaret Gregory, daughter-in-law of Augusta, Lady Gregory, a writer and close friend of W.B. Yeats; she was unhurt. RIC reinforcements coming to investigate found themselves under fire. A constable was fatally wounded and died six days later.

Kilmeena

The West Mayo Brigade Flying Column was not formed until the spring of 1921. It was able to draw from three battalion columns based at Castlebar, Westport and Newport. Michael Kilroy was appointed its commandant. Up until this time the county had been fairly quiet, and the formation of a Brigade flying column was designed to produce greater commitment to the fight. Poor intelligence had led to a number of abortive engagements, but the killing of an RIC sergeant and the wounding of a constable led to the expectation of a British patrol in the area either between Newport and Castlebar or between Westport and Newport. On 19 May, forty-one Volunteers of the West Mayo Column under Kilroy prepared an ambush at Kilmeena, in County Mayo. By dawn the column, consisting of units drawn from the Newport, Westport and Louisburgh battalions, was at the crossroads at Knocknaboly Bridge. The ambush site chosen was some forty yards below the bridge, set in a little way from the road. The main party of the IRA men were positioned behind a bank. A smaller party were placed behind a bank a little further down, on the opposite side of the road, to protect the flank of the main body. The road was blocked to prevent trucks discharging their men and thus outflanking the Volunteers' lines. Beyond the brow of the hill, south of the main position, an outpost of four men was placed on a ridge about one hundred feet above the road, where they would dominate the Newport road. On a hill to the north, about eight hundred yards away towards Westport, was an observer who would signal the British approach. It was textbook positioning for the terrain and the conditions prevailing — but there were insufficient men to protect the line of withdrawal, and this led to the defeat of the column with heavy losses.

The day wore on. It looked as if the enemy would not venture forth that day. Then about 3:00 P.M. the alert was given that a truck was approaching. It was traveling at speed. As it entered the ambush site it was fired upon. Lurching from side to side across the road, it succeeded in reaching the bridge and was soon safely away. There was more firing as the truck passed the outpost, then silence. The ambush had been a failure.

Above the bridge on the Westport road a second police truck and a car, carrying RIC men and Black and Tans under the command of District Inspector Donnellan, came to a halt as they heard the firing. The Black and Tans piled out of the truck, and as they did so they received fire from the IRA outpost. They sought cover to ascertain the position of the enemy, and having done so, sprayed the hill with a Lewis gun. The Volunteers withdrew to a safer position, and in so doing they exposed the flank of the main body of the ambushers. From the bridge, fire from the Lewis gun covered the police as they moved into position behind a tailor's house. The hedge behind the house turned into a small sunken lane. Down the lane the Tans proceeded until they had outflanked the main body of Volunteers behind the bank. As they opened fire upon the Volunteers, Kilroy ordered his men to fall back. The smaller group of Volunteers along the other side of the road now attempted to cross the road and join their comrades Along the spine of the second bank to which Kilroy had withdrawn his men ran another bank at right angles to the main road. Down this, Kilroy attempted to get his men; but there were gaps in the bank where the IRA men were exposed to enemy fire. Volunteers John Staunton and James MacEvilly were fatally wounded, as was Paddy Jordan. As the column made its escape Paddy Mulloy was wounded in the back. The column eventually got to a slight rise of ground above a diagonal bank where Kilroy and his men were now sheltered. Nearby was the house of Father Conway, a local priest, which gave extra protection from enemy fire. Here Kilroy found men from the other section already in position. They had wounded men. Paddy O'Malley's shin was shattered by a bullet. Tom Nolan lay nearby, wounded in the leg. There was little Kilroy could do for them. The Tans were now in close pursuit. A Volunteer named Pierce insisted on remaining with the wounded men, even though capture meant certain death. Kilroy moved his men out. As they proceeded they heard gunshots. The Tans had fired at Mulloy as he lay wounded on the ground. At this point the British broke off their pursuit. Kilroy and his men, including two other wounded men, Michael Hughes and James Swift, made their escape across the fields. The dead and wounded Volunteers left in the withdrawal were dragged across the fields to the British trucks and taken back to the police barracks at Westport. There were four men dead, James MacEvilly, Tom O'Donnell, John Stanton and Sean Collins, and five wounded. The British lost one man killed, shot through the eye, and another who was wounded.

Kilroy realized that British reinforcements would be all over the district in a matter of hours. He had to get his men outside of the triangle formed by Castlebar, Westport and Newport. The men, largely inexperienced, were shell-shocked, and demoralized at their losses. Aghagower, Kilroy's intended stopover for the night, had to be abandoned in favor of somewhere nearer. Kilroy had to drive his men on. They marched northwards towards Skerdagh carrying their wounded with them. If the British caught up with them, his men were in no position to put up a fight. They waded through the River Newport, and kept on until they reached the village, where, watched over by local Volunteers, they spent the night.

The police trucks arrived back at Westport. The dead and dying Volunteers were thrown out onto the road, and there left, the Tans gloating at their victory. Any attempt by the villagers to assist the dead or wounded was prevented by force. The Marquess of Sligo, a Unionist who lived locally, visited the police station to remonstrate at the behavior of the Crown forces. Following his visit the dead and wounded were brought into the barracks and the dead, at least, were treated with some respect.

Meanwhile, the fleeing Volunteers had rested for three days among the scattered cottages of Skerdagh. Kilroy strove hard to restore their discipline. At about four o'clock in the morning shots rang out as a local Volunteer opened fire upon an approaching British search party. Kilroy sent Jim Moran, a local man, to organize the removal of the wounded, while he and John Connolly, another local man, set off in the direction of the gunfire. As they walked towards the sounds, Kilroy saw a figure up ahead. He signaled towards Connolly to get down. Turning back he saw the figure up ahead take aim. As he fired Kilroy threw himself to the ground. The figure spoke to other policemen who now came into view. "Wasn't that a good shot so early in the morning?" Kilroy heard an English voice say. The soldiers believed that they had killed the Volunteer. Then from a prone position Kilroy and Connolly returned fire. There were cries of "Take cover! Take cover!" as the Black and Tans realized that they had now come under attack. As Kilroy and Connolly held off the police, twenty-four in number from Newport RIC barracks, the other Volunteers regrouped and under brigade officer John Madden, a doctor, collected up the wounded and withdrew. Volunteers Kitterick, Canon, MacDonnell and Gibbons came to Kilroy and Connolly's assistance, and they succeeded in making an orderly withdrawal.

Cautiously the British pursued them. As the rearguard made its way up the hill, they observed a line of trucks coming along the road from Newport. The enemy vehicles halted at Skerdagh School, and the soldiers disembarked then began proceeding up the slopes. The Volunteers moved off again. Every so often they heard a burst of machine-gun fire as the police swept the hillsides, hoping to draw out the fleeing IRA men. The Irishmen found a brief breathing space in a hollow overgrown by moss and rushes, then it was off on the move once more, to avoid the British encirclement. Hearing a noise somewhere off on their flank, they threw themselves to the ground. They caught sight of one Tan, the last man in an enemy line as he passed by and away. After some time when they thought it safe, the Volunteer rear-guard moved off again. They continued climbing until they reached a peak. Here they rested. Way off in the distance they heard more machine-gun fire.

More troops were searching for the main party of Volunteers. This party had gone up Shrahmore to the west by the side of Lough Feeagh. There were at least three bodies of Crown forces now in pursuit. The rearguard decided to make for the hills near Aghagower.

Dusk was falling. They stopped at the house of Jack MacDowell, where they were given something to eat and drink. It was dark as they left. They crossed the Newport river by a small bridge. It was now midnight. Away in the distance they saw beams of light moving in their direction. More troops were arriving to complete the encirclement. The rearguard had to get down to the Crossmolina road before the British arrived. If they could manage it they would be outside of the encirclement. Down the hill they ran, even though exhausted after twenty-four hours on the go. They made the road and crossed it, finding the safety of a bog drain. A matter of moments later the trucks, their headlights blazing, arrived and stopped a short distance away. The soldiers disembarked. The British officers discussed what to do and decided to put a guard on the bridge near Divers that the Volunteers had so recently crossed. The troops got back into their trucks once more, and the motorized convoy moved on.

The main body of Volunteers, meanwhile, were met by John Chambers, a lieutenant in a local mountain company who led them off to safety across the mountains with their wounded. They crossed the ridge between Mount Eagle and Bireencorragh and marched on towards Leamadartaun to the northwest. An airplane engine was heard in the distance. The Volunteers scrambled for cover. The airplane came over and circled once or twice before flying off. It did not spot them. The column then continued on to Leamadartaun where they took a break as scouts kept watch upon the surrounding valleys. In their continued trek, field glasses of the RIC picked them out as they crossed a ridge over two miles away. The police were themselves exhausted, and without any means of contacting the other encircling troops, they watched as the Volunteers disappeared from sight. The column continued on and about nine o'clock they were met by men from the Castlebar Battalion with guides, who led them away to safety. Later that same month a Black and Tan was shot dead by a sniper in Ballyhaunis. An innocent man, Michael Coen, was shot dead outside the town as a reprisal.

Carrowkennedy

As they had been badly defeated at Kilmeena, only a victory could restore the morale of the West Mayo Flying Column. Michael Kilroy, its Commandant, looked for an opportunity. On the evening of 3 June a scout brought word that a joint RIC/Black and Tan motorized convoy of two trucks and a car had forced local men at gunpoint to fill in a trench along the road that they were traveling. The convoy had then driven off. Analyzing the situation Kilroy came to the conclusion that, because of other trenched roads and a destroyed bridge, the convoy would have to return by the same route. He assembled twenty-five brigade members from the Westport Battalion and outlined a plan to ambush the convoy. The site chosen was along the Westport to Leenane road at Carrowkennedy. The first section, under Brodie Malone, vice-commandant of the Westport Battalion, was placed on a hillside about one hundred and fifty yards from the road. In front, down on the road, was a stone wall running from knee high to about five feet in height. This section was detailed to deal with the first vehicle, which would be allowed to pass through the other two ambush positions. The second section under Tom Kitterick, was placed about one hundred and fifty yards away. Between them was cottage and a lane which would afford extra cover should it be needed. The second position was a burned out police station destroyed at Easter 1920. This section had orders to deal with the second vehicle. On the slope of a hill on the other side of the road, about one hundred feet high and to the rear of the McGrale family cottage, Kilroy placed his third section of ten men, commanded by himself. The position was screened from the road by a small grove of trees. From here the Volunteers had a good view of the road for about eight hundred yards. The designated line of withdrawal was down the road to Clady, which was about one and a half miles away.

A scout brought word that the convoy was at Darby Hastings' pub, about a mile down the road and heading towards the ambush site. The first truck approached and passed through the ambush site until it reached Malone's position. Rifle fire was opened up on it and the vehicle slew to one side and halted by the bank. The police piled out of the truck and sought the shelter of the bank, but it gave them no protection from the men up on the hill. District Inspector Stevenson, who had taken over as driver, and the man sitting next to him were killed; Stevenson was shot in the head. From the second truck a Lewis gun was thrown down onto the road and some of the policemen started firing at the third section, who were also firing at them. The machine gunner was killed. A second machine gunner opened fire on the third section, but Volunteers up on the hill at section two shot him dead. The men from the second truck ran towards McGrale's cottage and gained access. The motor car, which was some distance behind the two trucks, halted by the cottage. From it jumped three policemen who sought cover. Volunteer Jim Flaherty, a former Connaught Ranger, shot one of them. The firing continued.

By now two hours had passed. Kilroy was concerned at the progress of the fight. He ordered men down to outflank the police. At the first truck the police had been firing grenades from their rifles. Now one of grenades accidentally exploded within the truck, killing or wounding all the men within. From inside the vehicle a handkerchief, tied to a rifle, was raised in surrender. Warily some Volunteers advanced upon it, fearing a trick, but it was genuine. Only one policeman was unwounded. The Volunteers gathered up the enemy rifles and ammunition. Included in the haul was a Lewis gun. The unwounded policeman was sent under a flag of truce to demand the surrender of his colleagues in the cottage. They did not reply at first, but a burst of fire from the captured Lewis gun brought a response in the form of a dishcloth tied to a rifle. They too surrendered, but on the understanding that the Black and Tans with them would not be shot out of hand. Kilroy agreed, and seventeen policemen emerged from the cottage with their hands raised. The Volunteers gathered up twenty-two rifles, a Lewis gun with eight drums of ammunition and six thousand rounds of rifle ammunition. Petrol was thrown over the three vehicles and they were set ablaze. Volunteer Dr. John Madden gave first aid to the wounded policemen, and one of their number was given a bicycle to ride off to Westport to get help for his wounded colleagues. Six policemen had been killed and four wounded, of whom two died during the night. The Volunteers moved off in good order. The defeat at Kilmeena had been avenged.

The British Army conducted a huge three-pronged encirclement around Ballycastle on 23 June 1921. They made brief contact with a unit of Volunteers, when, after a bloody firefight, one IRA man was killed and seven captured.

Culleens

On 1 July a seven man RIC patrol was ambushed at Culleens, County Sligo by the Sligo, Column led by Liam Pilkington. The IRA plan had been to lure the police into the ambush site by robbing the Culleens Inn, also known as Tuffy's shop. The column moved into Culleens at dusk on the evening of 30 June. On the morning of 1 July, at about 8:00 o'clock, two of the Volunteers, disguised as tinkers, robbed the shop of between £60 and 70. Returning home a little later, the proprietor, Tommy Joe Tuffy, was told by his sister what had happened. He immediately sent for the police at the RIC barracks at Dromore West. At 10 o'clock the column took up its ambush position. The two "tinkers" returned the money to the shop and rejoined their comrades. At almost 12 o'clock the strung-out seven-man RIC bicycle patrol arrived. The column, some thirty in number, had divided into two groups. The first two constables, King and Higgins, were allowed past the first group of ambushers. As they drew abreast the next group, the Volunteers opened fire. Both King and Higgins were wounded. Another policeman, Constable Curry, was shot in both arms. Just then a motor car approached, and the other policemen commandeered it and made good their escape, ordering the driver to take them to Easky Barracks. King and Higgins were left to their fate. The Volunteers gathered up the police guns, and after dressing the wounds of their two prisoners led them off towards the Gleneasky Mountains and escape. British reinforcements were soon on their trail. Proceeding through the bog land, the wounded policemen slowing them down, the IRA men decided to callously shoot their prisoners rather than just leave them. The excuse given was that Constable King, a regular RIC man, knew them all and could identify them. The prisoners were given a brief opportunity to say their prayers before they were shot. One of the constables was killed instantly, the other was found by his comrades, still alive. He was given the last rites before he died. The IRA column escaped into the mountains near Bonniconlon.

The Irish Midlands

Sean MacEoin, a blacksmith from Balinalee, County Longford, took charge of the Longford Brigade at Michael Collins' bidding. He and the column engaged the enemy just outside Ballinalee on 5 November 1920, killing twenty Auxiliaries and Black and Tans. In response the authorities embarked on an all-out campaign to destroy the Longford Brigade. On 7 January 1921, following a major sweep of the area, a patrol of the RIC came across the cottage where MacEoin was staying. Seeing them approach, MacEoin stepped out of the cottage, firing as he did so. District Inspector Thomas McGrath of the RIC was killed, and a constable was wounded before the remaining police were put to flight. Once more back with his men, MacEoin led the North Longford Flying Column in a successful ambush on 1 February. Two trucks of Auxiliaries were ambushed at Clonfin. A land mine was exploded under the leading truck, killing its driver and injuring several men. The Auxiliaries disembarked and a firefight lasting the better part of two hours followed. With five Auxiliaries killed and eight wounded, the British paramilitaries surrendered. MacEoin congratulated the surviving Auxiliaries on their courage and did what he could for the wounded before sending them back to their barracks in the surviving truck. The column captured 18 rifles, 20 revolvers and a Lewis gun.

The North Longford Column suffered a great loss on 1 March when Sean MacEoin was recognized as he was traveling home and taken off the train at Mullingar Station. He tried to escape but was shot through the lung. As he lay on the platform he was severely beaten with rifle butts. The arrival of a doctor saved his life. MacEoin was charged with the death of Inspector McGrath. Three of the Auxiliaries who had surrendered to him at

Clonfin paid tribute to him at his subsequent court-martial, and his life was spared. He spent the rest of the war in custody. Further tragedy struck the Longford Brigade that same month. It was ambushed at Selton Hill near Mohill, County Leitrim, by British troops. Senior officer Sean Connolly and five other Volunteers were killed before the column managed to extricate itself. Their location was said to have been betrayed by a local Orangeman.

Scramogue

An ambush along the Strokestown to Longford road at Scramogue in County Roscommon had long been considered. It was a busy military road. That fact had mitigated against an ambush. Military convoys traveled along the road in both directions and at unspecified times. A flying column attacking one convoy might find itself involved in fighting off another convoy, either following on or coming from the other direction. Any ambush had to be short and decisive and coupled to a secure line of withdrawal. GHQ's constant urging that less active parts of the country must get involved to take the pressure off counties like Cork brought matters to a head. In March 1921, Pat Madden, commandant of the South Roscommon Brigade and leader of its flying column, made plans to stage an ambush. His priority was to ensure that the column was protected while it conducted the action. He called in support from the other local battalions and from the men of the North Roscommon Brigade. Careful observation revealed that individual trucks or smaller convoys passed along the road most regularly in the morning. The Volunteers from North Roscommon were better armed, and it was decided that they should be used to secure the safe withdrawal of the column. Though Madden's column was mainly made up of local farmers' sons drawn from the Kilgeffin Battalion, he also had a number of ex–Irish Guards with World War I experience. The 23rd of March was selected as the day of the ambush.

The Volunteers arrived at the ambush site at about three o'clock in the morning. Men from the two adjoining battalions of Strokestown and Elphin were detailed to construct roadblocks to hinder British reinforcements. The site for the attack was a bend in the road, which rose some six feet above it and commanded a view of about five hundred yards. Here a Volunteer party dug a trench behind the hedge. The hedge itself was cut back to reduce exposure. Gaps were cut in it at right angles to the road to assist communication. In the barn just behind them an exit hole was cut in the far wall to assist the men to escape should it become necessary for them to make a rapid withdrawal. Just across the lane a roadside house was commandeered, its inhabitants taken away to safety. Loopholes were cut in its wall. Men guarding the line of withdrawal were placed on the rising ground looking down on the Strokestown road. A reserve of ten men to be deployed where required were placed a short distance away on the rising ground.

Apart from the danger of unexpected trucks coming along the road, barely a mile and a half away was Strokestown House, garrisoned by the 9th Lancers. The Lancers could move quickly across country on their horses at the first sound of rifle fire. This factor also had to be taken into account. There were also other garrisons nearby. Longford was twelve miles away, as was Roscommon. Castlereagh and Boyle were a little further away, but combined they formed a ring around the ambush site.

Orders were drummed into the Volunteers as to their duties, then all was ready. The men settled down to wait. The morning wore on. Then the sound of trucks was heard. The

Volunteers had expected two trucks and it was agreed that the first truck should be allowed to progress into the ambush site as far as the shotgun party, just beyond the bend. As the first truck, containing soldiers from the Lancers, entered the ambush zone, the second was some considerable distance behind and well out of the ambush site. The first truck was fired upon, as per orders, by riflemen in the house. It juddered to a halt and its passengers jumped from the vehicle and sought the shelter of the wall on the other side of the road. Others lay on the ground where they had fallen. A corporal in the truck, armed with a Hotchkiss gun, got in a burst of fire on the men in the house before he was wounded by the flanking group in the trench. Those Lancers behind the wall now came under attack from the men in the trench, who had a complete view of that side of the wall. Within minutes it was all over.

Captain Sir Alfred Peeke, DSO, a nephew of Lord Middleton, was wounded but continued running back towards the second truck seeking help, and he was cut down and killed. This second truck, carrying RIC and Tans and still some considerable distance away, was fired upon by the Volunteers in the trench. It came to a halt, then reversed out of danger. The Lancers later blamed the Black and Tans for their cowardice in not helping the soldiers under attack. Captain Peeke was dead, as were two policemen riding with the Lancers. Most of the others were wounded. The Volunteers lost one man killed. Arms and ammunition captured included Lee Enfield rifles, Webley revolvers, and the Hotchkiss machine gun so recently used against the Volunteers. Two Black and Tans who were in the custody of the policemen survived unscathed. They were led off with the column as it withdrew, and both were subsequently shot.

Sent into Cavan for training, one of the Belfast columns of Volunteers, consisting of thirteen men, found themselves surrounded in the Lappinduff mountains, on 8 May, by British soldiers. There was a brief firefight and one Volunteer was killed and two wounded before the remainder ignominiously surrendered. On 16 May eight Volunteers from County Kildare's B Company, 5th Battalion, Carlow Brigade, led by their Captain, Joe Maher, ambushed an RIC bicycle patrol at Barrowhouse. The policemen were traveling from Ballylinan Barracks to Grangemellon Barrack, when they were attacked. Though the Volunteers had the advantage of surprise, they were poorly armed. The eight Volunteers involved were Captain Joe Maher, Lt. Joe Lacy, Paddy Dooley, Mick Maher, Jack O'Brien, Joe Ryan, James Lacy and William Connor. Though the assault was successful and they captured arms and ammunition, two Volunteers, James Lacy and William Connor, were killed. Six days later, on 22 May, A Company under its captain, John Hayden, attacked the RIC barracks in Barracks Lane, Athy. Without explosives the attack was no more than a gesture. After half an hour, neither side suffering any casualties, the Volunteers withdrew. Two RIC men were killed in an IRA ambush at Kinnity, County Offaly (King's County), on 20 March. Following an abortive attack in Mullinglow, County Carlow, several Volunteers were arrested on 9 April 1921.

The Northeast

On 1 January 1921 the Monaghan Flying Column, led by Eoin O'Duffy, carried out an ambush at Ballbay, Monaghan. One RIC man and a "civilian" were killed. Three Auxiliaries were wounded. The following day in an opportunist killing two RIC men were shot dead in a hotel in the center of Belfast. Volunteer John Doran was abducted from his home in Camlough, County Armagh, and killed by unknown gunmen. On the 25th, one of the hated Ulster Special Constables, many being former members of the U.V.F., was shot dead in Crossmaglen, County Armagh. That same month in an IRA ambush at Freeduff, County Armagh, two RIC men were killed and a number wounded. Two Black and Tans were shot dead in Belfast by men from the West Belfast IRA, on 12 March. On the 22nd of March, Volunteers in Fermanagh burned the homes of ten local Protestants who were members of the Ulster Special Constabulary. Two of the constables, noted for their brutality to Volunteer prisoners, were shot dead in their beds. In Donegal that same month, a Flying Column under the command of Peader O'Donnell, attacked the RIC barracks at Falcarragh. One policeman was reported killed.

April saw a number of tit-for-tat killings in County Tyrone. An RIC constable was killed and four Special constables were wounded in an IRA ambush near Dromore. The following day an RIC officer shot a Catholic girl, Eileen Doherty, in the legs. Her brother, who was a Volunteer, sought out the policeman and shot him dead. The next day a group of Special constables abducted three known Volunteers and shot them dead, dumping their bodies half a mile outside the town. Later that month in an ambush four RIC men were wounded. The Volunteers lost one man killed. Elsewhere in the province an IRA unit held the congregation of a Protestant church in Creggan, County Armagh, hostage as they arrived for a service and ambushed the local B Specials as they arrived. A grenade and small arms were used in the attack, which left one constable dead and another wounded. The congregation were then released unharmed. In Belfast two Auxiliaries were shot dead in Donegal Place, in the city center. That same night two Catholics were killed in reprisal in the Falls road.

On 23 April two Auxiliaries were shot dead in Donegall Place, central Belfast, by two Volunteers. The IRA men exchanged shots with other RIC men as they made their escape. Two civilians were killed in the crossfire. Loyalist gunmen murdered two Catholics in reprisal, and uniformed RIC men killed two Republican activists, the Duffin brothers, in revenge for the shooting of their colleagues.

Units of the Monaghan Flying Column were surrounded by British soldiers in the Lapinduff Mountains on 8 May 1921. One Volunteer was killed and two wounded in the ambush. Thirteen Volunteers were taken prisoner. That May Ulster Special constable George Lynas was shot dead in County Armagh. The B Specials shot dead two local Catholics in reprisal. On 12 June three RIC men were shot dead by the IRA in the Falls Road in Belfast. One of them subsequently died of his wounds. In reprisal the RIC and Black and Tans arrested and murdered three innocent Catholic men in north Belfast. One of the murderers was identified as Detective Inspector Nixon of the RIC. Over the next few days Loyalist gunmen killed six more Catholics at random. In response the IRA murdered three innocent Protestants in the city.

In June 1921 four Catholics with no known involvement in the IRA, were taken from their homes in Bessbrook and Altnaveigh, south Armagh, and shot dead by the sectarian B Specials. On 23 June the South Armagh Flying Column ambushed a train as it passed along the Belfast to Dublin line between Aghdavoyle and Jonesborough. A mine was exploded under the train, derailing it and killing four soldiers of the 10th Royal Hussars. The driver and fireman were also killed. British troops later shot dead a local man when he failed to stop when challenged, and a truck of Black and Tans shot up the local Catholic infant school, the children diving for safety under their desks.

On 10 July the IRA mounted an ambush in Raglan Street, Belfast. Two policemen were killed. In the following week sixteen Catholics were killed as a reprisal, and 216 Catholic homes were burned in the city. Elsewhere in the province the Black and Tans and elements of the newly created Royal Ulster Constabulary were burning cooperative creameries owned by Roman Catholics. Where possible the IRA reciprocated by burning Protestant creameries. On the morning of the truce, at half past ten — half an hour before the truce came into being — Volunteers from the Tyrone Brigade under James McElduff, set fire to Doon's Creamery, Dunnamore. Its manager was a B Special, a part-time policeman in a force that was to enjoy the same notoriety among Catholics as the Tans. The ASU commandeered two motor cars, and proceeded towards Dunnamore. On the way they intercepted a policeman on a motorcycle and took him prisoner. As they prepared to destroy the creamery a Black and Tan from the nearby RIC barracks approached them. McElduff fired a warning shot, and the policeman raised his hands in surrender. Volunteer Frank Curran dragged the creamery manager out of his office and led him to safety as the building went up in flames.

12

Between Truce and Treaty

The year 1921 at the height of summer, with its long sunny days, mitigated against guerrilla warfare. Actions were scaled back until the coming autumn. Rumors now reached the guerrillas of a possible truce. Curiously GHQ had not consulted with its commanders in the field as to their capacity to continue the struggle, this at a time when Liam Lynch in County Cork was, if he could secure more arms, intending to resume the struggle on a larger scale. Tom Barry had previously been asked by de Valera how long the guerrillas could continue. His response had been that it all depended upon British reinforcements and whether they, the Volunteers, could obtain more arms. His comments, and those of other guerrilla leaders in reports to IRA GHQ, cast doubts in the minds of de Valera, Cathal Brugha and Richard Mulcahy as to whether the war could be sustained.[1]

Meanwhile the war continued, its brutality a way of life. In Britain many felt shame at what was being done in their name. There was mounting opposition. "When is this going to end?" the *Nation and Athenaeum* asked:

> The government still cling to the belief that they can crush the Irish spirit, destroy some of the bravest and most promising of Ireland's young men, and win by these means an outward victory. They are wrong.... Men of noble spirit and unfaltering courage are dying, but their race does not perish.... We can spread ruin; that we are doing. A week ago a deputation from the American Relief Committee waited upon General Macready and Sir John Anderson to explain that America proposed to raise thirty million dollars for repairing the havoc caused by the armed forces of the British Empire in Ireland: there have been prouder moments in our history. We can spread death; that we are doing. We can do to Ireland just as much as Austria did to Italy, or Germany to Belgium. But the end is as certain in this case as in those, for the Irish people, supported as they are by their own spiritual vitality, and by the sympathy of the world, can keep this struggle alive till it ceases to be merely a struggle between Government and a Nation. The Government which refuses to give peace to Ireland may find, sooner or later, that it has broken the peace of the world.

The British prime minister, David Lloyd George, was coming under increasing pressure both in Britain and internationally to stop the atrocities being carried out by Crown forces, and to bring the war to an end. British intelligence informed him that the war would have to continue for another twelve months, and there was no guarantee that it could be won even then. How to end the war without losing face was the dilemma presented to him and his cabinet. Then the problem resolved itself. On 22 June 1921, King George V spoke in Belfast to the newly established Northern Ireland Parliament. His theme was one of conciliation:

I speak from a full heart when I pray that my coming to Ireland today may prove to be the first step towards the end of strife among her people, whatever their race or creed. In that hope I appeal to all Irishmen to pause, to stretch out the hand of forbearance and conciliation, to forgive and forget, and to join in making for the land they love a new era of peace, contentment and goodwill.

It is my earnest desire that in Southern Ireland, too, there may, ere long, take place a parallel to what is passing in this hall; that there a similar occasion may present itself, and a similar ceremony be performed. For this the parliament of the United Kingdom has in the fullest measure provided the powers. For this the Parliament of Ulster is pointing the way.

The future lies in the hands of my Irish people themselves. May this historic gathering be the prelude of the day in which the Irish people, North and South, under one parliament or two as these parliaments may themselves decide, shall work together in common love for Ireland upon the common ground of mutual justice and respect.

On the afternoon of that same day good fortune smiled on Lloyd George. Eamon de Valera was arrested at a house in Blackrock, in Dublin. Twenty-four hours later he was released. Who he spoke with in those twenty-four hours was not revealed, but it seems highly probable that one of those people was Andy Cope, the assistant under secretary for Ireland, a man who had apparently already established a link with Michael Collins through the imprisoned Arthur Griffith. Two days later de Valera received a letter from Lloyd George asking him to come to London for a conference with Sir James Craig, the Northern Ireland prime minister, and himself to explore the possibilities of a settlement. The acceptance of the partition of Ireland was implied as a prerequisite to the meeting.

Accordingly, de Valera turned down the invitation, but he was interested in talking. He in turn invited "representatives of the political minority" in Ireland to attend a meeting to be held at the Mansion House in Dublin on 4 July. While Craig refused to attend, other members of the Unionist Party did so. As a result of this meeting, which arrived at some sort of agreement, de Valera telegraphed his willingness to meet Lloyd George in London on 14 July. In Dublin a truce was agreed between de Valera and General Macready, commander-in-chief of the British Army in Ireland. It did not signify a military victory for either side, but the decision by Sinn Fein to negotiate inevitably meant that the demand for an Irish Republic would be compromised. Under the agreed terms the IRA was to retain its arms and the British Army was to remain in barracks for the duration of the peace negotiations. On 9 July brigade commanders throughout Ireland received a communiqué from GHQ in Dublin:

> In view of the conversations now being entered into by our Government with the Government of Great Britain, and in the pursuance of mutual conversations, active operations by our troops will be suspended as from noon, Monday, 11th July.
> Risteard Ua Maolchatha,
> Chief of Staff.

Many IRA brigade officers in the more active areas, those who were prosecuting a successful campaign, could not understand why a truce had been called. Ernie O'Malley recalled:

> One evening in July 1920 a dispatch rider asked to see me. He was shown into the kitchen of Mrs. Quirk's in Donohill, in south Co. Tipperary. The dispatch was from General Headquarters and stated that hostilities would cease after forty-eight hours by twelve noon on 11 July. Immediately Con Moloney, the Divisional Adjutant, typed orders to the five brigades and

arranged for their dispatch. Then we sat down to consider the situation. It was the first official intimation we had received and we did not understand it.

Con, Mickey Fitzpatrick and I discussed possible angles and reviewed areas in our own and in other Commands, but we failed to arrive at a satisfactory solution. Why had the truce been ordered? We were gaining ground, each day strengthened us and weakened our enemy; then why was it necessary to put a stop to hostilities? ... [T]he day of the truce dawned leaving us in a state of uncertainty.[2]

Other brigade officers interpreted the truce as only a temporary break in the fight. They continued to recruit and train volunteers. Training was done quite openly. Seven training camps were established around Dublin, the main camp being in the Wicklow hills. Here up to a few hundred men would drill, skirmish, and practice with rifle and revolver each week. This training was monitored by the British using aerial photography.

IRA records as of July 1921 give a membership figure of 112,650 Volunteers, though it should be emphasized that only a small fraction of this number were armed or properly trained:

IRA Strength, July 1921

1st Northern Division	5,000	Midland Division	6,600
2nd Northern Division	2,800	1st Western Division	8,500
3rd Northern Division	1,200	2nd Western Division	4,000
4th Northern Division	2,300	3rd Western Division	7,700
5th Northern Division	2,200	4th Western Division	8,400
1st Eastern Division	3,700	1st Southern Division	33,500
2nd Eastern Division	5,100	2nd Southern Division	12,500
3rd Eastern Division	3,100	3rd Southern Division	6,000
	Total 112,650		

By comparison the British Army in Ireland appears much smaller, but the emphasis here is that they were trained, and, excluding support corps, armed:

British Army in Ireland, 1920 and 1921

	1920	1921
Infantry	32,627	39,514
Cavalry	4,329	3,535
Royal Horse & Field Artillery	2,996	4,073
Royal Garrison Artillery	1,393	1,280
Machine Gun Corps	1,060	890
Tank Corps	226	275
Royal Ordnance Corps	443	529
Royal Engineers	1,630	1,409
Royal Army Service Corps	3,103	3,848
Corps of Military Police	248	298
Royal Corps of Signals	2	746
Royal Army Medical Corps	532	456
Army Dental Corps	0	20
Royal Army Pay Corps	42	58
Corps Of Military Accountants	55	113
Royal Veterinary Corps	54	71
Total	48,740	57,116

Many in the Republican movement saw no reason for a truce. Sean MacBride, son of Major John MacBride, who executed after the failure of the Easter Rising, was one of them, as was apparently Michael Collins. MacBride reveals that "Collins did not give me the impression at that time, which other people are said to have got from him, that things were at a low ebb in the Army; I could not see that, nor could he. He told me that there was no necessity for the Truce, but that de Valera and the others were keen on it. He may have meant Mulcahy, whom at that time he did not like." MacBride's opinion was echoed by Edward Broy, Collins' spy in the Castle. In his witness statement to the Bureau of Military History he remembered the following: "I went to Dublin on July 12th or 13th and reported at GHQ. Collins, Mulcahy, Gearoid O'Sullivan and others all emphasized that they didn't expect the Truce to last very long and that it must be used to improve our organization and training. I left them quite convinced that we had only a breathing space and that a resumption of the fighting was an absolute certainty."

Mulcahy had an almost obsessive belief that winning the war in Dublin was more important than winning the war in the country. The increasing pressure on the Volunteers in Dublin by a resurgent intelligence-led military would have led him to believe that the IRA was close to defeat. By July 1921, over 4,000 officers and men had been interned throughout Ireland, including 19 brigade commanders, 90 battalion commanders and 1,600 company officers. For this reason, and his intimate knowledge of the situation in Dublin, he would have supported a truce, hence perhaps the tensions between him and Collins that MacBride hints at. Seeing the bigger picture, the state of the country as a whole, MacBride was far from convinced that the IRA was losing. Those men captured were replaced, and, it might be argued with a few notable exceptions that the men interned were often the least rather than the most capable. MacBride continues:

> I was myself quite satisfied that we could intensify our activities very considerably at the time. I knew that from my own experience in the south-east over the last couple of months where, from almost nothing, we had begun to get things done, particularly in Wicklow. I also knew what possibilities lay in getting arms landed in the country. I had been down to see Pax Whelan and his friends around Helvick, and we had a number of shipments planned. One ship that I recall, the *Sancta Maria* was brought in by [Charlie] McGuinness....[3] So I felt from the experience we were gaining in purchasing arms that we were on the threshold of being able to mount a much larger campaign than we had mounted until then. I felt that with the arrival of these guns, we could step up the fight considerably. I also considered that the morale of the organization was good and that there was no weakness in the determination of the Volunteers to see the thing through. I was therefore very much against the Truce.... I saw Collins, and for the first time I was angry. I said the Truce was a terrible mistake.
>
> "Oh ho," said Collins laughing, "we can use it to reorganize and to get more arms in; I want you to start working on that immediately." I was sent abroad to Germany on the various arms procural missions."[4]

One of those missions was the successful import of arms aboard the *Frieda*. Pax O'Faolain saw the ship's arrival off Helvick Head, County Waterford: "The 'Frieda' arrived here off Helvick on November 11th 1921. There was a fog at Helvick, so she moved down and up the Suir to Cheekpoint, where we unloaded most of our cargo. It consisted principally of Peter the Painters, Parabellums, rifles, all new, and of course ammunition."[5]

On the British side there were those who also questioned the need for a truce. They felt that they were winning. The military certainly did. What was required were extra troops to swamp the country. General Macready advocated that martial law should be imposed throughout the entire country with the exception of the six counties that were to make up Northern Ireland. Garrisons would need to be reinforced with an additional 19 battalions and a strong force of marines. British Army strength needed to be brought up to 150,000 men for a military solution to succeed. Field Marshal Sir Henry Wilson also supported a military solution. In his published diaries he wrote the following: "18th May [1921]: I said that directly England was safe, every available man should go to Ireland that even four battalions now serving on the Rhine ought also to go to Ireland. I said that the measures taken up to now had been quite inadequate, that I was terrified at the state of the country, and that in my opinion, unless we crushed out the murder gang this summer we shall lose Ireland and the Empire." This was the view of many serving officers on the ground in Ireland. Major General Hawes, then a junior officer serving in Ireland wrote of it: "More and more troops were poured into Southern Ireland until there were some 100,000 of them. Techniques for quelling the rebellion were perfected and the rebellion was being subdued. H.M. Government chose this moment to give in. All the casualties we had suffered were wasted. While it might have been wise to give Southern Ireland independence, I feel this might well have been done earlier or kept until we had made it quite clear that we were acting from a position of strength."[6]

Simply swamping the country with extra troops was not necessarily the solution to the problem. British Army commander Hugh Elles had come to the conclusion that big war tactics against guerrillas did not work. They had been fighting without a defined front, and large-scale sweeps were ineffective unless there was a defined target. A major rethinking of strategy was necessary. More objectively, perhaps, in February 1921 Sir Warren Fisher, head of the British Civil Service and appointed by the government to look into administration in Ireland, seemed to infer that even given more men the I. R.A. would still retain the tactical advantage: "[T]he gunmen did exactly what any ordinarily intelligent fellow would do — they concentrated in the martial law area ... most of their best organizers and most of their best trained fighters in order to make martial law look silly. The police (as gallant and stupid as the Six Hundred at Balaclava) have given the gunmen every opportunity of practice — and the rest of Ireland (outside Dublin where the Court Martial trials have needed a counter) has been comparatively quiet."[7]

While those IRA officers operating in more active areas disputed the need for a truce, the ordinary Volunteers welcomed an end to the fighting. They were given leave to return to their homes, to family and friends, but were ordered to keep in touch with their units and hold themselves ready for mobilization at short notice. There was a holiday atmosphere. Volunteer Dan Gleeson recalled it:

> When the truce came I had no doubt about it. It was a pause, but not a victory. Unfortunately the great bulk of the lads thought they had won, and were lulled into this by the accolades poured upon people like Collins as *the man who had won the war*. In the circumstances, the fact that it was the contribution of the whole people and not the effort of any single person or personalities was overlooked.... Meanwhile the Truce was availed of in many ways. Lads on the run could come home again. Some were released from prison. There were celebrations and a general air of relaxation. I have to hand it to the English that they understand so well the psychology of this kind of thing. They knew what would happen. Once the lads came home, frequently as conquering heroes, they would have no wish to go out again. That is the great danger when a volunteer army stands down.[8]

To the ordinary people of Ireland the truce brought a sudden return to normality, an end to the intolerable strain of British reprisals and a sense of hope for the future. In this holiday atmosphere former enemies rubbed shoulders. There was some triumphalism on both sides with jibes and taunts, but on the whole the truce was observed. Lt. Frederick Clarke of the Essex Regiment recalled one such unexpected meeting with his opposite number in the IRA: "A strange meeting took place at a chemist's shop in the town [of Bandon, Co. Cork] when a big middle aged man unknown to me said 'Good Morning Mr. Clarke.' I made an appropriate reply and he added: 'We could not have met like this a few weeks ago.' Then nodding to me he left the shop and the chemist said 'Do you know who that was?' I shook my head and he replied 'That was John Hales.' How did he know my name? Now John Hales, a big farmer, was said to have been descended from one of Cromwell's settlers, nevertheless, he had been the rebel leader over most of Cork."[9]

One officer, commanding L Company of the Auxiliaries based in Millstreet, County Cork, had reason to complain to GHQ in Dublin Castle at a seeming provocation:

Non observance of the Truce

I have the honor to report, with regard to the above subject, an incident which occurred in this area today.

At about 12.00 hours there arrived in Millstreet from the direction of Rathmore, two open motor cars and one motor cycle. These cars contained ??? men, while one rode the motor cycle. All of them obviously members of the I.R.A. I ascertained that they were in this village for the purpose of holding an inquest! Upon an individual named Murphy of this place, who was knocked down and killed by a railway train yesterday.

The man who appeared to be in charge of the party was appareled in full I.R.A. uniform, including "Sam Browne" belt. This person with his bodyguard walked boldly through the town and was observed by my second-in-command and myself. Just outside the lodge gates of Mount Leader House, our billet. What the motive was in walking all the way out to what is practically the Company billet, I cannot say. But to my mind it would appear that this fellow (Moynihan by name and as far as we know a stranger in this district) was simply out to provoke Crown Forces. "Commandant" Meaney (one of the local "heroes") was also in attendance on the man Moynihan in the town, and was wearing a "Sam Browne" over his mufti. The numbers of the cars that the party arrived in were P.I. 245 & I.F. 730 and the motor bike number was P.I. 935.

For your information I would point out that the above is not an isolated case by any means. Frequently is the Truce being broken and ignored with impunity by these ruffians and when so provocative and flagrant an insult is offered, as was the case today, the position becomes exceedingly delicate and acute.[10]

On 12 July, President de Valera and a party of senior Irish government ministers and prominent Sinn Fein members, including Arthur Griffith, Robert Barton, Count Plunkett, Austin Stack and Erskine Childers, crossed to London. Two days later de Valera met Lloyd George in a private meeting. It was an opportunity for the two men to get to know one another. They discussed the Welsh and Irish languages, Lloyd George remarking that there was no equivalent for the word "Republic" in the Welsh language. He asked whether one existed in Irish. De Valera revealed that there were two possible words, "Poblacht" and "Saorstat," though the linguists preferred "Saorstat." Lloyd George asked for the literal translation of "Saorstat." De Valera replied, "Free State." Lloyd George smiled, for what he had in mind was a Free State for Ireland within the British Empire, an illusion of independence.

On Wednesday, 20 July, Lloyd George's proposals for a treaty were passed to de Valera. It was a lengthy, very carefully worded document with some contentious issues, including an invitation for Ireland "to take her place in the great association of free nations over which

His Majesty reigns." While Ireland would be offered the autonomy of Dominion Home Rule, as enjoyed by Australia, Canada and South Africa, there were restrictions levied on Ireland that were not levied on the other dominion states. Then there was the thorny issue of Ulster, in that an Irish Free State must recognize "the existing powers and privileges of the Parliament of Northern Ireland, which cannot be abrogated except by their own consent." De Valera responded that he could not recommend such terms for acceptance by the Dail; in fact he would not even bring them back for consideration. This angered the British prime minister, who threatened an immediate resumption of hostilities. De Valera was not to be bullied though. He was not that sort of man. Lloyd George then softened his approach. He asked for a considered written reply, and this de Valera agreed to, provided that he be allowed to consult his team. De Valera and his colleagues returned to Ireland. He called a meeting of the Republican ministry where the proposals were discussed—and rejected. Lloyd George persuaded General Smuts, a South African, to write to de Valera, which he did, urging the Irish president to accept partition for a time and arguing that "I believe that it is in the interests of Ulster to come in and that the force of community of interests will, over a period of years, prove so great and compelling that Ulster will herself decide to join the Irish State."

Smuts was not aware that Ireland had not been offered full dominion status, or, being the honest man that he was, he would not have written. His letter and the Irish refusal were given to the press without de Valera's consent, framed in a way that showed Ireland to be intransigent. A series of letters passed between the two statesmen with demands and refusals.

On 6 August, in a goodwill gesture, all interned and imprisoned members of the Dail were released. On 16 August the Second Dail met in the Round Room of the Mansion House. The program for the session allowed two days of public meetings followed by a private session to which the reply of the Dail to Lloyd George would be submitted. Even as they discussed their reply, threats of renewing the war were being urged in the houses of Parliament and the more right-wing English press. This talk of renewed war was designed to intimidate the Irish into submission. Far from being intimidated, Ernie O'Malley, OC of the Second Southern Division, recalled that his men were actively training for a renewal of the war. Eoin Duffy, the deputy chief of staff, on a visit to the area, after intense questioning of O'Malley and his men even suggested that should negotiations reach deadlock, he, O'Malley, should attack British posts without giving the agreed seventy-two hours' warning. A number of officers were in favor, believing that the British would do exactly the same. Soon afterward, senior IRA officers were summoned to Dublin for discussions. Michael Collins, the director of intelligence, Richard Mulcahy, chief of staff, Eoin Duffy, deputy chief of staff, and Emmet Dalton, director of training, were present. O'Malley remarked that, curiously, Liam Lynch of the First Southern, Tom Maguire of the Second Western, Billy Pilkington of the Third, Michael Kilroy of the Fourth Western, and Frank Aiken of the Fourth Northern, the most active commanders, were not there. The officers submitted verbal reports of conditions in their areas, gave details of arms and ammunition and reported on training. Some seemed pessimistic of a resumption of war. These were officers from former inactive areas now re-formed into divisions. O'Malley was angered by their responses. The next day the officers met the president, Eamon de Valera, and Cathal Brugha, the minister of defense. The officers were questioned about the morale of the people and the support they could be expected to give in case of a renewal of hostilities. Their views evidently influenced further Irish negotiations, but why had the senior officers from more active areas not attended?

Despite threats of renewing the war, the Dail rejected the English terms. Lloyd George responded to the Irish rejection on 26 August with a letter to de Valera. A copy was sent to the press. It was a detailed letter, more for home consumption, with spurious historical references, pointing out the Irish president's intransigence. De Valera replied on 30 August, agreeing that progress should be made towards a basis upon which further negotiations could usefully proceed. More letters passed to and fro, neither side giving ground. On 29 September Lloyd George sent an invitation to a conference in London on 11 October. De Valera accepted. The basis for the discussions was to be "How the association of Ireland with the community of nations known as the British Empire may best be reconciled with Irish national aspirations."

Irish cabinet ministers urged de Valera to attend the conference, but he demurred, insisting that as head of state his place during the crisis was at home. The Irish delegation appointed consisted of Arthur Griffith, minister for foreign affairs, Michael Collins, minister for finance, Robert C. Barton, minister for economic affairs, Edmund J. Duggan and George Gavan Duffy. The secretaries to the delegation were Erskine Childers, Finian Lynch, Diarmuid O'Hegarty and John Chartres. Childers was appointed because of his intimate knowledge of British politics and mentality. The same could be said of John Chartres, who may well have been a British agent. The British delegates appointed were Lloyd George; Lord Birkenhead, the lord chancellor; Sir L. Worthington Evans, the secretary of state for war, Austen Chamberlain, leader of the House of Commons; Winston Churchill, secretary of state for the colonies; and Sir Hamar Greenwood, chief secretary for Ireland. Sir Gordon Hewart, the British attorney general, was appointed to act as a member of the conference to clarify constitutional questions. Lionel Curtis acted as one secretary; Thomas Jones, Lloyd George's secretary, acted as the other.

The Irish delegates arrived in London on 9 October. They were taken to their quarters at Cadogan Gardens and 22, Hans Place. On the morning of 11 October they drove to the official residence of the British prime minister at 10, Downing Street. Lloyd George, after introducing his colleagues, opened the debate, asking for a statement of the Irish attitude to the six conditions contained in the British offer. The problem of Ulster was discussed as an opening gambit, with Lloyd George promising that he would stand aside and act as a "benevolent neutral" while the Irish attempted to induce Ulster to unite with the rest of Ireland. The other conditions briefly touched upon that

The Irish peace delegation arrive at Euston Station, London. Arthur Griffith is pictured third from right.

opening morning included dominion status and Ireland's intention of becoming a neutral state, the retention of naval bases, and the relationship of the Crown and the Irish state. It was suggested, and accepted, that the appointment of subcommittees would help matters along. The conference became bogged down with a lack of resolve over concessions, though it appeared that the Irish were the ones expected to make the concessions. The conference was adjourned for three days.

When it reconvened the question of the Crown was raised, and the form of "Association" proposed. As leaders of the delegations, the prime minister and Winston Churchill expressed a wish to meet Arthur Griffith and Michael Collins in a private conference. The Irishmen agreed, and as Dorothy Macardle put it in her book, *The Irish Republic,* "from that moment the character of the negotiations changed." The Welsh wizard had split the delegates, who never sat together again in the conference room. Pressure now was upon Griffith and Collins. During the adjournment de Valera had urged them to push the Ulster question. The British were ready to discuss Ulster, if the position on the Crown was accepted. Griffith told them that he was not in a position to accept the position, but believed that some form of association might be considered if Ireland's unity was secured. Then there was the matter of facilities in Irish ports for the British naval and air forces and a free trade agreement. The reply came back from Ireland expressing a willingness to consider the granting of temporary coastal facilities under license from the Irish government to the British naval and air forces, on condition that there should be no armed occupation of Irish soil. This seemed acceptable to the British.

Fresh proposals for "Association" were raised once more, and the Irish delegates suggested a compromise wording, they hoped would be acceptable to the British. They agreed their willingness to recommend that the "elected Government of a free and undivided Ireland, secured in the absolute and unfettered possession of all legislative and executive authority, should, for the purposes of the association, recognize the Crown as symbol and accepted head of the combination of signatory states." The British agreed to consider the proposal.

As the days went by Lloyd George found himself coming under increasing pressure from the opposition in Parliament to bring negotiations with Ireland to an abrupt halt. He was faced with strong opposition from the Ulster Unionists and their Conservative supporters. Lloyd George gave assurance to the Ulster Unionists that he would take immediate steps to have the powers conferred by the 1920 Act on the Northern Government transferred to them with the minimum of delay. In private he succeeded in convincing them that the Irish delegates would accept inclusion in the Empire and allegiance to the Crown. It was his hope, that believing this, the Unionists would accept local autonomy under an all-Ireland Parliament.

On the evening of Sunday, 30 October, Griffith met with Lloyd George at Winston Churchill's house, where the prime minister explained to Griffith the difficulty facing him from the Unionists. He assured Griffith that if he would concede to "free partnership" within the British Empire, then he, Lloyd George, would fight for Irish unity. Realizing that the negotiations were breaking down Griffith agreed, believing that any blame for the failure of the talks would be attached to the Ulster Unionists. Lloyd George discussed the setting up of a Boundary Commission which would decide the area that would come under a subordinate Northern Ireland Parliament. The wishes of the Nationalist inhabitants would be taken into account, which would inevitably mean that two of the proposed six counties of

Northern Ireland, Fermanagh and Tyrone, as well as parts of other counties, would be ceded to the Free State, leaving an area so small that those people remaining under the jurisdiction of the Northern Parliament would have everything to gain, economically and socially, by uniting with the rest of Ireland. Griffith rather foolishly agreed to the temporary partition of Northern Ireland on this basis. A memorandum to this effect was drawn up by Thomas Jones, Lloyd George's secretary.

On 12 November Griffith met with Lloyd George, again in private, at Sir Philip Sassoon's house in Park Lane. Lloyd George explained he was having difficulties with the Unionists but had managed to get them on board by promising them if they became involved in an All-Ireland Parliament, he would ensure them the right of withdrawal within twelve months if they were so inclined. He told Griffith that they had agreed to this on the understanding that the proposal had come from the Southern delegation. Would Griffith now agree to this? The Irishman was in a dilemma, for to do so would imperil Ireland's unity and make partition possible on his say so. Nonetheless he agreed. Thomas Jones duly recorded what had been agreed. Though there was no verification, Griffith may very well have put his agreement in writing.

The Irish delegates had reconciled themselves to a temporary partition being offered to the Unionists in the North, but they consoled themselves that the findings of the Boundary Commission would convince the Northern government of the necessity of unity. On 22 November the Irish delegates submitted a new memorandum to the British, with the rider that it was submitted "upon the assumption that the essential unity of Ireland is maintained." The new proposal indicated that if the Northern Parliament accepted its position under the National Parliament it would be confirmed in its existing powers, and safeguards would be put in place to protect its special interests. The delegates could not, however, agree to any breakaway of any part of Ireland from the Irish State.

Turning to the question of sovereignty, the Irish reiterated their position as laid down in their terms of reference when appointed as delegates. They could not agree to being part of the British Empire, nor accept the king as being king of Ireland. In a break in the meeting Jones now approached Griffith telling him that Lloyd George was considering terminating the conference because of the Irish delegates' intransigence. Crown and Empire had to be dealt with. Griffith refused to compromise further, declaring that "External Association" must stand.

The next day the British made concessions regarding trade and defense. Meanwhile a sub-conference had met to discuss the position of the Crown. John Chartres was part of the Irish party. He put forward a compromise whereby Ireland would recognize the British Crown as the symbol and accepted head of the combination of Associated States, of which Ireland would be a member. On Monday the 28th a memorandum on external association was submitted by the Irish delegates to the British. The British responded by declaring that the Irish proposal was impossible. Griffith told them that the Irish delegates had no authority to deal with them on any other basis, than the exclusion of the Crown from Irish affairs. A compromise was offered — that the function of the Crown would be no more than in the other dominions — and the oath could be altered accordingly. It was decided that both sides should discuss the proposal amongst themselves and present their final proposals at a meeting to be held on 6 December.

James Craig, on behalf of the Northern Ireland Parliament, made known the position of the Northern Unionists once again to Lloyd George: they would not go into an All-

Ireland Parliament. The right-wing British press were becoming impatient for a solution and denounced the government for not dealing more firmly with Ireland. Senior British officers pressed for a military solution. All of this was leaked to the Irish delegates. Pressure was being brought to bear on the delegates for further compromise. In Ireland the Republican government prepared for a resumption of war.

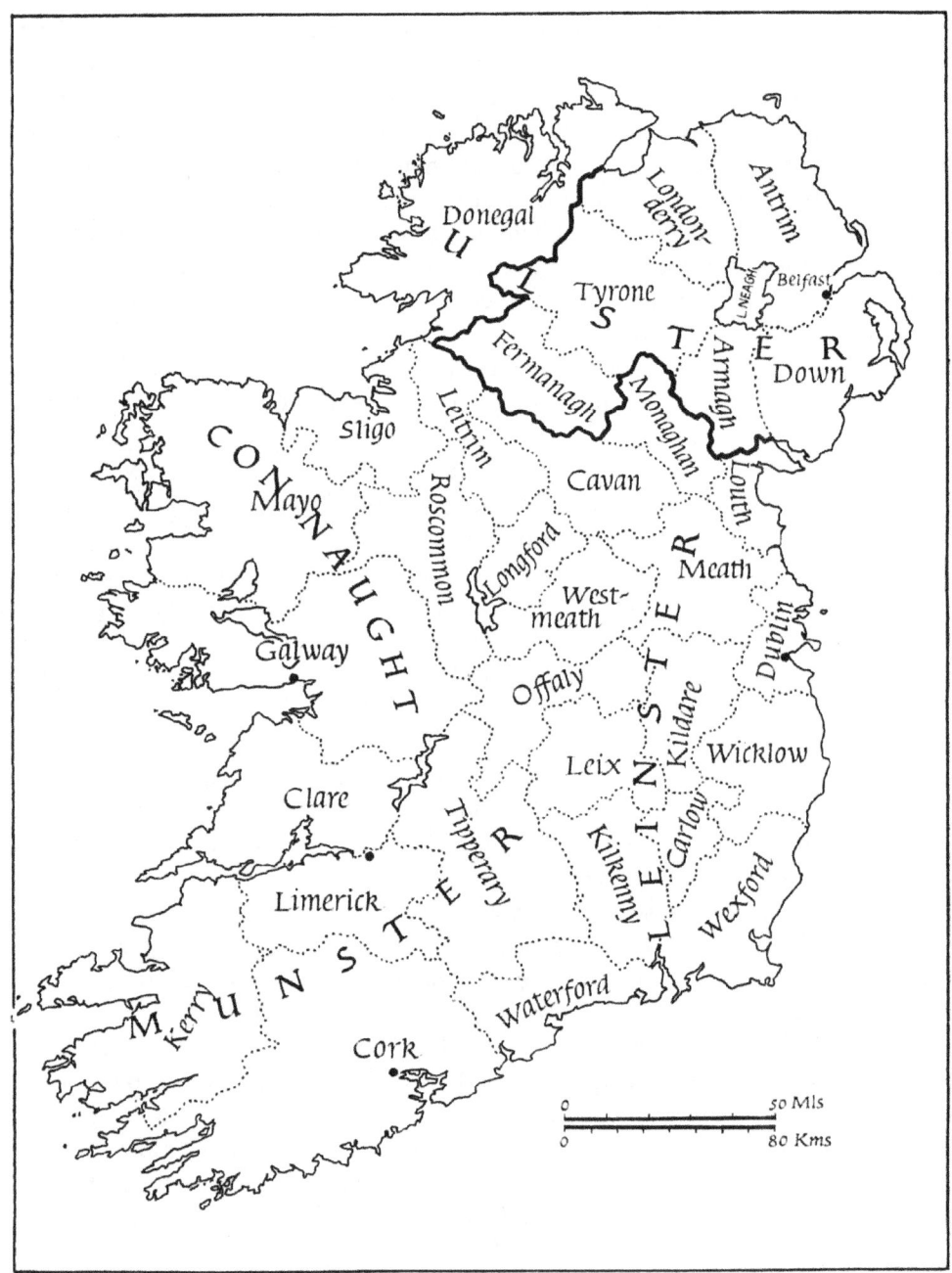

A map of Ireland showing the political divisions.

Griffith and Michael Collins were summoned to Downing Street where, through the night, they discussed amendments with the British delegation. The next day, leaving Collins, the Irish delegates led by Griffith traveled back to Ireland. That evening Collins, Gavin Duffy and Erskine Childers caught the later 8:45 P.M. train from Euston. They were seen off by Lloyd George's secretary, Thomas Jones, who handed them the latest revision to a proposed draft. The three men arrived in Dublin the next morning at 11:00 A.M. A cabinet meeting followed where the British proposals were discussed. Under the latest revision Ireland was to be offered the status of a British dominion and the title of Irish Free State. Under this arrangement the form of oath offered required read as follows: I ... solemnly swear to bear true faith and allegiance to the Constitution of the Irish Free State; to the Community of Nations known as the British Empire; and to the King as head of the State and of the Empire."

The northern government, according to the latest British offer, was, if it so wished, to be excluded from the Irish Free State. What was on offer was substantially what had been on offer originally. De Valera was opposed to the latest proposals. Griffith stressed that it was not worth breaking up the conference. Under the proposals Ireland would be recognized as a republic in all but name. Collins gave support to Griffith's proposal, and regarding the oath, while it would be twelve months before the oath would come into force the British could arrange a war in Ireland within a week. A number of the other members of the cabinet also urged the acceptance of the proposals. The cabinet was split. De Valera said that it was now for the Dail to decide. Meanwhile the delegates would return to London and see what concessions could be obtained. Until the Dail decided, Ireland's position should remain as already stated. They could not accept the oath and were prepared to face a continuation of the war rather than accept partition.

Back in London, members of the Irish delegation prepared draft counter-proposals. To their surprise both Collins and Griffith rejected any counterproposals. After some reluctance Griffith agreed to head the delegation when it renewed talks with the British. Collins refused to attend. When the British delegates read the proposals they adjourned the meeting to discuss them. They returned and announced that the new Irish proposals went back on previously accepted agreements. Griffith responded that Craig's refusal of an All-Ireland Parliament was a problem. The British responded that if the Irish delegates signed the treaty, the prime minister would call Parliament together immediately and pass an act to ratify it before Christmas. British troops would then withdraw from Ireland. Irish delegate Gavin Duffy began to speak of the difficulty of coming into the Empire, to which the British reacted angrily and left the room. Later that evening Thomas Jones spoke to Griffith in private, asking him if Collins would meet with Lloyd George alone the following morning before he went to see the king. Collins agreed to the private meeting. The discussion concerned the inclusion of the Six Counties. Lloyd George insisted that the boundary Committee would save Ireland from partition and asked for a resumption of talks that afternoon. Copies of the articles of agreement, with a few minor alterations, were put before the delegates. Lloyd George resumed the discussion by announcing that Griffith had already agreed to partition, referring to their two private evening meetings. Collins insisted that every proposal made by the Irish delegates had been based upon the unity of Ireland, and that Craig's acceptance had to be assured. But Craig had not given that assurance. After a break the delegates met again. The prime minister produced Griffith's written statement as drawn up by

Thomas Jones and accused Griffith of letting him down. The Irish delegates, Collins included, had no idea what was going on. The document was passed to them to read. Griffith declared that, while he was in agreement, his colleagues were in a different position. They were not party to his promise. He, however, would sign the treaty.

Lloyd George then said that he understood that Griffith spoke for the delegation. There could be no agreement unless every member of the delegation signed and promised to recommend the treaty. Any delegate refusing would have to take full responsibility for resumption of the war. The prime minister produced two envelopes, one of which would be sent to Sir James Craig, he announced. The first enclosed the articles of agreement, the second recounted their refusal, which would mean a resumption of war within three days. Griffith asked for an adjournment with the promise that he would give the decision of the Irish delegates at nine o'clock that evening, adding that he personally would sign. The specter of a renewed, more cruel war hung over the Irish deliberations at Hans Place. It was past midnight before the Irish delegates returned to Downing Street. At 2:15 A.M. on the morning of 6 December 1921, the articles of agreement for a treaty which partitioned Ireland were signed. Amidst much rancor, on 7 January 1922, the treaty was approved in the Dail by the narrowest of margins.

Lloyd George's threat to renew the war was an important factor in the Irish delegation's decision to agree to terms with the British. Between truce and treaty the Irish people experienced five months of peace, and few wanted to return to the terror they had known for the past two and a half years. The prime minister had threatened to send a further 150,000 soldiers into Ireland. Mulcahy, despite later claims, was not fully aware of the true state of the IRA out in the country. This being so, owing to a lack of accurate information, IRA GHQ briefed the Irish government that it could not sustain a renewal of the war. However, with the successful import of arms from Germany, the IRA, now 112,650 strong, though a large part of them were inexperienced, could have contained the British Army of occupation and produced a stalemate. Lloyd George's introduction of a further 150,000 British troops would have tipped the balance in favor of the British, but where would Lloyd George have raised such a number?

The number of soldiers on the army establishment, including Reserves and the Territorial Army as of 18 April 1921, was 341,000.[11] This figure was expected to fall during the year to about 235,000 with demobilization. *Whitaker's Almanac* for 1921 gives a breakdown of the displacement of British troops:

DISTRIBUTION OF BRITISH FORCES

Home	140,523
Colonies	12,290
Rhine and Plebiscitary Areas	14,200
Constantinople	4,300
Egypt	10,300
Palestine	4,500
Mesopotamia (Iraq)	14,300
Total	**200,413**

Not included in this list is the part-time Territorial Army and the Reserves (former soldiers who theoretically could be called up in an emergency). Also not included are the soldiers in Northern France and Flanders or the Colonial Troops, who numbered 62,600. Given this incomplete set of figures it is still difficult to see where Lloyd George could have obtained his proposed 150,000 troops. Field Marshall Sir Henry Wilson advocated bringing back the four battalions that formed the British Army of the Rhine. Such a move would have been opposed by the French and the Belgians. There were tensions in Germany and right-wing militia groups were springing up. Germany had stopped paying reparations, and the French sent in troops. The Rhineland was in turmoil, threatening to break away from Germany and form its own state. There were riots in Iran and Iraq, countries that had believed they would gain independence at the end of World War I but now found themselves under British control. With British oil companies exploiting the mineral wealth of these countries, Britain could not withdraw troops. Palestine, now a British Protectorate, was also in rebellion, and there were religious and anticolonial riots in India. In Britain there was a series of strikes and civil unrest, attributed to attempts by the Communists to foment revolution. British forces were stretched to fulfill international commitments and to hold together an empire tearing itself apart. Lloyd George's threat to send additional troops into Ireland seems to have been a bluff.

Michael Collins, commander in chief of the Irish Army.

The official British Army *Record of the Rebellion in Ireland 1920–1921* (vol. 2, part 3) openly admitted that by "September the situation had altered and the country was no longer controlled by the Crown forces. The British Government had permitted the IRA to usurp authority unchecked, and no action by the Crown forces against this procedure was encouraged. Gradually the country was passing under the control of Sinn Fein. The small detachments of Crown forces previously adequate to maintain control were now in danger themselves."[12]

Some two years after Britain's withdrawal from southern Ireland Major Percival, in preparation for a two part lecture on guerrilla warfare using Ireland as his model, wrote to his old friend, the Anglo-Irish officer (major, later field marshal), Bernard Montgomery, asking his advice. Montgomery wrote back on 14 October 1923:

> My Dear Percival,
> My own view is that to win a war of this sort you must be ruthless. Oliver Cromwell, or the Germans, would have settled it in a very short time. Nowadays public opinion precludes such methods, the nation would never allow it, and the

First stamp of the Irish Free State, overprinted on King George V's head.

politicians would lose their jobs if they sanctioned it. That being so I consider that Lloyd George was really right in what he did, if we had gone on we could probably have squashed the rebellion as a temporary measure, but it would have broken out again like an ulcer the moment we removed the troops. I think the rebels would have probably refused battles, and hidden away their arms etc. until we had gone. The only way therefore was to give them some form of self government, and let them squash the rebellion themselves, they are the only people who could really stamp it out, and they are still trying to do so and as far as one can tell they seem to be having a fair amount of success. I am not however in close touch with the situation over there, but it seems to me that they have had more success than we had. I arrived at the above conclusion after a great deal of thought on the subject. You probably will not agree.

Yours ever,
B.L. Montgomery[13]

It was an honest opinion, a statement of reality. Barely two months after the truce, yet before the treaty was signed, the Irish State was functioning quite openly, while the British looked on. Lloyd George did not have the troops to send, but he had so outmaneuvered the Irish delegates that the only outcome of the negotiations was a semi-independent Irish Free State within the British Empire. If the troops had been available and Britain had ignored world opinion, used extreme brutality towards the Irish people, Britain could have regained Ireland. But how long would it have been before the people rose up again? While it is true that British forces were withdrawn from the 26 counties that made up the Irish Free State, by analyzing the war it can be said that neither side truly won. Perhaps the real winner was the innate decency of the British people. People with influence in Britain stood up and declared that they were not prepared to countenance the brutality towards the Irish people carried out in their name. With outside pressure also being brought to bear, the British government, though it was totally opposed to giving Ireland independence, was forced to grant it a measure of independence. As Erskine Childers pointed out, £50 million was coming out of Ireland to fill British coffers, but the British government was spending £100million on administration, military and police. Ruling Ireland was no longer commercially viable. The Boundary Commission that it was thought would give so much of the North to the Free State, thus making it unviable, was not completed. Craig, the prime minister of Northern Ireland, refused to cooperate with it; and the passage of time while the civil war raged in the south meant that the border drawn up in 1920 remained. Trapped in a "Protestant State for a Protestant People," the Roman Catholic Nationalist population, feeling a keen sense of betrayal by the politicians in Dublin, continued to suffer state sponsored repression for another seventy years.

13

Conclusion: Prelude to Civil War

In the Irish general election of 24 May 1921, despite the expulsion of thousands of Catholics from Ulster, the Nationalists and Republicans were elected to nearly one quarter of the seats contested in the Northern Ireland Parliament—12 out of 52. Among those elected were de Valera for Down, Collins for Armagh, Eoin MacNeill for Derry, and Arthur Griffith, Sean Milroy, and Sean O'Mahony for Fermanagh and Tyrone.

The truce, which heralded an end to the killings in the rest of Ireland, triggered an anti–Roman Catholic pogrom in Ulster. The U.V.F., in their new guise as the Ulster Special Constabulary, carried out numerous assaults, intimidations and even murders in an attempt to drive the Catholics out. The pogrom lasted from the 10th until the 17th of July. In Belfast sixteen Catholics were murdered and 216 Catholic homes destroyed. Over the period from 29 August to 1 September there was further rioting in north and west Belfast, leaving twenty people dead. From the 21st to the 25th of November there were further killings in the city. Thirty people, most of them Catholics, lost their lives within four days. Seven Protestants were killed when the IRA bombed a tram taking them to work. The IRA had turned to sectarian killing in a bid to stop the killing of Catholics in random murders.

On 6 December 1921 the Anglo-Irish Treaty was signed. British forces in the south were moved to Northern Ireland in a bid to crush IRA resistance there. Previously, with the coming to power of the Northern Ireland government in March 1921, a special powers act was brought into being which imposed the death penalty for the unauthorized possession of arms. Trial by jury was suspended in political trials and coroners' inquests in similar cases were also abolished. Thirteen battalions were added to the Royal Ulster Constabulary and the Ulster Special Constabulary. Early in 1922 Sir Henry Wilson was appointed Military Advisor to the Northern Ireland government. Meanwhile, an unofficial system of state-sponsored terrorism was being waged against the Roman Catholic Nationalist population. In the two years ending June 1922, a total of 23,000 Roman Catholics had been driven out of Ulster in what today we know as "ethnic cleansing." Nearly 500 had been killed, and over 1,500 had been wounded or brutalized. Northern Ireland had been created as a "Protestant State for a Protestant people," and there was no place for Catholics.

In January 1922 Dan Hogan and a number of 5th Northern Division officers traveling through Northern Ireland to Derry were held up and searched by Special constables at Dromore, County Tyrone. Handguns were found in their possession and they were detained as prisoners. Their arrests and the intention to execute other Republicans held by the Northern government presented a challenge to Michael Collins. He had appealed for clemency, but this had been turned down. On 8 February 1922, IRA units headed by Commandant Sean

Changing the Guard: The National Army (on the right) taking over from the British garrison (marching away) at Richmond Barracks, 1922 (courtesy the National Library of Ireland).

MacEoin kidnapped forty-two Loyalists in Counties Tyrone and Fermanagh and took them over the border as hostages. They threatened to shoot the hostages in reprisal, and Hogan and his men were released and the condemned Derry men were reprieved. The Loyalist hostages were released unharmed.

On 11 February 1922, a substantial number of Ulster Special Constabulary traveling by train were stopped at Clones, County Monaghan, then in the agreed Free State part of Ulster. A firefight broke out in which four Special constables and an IRA officer were killed. The remaining Special constables then surrendered and were disarmed. Reprisals in the North were swift in response to the deaths of the constables. Violence erupted in Belfast that same day and lasted until 13 February. Thirty people were killed, six of whom were Catholic children who died when Loyalists in a sectarian attack, threw a hand grenade at them while they were playing in a schoolyard on Weaver Street. Forty other children were wounded in the attack. Sectarianism had reached a new low.

On 18 March 1922 a combination of the old RIC and the new Ulster Special Constabulary staged a raid upon the Belfast IRA headquarters at St. Mary's Hall. Their seizure of arms was secondary to their intelligence gains, including a list of names and addresses of IRA members in the city. While they planned a roundup of those listed, the IRA struck, the next day. A unit of twenty IRA men captured the RIC barracks at Pomeroy, County Tyrone, completely by surprise. They tied up the police and took away 75 rifles and large amounts of ammunition, including hand grenades. That evening another IRA unit overpowered the RIC garrison at Maghera and took their weapons too. Along the border of the two new Irish states, the IRA shot two policemen and a civilian who was with them. The civilian and one of the policemen died of their wounds. On 20 March an IRA column from Monaghan attacked the USC barracks just across the border in Aughnacloy. The Protestant response came on 26 March when uniformed members of the USC murdered six members of the Catholic McMahon family in their own home in Belfast. By the end of that month 60 people had been murdered in the city. The pattern was the same; the IRA would kill policemen, the Loyalists would respond by killing Catholics as a deterrent against further assaults.

On 28 March 1922, a column of 50 Volunteers attacked and captured the Belcoo Barracks in County Fermanagh after a three hour gun battle. Fifteen policemen were taken prisoner and marched over the border into the Free State, where they were held as prisoners in Athlone until 18 July as possible hostages against the killing of captured IRA men. Right at the end of the month, on the 31st of March, an IRA unit ambushed a Special Constabulary patrol in Newry, killing one policeman. In South Armagh, an IRA unit ambushed another USC patrol, killing two policemen and wounding five others.

On 1 April an RIC constable was shot dead by the IRA on the Old Lodge Road, Belfast. The Protestant reply was swift and brutal. Five Catholics who had nothing to do with the killing were murdered in Arnon Street, Belfast, by uniformed policemen. That month 30 people were murdered in Belfast. May was an equally bloody month in Ulster. On the 2nd of the month the IRA, reinforced by Volunteers from the South, launched a series of attacks on RIC barracks in Counties Londonderry and Tyrone. Six RIC and USC men were killed in the attacks. In reprisal for the death of their comrades the Ulster Special Constabulary murdered nine Catholics in two areas — two on 6 May and three on 11 May at Magherafelt and four on 19 May at Desertmartin.

A joint Free State/Republican military campaign, organized by the IRB, was launched against the North on 17 May 1922. Experienced officers from Liam Lynch's Southern Division, some twenty in number, were sent north to take charge and coordinate activity within Northern Ireland. The plan was to attack from inside and outside the Northern Ireland border on three fronts: Donegal in the west under Charlie Daly and Sean Lehane, and in Armagh and beyond its border in Louth in the Free State under Frank Aiken. There was concern that arms supplied by the British government to the Free Staters to subdue the Republicans (10,000 rifles, 2,000 revolvers, 5 machine guns and 80 tons of explosives) should not be used in the campaign for fear that they might be

Sectarian riots broke out in Belfast and Derry as more than 23,000 Roman Catholics were driven from their homes in a northern Irish state designated as a "Protestant State for a Protestant People."

captured, thus implicating the Free State government. As a consequence, even though civil war was very much a reality, the Irish government and the Southern division agreed to a swap of arms. Arrangements were made and British-supplied arms were sent down to Cork. In reply the First and Second Southern Divisions sent their arms north.

Between the 17th and 19th of May 1922, the combined IRA including units of the 5th Northern and 1st Midland divisions, carried out a series of attacks across Northern Ireland. The RIC barracks at Martinstown, Ballycastle, and Cushendall, County Antrim were all attacked, but none were captured. In Belfast commercial premises were targeted, and between 80 and 90 businesses were destroyed over the following two months. On 18 May a 20-strong unit of the IRA under Roger McCorley attacked Musgrave Street Barracks in Belfast. Two RIC men were wounded and a third fatally, 50 in the attack. A number of Volunteers were also wounded. McCorley's men succeeded in capturing some weapons in the process. Loyalists responded by boarding a tram in central Belfast and killing three workmen they identified as Catholics. In a tit-for-tat killing the next day, IRA men entered Garret's cooperage in Little Patrick Street, Belfast, and shot four Protestants, killing three of them. On 22 May, Unionist MP William Twaddell was assassinated by an IRA hit squad in Belfast city center. The Northern Ireland government responded by introducing internment without trial. The names and addresses of the Belfast IRA having been discovered in an earlier raid, up to 350 Republicans were rounded up. The internments gradually rose to 724 by 1924.

Gun battles broke out along the Falls road, Belfast, on 24 May, as Protestant paramilitaries opened fire on Catholics. The badly outnumbered survivors of the government roundup defended their coreligionists as best they could. Three people were killed and twenty injured in the attacks, which lasted several hours. On the 26th, the IRA launched its own sectarian attack in reprisal when it bombed the Protestant Model School in Divis Street, Belfast. As the school was not being used at the time, there were no casualties. But it was a warning as to what could happen.

Battle of Pettigo

The County Donegal Flying Column, assisted by men of the South Tyrone Column, comprising some 100 Volunteers, raided the town of Pettigo, just within the Northern Ireland border in County Fermanagh, on 28 May 1922. A fierce gun battle ensued between them and some 250 plus Ulster Special constables. A battalion of British soldiers and an artillery battery of six guns was brought up to drive the column off. Seven IRA men were killed, six wounded and four captured. One USC man was killed and one soldier. The British succeeded in cutting off another fifty Volunteers and taking them prisoner. The remainder of the column succeeded in recrossing the border to safety. A detailed account of what amounted to a full-scale battle is documented in the witness statements of John Travers and four other Volunteers who were there:

> [It] began on Saturday, May 27, 1922. On that day, a hundred Specials crossed Lough Erne in a pleasure steamer called *The Lady of the Lake,* towing a number of small boats, and landed above Belleek. They marched to Magherameena Castle, the residence of the late Reverend L. O'Kierans, then P[arish] P[riest] of Pettigo, and ordered [him] to leave immediately, which he did. A party of thirty I.R.A. Volunteers advanced down the railway line towards Magher-

ameena Castle. On their way there they were intercepted by a patrol of Specials, who engaged them and then retreated to Magherameena Castle, pursued by the I.R.A. Volunteers. The Specials then abandoned the castle for good, retreated to their boats on the Lough Erne and withdrew to the Buck Island in Lough Erne, where they were reinforced by another hundred Specials with medical attendants who treated their wounded. The Volunteers had suffered but a few minor injuries.

On Sunday 28 May, a number of [Specials in] Crossley tenders accompanied by an armored car left Enniskillen to assist their comrades at Magherameena Castle, but they were intercepted as they crossed into Donegal at Belleek by the I.R.A. Volunteers. After a short but sharp engagement , in which the driver of the armored car was killed [the occupants of the car] retreated, leaving the Crossleys and the armored car, which were taken possession of by the Volunteers.

That evening the I.R.A. Volunteers in Pettigo got information that large contingents of A and B Specials were converging on Pettigo. The Volunteers blocked the bridges at Pettigo between Donegal and Fermanagh and took up defensive positions. That night, a substantial contingent of Specials advanced from their headquarters at Clonally, County Fermanagh, to Pettigo. They then opened fire on Pettigo with a view to obtaining a right of way through it to their beleaguered men on the Buck Island in Lough Erne. The Volunteers returned fire and, after a two hour engagement, the Specials retreated to their convoy of Crossleys. Then on Sunday night, they attempted an outflanking movement with the aim of reaching their comrades on the Buck Island through Lowry. They would have to cross a narrow isthmus of Donegal territory, known as the Waterfoot, which juts out into Lough Erne between Letter and Lowry, both of which are situated in County Fermanagh. A section of the I.R.A. Volunteers were sent to this isthmus on Monday morning, 29th May, where they entrenched themselves and prevented the Specials from crossing it. From then until Thursday 1st June, the Specials contented themselves with sporadic firing into the tower from the surrounding countryside.

On 1st June, a number of lorry-loads of British soldiers. Followed by four Crossley-loads of Specials, advanced on the town of Pettigo. The Specials opened fire with rifles and machine guns on the I.R.A. Volunteer outposts stationed on Drumharrif hill and at Pettigo railway station. The I.R.A. returned fire, and then the British soldiers joined in with rifles and machine guns. This engagement lasted an hour and a half, during which a number of British soldiers were killed and others wounded. They then retreated. During Thursday and Friday nights, there was intensive sniping at Pettigo by Specials, who were now reinforced from Belfast. During Friday 2nd June and Saturday 3rd June, the British commandeered all the boats on Lough Erne and assembled them at Portonode. They used the boats to transport a Battalion of British soldiers across the Lough to Boa Island. The soldiers were marched through the island and from there were transported in the boats to [the village of] Letter, which is two miles below Pettigo.

In the meantime, another Battalion of British soldiers had advanced from Kesh to Lowry, with a view to joining the Battalion at Letter. This would entail them crossing the isthmus at the Waterfoot, but the I.R.A. Volunteer outpost, which had been in place since Monday, was determined to prevent this from happening. Throughout Saturday night, both Battalions of British soldiers made repeated attacks on the I.R.A. Volunteers at Waterfoot in the hope of dislodging them, but they failed to do so. During the intense fighting, a section of the I.R.A. Volunteers crept from Pettigo, a distance of a mile, to assist their comrades at the Waterfoot.

During the week, a large party of Specials had gone into Donegal through Letteran, which is five miles from Pettigo, and had terrorized the people. Among other things, they shot and seriously wounded two girls. Now on the night of Saturday 3rd June, the party of almost two hundred Specials tried to cross at Letteran from Fermanagh into Donegal, so as to attack Pettigo from the rear. A party of I.R.A. Volunteers, foreseeing their intentions, intercepted them there and, after a fierce engagement, put them to flight, burdened with their dead and wounded.

> The third engagement of this eventful night took place in Pettigo town. Two British Battalions tried in vain to take the town. Then on the morning of Sunday 4th June, a fleet of armored cars and infantry again attacked the town, but the driver of the leading armored [car] was shot dead through the head, and the car overturned and blocked the road. Fire from the Volunteers prevented the British from clearing the way for some time. At this stage, a battery of howitzers artillery was brought into action by the British. Under this artillery fire, the unit of Volunteers covering the bridge was forced to withdraw to new positions, and the British then cleared the obstructing car and the barricade at the bridge and advanced into the town.
>
> As this main thrust was being made, two other Columns of British troops, one which had been stationed at Letter and another from the right by Lough Derg road, attempted to join forces so as to encircle the town. Fire from the Volunteers on each flank kept them at bay and left the escape route open to the main body of the Volunteers, who withdrew to the hills and kept up a running fire until 5 P.M., when they retreated to Donegal town. The machine-gun post of about eight Volunteers, which manned Drumhariff Hill covering the approach to the town, held their position until their ammunition was exhausted, and then the post was surrounded and captured. Three of the gallant defenders, Patrick Flood of Pettigo, and Bernard McCanny and William Kearney of Drumquin, were killed at their post.
>
> While the fighting was taking place in Pettigo town, the post which manned the Waterfoot was heavily engaged by vastly superior numbers of British forces and was forced to surrender after two hours. Thus ended the Battle of Pettigo, a battle that is unique in the War of Independence in two respects: it is the only place where there was a stand-up fight with a defined battle line, and the only place in Ireland where artillery was used against the I.R.A.

On the last day of the month the IRA shot dead a Special constable in central Belfast and wounded another. That night Loyalists and Special constables in uniform murdered nine Catholics in retaliation. Before the night was out two Protestants were killed in reprisal. Throughout the month of May, 75 people were killed in Belfast.

In preparation for an enlarged campaign in Northern Ireland 500 officers from the 2nd and 3rd Northern divisions were sent south to the Curragh on an intensive two week training course. Civil war was now very close. On 7 June Lynch met Free State commandant Richard Mulcahy in a bid to prevent it. Compromises were made to avoid confrontation in the hope that the war in the north would bind both factions in the one struggle. The British became insistent that the Free State government should crack down on the Republicans. What drove a wedge between the two Irish parties was the publication of the Free State Constitution on 16 June 1922. It included an oath to the British monarchy and the acceptance of the Free State as being part of the British Empire. At a meeting of senior IRA military staff in Dublin, rancor led to members' walking out. Attitudes were hardening. Collins portrayed the Free State as a stepping-stone to an Irish republic. Those Republicans who had actually taken part in the war, those who had borne the brunt of the war, saw it as a betrayal of everything that they had fought for. A thirty-two county Irish Republic was within their grasp, they believed.

In Northern Ireland the tit-for-tat killings continued. On 17 June, in revenge for the murder of two Catholic men and the serious sexual assault of a Catholic woman, units of Frank Aiken's column attacked a number of Protestant-owned farms in Altnaveigh, South Armagh, killing six Protestant Loyalists. On 20 June three carters, identified as Catholics, were shot dead by Loyalists as the Carters made their way to work in Belfast.

On 22 June 1922, Field Marshal Sir Henry Wilson, military advisor to the Northern Ireland government, was assassinated in London in reprisal for attacks on Catholics in Ulster. The British government believed that the death was ordered by Republicans, who had established a barracks at the Four Courts in Dublin. General Macready, still in charge of the remaining British forces in Dublin, was ordered to attack the Four Courts the following day. To have done so would have united Free Staters and Republicans and would inevitably have led to the resumption of the Anglo-Irish war. Crisis talks followed between the British and the Free State governments. The British gave the Irish an ultimatum, demanding that the occupation of the Four Courts be ended or they would face the resumption of war. There was some division among the Republican military leaders, who believed that they should unite with the Free Staters in an all-out war against the north. The Irish government thought swift and decisive action against the Four Courts would bring an end to the threat of civil war. At 3:40 A.M. the provisional government issued an ultimatum to the Four Courts garrison to depart. This was refused, and an hour later an artillery assault on the Four Courts was begun. The Irish civil war had started, and with it died the hopes of continuing the war of liberation in the North.

Field Marshal Sir Henry Wilson was appointed military advisor to the new Northern Ireland government. His assassination in London in June 1922 precipitated the civil war in the South.

The struggle for Irish independence, though incomplete, was to have a lasting legacy. The overthrow of British rule in Ireland became the model for the overthrow of British imperialism in Africa, Asia and elsewhere, to the extent that within fifty years the British Empire ceased to exist. So too did the French Empire in North Africa and Indo-China. When accounts of the Irish struggle began to appear in print, they became required reading at the military colleges of Saint Cyr in France, Sandhurst in England and West Point in the United States. But if military colleges were studying the works of men like Tom Barry, so too were the emerging guerrilla leaders. Mao, Giap, Begin, Grivas and Castro all studied the Irish method of guerrilla warfare and applied it to their struggles. Meda Ryan, in her biography of Tom Barry, records that both Menachem Begin in Israel and Che Guevara (who had an Irish grandmother) in Cuba wrote to Barry asking for his assistance in training their young men and women. Post–World War II history has shown us that guerrilla armies can take on the mechanized might of the armies and air forces of the great nations — and defeat them. Vietnam is the prime example. Afghanistan, a complex war without a timetable as far as the guerrillas are concerned, might prove to be another example. Will the Afghan guerillas wear down the resistance of the United States and Great Britain, forcing them to retire? Only time will tell.

Appendix I

"Patrolling in the City"

This extract originally appeared in *Record of the Rebellion in Ireland 1920–1921*, vol. 4 (Dublin District Historical Record).

THE FOLLOWING SUGGESTIONS are issued as a guide to patrol work in towns in aid to the civil power.

1. Abandon all fixed beats.
2. Each battalion should divide its part of the city into patrol areas.
3. The objective is to gain control of the streets and break up resistance.
4. Examine each sector in the light of local circumstances and calculate the form and extent of likely resistance, then dispose forces accordingly.
5. In some parts patrols of eight or ten fully armed men will suffice. In others it may be necessary to employ up to the strength of platoon. Patrols should not move in mass [*sic*], but should work in groups, and in the case of strong patrols scouts should be used to watch the front, rear and flanks.
6. Where police are co-operating a preliminary conference between the officer in charge of the patrol and of the police concerned should be carried out.
7. As the situation develops the concentration of patrols in those parts where resistance continues should be considered.
8. Patrols should not remain out for fixed periods of time but should come back into barracks or billets for rest, so that the men may not be over-strained.
9. A strong line should be taken by searching persons, motor cars, other vehicles, and houses, so that it may become difficult for ill-disposed persons to carry arms.
10. Searching should be carried out by one or two men covered by the remainder. The searchers should carry out their work quietly and quickly. Altercations or arguments should be avoided.
11. Patrols should work in groups, moving on both sides of the street some distance apart, so as to avoid offering a concentrated target.
12. Loiterers, groups and collecting crowds should be promptly moved on or dispersed.
13. Patrols should frequently halt and take stock of the situation.
14. When fired on men should at once lie down and return the fire. All crowding together on the part of the patrol should be avoided.
15. As far as possible men on patrol should be lightly equipped and wear rubber soles, or the equivalent.
16. During the night halting near street lamps or other lights may prove fatal.
17. Foot patrols can be supported by motor lorry or motor car patrols; these should cover a wider beat, but keep in touch with foot patrols. At night the more mobile patrols can also search persons, motor cars and other vehicles.
18. All patrols should be prepared to lay in ambush.
19. In time of actual or expected disturbances, strong patrols should at once take over con-

trol. The confinement of troops and police to barracks on such occasion is damaging the moral[e] of men and discouraging to loyal elements.

20. When there is excitement owing to the assembly of large numbers of persons, the patrols of police and troops should be sent out on strength to assert the law. They should see that motor cars are complying with the motor regulations, search cars and strongly suppress any disorder.

21. Searching of motor cars should be thorough; the hood, seats, cushions, toolbox, spare wheels and bonnet should be carefully examined. Cases have occurred where revolvers and ammunition were found in the horsehair of cushions.

22. Houses of suspicion should receive continual attention especially by night. Such action is disconcerting to the inmates concerned.

23. When order has been restored patrols should not slacken. All breaches of ordinary law should be dealt with so that the public may realize that order has been restored.

Appendix II

Tom Kelleher's Account of Crossbarry

Witness Statement to the Bureau of Military History

"Crossbarry on the 19th March 1921, was a great fight.... It all happened by accident. There was a convoy of 300 British military moving from Kinsale to Bandon. We were lying in wait for them at Shipool near Inishannon, but they got to hear of it and decided to round us up instead. We knew nothing about that. We moved off into the town land of Skough and then northwards to Crossbarry. We were particularly careful now because we were out of contact with the enemy. I was instructed to move my section ahead of the main column through the fields and at 1.00 A.M. on the 19th we arrived at Crossbarry. We had no inkling that it was to be the morning of the biggest fight in the war. I'll start by giving you the names of all that led the action there. There was Tom Barry, the Brigade Commander, Liam Deasy, the Adjutant, Tadhg Sullivan, the Quartermaster, Dr. Con Lucey was Medical Officer. He was assisted by Eugene Callanan, then a student. There were seven sections, each of fourteen men inclusive, commanded by the following: Sean Hales, Ballinadee, a farmer, John Lordan, Newcestown, a farmer, one of the best men in Ireland, Mick Crowley, Kilbrittain, an engineer, Denis Lordan, Ballinhassig, myself on no. 5, Peter Kearney, Dunmanway, and Christy O'Connell, Castletownbere. Florence Begley, who played *The Men of the West* on the pipes inside Harold's farmyard, completed the complement of 104 men.

"Mick Crowley and I had no sleep. We were out looking for scouts, but a good job we were. We heard the lorries leaving Bandon at 2 A.M. They were coming and stopping, coming and stopping. Tom Barry was in bed, fully clothed and on the alert.... I said, 'you'd better get up and get up quickly. They are coming along very near ... we have a fight.... They are coming along, coming and stopping.'

"He got ready quick and we made down the road. We were after coming from Brinny Cross, halfway between Crossbarry and Bandon. We were locating our scouts, all local men, strung out in all directions. That was our mission, Mick Crowley and I. The lorries were still advancing so we had to hop back lively. They were traveling slowly however, because they were raiding as well. We could hear them distinctly coming in to Kilpatrick. The night was very calm. A strange thing happened then. They arrested a man there by the name of White. He was a prisoner. I would say, in the second lorry. There were 24 lorries in the sweep. I had a scout counting them. You had nine, seven, five and three. Of the first convoy, the nine, only three got into the fight. A soldier in the fourth lorry spotted a man with a rifle at a window, and the rest stopped. Tom Barry used [to] always criticize that man, but I clap him on the back because if the nine lorries got in, the occupants of the nine lorries would make a fight and we had only three sections there to face them. We had Sean Hales, John Lordan and Mick Crowley. Three times fourteen would be 42; begod 42 men could never fight nine lorries. That was my opinion; Barry was of a different opinion, but I had mine.

"The man White, who was captured in Kilpatrick, jumped out of the lorry as soon as it entered the ambush, got inside a gate, and there, a rifle was put into his hand right away. He stayed with us after. Con McCarthy, a butcher of Bandon, a great fighter was also with me. We were covering the back. Con was very anxious to know how things were going, and he forced me hard to have a look. I knew it was wrong to go down any road because I had the responsibility of my section. Anyway we rushed down very quickly and we asked Mick Crowley who was in charge of No. 3 Section.

"We saw the driver of a lorry with his two hands on the wheel, and the poor man, a British fellow, was dead. I put up the rifle to fire at him because I thought he was alive.

"We had however dealt with the column trying to encircle us from the west. There were still about 600 men in the lorries approaching from Cork, from the north-east. That is the group that came upon and killed Charlie Hurley a few hours before. There was a third facing us to the south along the Cork/Bandon railway line—not there now. They were all under the command of Major Percival who, as General Percival, surrendered Singapore to the Japanese without firing a shot in 1942. He divided his men at O'Brien's Cross, a mile to the north, and he lined the east and he lined the south, consequently making it half a square. Barry had said to me, 'you will have the hardest fight this day,' and he was right.

"We were attacked from the north. I was just after sending two scouts towards Driscoll's house which would be in line with O'Brien's Cross. They were just north of Driscoll's house, in a boreen, when they heard them coming on at the double. They ran back and they took refuge in a shed where they pretended to turn potatoes, the bloody rascals. They had a right to send word back to *mise*,* but they did not. By some good luck at that moment I saw them myself. They were in a remarkable formation. They were in bunches together, twenty five yards apart, lovely targets for us. They opened up a volley of fire. The field we were in was ploughed, and Jim Beasley, who was a very *sleachtach*† farmer, was after digging a furrow, so that it made a cover for us. We slipped into it. Prior to that I had been at the northern end with my men behind me. Connie O'Leary was in the far half of the field facing east; he was in charge of the other half section. I fell back to my section, because if they took fright I would be without a command. Fire had been opened on us, as I say. Bob Hales was in front of me and this fellow who was shot in the ankle was just behind my back. In other words, and you can take it this way, they were running away from the firing. I got them over the fence and I said: 'Look here I have orders to shoot the first man that runs.' And then I said, 'we have two men in the castle'—t'was a heap of stones, no more—'and we have got to help them.' the two, Den Mehigan and Con Lehane, had been placed there specially to attract the enemy round it. They were exposed before but we had cover now going back helping out the two in the castle because there was a fence on our right. When we got up across from the castle, we were in a grand position without the British

---

*Mise—*myself.*
†Sleachtach—*tidy or neat*

knowing it. Our two men in the castle, once they had the enemy in line, opened up and shot two officers. Grand job. They were surrounding the castle, and to look at them, they were like bees in a hive. You could not miss them. I was reinforced then by Spud Murphy. I said to my squad: 'Get ready now, I am going to dish out the orders. Section! Ready! Volley fire!' I repeated that order, and then I said 'rapid fire. Spud,' I said 'I'm going flanking.' I wanted to get out in the direction of the cottage before Percival could complete his encirclement. We had a bit of a difference. 'You are in charge,' said Spud, 'and you should stay.' 'You are quite right,' I said, 'I am in charge. I agree with you. But when I am in charge you must do as you are told, and you will stay here.' was no good for anything else, being already wounded in one hand. 'And you can't use a rifle with one hand.'

"I took two men up over a fence to the right where there was a big long fence about 300 yards long. Jim Beasley had it all cut and drawn away, as I said he was a very *sleachtach* farmer. Up we went and I decided we would stay here. What did the British do? They came at the northern side of the fence. And if they came over the fence they could enfilade Spud and his men. Do you know what was the beating of them? They were going according to plan. That is my guess. Every movement was according to plan. If they had not gone according to plan but had moved over the fence we would have been destroyed. Anyway I had my two men. And I am sorry to say that they were not two good men. The man on the left I don't think he fired a shot. I had ten in my magazine and one up the breech, that was eleven. I fired eleven and eleven fell. I reloaded with five and five fell. I reloaded again and five more fell. That was twenty one. That is gospel truth. Of course some had thrown themselves down, and some were only wounded. I looked left for my own man on the left. He was gone, and I have not seen him since. And that is 59 years ago.

"The man on my right had his rifle pointed away at the horizon, and he pulling away, wasting ammunition. I stood back and I gave him a toe up the tail. 'Can't you fire?' I said, and he did. That fellow did very good after. The next thing I got a tap on my left shoulder. Who is it, I thought; is it a British officer about to kill me? I wheeled around and who was there but Barry. 'I thought you were wiped out,' said he. 'I am not wiped out. When are we going for their guns?' They were all lying down there. Now you could not prove they were dead. Maybe they were not. But they were not able to get up. If they were able to get up they'd have got up, and hopped it. They were laid out there the twenty one of them. 'No, no,' said Tom. 'We are not going for their guns. We have more guns than we can carry including a machine gun.' 'Splendid,' says I; I was mad for guns. 'Let us take the lot!' 'No,' he said, 'we haven't time.' And I didn't realize time at all, but he did. He had a weather eye cocked for the inevitable reaction from the British.

"That was a great thing about Tom Barry. He was more experienced than we were. He knew the time to pull out. We'd fight away like billeo, but that wouldn't win the fight in the finish. 'Where is your section?' says he. 'I'll get them,' but he wouldn't let me move an inch. He sent a man on my left down a field and a half to get them. And the 21 dead men were lying there all the time. And we left them there too, rifles and all."

APPENDIX III

Analysis of Crossbarry by Tom Barry

In her biography of Tom Barry, *Tom Barry, IRA Freedom Fighter*, author Meda Ryan includes an analysis of the action at Crossbarry drawn up by Barry (394–6):

British Mistakes at Crossbarry

1. The OC of the Essex made a stupid error of having his lorries travel in advance of his ground forces, thus allowing three or four lorries to be attacked by the IRA. Had his ground forces met O'Connell's flankers before the lorries were attacked, a very serious situation would have arisen; several hundred British could have been deployed on our right flank to attack while the Kinsale, Cork and Ballincollig troops, close by, were closing in from the south, east and north-east.

2. Whoever was in charge of the Essex cannot have made any attempt to rally or control his troops. I, and many others, saw them race away from at least seven or eight lorries beyond those attacked and outside our range of fire, and make off cross-country to the south. The Essex were no problem after the first five minutes; perhaps, too, they had memories of a few hammerings and of our contempt for them as fighters.

3. The efforts of the British from the south, east and north-east appeared to have been completely uncoordinated. Their north-eastern units, estimated at 200, made an attempt to narrowly encircle Kelleher and Spud, which was quickly countered. Instead of this, any OC worthy of the rank would have sent half his troops northward, direct from their positions, for a quarter of a mile, within instructions to turn west there, and extend westward to cut off any escape to the north.

4. All the British seemed to have been mesmerized by the IRA going over to the offensive, thus destroying the plans they had for a complete encirclement of the Brigade Flying Column and its destruction when one of our lines was smashed.

Mistakes of the Flying Column at Crossbarry

1. The man who exposed our presence lost us at least three more lorries.

2. Our hardest-hit section commanded by Denis Lordan was in a bad position. The cover was bad, but when I first saw it at daybreak, it was too late to seek another to command the road from Crossbarry Cross, as the British from the west were already on us.

Our Advantages

1. The far superior qualities of our troops as fighting men and the excellence of the officers and their section commanders who could out-think and out-fight any of the enemy commanders. I did not see one man over-excited during the day.

2. Our sections were properly deployed to counter encirclement, as events proved.

3. Our luck in getting in the first half dozen blows.

4. When the IRA commenced its retirement in column of sections in extended order, they moved as if on a parade ground.

Chapter Notes

Introduction

1. Erskine Childers, *Framework of Home Rule* (Dublin: Talbot Press, 1911), 89.
2. Dorothy Macardle, *The Irish Republic* (London: Corgi, 1968), 85.
3. To the best of its ability British intelligence in Ireland compiled a list of armaments held by the Irish Volunteers:

	10 Dec. 1914	31 Dec. 1915	29 Feb. 1916	31 Mar. 1916
Lee-Enfields and other recent English patterns	1,010	1,231	1,256	1,280
Mauser & Mannlicher	242	197	198	199
Italian	97	177	210	213
Others	99	144	155	194
Total rifles	1,448	1,749	1,819	1,886
Total shotguns*		1,063	1,322	1,654
Total revolvers and pistols*		709	847	925
Total Arms*		3,521	3,988	4,465

Source: Parliamentary Papers, 1916: Cmd 8279.
*The survey for 10th of Dec. 1914, was incomplete and provided no figures for these types of arms

4. The Citizen Army crossed the sectarian divide. A number of its soldiers were Protestant. One of Connolly's daughters, Aghna, married Archie Heron, a Protestant radical from Portadown. David Boyd, another Protestant radical, from Belfast, was also very influential in the Trade Union movement.

Chapter 1

1. *Sinn Fein*, 8 August 1914.
2. *Workers' Republic*, 6 November 1915.
3. Joe Good, *Enchanted by Dreams* (Dingle, Ireland: Brandon), 17–18.
4. Dorothy Macardle, *The Irish Republic* (London: Corgi, 1968), 143.
5. In 1915 Weissbach was a torpedo officer aboard the U-20 that sank the passenger liner *Lusitania* off the Old Head of Kinsale.
6. Macardle, *The Irish Republic*, 161.
7. Hansard, *1920–21*, British Government, 1916.
8. *Proletary*, 11 September 1906.
9. R.M. Fox, *History of the Irish Citizen Army* (Dublin: James Duffy, 1943), 172.

Chapter 2

1. Sean O'Luing, *I Die in a Good Cause: A Study of Thomas Ashe* (Tralee, Ireland: Anvil, 1970), 189.
2. Some Sinn Fein members had successfully been elected to more than one seat. Eoin MacNeill had been elected both in Derry City and for the National University of Ireland. Eamon de Valera had been elected to East Clare and East Mayo, and Liam Mellows was elected to east Galway and North Meath.
3. Maire Comerford, *The First Dail* (Dublin: Joe Clarke, 1969), 51.
4. Frank O'Connor, *An Only Child* (London: Penguin, 2005), 41.
5. *Irish Times*, 15 July 1920.

Chapter 3

1. Commandant Andy McDonnell, interviewed by Sean White for the *Irish Press*, April 1964.
2. Sean O'Faolain, *Vive Moi* (London: Frank Hart Davis, 1965).
3. An assassination squad under Cathal Brugha had been assembled to kill members of the British cabinet if they were to implement the Irish Conscription Act. The squad consisted of Joe Good, a London-born Irishman, Bill Whelan, Sammy Reilly, Matt Furlong, Martin Gleeson, Peter Murtagh, James Mooney, James McNamara, and an unnamed Irishman. The men found lodgings in London. Brugha and two other members of the squad, fully armed, tested British security by actually entering the House of Commons and from the Strangers' Gallery watching the debates. In the end the assassinations were called off in August 1918, and the operatives returned to Ireland.
4. PRO, War Office Papers, WO 35, 180 part 1.
5. "Periscope," "The Last Days of Dublin Castle," *Blackwood's*, August 1922.

6. Tom Barry, *Guerilla Days in Ireland* (Dublin: Irish Press, 1949), 47.
7. Ibid., 19–20.
8. Sean Moylan, *Sean Moylan, In His Own Words* (Cork: Aubane Historical Society, 2005), 45–46.
9. Ernie O'Malley, *On Another Man's Wound* (Dublin: Anvil, 1979), 79.
10. Good, *Enchanted by Dreams,* 164–165.
11. O'Malley, *In His Own Words,* 105.
12. Barry, *Guerilla Days,* 21–22.
13. Ibid., 133.
14. Liam Deasy, *Towards Ireland Free* (Cork: Mercier, 1973), 30–31.
15. Barry, *Guerilla Days,* 25–26.

Chapter 4

1. Lord Riddell, *War Diary, 1914–1918* (London: Ivor Nicholson & Watson), 130.

Chapter 5

1. "Periscope," "The Last Days of Dublin Castle,"169.
2. Jim Slattery, WS445, Bureau of Military History Statements, National Archives, Dublin.
3. "Periscope," "The Last Days of Dublin Castle," 166–7.
4. Dan Breen, *My Fight for Irish Freedom* (Tralee, Ireland: Anvil, 1964), 138–9.
5. William Sheehan, *British Voices: From the Irish War of Independence 1918–1921* (Cork: Collins, 2007), 88.
6. There was some controversy over the shooting of Captain McCormack. Nominally he was a veterinary corps officer newly arrived from Egypt, though why he was in Dublin and staying at an expensive hotel has never been explained. It has been suggested that he had expertise in germ warfare. He was not on the original list drawn up by Collins. His name appears to have been added by the intelligence officer of the Dublin Brigade.
7. Sheehan, *British Voices,* 89.
8. "Periscope" (may well be Captain J.L. Hardy, given that their literary styles are so similar) took a different slant on Bloody Sunday in an article, "The Last Days of Dublin Castle," which appeared in *Blackwood's* magazine of August 1922, (164–5):

"Sinn Fein was making desperate efforts ... and on 14th November 1920 it achieved what it may have regarded as its master-stroke, but what no honest Irishman can ever think of but with a sense of shame and disgust. About 9 o'clock on a Sunday morning, when the streets were filled with those returning from mass—the symbol of a Christ who gave his life to save the souls of men—some dozen houses in the best residential parts of Dublin were entered by bodies of armed men, and there were murdered, many before the eyes of their wives, fourteen men, most of them military officers, others auxiliaries, one or two apparently in error. Any one who was in the streets of Dublin that day can never forget the feeling of intense Expectancy that brooded everywhere, as though people were waiting for the Destroying Angel to strike once in wrath, and Dublin would be one with the ruins of Ninevah and Tyre." The statement is unbelievable in its breathtaking self-righteous hypocrisy. "Periscope," if he is indeed Hardy, would have been fully aware of the torture and murder of Republican prisoners that took place in the Castle at the hands of these assassinated intelligence agents, the "Cairo Gang." These were the men who were responsible for the targeted murders of seventeen Irishmen in the previous month. Oddly, "Periscope" makes no mention of the murder of twelve men and women and the wounding of sixty others in revenge by the Black and Tans that afternoon at Croke Park.

9. Barry, *Guerilla Days,* 178.
10. (Captain) R.D. Jeune, quoted in *British Voices,* 86.
11. Uinseann MacEoin, ed., *Survivors* (Dublin: Argenta 1987), 317.
12. O'Malley, *On Another Man's Wound,* 333–4.
13. This was a claim made by the revisionist historian Peter Hart. It is a claim proved to be palpably false by historian Meda Ryan in her biography, *Tom Barry: IRA Freedom Fighter.* Hart was somewhat misleading in what he quoted and, more important, in what he did not quote.

Chapter 6

1. MacEoin, ed., *Survivors,* 314.
2. "Periscope," "The Last Days of Dublin Castle," 142, 165–6.
3. Sheehan, "The Diary of Private J.P. Swindlehurst," in *British Voices,* 17.
4. Ibid., 21.
5. "Periscope," "The Last Days of Dublin Castle," 163.
6. McEoin, ed., *Survivors,* 314.
7. McEoin, ed., *Survivors,* 425.
8. The British version of the customs house debacle appears in the unpublished "Records of the Rebellion in Ireland 1920–21," vol. 4, part 3 (PRO Kew): "Destruction of Custom House (25 May)—On 25th May the destruction of the Custom House by the active members of the 2nd Bn. Dublin brigade took place. On 25th May at about 13.10 hours, information was received from DMP that the Custom House had been rushed by approximately 100 civilians. An armored car was at once dispatched, followed by 'F' Company, Auxiliary Division, RIC with another armored car. The leading armored car arrived about 13.25, endeavored to prevent the raiders escaping from the Custom House, and succeeding in covering the southern side. 'F' Company, on arrival, made for the northern side, and were heavily fired on and bombed on reaching the railway bridge,

suffering four casualties. About a dozen raiders were seen to run from the Custom House, and were fired on and believed to be hit, but definite report is not to hand. About four minutes later 'Q' Company, Auxiliary, RIC (from North Wall), who had also been warned, arrived and covered the eastern side of the Custom House. By this time the Custom House was surrounded but in flames. The Auxiliaries entered the front door of the Custom House and found many revolvers and petrol tins. Some of these were taken out, but owing to the heat of the flames the Auxiliaries were compelled to withdraw. A large number of civilians came out of the Custom House when it burst into flames, with their hands up; these were marshaled by the Auxiliaries and head Custom officials were asked to identify their own employees, who were not detained. On completion of identification, about 70 civilians remained. These 70 civilians were arrested. Meanwhile, orders had been issued for troops to move from the Royal barracks and the Castle, those from the Royal Barracks (Wiltshire Regiment) being in charge of a field officer, who had orders to take over command of the whole operation. This was done, and arrangements were made to withdraw the Auxiliaries and piquet the area with troops. The fire brigade arrived and were assisted in their endeavors to extinguish the fire, but the Custom House could not be saved. Intermittent explosions continued, evidently from ammunition and bombs left in place by raiders. The casualties that can be definitely reported are 7 civilians killed, 4 Auxiliaries wounded, and 10 civilians wounded, one of whom was known to be a raider. The wounded civilians other than the raider were not detained in King George V Hospital. Over 100 civilians were ultimately arrested in this affair. They composed the whole of the active portion of 2nd Bn. Dublin Brigade, IRA."

9. Tim Pat Coogan, *Michael Collins: A Biography* (London: Hutchinson, 1990), 70.

Chapter 7

1. Lil Conlon, *Cumann na mBan and the Women of Ireland* (Kilkenny: Kilkenny People, 1969), 299–300.
2. (Countess) Constance Markiewicz, Prison Letter, 1934, quoted in *Dublin 1916*, ed. Roger McHugh (Dublin: Arlington, 1966), 122.
3. R.M. Fox in his book, *The History of the Irish Citizen Army,* lists by garrison the women soldiers of the ICA who took part in the Rising: **GPO:** Winifred Carney; **Stephen's Green:** Mary Devereux, Nellie Gifford, Margaret Ryan, Bridget Gough, Sergeant Madeline ffrench-Mullen, Rosie Hackett, Mrs. Joyce, Chris Caffrey, Annie Kelly, Mary Hyland, Lilly Kempson, Lieutenant Constance Markiewicz (second in command), Mrs. Norgrove, Kathleen Seerey, Margaret Skinnider (wounded in action); **City Hall:** Mrs. Connolly Barrett, Bridget Brady, Mollie O'Reilly, Bridget Davis, Annie Norgrove, Bessie Lynch, Dr. Kathleen Lynn (Chief Medical Officer, ICA), Helena Moloney, Jennie Shanahan; **Imperial Hotel:** Martha Walsh.

4. Markiewicz, 124–5.
5. Conlon, *Cumann na mBan,* 25.
6. Prison Letters, 125.

Chapter 8

1. Crozier, 91.
2. O'Malley, *On Another Man's Wound,* 172.
3. Ibid., 203.

Chapter 9

1. O'Malley, *On Another Man's Wound,* 338–9.
2. Ibid., 332.
3. Good, *Enchanted by Dreams,* 162–3.
4. Interview with Tom Kelleher in *Survivors,* ed. MacEoin, 217–18.
5. Barry, *Guerilla Days,* 46.
6. Revisionist historian Peter Hart, a Canadian, has questioned Barry's account of the ambush at Kilmichael, alleging that it is "riddled with lies and evasions." He claims that the false surrender did not take place and that Barry's claim that it did was to mask the fact that the Volunteers murdered the wounded. Hart's version is based on the discovery of an account, "A Rebel Commandant's Report," discovered in the Imperial War Museum. The report does not actually bear Barry's name, which is extraordinary if he was reporting to GHQ. The account is also factually inaccurate. In Barry's book, *Guerilla Days in Ireland,* he recounts that at the end of the ambush there were two dead Volunteers and one badly wounded. In the "Report" this becomes one man dead and two wounded. Barry, who actually names the three casualties, would not have made such a mistake. Brian Murphy, author of *The Origins and Organisation of British Propaganda in Ireland,* argues convincingly that the "Report" is a forgery that was never used because of its inaccuracies but was filed away, for later discovery. Hart also alleges that on 19 November 1989 he interviewed two Volunteers who took part in the ambush, one a rifleman and the other a scout. The first of these witnesses, the rifleman, according to Hart, denied that the false surrender had taken place. The other claimed that he was unaware of it. These supposed interviews by Hart were clearly impossible, for all the scouts were dead by 1971 and the last rifleman, Ned Young, had died six days before the supposed interview. Meda Ryan, researching her own book on Tom Barry, was informed by Young's family that the alleged interview had not taken place. Controversially, Hart alleges that the Cork IRA embarked on a campaign of ethnic cleansing of the Protestant/Loyalist community in the county. This hypothesis does not stand up to ex-

amination. Of the 30 civilians executed as spies by the IRA in West Cork, only 5 were Protestants. Hart, it would appear, was highly selective in his quotes, taking material out of context and thus giving it a meaning never intended. His revisionism has produced a distortion of history to fit his thesis. For more on this subject see Meda Ryan, *Tom Barry: IRA Freedom Fighter,* Brian Murphy, *The Origins and Organisation of British Propaganda in Ireland,* and John Borgonovo, *Spies, Informers and the Anti-Sinn Fein Society.*

7. O'Donaghue Papers, National Library of Ireland, quoted in Michael Hopkinson, *The Irish War of Independence* (Dublin: Gill & Macmillan, 2004), 83.

8. Deasy, *Towards Ireland Free,* 188–9.

9. Good, *Guerilla Days,* 160.

10. Ernie O'Malley, *Raids and Rallies* (Dublin: Anvil, 1982), 88–9.

11. Barry, *Guerilla Days,* 73.

12. Public Record Office, Kew, WO 35/88B.

13. For Tom Kelleher's account of the fight at Crossbarry see Appendix II.

14. PRO (WO35/88B).

15. Sheehan, *British Voices,* 224–5.

16. Interview with Tom Maguire, Commandant General, IRA, in *Survivors,* ed. MacEoin, 283.

Chapter 10

1. The lack of communication between the brigades in the country and GHQ in Dublin led Mulcahy to brief the Irish delegates at the treaty conference that the IRA could not sustain the war. Piaras Beaslai, in his book, *Michael Collins and the Making of a New Ireland,* put forward the following theory: "It was about this time [the spring of 1921] that Liam Lynch and some other Southern IRA Officers went on a deputation to GHQ in Dublin to state that owing to the shortage of arms and ammunition and enemy pressure that they were unable to continue the fight." Tom Barry was quite vehement in denying this calumny. No deputation of southern officers had ever visited GHQ, much less at the date quoted, 12 May 1921. Lynch never left the divisional area between 1 April and the time of the truce in July 1921. Beaslai wrote his book after the end of the civil war, and it appears as if he is looking for justification in Ireland to accepting a Free State rather than fighting for a Republic by blaming Lynch, who was then dead, having been killed by Free Staters.

2. O'Malley, *The Singing Flame* (Dublin: Anvil, 1978), 13.

3. Charlie McGuinness was from Derry. His father was a former sea captain, and he himself was an officer in the North German Lloyd's. He spoke fluent German.

4. MacEoin, ed., *Survivors,* 114.

5. Ibid, 141.

6. Sheehan, *British Voices,* 234.

7. Hopkinson, *The Irish War of Independence,* 95.

8. MacEoin, ed., *Survivors,* 266.

9. Sheehan, *British Voices,* 40.

10. PRO Kew, CO/904/52.

11. Parliamentary Report XX 195, 1921. Number of Men on the Establishment of the Army.

12. Sheehan, *British Voices,* 71.

13. Montgomery Papers, Imperial War Museum (British Voices p. 145).

Bibliography

Primary Sources

Public Record Office, London
PRO Record of the Rebellion in Ireland, 1920–1921.
PRO HO 184/50-1, Royal Irish Constabulary, Auxiliary Division Register.
PRO WO 35.180. War Office Papers.

Birmingham (England) University
Austen Chamberlain Papers.

Bureau of Military History, Dublin
Witness Statements, 1947–1957.

University College Dublin Archive
Richard Mulcahy Papers.
Ernie O'Malley Papers and Notebooks.

British Government Publications

Hansard, 1920–21

Parliamentary Papers
Army Estimates, 1921 XX.
Royal Commission on the Rebellion in Ireland, 1916 (Cmd. 8279 and Cmd. 8311), 1916.
Royal Commission on the Arrest and Subsequent Treatment of Francis Sheehy.
Mr. Thomas Dickson Skeffington and Mr. Patrick James McIntyre (Cmd. 8376), 1916.
Outrages (Ireland) (Cmd. 63 and Cmd. 709), 1920.
Outrages (Ireland), Return Showing the Number of Serious Outrages (Cmd. 1165), 1921.
Parliamentary Report XX, 1921.
Documents Relative to the Sinn Fein Movement (Cmd. 1108), 1921.
Intercourse between Bolshevism and Sinn Fein (Cmd. 1326), 1921.

Irish Government Publications

Dail Eireann: Minutes of Proceedings of the First Parliament of the Irish Republic, 1919–1921.
Arrangements Governing the Cessation of Active Operations in Ireland (Cmd 1534 XIX), 1921.

Books

Ambrose, Joe. *Sean Treacy and the Tan War*. Cork: Mercier, 2007.
Barry, Tom, *Guerilla Days in Ireland*. Dublin: Irish Press, 1949.
Bennett, Richard. *The Black and Tans*. Stroud, UK: Spellmount, 2007.
Breen, Dan. *My Fight for Irish Freedom*. Tralee, Ireland: Anvil, 1964.
Buckley, Donal. *The Battle of Tourmakeady*. Dublin: Nonsuch, 2008.
Childers, Erskine. *Framework of Home Rule*. Dublin: Talbot, 1911.
Childers, Erskine. *Military Rule in Ireland*. Dublin: Talbot, 1920.
Comerford, Maire. *The First Dail*. Dublin: Joe Clarke, 1969.
Conlon, Lil. *Cumann na mBan and the Women of Ireland*. Kilkenny: KilkennyPeople, 1969.
Connolly, James. *Revolutionary Warfare*. Dublin: New Books, 1968.
Coogan, Tim Pat. *Michael Collins: A Biography*. London: Hutchinson, 1990.
Cottrell, Peter. *The Anglo-Irish War*. Oxford, England: Osprey, 2006.
Curtis, Edmund. *A History of Ireland*. London: Methuen, 1964.
Deasy, Liam. *Towards Ireland Free*. Cork: Mercier, 1973.
DeBlacon, Aodh. *What Sinn Fein Stands For*. Dublin: Mellifont, 1921.
Dwyer, T. Ryle. *Big Fellow, Long Fellow*. Dublin: Gill & MacMillan, 1998.
———. *The Squad*. Cork: Mercier, 2007.
———. *Fifty Years of Liberty Hall*. Dublin: Three Candles Press, 1960.
Foster, R.F. *The Oxford Illustrated History of Ireland*. Oxford: Oxford University Press, 1998.
Fox, R.M. *The History of the Irish Citizen Army*. Dublin: James Duffy, 1943.
Good, Joe. *Enchanted by Dreams*. Dingle, Ireland: Brandon, 1996.
Hart, Peter. *The IRA and Its Enemies: Violence and Community in Cork, 1916–1923*. Oxford, England: Clarendon, 1998.

Holmes, Richard. *The Little Field Marshal.* London: Cassell, 2005.
Hopkinson, Michael. *The Irish War of Independence.* Dublin: Gill & Macmillan, 2004.
Kee, Robert. *Ireland: A History,* London: Widenfeld & Nicholson, 1980.
Lord Riddell. *War Diary, 1914–1918.* London: Ivor Nicholson & Watson, 1970.
Macardle, Dorothy. *The Irish Republic.* London: Corgi, 1968.
MacCarthy, J.M., ed. *Limerick's Fighting Story.* Tralee, Ireland: Anvil, 1966[?].
McCay, Hedley. *Padraic Pearse.* Cork: Mercier, 1966.
MacEoin, Uinseann, ed. *Survivors.* Dublin: Argenta, 1987.
McHugh, Roger, ed. *Dublin 1916.* Dublin: Arlington, 1966.
McNally, Michael. *The Easter Rising 1916.* Oxford, England: Osprey, 2007.
Moody, T.W., and F.X. Martin, eds. *The Course of Irish History.* Cork: Mercier, 1967.
Moylan, Sean. *Sean Moylan, In His Own Words.* Cork: Aubane Historical Society, 2005.
Neeson, Eoin. *The Life and Death of Michael Collins.* Cork: Mercier, 1968.
Neligan, David. *The Spy in the Castle.* London: Macgibbon and Kee, 1968.
O'Cathasaigh, P. *The Story of the Irish Citizen Army.* Dublin: Maunsel, 1919[?].
O'Connor, Frank. *An Only Child.* London: Penguin, 2005.
O'Donoghue, Florence. *No Other Law.* Dublin: Anvil, 1954.
O'Faolain, Sean. *Vive Moi.* Frank Hart Davis: London, 1965.
O'Luing, Sean. *I Die in a Good Cause: A Study of Thomas Ashe.* Tralee, Ireland: Anvil, 1970.
O'Malley, Ernie. *On Another Man's Wound.* Dublin: Anvil, 1979.
_____. *Raids and Rallies.* Dublin: Anvil, 1982.
_____. *The Singing Flame.* Dublin: Anvil, 1978.
Ryan, Annie. *Comrades: Inside the War of Independence.* Dublin: Liberties, 2007.
Ryan, Meda. *The Real Chief.* Cork: Mercier, 1986.
_____. *Tom Barry: IRA Freedom Fighter.* Cork: Mercier, 2005.
Sheehan, William. *British Voices.* Cork: Collins, 2007.
_____. *Fighting for Dublin.* Cork: Collins, 2007.
Smith, Michael. *The Spying Game.* London:Victor Gollancz, 1996.
White, G., and B. O'Shea. *Irish Volunteer Soldier 1913–23.* Oxford, England: Osprey, 2003.

Newspapers and Periodicals

Bowden, T. "Bloody Sunday — a Reappraisal." *European Studies Review* 2, no. 1 (1972).
Daily Herald (London), issues from 1920 and 1921.
Fitzpatrick, David. "The Geography of Irish Nationalism 1910–21." *Past & Present* 78 (February 1978).
Hart, Peter. "The Geography of Revolution in Ireland, 1917–23." *Past & Present* 155, (May 1997).
Harvey, A.D. "Who Were the Auxiliaries?" *Historical Journal* 35, no. 3 (1992).
Irish Bulletin (November 1919-June 1921). "Irish War of Independence."
Observer (London),1920–21.
"Periscope." "The Last Days of the Castle." *Blackwood's,* August 1922.
Times (London), 1920–21.
Townsend, Charles. "The Irish Railway Strike of 1920." *Irish Historical Studies* 21, no. 83 (March 1979).
_____. "The Irish Republican Army and the Development of Guerrilla Warfare, 1916–21." *English Historical Review,* April 1979.
Whitaker's Almanac, 1919–22.

Index

Aghdavoyle 183, 248
Aiken, Frank 56, 182, 256, 267
Allen, John 191
Allihies Barracks 136
Ames, Lt. Peter Ashum 84
Amiens St. Station, Dublin 19
Anderson, Sir John 250
Andrews, Dr. Christopher 79
Angliss, Lt. 84
Anglo-Irish Treaty 234
Arbor Hill Prison 105
Asgard 5, 6, 7
Ashbourne Barracks 30, 31
Ashe, Thomas 25, 26, 28, 30, 31, 38, 39–40, 45, 97
Asquith, P.M. Herbert 4, 28, 184
Athenry 27
Athlone 25, 71
Aud 14, 27
Aughnacliffe 131
Auxiliaries 73, 101, 106, 121, 186, 236
Aylesbury Prison 38, 114

Bachelor's Walk, Dublin 22
Baggalley, Capt. G.T. 85
Bailey, Daniel 15
Ball Vaughan 235
Ballaghderren Barracks 181
Ballinspittle Barracks 138
Ballycrovane Coastguard Station 144, 146
Ballydehob Barracks 138
Ballydrachane 150–1
Ballygurteen Barracks 138
Ballyhahill 224–5
Ballylanders Barracks 163
Ballyvarey Barracks 180
Bandon 189
Bandon, Lord 217
Bantry 128
Barret, Ben 76
Barrett, Dick 44
Barrington, Miss 229
Barry, David 173
Barry, Kevin 102
Barry, Paddy 226
Barry, Tom 43, 44, 48, 50, 53, 55, 56, 62, 65, 87, 149, 152,
155–6, 188, 189, 190, 192, 199, 202, 203–8, 213, 250, 278
Barton, Det. Sgt. John 76
Barton, Robert 34, 255, 257
Beaslai, Piarias 51
Begley, Flor 138, 197, 203
Begley, Joe 159
Begley, Neilus 197
Belfast 20
Belgooly Barracks 138
Bell, Alan 78
Bennett, Capt. George 84
Bennett, Louie 109
Benson, Patrick 228
Bere Island 43, 58
Bicycle War 211
Biggs & Co. 139
Birkenhead, Lord 257
Black and Tans 70, 86, 100, 106, 120–1, 133, 143
Bluebell 14
Boer War 39, 53
Boland, Harry 38
Boland's Mill, Dublin 13, 22, 23, 112
Bolster, John 149
Bonar Law, Andrew 69
Borriskane Barracks 167
Boundary Commission 258–9, 264
Bowen-Colthurst, Capt. 28
Boxold, Sgt. 194
Boylan, Sean 56
Boyle, Con 220
Boyne, Battle of the 182
Bracken, Peader 22
Brady, Inspector 180
Brandsfield, Willie 211
Breen, Dan 60, 61, 82, 99, 129, 135, 226, 227
Brennan, Michael 48, 56, 95
Brennan, Robert 27
Brest-Litovsk Treaty 40
Bridges, Constable 213
Briggs, Det. Inspector Harry 229
British Army 252, 262
Broderick, Albinia 109
Brooke, Frank 76
Brosna Barracks 175
Brosnan, Tadh 215
Broy, Edward (Ned) 74, 77, 90, 253
Brugha, Cathal 32, 33, 36, 39, 80, 147, 250
Buckley, Sean 44, 138
Burgatia House, County Cork 191–2
Burgery 222, 226
Butler, John 197, 198
Byrne, Brig.-Gen. 80
Byrne, Charlie 73
Byrne, John 180
Byrnes, John Charles 77
Byrnes, Robert J. 68, 128, 140
Byrnes, Vinnie 76, 84

Caherguillamore House, Limerick 174
Cahill, Paddy 147
Cairo Gang 83, 84–86, 87, 134
Caldow, John 84
Callaghan, Daniel 191
Callaghan, Maj. 84, 85
Callaghan, Michael 139
Camlough Barracks 182
Canterbury, Archbishop of 185
Carney, Winifred 112
Carolan, Prof. John 82
Carrigtwohill Barracks 135
Carrol, Sean 221, 229
Carrowkennedy 243–4
Carson, Sir Edward 3, 4, 28, 182
Carty, Frank 180
Casement, Sir Roger 5, 14, 15, 16, 28, 78
Casey, Patrick 229
Castle Barnard 217
Castletownbere Coastguard Station 144, 212
Cat and Mouse Act 43
Ceant [Kent], Eamonn 12, 13, 19, 28
Chamberlain, Austin 257
Chartres, John 257, 259
Chatfield, Capt. 237
Chenevix, Helen 109
Childers, Erskine 3, 6, 107, 255, 257, 264

Chotah 6
Christian, Francis 83, 102
Churchill, Lord Randolph 3
Churchill, Winston 257
Clancy, David 166
Clancy, George 184, 228
Clancy, Patrick 140, 141
Clancy, Peader 84, 86, 89, 166
Clanwilliam House, Dublin 23
Clarke, Constable 130
Clarke, Lt. Frederick 194, 255
Clarke, Thomas 17, 28, 79
Clonbannin 201
Clune, Archbishop Joseph 84
Clune, Conor 84, 86
Clune, John 176
Coade 28
Coakley, Paddy 197
Coen, Michael 243
Colbert, Con 13, 28
Colbert, Jim 225
Coleman, Capt. Richard 25
Coleman, Sgt. 213
Collins, James 175
Collins, Michael 5, 31, 33, 34, 36, 39, 51, 73, 76, 80, 87, 90, 91, 114, 133, 147, 186, 251, 252-3, 254, 261, 265, 270
Collins, Sean 241
Collison, Jack 231
Condon, Larry 127, 140
Connaught Rangers 5, 244
Connolly, Con 208, 212
Connolly, James 181
Connolly, James (Labour leader) 8, 11, 12, 13, 17, 23, 25, 28, 29, 39, 98, 110, 112
Connolly, Sean 48, 113, 180, 246
Conroy, James 76
Conroy, Martin 237
Conscription crisis 40, 66
Conway, Andy 115
Conway, John 178
Conway, Martin 174
Coogan, T.P. 106
Cookstown Barracks 182
Cooney, Andy 55
Cooney, Constable 181
Co-operative Society 6, 36
Cope, Andy 87, 251
Corbally, Dick 59
Corcoran, Sean 179, 238
Cork 134, 159-60
Cork 1st Brigade 125, 135, 136, 148, 150, 159, 197, 198, 207, 215
Cork 2nd (North) Brigade 125, 135, 148, 149, 187, 191, 196, 200
Cork 3rd (West) Brigade 52, 125, 128, 137, 138, 139, 144, 148, 149, 154, 161, 187, 189, 191, 192, 197, 200, 202, 213-4
Corkery, Jack 208, 212
Cosgrave, W.T. 31, 34
Cosgrove, Patrick 180
Costello, Michael 237

Coughlan, Sgt. 238
Craig, Sir James 185, 251, 259, 261, 262
Crake, Col. 157
Crawford, Capt. 85
Creedon, Siobhan 92
Creighton, Constable 213
Croke Park killings, Dublin 84, 86
Crossbarry 202-7, 275, 278
Crossey, Lt. W.E. 215
Crossmaglen 248
Crowe, Tadhg 169
Crowe, Tim 61
Crowley, Daniel 207
Crowley, Mick 138, 139, 161, 203, 205, 213
Crowley, Paddy 192
Crowley, Tadhg 166
Crozier, Brig.-Gen. F.P. 86, 121, 184
Culleens 244-5
Cullen, Tom 73, 78, 83
Cullenswood House 78
Cumann na mBan 13, 31, 111-2, 118, 144
Cummins, Brig-Gen. H.R. 202
Curragh Camp 4, 13, 19, 20
Curtin, Michael 177
Curtin, Owen 140, 141
Cusack, Brian 34
Custom House, Dublin 35, 106

Dail Eireann 32, 34, 36
Dail Loan Scheme 34
Daily Bulletin 69
Daily Express 19, 21
Daily Mail 19, 28, 184
Daily News 72
Dalton, Charlie 73, 88
Dalton, Detective Constable 76
Dalton, Emmett 43, 256
Daly, Charles 56, 267
Daly, Constable 153
Daly, Edward 13, 20, 28
Daly, Paddy 71, 107, 231
Danford, Col. 140-1
Dartmoor Prison 38
Davin, Jerome 58
Dawn of Russia 30
Dawson, Paddy 128
Deasy, Liam 44, 138, 139, 147, 153-4, 158, 161, 188, 189, 190, 203
Deasy, Pat 158
Deasy, Sean 206
Deasy, William 207
deCourcy, Bob 229
Defence Barracks Sergeants 120
Defence of the Realm Act 121, 132
The Defiance 59
Derry 182
Derrypark Barracks 239
Deserters 95, 180
Desmond, Denis 197
Despard, Charlotte 109

de Valera, Eamon 13, 22, 23, 28, 31, 33, 34, 36, 38, 66, 80, 90, 106, 112, 114, 250, 255, 256, 257, 261, 265
Devins, Jim 114
Devitt, Mauteen 48
Devlin, M.P. Joseph 180
de Wett, Christian 39
Dickson, Thomas 28
Dieces, Gen. Prescott 93-4
Dillon, Col. Hill 78
Dillon, John 66, 67
Dillons Cross 159
Dixon, Capt. 154
Doherty, Eileen 248
Dolan, Joe 78, 85
Donabate Garrison 25
Donegan, Maurice 128, 137, 142
Donnellan, District Inspector 241
Doolan, Denis 197, 198
Doran, Edward 234
Doran, John 247
Dowling, Maj. 84, 86
Doyle, Martin 43
Doyle, Patrick 72
Doyle, Sean 76, 84
Drangon Barracks 167
Drimoleague Barracks 193
Drishanebeg 194-6
Dromkeen 220-2
Drumbane Barracks 162
Drumcondra 89, 104, 182
Drummin *see* Rineen
Dublin Castle 17, 19, 20, 43, 74, 82, 98-9
Dublin Home Defense Force 20
Dublin Lock-Out 6, 110
Dublin Mansion House 32, 33, 71, 98, 251, 256
Dublin Metropolitan Police 9, 20, 28, 79, 98, 118
Dublin Women's Suffrage Association 109
Duffy, George Gavan 257, 261
Duffy, Sean 228
Duggan, Eamon 73, 257
Dundon, Commandant David 93
Dunleavy, Detective 76
Dunmanway 212-3
Dunne, Eugene 58
Dunne, Peader 128
Durrow Station 222
Durrus Barracks 138
Dwyer, Frank 169
Dwyer, Liam 212
Dwyer, Ned 169
Dwyer, Nicholas 174

East Clare 31
East Limerick Brigade 220
Egan, Patrick 160
Emly 166-7
Engels, Frederick 7
Ennis, Tom 106

Enniscrone Coastguard Station 179
Enright, Constable 130
Essex Regiment 94, 147, 148, 152, 159, 188, 189, 204, 213, 255
Evans, Sir L. Worthington 257
Eyeries Barracks 57, 59

Fahy, Constable 168
Falvey, Batt 197
Fanning, John 140
Fastnet Rock 217–8
Federation of Dublin Employers 6
Fermoy Barracks 113, 127
Finn, Jackie 47
Finn, Seamus 166, 225
Finn, Sean 147, 168, 224
Fisher, Sir Warren 254
Fitzgerald, Desmond 38
Fitzgerald, Jack 142, 143
Fitzgerald, John 223
Fitzgerald, Sgt. John 84
Fitzgerald, Michael 140
Fitzgerald, Tim 148
Fitzpatrick, Constable J. 128
Fitzpatrick, Michael 170, 252
Flaherty, Jim 244
Flanagan, Mick 84
Flood, Francis 72
Flood, Patrick 270
Flynn, Con 151
Forbes, Det. Insp. 79
Ford, Liam 229
Ford, Sean *see* Tomas Malone
Four Courts 13, 19, 20, 23, 24, 271
Fouvargue, Vincent 89
Freeman's Journal 72, 139
French, Gen. Lord John 32, 77, 80, 99, 109, 117, 119, 132
ffrench-Mullen, Madeleine 109, 111, 113
Frieda 186, 253
Frongoch P.O.W. Camp 28, 38–9

Gaelic Athletic Association 5, 74
Gaelic League 5, 32, 39, 74
Gallagher, Dan 234
Galligan, Commandant Paul 27
Galvin, John 159
Galway, Mary 110
Garniss, Cadet 85
Garrykerin House 222
Gay, Thomas 73
Gaynor, Sean 91, 167, 229, 231
General Post Office, Dublin 12, 17, 23
General Strike 70–1
George V (King) 250–1, 263
Gerard, John 174
German Plot 31, 80
Gifford, Grace 28
Gilbride, Eugene 115

Gill, Patrick 180
Gleeson, Dan 254
Gleeson, Tim 232
Glencurrance 160
Glencurrane, Limerick 172–3
Glennon, Sean 231
Gonne, Maud 109, 111
Good, Joe 12, 47, 141, 173
Gore-Booth, Eva 109
Gorman, Jim 164
Gough, Sir Hubert 4
Gouldron, Sgt. J.F. 128
Grange, Co. Limerick 170–1
Grant, Maj. 199
Greenwood, Sir Hamar 80, 82, 257
Gregory, Margaret 240
Griffin, Fr Michael 180
Griffith, Arthur 11, 31, 34, 36, 87, 134, 251, 255, 257, 258, 259, 261, 262
Griffith, Lt. 222
Guerilla Days in Ireland 48, 55, 62, 199
Guerin, Capt. D. 221
Guilfoyle, Joe 73

Hales, Sean 148, 151, 182, 255
Hales, Tom 52, 125, 147
Hampshire Regiment 215
Hampson, Sgt. 132
Hanley, Mary 236
Hannigan, P. 165
Harcourt St. Station, Dublin 19
Hardy, Capt. J.L. 83, 85, 86, 88
Harnett, Larry 234
Harnett, Mossie 175
Harrington, John 73, 104
Harte, Dan 140
Harte, Pat 138, 142, 147
Harte Auxiliary 160
Hawes, Maj. Gen. 254
Hayden, John 180, 247
Hayes, Liam 222
Hayes, Richard 34
Hayes, Sean 138
Headford Junction 234
Healy, T.M. 67
Helga (gunship) 21, 23
Hennessy, Tim 229
Heuston, J.J. 28
Hibernian Rifles 17
Hickey, Sgt. 222
Higgins, Patrick J. 136
Highland Light Infantry 132
Hobson, Bulmer 5, 12, 15
Hodnett, Jim 143, 144
Hoey, Det. Daniel 76
Hogan, Dan 56, 129, 265
Hogan, Sean 99
Holland, Sgt. Tim 181
Hollyford Barracks 164–5
Hollyhome, Private 196
Holmes, Gen. 201
Home Rule 3, 32, 134

Horan, James 221, 229
Hostages 158, 187, 191
Houlahan, James 178
Howes Strand Coastguard Station 142, 143–4
Howth 6
Huckerby, (Black & Tan) 169
Hudson, Col. 193
Hugginstown Barracks 163
Hunt, Det. D.I. 90
Hunt, Auxiliary Cadet William 108
Hurley, Charlie 43, 57, 58, 139, 142, 143, 144, 153, 188, 189, 197, 198, 206, 207
Hurley, Dick 137, 139
Hurley, Jim 212

Igoe, Head Constable Eugene 88
Inghinidhe na hEireann 111, 113
Irish Bulletin 239
Irish Citizen Army 7, 8, 12, 17, 19, 22, 39, 59, 109, 110
Irish Guards 48
Irish Independent 166
Irish Labour Party 70, 71
Irish National Party 3, 4, 31, 32, 66
The Irish Republic 8
Irish Republican Army 29, 42, 63, 90, 121, 252, 269
Irish Republican Army Divisions 56
Irish Republican Brotherhood 4, 11, 14, 36
Irish Self-Determination League 35, 77
Irish Times 35, 100, 140
Irish Transport and General Workers Union 6, 7, 59, 110
Irish Volunteers 12, 36, 43
Irish War News 21
Irish Women Workers' Union 110, 113
Irish Women's Franchise League 109
Irish Women's Suffrage Federation 109
Irish Worker 8
Isham, Lt. Ralph 77

Jennings, Col. 85
Jeune, Capt. R.D. 83, 86, 87
Jones, Thomas 257, 258, 261

Kavanagh, Det. Joseph 73
Kearney, Peter 205, 208, 213
Kearney, William 270
Kearns, Linda 114, 180
Keating, Patrick 223
Kell, Vernon 79
Kelleher, Det. Inspector 90
Kelleher, Tom 96, 151, 198, 203, 204, 205, 206, 208, 275
Kelliher, Ned 88
Kells, Det. Constable Henry 76

Kelly, Capt. M. 59, 98
Kelpie 6
Kenna, Constable 212
Kennedy, Mick 76
Kennedy, Patrick 89, 105, 184, 231
Kennelly, Dan 176
Kennlyside, Capt. 84, 86
Kent, Eamonn *see* Ceant, Eamonn
Keogh, Margaretta 112
Keogh, Tom 76, 84
Keon, Constable 114
Kerry Brigades 235
Keyes, Ralph 128, 139
Kilbrittain Barracks 160–1, 188
Kilfall 237–8
Kilkenny 31
Kilmainham Prison 28, 89
Kilmallock 165–6
Kilmeena 240–1
Kilmichael 155–6
Kilroy, Michael 238, 240, 243, 256
King, Capt. W.L. 84, 89, 105
King, Constable 245
King, Maj. 85
King's Liverpool Regiment 128, 137, 193
King's Own Scottish Borderers 6
Kingstown (Dun Laoghaire) 13, 21, 22
Kinnane, Paddy 162
Kitterick, Tom 243
Knocklong Station 129–30

Labour Party 6, 36
Lacey, Dinny 168, 228
Lacey, Joe 247
Lafferty, Constable 114
Larkfield, Kimmage 12
Larkin, Delia 110
Larkin, James 6, 7, 8, 110
Lawson, Lt.-Gen. Sir H. 42
Leahy, Mick 186
Lee-Wilson, Capt. 79
Lehane, Con 143, 151
Lehane, Sean 152, 159, 213, 267
Leitrim Observer 236
Lemass, Sean 85
Lendrum, Resident Magistrate 178
Lenin, V.I. 7, 30
Lennon, George 219, 222, 227, 234
Leonard, Joe 76, 84
Lessons of the Moscow Uprising 30
Liberty Hall 8, 16, 21
Liddy, Con 125
Limerick City Second Battalion 128, 130
Limerick Soviet 68–9
Lincoln Gaol 34
Lindsay, Mrs. J.M. 191
Linen Hall Barracks, Dublin 20
Lisnagaul, Tipperary 172
Lloyd George, P.M. David 31, 32, 40, 108, 118, 182, 250, 255, 257, 258
Long, Walter 120
Lordan, Denis 208
Lordan, John 157, 199, 204, 205, 213
Loughrane, Patrick 182
Lowe, Brig. Gen. 24, 113
Lowney, Con 58
Lucas, Gen. 140–1
Ludendorff, Field Marshal 40
Luggacurran Barracks 180
Lynas, Constable George 248
Lynch, John 83
Lynn, Dr. Kathleen 20, 109, 113
Lynch, Liam 52, 55, 56, 92, 102, 125, 127, 135, 139, 147, 148, 150, 152, 155, 191, 207, 210, 215, 217, 228, 267
Lynch, Patricia 110
Lynn, Robert 72
Lyons, John 191

MI5 79, 80
Macardle, Dorothy 14, 258
MacBride, Maj. John 28, 39, 109, 252
MacBride, Sean 252, 253
MacClean, Lt. Donald Lewis 84
MacCormack, Patrick 61
MacCurtain, Austin 91
MacCurtain, Tomas 27, 52, 79, 125, 133, 137, 182
MacDermott, Sean 15, 17, 28, 76
MacEoin (McEwan), Sean 48, 56, 106, 180, 181, 237, 245, 265–6
MacEoin, Uinsean 151
MacMahon, Sean 51
MacNamara, James 74, 77, 83
MacNamara, Tom 200
MacNeill, Eoin 12, 15, 16, 27, 29, 33, 38, 265
Macready, Sir Nevil 80, 250, 251, 253
Macroom Castle 155
MacSwiney, Terence 27, 133, 147, 148
Madden, Dr. John 244
Madden, Pat 246
Magherameena Castle 268
Magner, Canon 160
Maguire, Tom 238, 256
Maher, Joseph 180, 247
Mahony, Constable 169
Mahony, John 128
Mahony, Patrick 191
Maire Cait 217
Mallin, Michael 13, 28, 112
Mallow Barracks 149, 152
Malone, Brodie 238, 243
Malone, Seamus 91
Malone, Tomas (Sean Ford) 163, 165, 171, 173
Manning, Dennis 143, 144
Mannix, Sgt. 84
Marchmont, Josephine 93
Markievicz, Countess (Constance Gore-Booth) 8, 13, 22, 28, 34, 109, 112, 113, 114
Marx, Karl 7
Maxwell, Gen. Sir John 22, 28
May, Paddy 238
McAuliffe, Brig. Garret 173, 225
McCann, Pierce 32
McCanny, Bernard 270
McCarthy, Capt. 208
McCarthy, Dan 175
McCarthy, Fr. Dick 147
McCarthy, J.M. 54, 163, 221
McCarthy, Maurice 74
McCarthy, Michael 156, 158
McCarthy, Patrick 149, 155
McCorley, Roger 268
McCormack, Capt. 85
McCormack, Richard 39
McCrae, Pat 76
McCurtain Hill Barrack 212
McDonnell, Andy 38, 56
McDonnell, Constable 132
McDonnell, Constable James 61
McDonnell, Mick 75, 99
McDonough [MacDonagh], Thomas 12, 13, 15, 25, 28
McElduff, James 249
McEvilly, James 241
McGarry, Sean 34
McGowan, Sean 59
McGrane, Eileen 90
McGrath, District Inspector 106, 245
McGrath, Frank 167
McGrath, Martin 202
McGrath, Sean 219
McGuinness, Charlie 186, 253
McGuinness, Joseph 34, 82
McIntyre, Patrick 28
McKee, Dick 75, 84, 86, 126
McKelvey, Joseph 56
McKinnon, Maj. B.A. 179, 234
McLean, Constable 212
McNamara, Michael 178
McWhinney, Linda *see* Kearns, Linda
Meaney, C.J. 194, 255
Mellows, Liam 27, 51
Mernin, Lily 74, 78, 83
Merrigan, Paul 172
Middleton, Lord 109, 247
Milling, Resident Magistrate John 130
Milroy, Sean 34
Miltown Malbay 132
Modreeny 231–2
Moloney, Edward 174
Moloney, Helena 113
Moloney, Tom 208
Monaghan, Lilly 105
Monaghan, Madge 105
Monahan, Peter 161, 205

Monteith, Robert 15
Montgomery, Lt.-Col. 84, 86
Montgomery, Maj. Bernard 263–4
Moore, Col. Maurice 5
Moore St., Dublin 24
Moran, Jim 242
Moran, Patrick 72
Moriarty, Tim 58
Moscow Insurrection 12, 29
Mount Pleasant Barracks 136
Mountjoy Prison 70, 72, 87, 106, 132
Mourne Abbey 141, 198
Moylan, Sean 55, 62, 64, 140, 150, 187, 200, 201, 202, 213
Mulcahy, Richard 26, 33, 34, 51, 78, 87, 97, 103, 116, 135, 147, 236, 250, 251, 253, 256
Mulhern, Sgt. 146
Murphy, Constable 163
Murphy, Humphrey 55
Murphy, James, "Spud" 89, 90, 105, 140, 147, 156, 184, 192
Murphy, Tim 93
Murphy, William Martin 6
Murray, Capt. 86
Murtagh, Constable Joseph 137
Myles, Sir Thomas 6

Nathan, George 228
Nathan, Sir Matthew 16–17
Nation and Athenaeum 250
National Loan Scheme 34
National Volunteers 28, 98
Neligan, Det. David 75, 80, 86
Nevinson, H.W. 29
Newall, Thomas "Sweeney" 88
New Statesman 70
Newbury, Capt. 84
Newcestown 151–2
Newry 181, 182
Newtownhamilton Barracks 181
Nixon, Detective Inspector 248
Nolan, George 82
Nolan, Jimmy 231
Nolan, Paddy 231
Nugent, Sgt. 57
Nyhan, John "Flyer" 140, 156, 157

Oakes, Constable 239
O'Brien, Art 77
O'Brien, Conor 6
O'Brien, Constable 91, 128, 129
O'Brien, Dan 211
O'Brien, Eamonn 129
O'Brien, Joe 93
O'Brien, John 236
O'Brien, John Joe 129, 130
O'Brien, Maurice 202
O'Brien, Michael 238
O'Brien, Nancy 75
O'Brien, Paddy 155, 211, 212, 231, 232

O'Brien, Thomas 72, 191, 219
O'Brien, William 67
O'Callaghan, Michael 184, 228
O'Connell, Christy 57, 136, 144, 146, 205, 208, 212
O'Connell, Dick 220, 221
O'Connell, Jack 136, 150
O'Connell, J.J. 39
O'Connell, Liam 102
O'Connell, Constable Patrick 61
O'Connor, Frank 50
O'Connor, Katie 110
O'Connor, Rory 51
O'Connor, T.M. 175
O'Donaghue, Florrie 55, 72, 93, 197
O'Donaghue, Sgt. James 154
O'Donaghue, Jim 138, 159
O'Donaghue, Tim 212
O'Donahue, Joseph 228
O'Donnell, Capt. P. 167
O'Donnell, Peader 166, 248
O'Donnell, Tom 241
O'Donovan, Dan "Sandow" 199
O'Driscoll, Daniel 212, 214
O'Driscoll, Michael 157
O'Duffy, Eoin 180, 181, 247, 256
O'Dwyer, Liam 144, 145, 146
O'Dwyer, Patrick 61
O'Faolain, Pax 87, 253
O'Faolin, Sean 40
O'Foghludha, Michael 74
O'Gorman, Jim 169
O'Hanlon, Mick 84
O'Hannigan, Donncadha O. 54, 166, 220, 224
O'Hanrahan, Michael 28
O'Hegarty, Diarmuid 51, 257
O'Hegarty, Sean 55
O'Herlihy, Mick 156
O'Leary, Paddy 197, 198, 203
O'Loughlin, Constable 99
O'Mahony, Dan 58, 147, 197, 198
O'Mahony, Jim 54, 139, 212
O'Malley, Ernie 46, 48, 55, 57, 63, 95, 100, 105, 124, 131, 140, 150, 164, 167, 181, 209, 227, 228, 233, 251, 256
O'Malley, Paddy 241
O'Meara, Jack 61
O'Mullaine, Jeremiah 207
On Another Man's Wound 46, 95, 105
O'Neil, Billy 146
O'Neil, Miah 189
O'Neill, Ignatius 48, 176, 177
O'Neill, Jackie 188, 212
O'Neill, James 39
O'Neill, Mick 143
O'Neill, Peter 57, 212
O'Neill, Stephen 156
An Only Child 50
O'Regan, Constable 239
O'Regan, John 211

O'Reilly, Dan 189
O'Reilly, Joe 78
Oriel House 76
O'Riordan, Jeremiah 147
O'Riordan, John 172
O'Shea, James 98
O'Shea, Michael 228
O'Sullivan, Corney 135, 136
O'Sullivan, Gearoid 51, 253
O'Sullivan, Michael 207, 212
O'Sullivan, Pat 198
O'Sullivan, Sgt. 166
O'Sullivan, Ted 44, 141, 212
O'Sullivan, Thomas 234

Pallas Barracks 220
Pankhurst, Silvia 110
Paris Peace Conference 36
Parnell St., Dublin 24
Partridge, William 113
Paul, Paddy 219
Pearse, Patrick 12, 15, 17, 23, 28, 36, 112
Pearse, Willie 28
Peeke, Capt. Sir Alfred 247
Peel, Lt. 84
Percival, Maj. A.E. 94, 122, 147, 151, 152, 263
"Periscope" 74, 81
Perry, Sgt. 114
Pettigo, battle of 268–70
Phelan, Sean 198
Phoenix Park 20, 77
Pilkington, Liam 244
Plunkett, Count 33, 255
Plunkett, George 12, 222
Plunkett, Joseph 12, 28, 33
Portobello Barracks, Dublin 19
Portobello Bridge, Dublin 19
Potter, Gilbert 226, 228
Power, George 140
Prendeville, Constable Maurice 170
Price, Capt. Leonard 84, 102
Price, Inspector Ivon 79
Prison Letters 112
Prowse & Co. Keith 77
Punch, Ned 221
Purcell, John 220

Queenstown [Cobh] 14, 79
Quinlan, John 174
Quinlisk, H.H. 78
Quinn, Private 163
Quirk, Constable Maurice 172

Rahilly, Michael 23
Raids and Rallies 177
Rathcoole 215–7
Rea, Constable Isaac 172
Records of the Rebellion in Ireland 63, 86, 263, 273
Redmond, John 4, 5, 11, 27, 28
Redmond, Det. Insp. W.C. Forbes 77, 78, 80

Index

Regan, John 217, 218
Reilly, Constable 130
Republican Courts 35
Restoration of Order in Ireland Act 133, 148
Revell, Det.-Sgt. Richard 76
Rice, John Joe 55
Richardson, Capt. 152
Richmond Barracks, Dublin 113
Richmond Hospital 73
Rineen, Co. Clare 175–7
Ring, Constable 130
Ring, Joe 238
Riordan, John 172
Robinson, Seamus 60, 99, 129, 164
Rosscarberry Barracks 207–9
Rowe's Distillery 19
Royal Air Force 94, 122
Royal Dublin Fusiliers 19, 21
Royal College of Surgeons, Dublin 19, 21
Royal Irish Constabulary 9, 13, 26, 57, 79, 118
Royal Irish Regiment 19
Royal Irish Rifles 19
Royal Marines 106, 176, 235
Royal Shropshire Light Infantry 127
Royal Ulster Constabulary 249
Rumble, Sgt. George 99
Ryan, Bernard 72
Ryan, Freddie 113
Ryan, Lance Corp. John 89
Ryan, Constable Thomas 163
Ryan, Michael 61

St. Enda's School 47
St. Stephen's Green 13, 19, 20, 22, 112
Sancta Maria 186
Sasoon, Sir Philip 258
Satchwell, Constable 236
Saurin, Frank 73
Savage, Martin 77, 99
Scanlon, Jim 129
Schull Barracks 137, 152–3
Scramogue 246–7
Scully, Liam 166
Seeley, Col. 4
Shanahan, William 178
Sharkey, Jack 92
Shaw, Lt.-Gen. Sir Frederick 120
Sheehan, Daniel 174
Sheehy Mountains 214
Sheehy-Skeffington, Hanna 109
Shelbourne Hotel, Dublin 113
Sherwood Foresters 22, 23, 229
Shields, Dan (informer) 198, 202
Shrove, Capt. F. Harper 84
Simon, Sir John 185
Singing Flame 48
Sinn Fein 3, 31, 32, 79, 83, 133, 185

Skeffington, John Sheehy 28
Skibereen, loyalty of 192
Skinnider, Margaret 22, 112
Sligo, Marquess of 242
Smart, Miss 74
Smith, T.H. 84
Smuts, Gen. 256
Smyth, Maj. Gerald 82, 146
Smyth, Det. Sgt. Patrick 76
A Soldier in Ireland 42
"The Soldier's Song" 72, 193
Solemn League and Covenant 3
Soloheadbeg 58, 60, 82, 125
South Dublin Union 19, 23, 112
South Staffordshire Regt. 24, 28
Southern Division 1st. 207, 210, 211
Spillane, Constable 128
Spindler, Capt. Carl 14
Stack, Austin 14, 38, 255
Stack, Mick 128
Stafford Prison 38
Stanton, John 241
Stapleton, Bill 76, 84
Stapleton, Jim 90
Stapleton, Sean 221
Starr, Paddy 229
Staunton, John 241
Stephens, James 4
Stone, Maj. Gen. 219
Strickland, Maj. Gen. Sir Peter 91, 160, 191, 201, 210, 215, 217
Suffragettes 109–10
Sullivan, Jim 158
Swanzey, District Inspector 137, 182
Sweeney, Joe 47, 56
Swindlehurst, Private J.P. 99–100

Teahan, John 128
Teeling, Frank 86
Thomas, Capt. 222
Thornton, Frank 73, 78, 83
Tierney, Constable J. 128
The Times 32, 185
Timoleague Barracks 136
Tipperary Brigade 226
Tobin, Liam 73, 77, 83, 89
Toibin, Ned 163
Tone, Theobald Wolfe 3, 128
Toureen 153–4
Tourmakeady 238–9
Tramore Barracks 219
Travers, John 268
Traynor, Oscar 56
Traynor (Trainor), Thomas 226, 228
Treacy, Sean 58, 61, 82, 83, 89, 99, 102, 129, 135, 164, 167, 233
Trim Barracks 181
Trinity College, Dublin 20, 30, 47, 109, 185
Troy, Capt. P. 226, 230

Truro, HMS 217
Tudor, Gen. Hugh 75, 80, 118
Tuffy, Tommy Joe 244
Tureengariff 200
Twaddell, M.P. William 268
Tyrell, Col. 140–1

Ulster 32
Ulster Defence Force 118
Ulster Special Constabulary 118, 182, 248, 265, 266, 268–9
Ulster Volunteer Force 4, 118, 131
Unionists 32
Upton Station 196–7

Valentine, Capt. 219
Vane, Sir Francis 28
Vaughan, Peter 176
Vico Road, Dalkey 179

Wade, Henry 174
Wall, Sean 227
Wall, Tommy 178
Wallace, Sgt. 130
Walsh, Sean 179
Walshe, Det. Constable 76
Waltham Prison 115
Weekly Intelligence Summary 91
Weissbach, Kapitanleutnant Raimund 15
Wellwood, Sgt. 163
West Clare Brigade 236
Westland Row Station, Dublin 19
Wharton, Detective Thomas 76
Whelan, Dinny 231, 232
Whelan, Pax 147, 222
Whelan, Thomas 72
Wheeler, Capt. 113
White, Capt. Jack R. 7
Wiggins, Constable 223
Wilde, Capt. 85
Will, Alexander 175
Williams and Wood's factory, Dublin 23
Willis, Richard 149
Wilson, Pres. Woodrow 34, 36
Wilson, Field Marshal Sir Henry 254, 263, 265, 270
Wimberley, Maj. Gen. 59
Wimborne, Lord 16
Winter, Col. Ormonde de l'Eppee ("O") 81, 83, 86, 87, 88, 118
Women Workers' Union 67
Woodcock, Col. 84, 86
Woods, Tony 89, 98, 104
Workers Dreadnought 110
Workers' Republic 8, 11
Wormwood Scrubs Prison 138
Wynn's Hotel, Dublin 111

Yeats, W.B. 240
Young, Ned 157

www.ingramcontent.com/pod-product-compliance
Lightning Source LLC
Chambersburg PA
CBHW081541300426
44116CB00015B/2719